Knowledges

CULTURE
COUNTERCULTURE
SUBCULTURE

PETER WORSLEY

THE NEW PRESS

In memory of
Kulpidja – great informant
Minimini – great artist
Narakidjara ('Billy the Kid')
and Nakinyaba – two delightful children

First Published in the Great Britain in 1997 by Profile Books, London
Published in the United States by The New Press, New York
Distributed by W. W. Norton & Company, Inc., New York

The New Press was established in 1990 as a not-for-profit alternative
to the large, commercial publishing houses currently dominating the book
publishing industry. The New Press operates in the public interest rather
than for private gain, and is committed to publishing, in innovative
ways, works of educational, cultural, and community value that might not
normally be commercially viable. The New Press's editorial offices are
located at the City University of New York.

PRODUCTION MANAGEMENT BY KIM WAYMER
PRINTED IN THE UNITED STATES OF AMERICA

9 8 7 6 5 4 3 2 1

Contents

Figures

Acknowledgements

My thanks are due, first and foremost, to Dr Julie Waddy, as will become apparent; to Michael Rowlands, who read the first chapter for me and pointed me to useful theoretical literature; and to Lester Hiatt, who also kindly read a draft of that chapter. Steven Hooper and Edvard Hviding brought their expertise to bear on Chapter 3; Margot Jefferys subjected Chapter 4 to her scalpel; and Michael Bury was a masterly guide through the medical literature. Sami Zubaida critically inspected the material on Gramsci in the last chapter.

The Departments of Social Anthropology at University College London, the London School of Economics and the School of Oriental and African Studies welcomed me to their seminars and made it possible for me to use their libraries. The library of the Wellcome Institute and the British Library were also invaluable. And the UCL Central Computer Service solved all my word-processing problems.

Introduction

I never intended to write this book. But as Thomas Mann wrote of *The Magic Mountain*, 'It is possible for a work to have its own will and purpose, perhaps a far more authoritative one than the author's.'

I began with the very limited idea of writing an account, fairly quickly, of the scientific knowledge of one Australian Aboriginal tribe. Little did I know that I was to end up, four years later – after an examination of pre-European navigation in the Pacific and the rise of modern Western biomedicine – with an analysis of Thanksgiving, Christmas, the Statue of Liberty and Disneyland, as well as a theoretical examination of nationalism and a critique of the concept of culture.

As C. Wright Mills wrote, there is an interplay between history and biography.[1] A child of my time, I went up to Cambridge in 1942 committed to equality and to the fairer distribution of wealth in a society which produced a great deal of it. People are sometimes shocked, though, when I say at that time – the year of Stalingrad – it appeared, increasingly, that all that stood between us and the elimination of civilization was the Red Army.

If that seems to be a contradiction now, it was not then, any more than that I, a communist, should have become an officer in the colonial forces. In Kenya, I became interested in African cultures and societies, and on my return to college, like nine out of ten of those who returned from the war, I changed my subject – from English literature to social anthropology. Then, still idealistic, I went as a mass education officer to Tanganyika, on the Groundnut Scheme. But by now the Cold War was well under way, and McCarthyism was not just a US phenomenon. After years of preparing to do fieldwork in Africa, I found myself banned from a research post there.

I did eventually get the opportunity to do fieldwork, by taking up a research post in the Australian National University, at Canberra, from where I prepared to go to the New Guinea Highlands. I was again refused entry, so I turned to fieldwork among Aborigines.

Like everyone else, I had to respond to the major events of those times. Intellectuals, though, are trained to make a special kind of response: to try to make *systematic* sense of what they are looking at, in the light of general theories checked against demonstrable data (which does not prevent their making mistakes).

They are also involved in another set of ideas: debates within their discipline. When I reached Groote Eylandt, an island in the Gulf of Carpentaria in northern Australia, my mind was full of questions raised by the
great anthropologists who had pioneered Aboriginal studies, notably
Emile Durkheim in France [2] and, in England, A. R. Radcliffe-Brown, one
of my teachers, whose analysis of Australian kinship had opened a new
chapter in Aboriginal studies. [3] Even without his influence, though, like all
anthropologists who have studied the Aborigines, I was instantly mesmerized by the intricacies of their kinship system, and this was to be the core
of my Ph.D. thesis.

Purely as a by-product, I had also collected hundreds of references to
the plants and animals which constitute the Aborigines' living environment: not our man-made environment of bricks and mortar, roads and
railways, in which nature is dominated by things people have created (the
Aborigines didn't have any of that), but the natural environment – the sea
and the land, hills, billabongs, rivers, plants and animals. Trying to make
sense of the ways they thought about these things, I went back to what past
writers, notably Durkheim, had written about Aboriginal thinking.

Some Victorian thinkers had argued that totemism showed Aborigines
simply could not think straight at all, for they attributed mystical powers
to inanimate objects. Others argued they took plants and animals as their
totems because of their importance as foods. No, said Durkheim. They
were neither confused, nor materialists. Their ideas were very coherent –
yams and kangaroos were important to them, not because they were of
culinary or economic value, but because they were 'badges' of *identity*:
symbols of the clans and other social groups people belonged to.

After I came back from the field, I wrote three articles about Aboriginal knowledge of plants and animals. In the first, [4] I accepted Durkheim's
point that totems were indeed attached to clans, but argued that there was
no justification for his further assumption that the order of society – the
clans and the moieties (halves of the tribe) – provided the model for orderly thinking in general, and even less for his conclusion that religion was
the source even of *scientific* thought. Totemic thinking was only *one* kind of
Aboriginal thinking, for side by side with their religious beliefs they also
possessed a very considerable amount of biological knowledge based on
empirical observation over countless generations.

In a second article, I provided the evidence for this contention: my
notebooks contained references to no fewer than thirty different kinds of
land animals, seventy-eight kinds of birds, 102 kinds of marine animals,
122 kinds of plants and trees, fifty-six kinds of crabs and shellfish and
thirty-four kinds of insects and flying things the Aborigines recognized.

But it was not simply that they had an awful *lot* of knowledge about plants and animals – in the aggregate, as it were. They also had systematic ways, first, of distinguishing trees and plants from animals and, second, of identifying the latter as either land, water or marine animals, and creatures that lived in the air. They had, that is, a biological, quite non-religious taxonomy – a systematic way of classifying things.[5]

Then, in the early 1960s, another great French scholar, Claude Lévi-Strauss, wrote two books that not only drove Durkheim off the stage but formed part of a new kind of theory, not just about what he called 'the savage mind', but about human knowledge in general.[6]

Lévi-Strauss illustrated this general argument with a study of Australian Aboriginal totemism,[7] attacking reductionist arguments with Gallic wit. Yes, he said, many plants and animals used as totems were obviously important as food. But the idea that the Aborigines' interest in these things was, in his sardonic words, 'inspired by nothing other than the rumbling of their stomachs' was an insult to their intelligence – and ours. They were interested in plants and animals, in his celebrated formulation, not because they were 'good to eat' but because they were 'good to think with'.

Previous writers had divided totemism into 'clan totemism', 'sex totemism', 'individual totemism' and a hundred and one other kinds of totemism. But all of these, he argued, were simply different facets of one general way of thinking about the relationship between humankind and nature. Second, there was nothing peculiarly Australian Aboriginal about all this: their 'totemism' was only one of many cultural variations upon a universal human theme – the need to define our place in the world – all of which use one form or other of 'binary' thinking based on the two basic categories of likeness and difference.

It seemed to me, though, that Lévi-Strauss, no less than Durkheim, was still looking at Aboriginal thought as if it was all of a piece. I argued, conversely, that there were several distinct modes of thought in Aboriginal culture. Durkheim had concentrated on religious classification, and in some situations Aborigines did emphasize the religious significance of plants and animals. But they classified them quite differently when they were thinking about them simply as *food*, and differently again when they were thinking about them *biologically*. Yet another model for classifying plants and animals was built into the language.[8] There were, then, four distinct ways of thought, not one.

And that was that. Since I did no more fieldwork on Groote Eylandt, and having made my theoretical point, I wrote no more on the subject.

Two decades passed by. Then one day the two volumes of the *Classification of Plants and Animals from a Groote Eylandt Point of View*[9] arrived through my letter box, with the request that I review them. They were by someone completely unknown to me, Dr J. A. Waddy, who, I discovered, was not only a trained biologist and anthropologist but also a missionary who had arrived on Groote after my departure and had been there ever since. She had spent fifteen years doing her research, whereas I had spent less than that number of months! She was also able to draw upon the excellent early linguistic work of her predecessors at the Church Missionary Society mission station on the island and was therefore thoroughly at home with the language of the Groote Eylandters, Anindilyakwa, and was further able to follow up the pioneering work of a fellow missionary, Dulcie Levitt, on native knowledge of plants and animals.[10]

Waddy's first volume sets Groote ways of thinking about plants and animals within the framework of general theoretical debate not only in anthropology but also in biology and linguistics. The second is a careful listing of plants and animals as classified both by expert Aboriginal informants and in Western biology.

I lacked any such grounding in biology. Instead, I had taken my theoretical ideas from an unlikely source: the writings of a Russian specialist in child developmental psychology, Lev Semenovich Vygotsky.[11] I opened the Waddy volumes, therefore, in some trepidation, expecting that she would be dismissive of my amateur dabblings in biological theory, and that my fieldwork, over a mere ten months, would evoke, and merit, equal scorn. To my relief, she too had largely adopted the Vygotsky framework. As for my empirical research, she was kind enough to write that I had 'collected a remarkable amount of data in the time . . . available', especially when 'biological data was by no means the primary focus of [my] study'; that I had recognized the higher-level terms used to group plants and animals; and that though the 315 edible species I listed had to be revised downwards to 273, I had still identified most of the 332 species she herself had been able to record. Because her work is so authoritative, in Chapter 1 that follows I always draw upon her research rather than my own early efforts. Yet because it would be repetitive to keep acknowledging the exact bits of the text I have used, I have only occasionally inserted precise references to her work, usually where I have used a longish passage, or cited a particularly acute observation, or something which might seem challengeable, so that people might wish to consult the original.

I ruefully reflected though, that whatever my personal enthusiasm for her book, probably no more than a handful of people would read either my review, written in a journal read only by Pacific scholars, or her two outstanding volumes, since they were both published by a small branch of a university press in remote northern Australia. Furthermore Waddy's work, straddling several disciplines, is very technical, while Groote culture, encoded in a ferociously difficult language, is hard even for specialists to understand. And so it proved, for later, when I went on a lecture tour of Australia and spoke about her research, I encountered only one other anthropologist who had read it.

So I decided to write an account of her work in non-technical language that would be accessible to a general readership. Although I had written about the need to acknowledge the several modes of thought used by the Aborigines, I concentrated at first on the area that was usually most neglected: their biological knowledge. But the project soon started to develop in unexpected ways. It began to appear far too limited simply to represent what Dr Waddy had had to say. And as Chapter 1 will show, I found myself drawn towards other studies, not only of what is usually called 'ethno-science' but of similar modes of thought in other cultures too.

Ideally, I would have liked to confine myself to hunters and collectors, since most people think they are singularly 'primitive'. It would not have come as news if I had reminded people that non-Western cultures such as that of China had produced a vast amount of scientific knowledge – Needham alone had crammed five volumes with what is only an outline of Chinese science [12] – or to remind them of the contribution of the Arabs to mathematics. But it *would* have been news to many that hunters and collectors too had their own forms of science.

Were we living in the nineteenth century, there would have been a large audience for the latest information about Australian Aboriginal thinking, because evolutionism had spread from biology to the social sciences. Anything about the Aborigines was hot news, voraciously snapped up by the great theoreticians in Europe and North America. Thus the latest findings about the Aranda in central Australia, reported by Sir Baldwin Spencer and his co-worker, F. J. Gillen, were passed on to Sir James Frazer, the eminent author of The Golden Bough, in Cambridge. As a result, whole generations became acquainted with the Aranda. Likewise, Lorimer Fison, a Wesleyan minister, sent information about the Kamilaroi, north of Sydney, to Lewis Henry Morgan, the great American theorist of social evolution, who was also in regular communication with A. W. Howitt, an explorer and magistrate in Gippsland.

Social evolutionism has long been dead. For the most part, only regional specialists remained interested in the Aborigines, though Blainey has pointed out the significance of northern Australia as a border zone between two major but radically different kinds of economies: hunting and collecting, on the one hand, and – across the Torres Strait – agriculture. [13]

By the 1960s, people had begun paying attention to the Aborigines once more. Now, however, they were being used as a kind of Rorschach test by white Australians who projected on to them their own guilt about the murder of tens of thousands of their number in the nineteenth century, a genocide that white settlers had 'justified' on the grounds that Aborigines were only vermin – animals living at the lowest limits of mere survival.

Even in the nineteenth century, though, some thinkers had found Aborigines an inspiration – the primitive precursors of modern communism. By the hippie era, they were even being credited with paranormal powers, and anthropologists were arguing that, in areas well endowed by nature (such as Groote), they represented the 'original affluent society'. With the rise of the women's movement, nineteenth-century notions of 'matriarchy' were revived and women were seen as much more important in Aboriginal and other 'primitive' cultures, in contrast to Western society.

My work and Waddy's had been attempts to answer *cognitive* questions: how and on what basis did Aborigines classify plants and animals? To answer those questions, Waddy had consulted two noted Aboriginal specialists. But their models did not entirely match, nor do we know the extent to which their expertise was shared by others in their culture. By now I had become sensitized to two further kinds of question. The first was a comparative one, about the social distribution of knowledge: how uniform, in fact, was the thinking of people, not just in Western cultures but even in cultures most people think of as 'simple'? Were there not, rather, *sub*cultures, or even *counter*cultures, in any culture? My second question was a simple matter of identification: when we talk about the ideas of this or that 'people', who exactly are we talking about? For thought does not think itself; it is individuals who think. Furthermore, who precisely were the people who created, codified and transmitted the thinking we describe as the cultural ideas of, say, 'the Lilliputians' – or of what we describe as 'Western' thought? For although we are normally supposed to live in a culture which we describe as 'scientific', we do not in fact normally use scientific thinking in our everyday lives. Rather, we simply assume we 'know' about science, because we use technological devices – such as cars, microwave ovens and video recorders which have developed out of modern science – a kind of knowledge which has been called 'recipe knowledge', as it does not require any understanding of the underlying scientific principles.[14] In a recent survey of the distribution of scientific knowledge among British and American adults, more than half had no idea what DNA was, and only one Briton in three knew that the earth went round the sun once a year (30 per cent thought the sun went round the earth). And I for one would be hard put to provide a visitor from outer space – let us call him ET – with anything like a coherent account of what a virus or an atom is. But I firmly believe that they exist. If pressed, I would have to direct ET to a scientist.

So after looking at Aboriginal food classification, I made a 'lateral' leap that some may find puzzling (not to say irritating): I moved from Aboriginal food classification to Western food categories, and then back again. I had no books by nutritionists, or even books about diet regimens or fashionable fads. When I need to deal with food, I use a quite different kind of book – a cookery book. So I went to the kitchen and looked at the ways in which Mrs Beeton, Delia Smith and Fannie Farmer classify food.

I then dutifully returned to examining the second mode of classifying plants and animals which the Aborigines use: their biological classification. At this point I made another 'lateral' digression, into Western biology, but here I was brought up against a further problem: what *kind* of Western classification were we talking about?

I discovered that the ferocious debates between different schools of thought that I was familiar with in the social sciences – between 'ethnomethodologists', for example, and those they dub 'positivists' – had their parallels (such as the controversy over 'cladism') among biologists who worked on classification.

Being ill-equipped to handle such issues, I extended my 'lateral' inquiry further, by looking at popular biology in my own culture. Scientists, I found, had never possessed any monopoly on thinking about nature (and neither had the Church before them), and scholarly ideas about nature had changed greatly over time. In the Middle Ages, it had been quite common to put animals on trial for offences against human laws, both secular and canon. But by the eighteenth century, nature had become a realm *outside* the human sphere. Popular ideas, no less than scientific ones, have also changed. As more and more people abandoned agriculture and moved to the cities, even though they took with them traditional attitudes to nature, the countryside became a place for aesthetic contemplation, for recreation, even for study. Today, bird-watchers, gardeners and nature lovers use books which, though usually written by scientists, group plants and flowers not in accordance with the principles of taxonomy used by biologists but by following quite practical methods developed over hundreds of years of observation on the part of thousands of amateurs. But radically new attitudes have grown up too: for example, it is now being argued that animals have rights.

I went back again to the Aborigines, and carried on systematically examining the two remaining ways in which they classify plants and animals. First, thinking about Groote linguistic classification led me to a particularly shocking discovery: that though I spoke English well, and also had (I thought) a sound knowledge of its grammar, my theoretical understanding of my own language was sadly limited. Second, I looked once more at totemism, the area Durkheim and Lévi-Strauss considered so central, and concluded that it represented yet another mode of thought – *mythological* thinking – different in kind from any of the others.

So, although most people would consider Aboriginal cultures 'simple' or 'undifferentiated', Aborigines actually make intellectual sense of the environment in a number of different ways.

Plants and animals are, of course, only one part of nature. From there I wanted to look at knowledge of another part of the cosmos: the seas and the skies. I wanted, though, to retain what has always been the great strength of anthropology, its intensive, in-depth case studies of particular cultures, and again I would have preferred to stick to hunters and collectors. But case studies of cosmological ideas among hunters and collectors of the quality of Dr Waddy's – where meticulous and extended field research is combined with theoretical sophistication – are hard to come by; studies which look at different kinds of thinking, side by side (astronomical and religious, for example), *within* the same culture, are even rarer.

So I chose a set of studies (see Chapter 2) – fascinating in themselves – about the ways in which Polynesians and Micronesians, faced with the immense problems of how to navigate successfully from island to island across vast expanses of the Pacific, had developed a profound knowledge of the heavenly bodies and the sea, and the necessary technology to make their voyages.

In the process, I found it necessary to come to terms with another set of theories, this time those of psychologists who had studied the mental development of children, notably Jean Piaget and L. S. Vygotsky, as well as the use made of Piaget's theories by the anthropologist Hallpike, who purported (misleadingly, I concluded) to be able to shed light on the development of human thought.

In Chapter 3, I decided to look at yet another domain of human life, that concerned with the body and its ills, concentrating more this time on Western medicine, since this is generally seen as a field in which the West has triumphed, definitively displacing its older modes of thought and forms of therapy, as well as systems of medicine outside the West. We generally think of health and illness as phenomena confined to the boundaries of our own skins. But other cultures do not. So I began by considering an outstanding case study of the Kongo. For them, illness is not simply a physical problem, nor is the sick person's body a kind of machine which can be brought back to normal performance by fine-tuning, by cutting out and sometimes even replacing troublesome components, or by 'treating' it with man-made chemicals. Disorders of the body – and of the mind – are seen, rather, as caused by social stresses and strains, or by human malice or supernatural forces, not by viruses. These are notions we commonly dismiss as 'superstition', and the methods used in treating them as so much 'mumbo-jumbo'. Though the Kongo do use a wide range of natural medicines, their medical therapy involves social and even religious dimensions, so that the management of illness calls for the participation not just of specialists in medicine but of people connected to the patient by kinship and community ties as well.

Western medicine is also a quite recent phenomenon. As the main form of medicine used by and on the masses, indeed, it is only a couple of centuries old. I therefore found it necessary to ascertain what people (and not only ordinary people) had used before then. The answer turned out to be herbal remedies. So I next had to trace how science-based medicine, focused on the hospital and using chemical drugs, displaced older, popular forms of medicine – though these have still not entirely disappeared. In order to do this, I had to document the extraordinary story of the rise of the medical profession, which organized itself so effectively that within a few decades, in alliance with the state, it was able not only to build itself an entrenched position in Western systems of health provision but also to establish a virtual ideological monopoly.

To understand this intellectual monopoly, though, and the respect commanded by Western medicine, I found it necessary to spell out the *meta*-scientific assumptions which inform Western medicine and Western science in general, and the ways in which the gaps between the scientific ideas doctors are trained in and those of their patients vary from each other, and also from one Western culture to another. For at the end of the day, in serious cases, we ask the same questions of our doctors as the Kongo ask of theirs: 'Why *me*?', 'Why this innocent child?', 'Why *now*?' To which doctors (theirs and ours) have no answers. These elemental concerns, then, are not satisfied by scientific medicine. For minor illnesses, people use 'folk' medicine, and when more serious diseases threaten even life itself, they turn to 'alternative', even mystical forms of treatment. During the 1960s, young people began to explore Third (and 'Fourth') World cultures, from the Indians of India to the Indians of the Americas, including their systems of health maintenance and medical cure. By now the cultural practices of peoples such as the Aborigines were no longer denigrated as primitive mumbo-jumbo, but were celebrated as kinds of wisdom that drew on deeper conceptions about the ultimates of life and death than existed in Western biomedicine. The disillusion with orthodox medicine has grown *pari passu*, with a marked rise in the popularity of various kinds of alternative medicine. And in the Third World, systems of treatment that long predate Western medicine, from Chinese acupuncture to Ayurveda in India, have never been eclipsed and continue to flourish, not just among peasants but in the cities where most people live today.

Medical science, although extremely powerful, cannot solve many key problems of human existence. Faced with death or grave incapacity, people the world over turn to ancient or novel alternative and dissenting forms of therapy, including constantly changing fads, and are even prepared to alter complete lifestyles. The incidence of illness and death seems to be so illogical and monstrously unjust – in Max Weber's words, so 'meaningless' – that it drives many people to look for answers not in science but in religion.

In Chapter 4, therefore, I returned to Durkheim's key question: what is the part played by religion in sustaining social solidarity? I used a celebrated case study of the Dogon of West Africa, where religion is depicted as central in every area of life – a situation often assumed to be typical of most non-Western cultures in general. Religion does indeed supply the framework within which the Dogon classify not only plants and animals but everything else. But hidden within this framework, I found they also classify these things on the quite different basis of empirical observation.

Knowledge, then, is necessarily plural: there are knowledges, not simply Knowledge with a capital K. The social distribution of knowledge is plural too, for although everybody thinks, not everyone has the same amount or kind of knowledge. It is the distinctive social activity of 'ethno-intellectuals' to develop, consolidate and transmit these systems of thought.

So in Chapter 4 I considered three case studies of outstanding individual intellectuals in preindustrial societies. I then examined the extent to which people followed, or deviated from, religious orthodoxy during what is uncritically assumed to have been an 'Age of Faith' – in medieval Western Europe – looking at the evidence collected in a famous survey of medieval religious houses in France, plus a detailed case study of heresy in one village, as well as what Chaucer tells us generally of his society.

With the decline of religion – and of a Church with 'universal' pretensions – as both the major framework of thought and the cement which holds society together, new foci of identity have emerged, foremost among them the nation. Old empires were segmentary structures, containing numerous ethnic communities, brought together by conquest and held together by secular mechanisms such as dynastic ruling houses and cultural co-existence. But the modern nation-state was built on a different foundation – the attempt, for instance, to bring into existence a 'British'

identity which would not only transcend the older identities of the conquered Welsh, Scots and Irish but also involve replacing English identity
with 'British'. When Britain became a world empire, even wider symbols
of identity had to be invented.

This, then, was not what Antonio Gramsci called 'hegemonic' nationalism – a political identity designed and used by those who run the state, imposed, together with their culture, for example on *conquered* peoples. We
normally reserve the label 'nationalism', though, for something different
from, and newer than, either old-style hegemonic nationalism or the 'in-
tegrative' British kind – protest on the part of ethnic-minority communities *against* submergence in large, multiethnic states, demanding, instead,
that each nation should have its *own* state. I have illustrated this with studies of the renaissance of Scottish and Welsh cultural nationalism, looking at
two strands: the transformation of truly ancient elements – the tartan in
Scotland and Druidic ceremonies in Wales – and the invention of other,
quite new symbols of nationhood. A third, less well-known case – that of
the Shetland Islands – examines a much more 'submerged' nationality.

A tour round the museums of Europe by a non-European, the Australian Donald Horne, highlighted the materials from which symbols of
national identity are constructed and questioned the common assumption
that cultural nationalism necessarily develops into movements of political
self-determination. For whatever its vibrancy, neither Scottish nor Welsh
nationalism (let alone that of the Shetlands) has given rise to the formation
of autonomous nation-states. The latter, indeed, have more often come
into being as a consequence of political and military action by Great
Powers than as a result of successful movements of national liberation.

I then examined two outstanding attempts to formulate theories which
account for not only the overlap of culture and society but also cultural
identities that exist both within and across the borders of the state: Gramsci's ideas about culture and counterculture, and the concept of subculture
later developed by the Chicago school of sociology.

National identity is not only a question of the relationship of the individual or the group to the state; cultural identity, in what Gramsci called
'civil society', is also involved. Even such an eminently successful symbol
of national identity as the Statue of Liberty therefore reflects the building
of not just a new *polity* but a new kind of *society*, one in which the older
ethnic identities of tens of millions of immigrants went into the 'melting
pot' to be replaced by a new, American identity, achieved not by exposure
to the state's cultural rhetoric but by participation in the popular rituals –
such as Thanksgiving and Christmas – of a newly invented mass culture.

If identities persist at lower levels than the state, cultural community has also always transcended the boundaries of even the largest of states: great world religions like Islam have spread from North Africa to Indonesia; more recently, Christianity has implanted itself in Africa and South America, while secular philosophies from liberalism to communism have spread across the globe. Today, due to the revolution in communications, the world has become what Marshall McLuhan described as a 'global village', where 'transnational' corporations and 'world' music flourish.

In the epoch of global mass society, therefore, the symbols created by Walt Disney in his theme parks – at first populist, then technological – have been, subliminally, far more effective than any overt attempts to consciously construct an ideology of world capitalism.

At the end of the day, though, poverty is still a worldwide phenomenon, and the spectacular achievements of modern science have not resolved many central problems of human existence. It is thus no mere 'doomwatching' to observe that Western science has become part of the problem, for we have long been on the brink of global destruction, not only of the human species but of the natural environment too. Conversely, achievements in the natural sciences have not been matched by theoretical advances in the social sciences, and even when the latter have illuminated human behaviour, the response from governments (and peoples) is usually one of neglect or even contempt. I conclude, therefore, with an attempt to develop a key concept in the social sciences – that of culture – and to show how the dimension of culture, as well as Gramsci's conception of civil society, needs to be added to the political and the economic dimensions of society if we are to make serious sense of a world in which the collapse of communism has been followed only by new kinds of disorder from Russia to the Third World.

I have described my strategy as a kind of 'lateral' thinking. Others may find the term Arthur Koestler applied to the great pioneers of modern science, 'sleepwalking',[15] more apt, though I would argue that this is a pejorative and unjustifiable way of describing perfectly rational scientific procedures, for whatever handbooks of methodology may say, you do not always select a nice, clear field of study (it is often selected for you or is closed to direct inquiry), then choose an appropriate hypothesis and collect data which might falsify or confirm it. It is quite legitimate, instead, to have a number of major preoccupations clearly in mind, and to try out various kinds of theory, looking for evidence which might throw light on these problems in very different places.

In musical terms, therefore, I have not written a baroque symphony, with a neat, linear sequence of first and second subjects, developments, recapitulations, codas and the like. Rather, I have followed Sibelius, whose symphonies open with scraps of melody, followed by others, all of which swirl about until, at the end, they give rise to a major conclusion. (My other hero is Messiaen, who develops many separate segments and similarly waits to bring them to a final synthesis.) This may annoy more tidy-minded readers. But it does mean that you will not be confined to a fare of exotic Australian Aboriginal concepts (though I think you will find these interesting in themselves). Instead, you will see the relevance of these concepts to your own culture (and as a reward for your patience, you will also be treated to a trip to Disneyland at the end).

There is inevitably an ethical dimension to all this. As Nancy Banks-Smith, the doyenne of British TV critics, wrote after the screening of a *Disapppearing World* film on a tribal community, 'Anthropologists are people who tell you that human beings are the same the world over – except when they are different.' That quip enshrines a complex truth: at the end of the day, we cannot simply assume that our thought is scientific and theirs is not, and that as a result there is nothing to be learned from doing what anthropologists do – studying 'other cultures'.[16]

Indeed making comparisons between different kinds of knowledge in Western and non-Western cultures raises questions about the status of 'our' knowledge. I had a particularly nasty shock at an international conference on peace and war when, after somebody had talked about the importance of subjecting negative stereotypes of people belonging to 'other cultures' to critical examination, I added the suggestion that we might also look at more *positive* aspects of the cultures of peoples like the Aborigines – such as their ethno-science, because most people think of them as 'primitives'. This benign idea was immediately questioned, appropriately, by someone from a society where racism is the major issue. Frene Ginwala, then research director of the African National Congress, now speaker of the South African Parliament, replied, 'Yes, that's important, but why, Peter, do you call it *ethno*-science?' I have been trying to answer that question ever since, and this book is part of that attempt.

Several questions then arise. Are the kinds of scientific knowledge which are usually labelled 'ethno-science' simply part of a unitary and universal science which all cultures have developed to different degrees? Or are they different *kinds* of science? Is Western science always superior, across the board? Or do other knowledges possess special strengths that our science lacks? Is Western science, as Harold Garfinkel argues in Chapter 1, however distinctive and powerful a mode of thought, nevertheless only a subculture coexisting with other subcultures and subscribed to by people called 'scientists' who use specialized codes of procedure which most people do not normally use? And since scientists belong to different 'schools of thought', can the scientific community itself not be thought of as further divided into *sub*-subcultures?

There are, moreover, many forms of thought other than scientific thinking, and even scientists do not think scientifically all the time. Nor is the thinking Western scientists do in their laboratories typical of all the thinking they do. In this respect they are no different from non-scientists, who also use different kinds of logic in different social situations. As we saw, the scientific knowledge of the West has not solved the key problems of human existence; rather it has brought us to the brink of global destruction.

Questions ET might put to scientists about 'first and last things' – the *meaning* of life; the occurrence of good and evil; the place of human beings in the cosmos – cannot be answered in purely scientific terms. To deal with that kind of question, we often have recourse to another sort of explanation and to another kind of specialist altogether – people we call theologians or priests.

But there are many religions, and many ways of responding to the same problems, so the answers we get from these various authorities are often contradictory. Still, like the Aborigines, we do not spend most of our time wrestling with matters of life and death. We are too busy getting on with living, answering Chernyshevsky's famous question 'What is to be done?' not in terms of metaphysical ultimates but simply by coping with the problems of everyday life. Moreover, we often take our guidelines not from 'official' sources such as science or organized religion, but from ways of thinking embedded in popular culture, absorbed by virtue of our membership of various kinds of communities, from close-knit ones like family and neighbourhood to global religious or political communities which cross even national boundaries.

If, then, there are many kinds of knowledge in all societies, should we not, instead of contrasting 'their' knowledge and 'ours' across the board, specify *which* of their (and our) kinds of knowledge we are talking about?

I have embarked on my journey to try to answer these questions by looking at a supposedly very 'simple' culture – that of one Australian Aboriginal tribe. Because they lived by hunting and collecting and hadn't developed agriculture, the Aborigines are sometimes considered devoid of scientific thought; instead, it is often believed that they saw things exclusively in 'mystical' terms. Yet they depended for their very survival on observing plants and animals accurately, on coming to correct conclusions about their world and on reaching an understanding of cause and effect. So I have begun with the way the Aborigines classify plants and animals as *foods*; I have then shown how they have developed categories remarkably similar to those of Western biologists, zoologists and botanists and how, in the process, they use similar intellectual procedures. I have next looked at their linguistic and mathematical categories, and finally at their religious conceptions of the relationship of humankind to the rest of nature – which cannot, of course, be reduced simply to the requirements of survival.

Green Knowledge:
The Living Environment of an Australian Tribe

Life before the White Man

To the eyes of white men, Groote Eylandt, like northern Australia in general, is featureless. To the Aborigines it is anything but. Just as English farmers know and name every field and copse, so too Aborigines know their land in intimate detail. There are few prominent natural features on Groote; even Central Hill, the highest point not only on the island, but in the whole of the Gulf of Carpentaria, is only 600 feet high, and apart from certain large billabongs and bays, nothing much is obvious. Yet Waddy has recorded no fewer than 600 named places on the coast of Groote and its offshore islands, while David Turner, who, in 1969 and 1971, studied Bickerton Island, off the coast of Groote – only two or three miles across from north to south and from east to west – recorded ninety-three named spots on the coast alone.[1]

As the landscape is far from featureless to the Aborigines, I should not have been surprised at the results when I asked children to draw for me anything of interest to them on a map of the island which was just an outline, the shape of which they were familiar with from school. Many of them covered the maps with irregular criss-cross lines, explaining that these were 'roads'. Yet to whites, these were just 'tracks' across the island, at best barely discernible most of the year; the island was nothing but a tract of 'natural' environment, a stretch of 'bush', hostile to human purpose and bearing no imprint of human culture.

To the Aborigines, the land is culturally dense. It can be read as a Bible, for anyone can see for themselves the sacred sites where the great Beings passed when they created the world in the Dreamtime. It can also be read as a newspaper, written not in print but in footprints, for when an Aborigine looks at tracks in the sand, he can tell the sex of the person, and often even exactly who it is and how long ago they were there. And when an Aborigine sees a plume of smoke in the distance, he can also calculate which party it is likely to be, whose clan territory it is, the groups known to have started out recently, where they are likely to be heading, their rate of travel, how long the food resources of a given place will permit the group to stay there and how long it will take them to get to their next campsite.

White Australians do know that Aborigines have extraordinary skill as trackers. Some even think of these abilities as mysterious. But there is nothing mystical about the ways in which Aborigines subject a footprint to intense scrutiny, and then to sophisticated interpretation. Yet even anthropologists have at times contributed to the confusion. Thus Warner writes of the Murngin of the mainland: 'A little girl eight or nine years old can immediately tell one who made a particular footprint even though there are a hundred or more people who have placed their footprints on the earth about it.' [2]

This statement seemed to me so sweeping a generalization that I decided to test it. Back in the 1930s an American psychologist, Stanley Porteus, had devised a way of testing the ability of Aborigines to recognize footprints, contrasting their abilities with those of American whites and members of other ethnic groups in various countries (students in Hawaii, children of various ethnicities in a juvenile institution in Chicago, patients in a psychiatric hospital and a New York 'institution', plus 100 British Borstal 'delinquents', 'defectives' in Manchester, and Japanese, Indians, South Africans and Brazilians). Existing intelligence tests, Porteus rightly argued, privileged literacy: the ability to read, or familiarity with regular, abstract shapes such as triangles, squares, etc. which hardly occur in nature. He therefore devised a test which, he thought, did *not* place a premium upon literacy and would be consonant with Aboriginal culture – the test of their ability to recognize footprints.

I didn't have Porteus' book with me in the field, so I asked the Aborigines to look at actual footprints in the sandy soil. [3] But my memory played me false, for what Porteus had done was to use not actual footprints but *photographs* of footprints. He had separated photos of the left foot from those of the right and had then asked his subjects to sort the separated pictures into the correct pairs. His conclusion – that the Aborigines' 'ability... is at least equal to that of whites of high-school standards of education and of better than average social standing'[4] – is not as complimentary to the Aborigines as it might sound, because though he does say that the tests might have been easier for white children, he quite underestimates the cultural bias involved in presenting black-and-white photographs of a reality that is three-dimensional and in colour to illiterates, as well as the greater familiarity of white children with this kind of test situation, performed to order for white male authority figures. And some of the differences in test situation were quite gross: six of the Aborigines were tested in prison, wearing heavy leg chains and guarded by a policeman with a pistol. Despite this, they were quite glad of the diversion, which helped them 'while away a couple of hours of their imprisonment'.

One of the testees, a murderer, even gave Porteus a gift of a message stick, which he passed through the bars.[5]

What my tests showed was that the ability to recognize other people's tracks is not some abstract, absolute and general skill. Rather, who gets recognized by whom depends, not surprisingly, on the social position and experience of the recognizer and the social position of the person whose footprints are being looked at. Overall levels of skill were indeed high, but certain individuals were more often recognized than others – a large, tall man who made heavy prints, for instance, or a girl who was in charge of the others and whose footprints were therefore well known. Individual cases such as these apart, whole *categories* of people were more likely to be recognized widely, either because they were socially important or because people associated with them regularly. Distinctions of sex and age were the most important: older men, being socially dominant, were readily recognized by all groups except young females; older women were the next group most often recognized by both men and women, young and old; young men were the third most commonly recognized group; while young girls were the least recognized, except by other young girls. There were anomalies too. The best at recognition, overall, was a twelve-year-old girl, while some people failed to recognize even members of their nuclear family (and in one case, their own prints!).

The Aboriginal landscape, then, is full of features whites do not recognize. It is also conceptualized differently. A major difference is the significance of water – the sea, of course, because of its resources and because it is the major highway, but also inland bodies of water. The larger permanent rivers and related lagoons derive from Central Hill and other rings of hills in the interior, which is often referred to as 'on top'. The special importance of the coast and other well-watered areas is reflected in linguistic usage: the verb -*dorinda*, meaning 'to go down', usually implies going down from the hilly interior towards the coast, while the verb -*riberiga* usually implies 'coming ashore' or 'going inland'. But the reference point is not always the coast, for these words can also be used in relation to a billabong or other body of inland water.

Boundaries, too, are treated differently. While whites use clear natural features, such as a creek, to mark off a piece of land, the boundaries of Aboriginal clan territories are marked by reference to the *central* parts of a territory, its heartland we might say: to a watershed rather than a river.

Small and scattered as the Groote Eylandt population might be – there were only between 250 and 300 people living there in the first half of the century – for a hunting and gathering economy, the islands have nevertheless supported one of the highest densities in Australia: 2.6 to 3.3 people per square mile. As a result life there was very different from the conditions that Aborigines had to cope with in the harsh deserts of central Australia. (Though I speak throughout of 'the Aborigines', I usually mean only the Groote Eylandters.)

Groote Eylandt, to a hunter-gatherer, was a rich country. The islanders recognize no fewer than sixteen different ecological zones: eight for the land and eight for the sea. Inland, rivers and billabongs are stocked with fish, crabs, prawns, water goannas (monitor lizards), freshwater turtles, crocodiles and often ducks, geese and other birdlife, and with a rich variety of plants not found in drier areas, while larger game frequent their banks. 'Jungles', thickly overgrown with creepers and reeds, are favourite spots for wallabies, and there are fruit-bearing trees such as pandanus and paperbark and other trees for making objects of material culture. A few, like spears, spear-throwers and turtle harpoons, are refined and artistic works of craftmanship; some, like canoes, are major pieces of technology; and others, like coffins, are needed only periodically. But because the Aborigines are always on the move, for the most part equipment is kept to the mimimum and to what can be easily carried.

But it is the coast which is most important, so much so that the Aborigines distinguish between the deep sea, the shallow sea, the coral reefs, the intertidal rock platforms and outcrops, and the shallower intertidal zone close inshore, as well as the sand and mud flats, and the beach itself.

Because of the richness of the coast, camps are often located there. Among the Yanyuwa of Boroloola, on the mainland nearby, men and women have different perceptions of coastal campsites. For the men, the camp is centred on the river, which they use for canoe travel; women, on the other hand, emphasize the arrangement of family groupings, and the church.[6] And the coast is so important for the Lardil of nearby Mornington Island that most personal names are derived from the coast and the sea. People may be named after the sheen on the surface of the sea, after seaweed or stormy weather, or different kinds of sea birds, the different phases of the tides and the wind, and so on. Other names are poetic: the smoky, hazy appearance of the sea in the distance; the 're-laxed' nature of some waves; the 'frolicsome', laughing nature of some small waves and the power of others.[7] One woman, who belongs to a family particularly identified with the sea, has written a history of her own people; her family name, which she writes as 'Roughsey', actually means 'sea swell'.[8]

The land becomes a very different place in each of the two major seasons. In his great novel *Capricornia*, Xavier Herbert catches the contrast graphically. During the Wet, he writes, cattle wandered in a land of plenty, fat and sleek, till the buffalo-flies and marsh-flies came and drove them mad, so that they ran and ran to leanness, often to their death… mosquitoes and a hundred other breeds of maddening insects were there to test a man's endurance.

In the Dry, however,

the grasses yellowed, browned, dried to tinder, burst into spontaneous flames … exhausted cattle staggered searching dust for food and drink, till they fell down and died and became neat piles of bones … But to the original inhabitants of the land, there were mangoes and flying foxes to eat … pandanuses and other palms and giant paper-barks and native fig trees. [In the billabongs there were] yams and lily-roots … it was the haunt of duck and geese, and a drinking place of the marsupials … Still more food was to be got from the sea, which abounded in turtle and dugong and fish.[9]

This alternation of the seasons is the fundamental framework of life. It is marked by two great prevailing winds: the north-west wind, which brings the Wet, from late November or early December to late April or early May, culminating in the monsoon; and the south-east wind, which ushers in the Dry by about early May. This opposition is reflected in the use made by the Aborigines of the north-west and the south-east winds as major religious symbols – the 'totems' – of the two largest clans, each belonging to one of the moieties into which the tribe is divided. One anthropologist has even argued that the apparently abstract shapes of these two symbols, which are painted on the chests of boys during their initiation into adulthood, and upon bark paintings used in religious rituals, in fact derive from the different shapes the sails of a canoe take when blown along by the different kinds of wind in different seasons.[10] Though there are phases within and between, it is the two major seasons, the Wet and the Dry which predominate, governing the availability of plants and of animal, especially marine, life (see Figure 1 overleaf).

The early Dry is cold and misty, and deteriorates into a cloudy period, when hunger threatens. With the coming of the Wet, it gets hotter and growth revives. Energetic as the Aborigines are when hunting and gathering food, during the hot season, Baker notes, the Yanyuwa conserve energy by sleeping or resting during the heat of the day, and 'minimize physical activity in the steamy monsoon'.[11]

In April and May, the delicious wild yam can be eaten; in July and August, tamarind fruits. These seasonal changes in plant and animal life, as

Figure 1 **Chart of the seasons on Groote Eylandt**

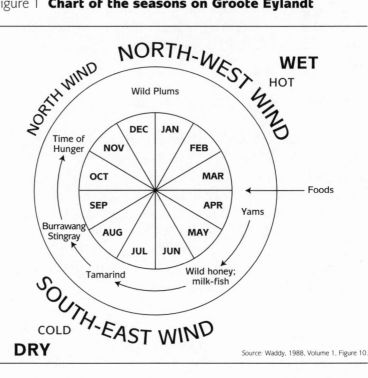

Source: Waddy, 1988, Volume 1, Figure 10.

Dulcie Levitt, the pioneer of Groote Eylandt biological research, has shown, constitute a 'bush calendar',[12] marked by changes in the weather. Thus the flowering of the cocky apple in September reminds the islanders that the time has come to look for turtles and their eggs on the beaches, a time also when certain kinds of stingrays are fat. Similarly, the flowering of the 'termite tree' in November/December means that the rainy season will soon be here; the flowering of the white berry bush in January brings lots of mosquitoes; the flowering of the rough-barked gum and the bunch spear grass in March signal the approaching end of the Wet and the arrival of the south-east wind, and with it the Dry. At the beginning, fruit is in short supply, so yams are in demand and it is a good time for fish such as snapper. Now that many Groote Eylandters are Christians, the flowering of the wattles reminds them that it is nearly Easter. Later in the dry season, the open forest is burned off, which makes hunting easier, and honey becomes available. With the flowering of the stringy-barks in July/August, the country begins to dry up and the billabongs can no longer be relied upon; by August/September people have to stay near the rivers to be sure of their water supplies. In October/November, the singing of the cicadas by day and of the crickets by night 'helps' the wild plums to ripen. Before long the Wet will begin, forecast by mangrove crabs leaving their holes and shifting to higher ground, and termites starting to build tiny 'hills' only four inches high. January is also the season when parrotfish are fat; April for snapper.[13] When a cyclone is approaching, people move to higher ground inland.[14]

Many of the vegetables collected by the Aborigines provide only small quantities of food, but a few, like the burrawang or the round yam, can be gathered and stored in large quantities. Routine hunting and gathering activities, normally a day-by-day necessity, can then be suspended or at least diminished, and large numbers of people are able to come together for important religious rituals, such as the initiation of boys.

However, the burrawang (or zamia palm, *cycas angulata*) is a singularly problematic food, since the nut inside the fruit contains a poison for which there is no known antidote. To remove it, the Aborigines treat the nuts by heating them, using hot stones and ashes, then pounding or grinding the nuts to make 'flour' — sometimes in the form of cakes that Australians call 'damper' — using bent-over fronds in running water as a strainer, which allows the poison to leach out without the food being washed away. According to the condition of the nuts, different methods are used: there is one for when they have been freshly gathered; another for when they have been left for a day or have just fallen from the plant; another for old nuts that have simply dropped off the tree; and yet another for old nuts with shrivelled, hard kernels. Really old nuts might need processing for as much as nine nights. Fresh nuts do not keep and therefore have to be eaten the next day; older nuts yield a 'porridge' which can keep for six days; nuts left with their kernels still inside can be stored in wet sand for a month, in extreme circumstances for five months.[15]

How the Aborigines developed these methods of removing poison, back in human history, raises a question to which no one has ever given me a satisfactory answer: how did they come to discover that the poison *could* be removed, especially when its removal took several days? Wouldn't many people have died in the process? Whatever the answers, the development of the necessary treatments must have involved a good deal of abstract reasoning and a lot of experimentation.

The round yam (*murungkwurra*) is also poisonous and is therefore called the 'cheeky' (i.e. dangerous) yam in pidgin English. The yams are covered with heated stones and leaves on which water is thrown in order to produce steam, and then covered with paperbark. Once cooked, they are then peeled by making a hole in a small snail shell to form a 'potato peeler', and the peelings (slivers of the flesh, not the outer covering) are soaked in running water overnight. Potato peelings are an apt comparison, for I found the taste similar to a rather chemical potato even after all this preparation.

The work of removing poison from plants is done by women, because vegetable food is their sphere. The basic division of labour, indeed, is based on gender. Feminists nevertheless might legitimately object to the title of an international conference some years ago, 'Man the Hunter', for 'hunting' is shorthand for hunting and collecting, in which the hunting is done by the men and the collecting by the women. But since it is vegetable food – yams and water-lily roots, wild plums and the burrawang – which provides the bulk of the diet, the women are the chief providers, not the men.

The productive sphere of men, hunting and fishing, is important, though, because it provides the main flesh component of the diet throughout the year. Hunting may bring in wallabies, but usually only smaller animals such as goannas, blue-tongued lizards, possums and bandicoots. In season, a good haul of flying foxes can be had by lighting fires under trees. But land game does not bring in a lot; nor do birds. Only the large birds – the jabiru, the jungle fowl and its eggs, the pelican, brolga and spoonbill – add much to the diet, and they are not often come across.

The really important flesh foods, in any quantity, come from the sea, whether in the spectacular form of the occasional large turtle or the much rarer dugong or porpoise, or regular catches of fish all year round. So important, indeed, are fish that the Aboriginal word for them, *akwalya*, is used not only to refer to animals in the sea (including large creatures like turtles and dugongs as well as fish proper) but also to talk about all kinds of flesh foods, including land animals and birds (though land animals can be distinguished, if necessary, by a different term, *yinungungwangba*).

If suitable yams or fruit are conveniently to hand, men will, of course, collect them, just as girls will collect eggs from nests and sandbanks. But because of the importance and regularity of the fish contributed by the men and the vegetables by the women, men are identified with the sea and women with the land, as reflected in an old word for women, *waringaribu-mandya*, meaning 'people of the land'.

Yet since it is vegetable food that people depend on most, the word for vegetable food, *aninga*, is used for food in general, just as the poor in European cities throughout history have used 'bread', their staple, as a synonym for food in general. But despite their crucial contribution to the food supply, the social status of women is not, as economic determinists might think, higher than that of men, or even equal, for women are excluded from the meetings at which the older men take the decisions which affect the life of the community. Only towards the end of her life does the occasional woman of strong personality participate in such gatherings.

Though we have talked about abundance, it is nevertheless seasonal and localized. Few bush foods provide as much as the burrawang. In a diary of the foods collected by several different hunting-and-collecting groups in Arnhem Land, Margaret McArthur, a nutritionist, recorded that on bad days there would be little to eat after nine or ten hours' foraging in the bush.[16] At times of hunger, people were reduced to subsisting on watered-down honey for days on end. On one occasion, on Groote, after a day when all our possessions, including our reserve food, had been swept off our heads while crossing a river, we had nothing to eat during a night of pouring rain except a smelly coconut which had floated over from New Guinea, some 300 miles away, and water too salty to drink.

For Groote, there is little information about how food gets distributed, but in the past it was mainly, as in all Aboriginal cultures, in accordance with sex and age. Norman Tindale, the last person to observe the islanders when they still lived entirely by hunting and collecting, states that there was a 'definite food-sharing custom' whereby one man always distributed the food, but the bringer of the food received nothing.[17] Large prizes like stingrays were taken to the senior men around – fathers and mothers' brothers, for example, or sometimes to the owner of the canoe, who also directed operations – and these senior men then undertook the distribution, in which they (and sometimes the senior women) got the titbits.

What conservation and storage techniques there are do not permit the building up of a food reserve. The Yanyuwa 'store' long-necked turtles and goannas in grass-lined holes with a rock on top, and also, nowadays, use hessian bags and even kitchen sinks and baths! They also tether them, and much larger marine turtles, to posts or trees with ropes, keeping them 'on the hoof', as it were, for later consumption. The Yanyuwa 'scramble' turtle and sea-bird eggs, then cook and seal them in paperbark bundles. Grass seeds are ground up to make 'dampers', as are cycads, pandanus nuts and water-lily seeds, while the fruit of the wild plum is pounded and made into a sweet paste and covered with red ochre, which prevents it rotting and allows it to be stored.[18]

There are a few other practices aimed at *conserving* wild plants. On Groote, women leave a small part of a yam tuber in the ground to allow regrowth, but we have no reports of more elaborate conservation measures such as the Yanyuwa practice. Among the Yanyuwa, flying foxes are not killed until April, when their young are weaned; there are rules against wasting food such as goanna meat and on the hunting of dugongs. Rights to hunt in particularly abundant areas, such as small islands rich in bird or turtle eggs, are jealously guarded. There are also ritual prohibitions on hunting in a dead person's territory, so that animals can 'breed up in hunt free havens', and rules which restrict the eating of flying foxes to initiated men only. The preservation of the resources of water holes is thought to be ensured by a taboo on the killing of the 'quiet' water snake.[19]

The Original Affluent Society?

In economic terms, then, the traditional Aboriginal world was not an egalitarian Eden inhabited by noble savages. Neither was it a wretched struggle for material survival. Because of the tropical climate and the abundance of sea and shore life, these coastal regions of the north are relatively well endowed.

Bill Harney, once described as 'one of the best bushmen' even seen, regarded Groote as one of the richest areas he knew,[20] while the nineteenth-century anthropologist Sir Baldwin Spencer remarked of the Boroloola mainland nearby: 'There is such a supply of food . . . that [the Aborigines] can do without what we have to give them easily; in fact, they fed just about as well as we do.'[21]

Though there are shortages at some times of the year, there are also periods when there is enough staple food to allow people to spend time looking for luxuries. With the basics assured, gourmet foods come to the top of the agenda. Thus, on one occasion when I was only too glad to sit down after hours of 'walkabout', many of the Aborigines immediately went off again into the bush – this time, looking for luxuries like pandanus nuts. On another occasion, when they had killed a wild bullock, one man, sated with meat, asked me for some turtle eggs I had buried in the sand. When I asked him why, he said he felt like a change from meat. McArthur, too, considers that Arnhem Land Aborigines could have collected enough food or yams to last several days, but preferred instead to collect food every day because they enjoyed what, to them, were social outings. She saw no sign that they disliked their work, or that walking and digging was looked on as either monotonous or 'drudgery'.

A second major luxury is honey, available from wild bee nests in June and July. 'Bee bread' (processed pollen) is very nutritious; it can also be used for medicinal purposes – to cure diarrhoea, skin infections, sore eyes and toothache.[22] But it is the wild honey itself which is the great delicacy, and it is often mixed with water and given to babies. Aborigines can unerringly spot the tell-tale signs of bee hives – the (to me) almost invisible droppings around the nests and the 'glue' on the tree trunks. Then they listen to hear whether the tree is occupied or not before they shin up, often a long way, to chop out the nests or to chop down the whole tree. Before they acquired metal axes, this had to be done with stone tools and must have been very hard work indeed. Even with steel axes, a particularly high price was sometimes paid when the wood was very hard, for my genealogies show that quite a number of people fell to their deaths satisfying a sweet tooth. An equally hazardous luxury is the pandanus nut, because to get the delicious kernel out you have to hold the very hard nut and chop the kernel out with an axe – which sometimes removes fingers as well.

With animal foods, it is fat that is particularly highly prized. In recounting a hunting success, one is always asked, 'Was it fat?' – in relation not only to land animals but also to marine foods. In paintings of stingrays, the fat glands are often shown.

The wider theoretical implications of such luxury, though, were not fully apparent, even to anthropologists, until Marshall Sahlins used them to challenge what was all too often taken to be common sense. In the 1960s, in an influential book generally seen as radical, J. K. Galbraith had argued that though advanced capitalism is the classic epoch of high production, mass consumption and even 'affluence', it is only '*private*' affluence which coexists with 'public squalor'. Far more radically, Sahlins now argued that this implicitly evolutionist view ignored the fact that hunting and collecting societies were the '*original* affluent societies' and not, as classical economics would have it, 'subsistence economies'. This latter, he said, is only so from the point of view of that kind of economic theory which assumes that human wants are infinite; that the technology of primitive hunters and collectors is so inadequate that they are engaged in a constant struggle to stave off hunger; and that they have no leisure in which to think, innovate or just rest.[23]

First, says Sahlins, you cannot judge the lives hunters led in the past by studying peoples today who have been forced out of the rich zones now appropriated for agriculture and urban settlement and who are now left only with remote deserts and jungles – the Kalahari, the Amazon, central Australia. Second, there is no justification for assuming that a boundless drive to maximize both production and consumption is a necessary, permanent and immanent part of the human condition. On that reasoning, the hunter would seem to be '*un*economic man'. In reality, Sahlins argues, the hunger lived in a 'Zen economy': one of limited means, but also of limited wants (which the hippies of the 1960s celebrated). Yet at least in the favourable areas which most hunters used to inhabit centuries ago, they were not 'poor'; they were *free*. A good case can be made for the following conclusion:

that hunters and gatherers work less than we do; and, rather than a continuous travail, the food quest is intermittent, leisure abundant, and there is a far greater amount of sleep in the daytime per capita per year than in any other condition of society.[24]

As to leisure, one of the crucial studies Sahlins cites was actually carried out on Groote by members of the Australian-American Scientific Expedition to Arnhem Land in 1948 on groups of Aborigines in the bush. Though the two groups they studied spent only a quarter of their time finding and preparing food, with little difference between men and women (the average length of time devoted to finding food and preparing it was only between four and six hours a day[25]), yet their diet was nevertheless 'adequate' when measured against the standards for the desirable consumption of calories and nutrients laid down in official US nutrition manuals. Once food had been procured, people spent their time talking, eating and, above all, daytime sleeping – women for nine hours a week, men for twelve hours – and, in the evenings, making music. One Arnhem Land group, Sahlins observes, 'maintained a virtually full-time craftsman whose true speciality... seems to have been loafing'. Similar attitudes to work and leisure have been recorded among hunters outside Australia. 'Why should we plant,' a Bushman in southern Africa classically asked, 'when there are so many mongomongo nuts in the world?'. And in East Africa Hadzapi hunters spent 'days on end' during the dry season gambling, often losing the bows and arrows they depended on for big-game hunting in the process. Sex and religion were major leisure-time activities too.

Since the resources of any one area rapidly become exhausted, hunters need to keep on the move – mobility is the name of the game. So they avoid accumulation: the possessions they have to carry are kept to the minimum and heavy items like pestles and mortars are buried where they can easily be found next time the site is visited. And when they do have a surplus, usually they do not (and often cannot) store it; they consume it.

That is why the myths about the creatures of the Dreamtime are stories of movement, for they, every bit as much as human beings today, necessarily kept on the move. Nalikena – 'on they went' – is intoned every few sentences in these sagas.

'Hunters,' Sahlins concludes, 'keep bankers' hours.' In contrast, one in three of those who rely on agriculture, or who live by selling their labour in cities, are officially classified today as 'poor'. And this is called 'progress' or 'development', while 'affluent' hunters are labelled 'backward' or 'primitive'.

Classifying People

This is an economy, then, that goes far beyond satisfying minimal calorific requirements. Yet the view of William Dampier, the first Englishman to encounter the Aborigines, in the seventeeth century, that these were 'the miserablest [people] in the world', still survives among whites three centuries later.

The Aborigines were singled out as the most primitive people on earth for other reasons, not just because they were hunters and collectors. The resistance they offered to the whites who fought them for the land proved that they were savages. 'Every acre,' Henry Reynolds has written, 'was won from the Aborigines by bloodshed and warfare'; in the continent as a whole, between 2,000 and 2,500 Europeans were killed, and at least 20,000 Aborigines.[26] Once their resistance was crushed, they became simply an encumbrance, useless as labour and at worst vermin to be exterminated.

But scientists also believed that the Aborigines were supremely 'primitive'. Nineteenth-century intellectuals, mesmerized by the triumph of evolutionism in biology, set about applying it to human society. On the basis of their technology, Aborigines were lumped together with hunters and collectors elsewhere in the world as 'Stone Age' peoples, even though the kinship systems and religious cosmologies of these peoples were very different from those found in Australia. There was no justification, either, for assuming that Aboriginal forms of social organization and culture were any more 'primitive' than those found in other continents. Even in economic, as distinct from technological, terms, Ernestine Friedl has distinguished four *different* ways in which the sexual division of labour is organized among foragers.[27]

It was particularly easy as well for incautious inquirers in the nineteenth century, often either missionaries or administrators influenced by racist assumptions, to conclude that the Aborigines were savages, incapable of clear thought about the facts of life and ignorant of civilized customs, in marriage or in anything else. It seemed to them that what they were confronting was 'group marriage', 'primitive sexual communism', even 'promiscuity'.

The Myth of 'Primitive Communism'

Aboriginal forms of social organization and culture were taken as 'fossil' remains of a way of life: the archetype of a 'primitive communism' which had died out elsewhere and been replaced with superior forms, a communism which had been not merely economic but also sexual – a myth which remains potent even today.

The 'evidence' lay not just in Stone Age technology but also in Australian social institutions, particularly their forms of kinship terminology, their marriage classes and their religious beliefs and practices, dubbed as 'totemism'.

Aboriginal kinship terminologies – the sets of labels used for different categories of kin – were considered by writers like Morgan and Engels to reveal traces of earlier forms of social organization, based on systems of marriage that no longer existed. True, not every nineteenth-century writer believed this, but those who did not are generally only known to specialists. By contrast, ideas about 'primitive communism' had become widely known to millions by the end of the nineteenth century because they had been taken up by the founders of modern communism, notably by Friedrich Engels, whose *Origin of the Family* was based largely on the work of the American ethnologist Lewis Henry Morgan.[28] And modern radical feminists continue to study Engels even though his schema is no more or less valid than the theories of other nineteenth-century writers like McClellan or Bachofen, now long forgotten.

Engels believed that humankind had originally lived in a condition of 'primitive promiscuity', in which no barriers existed to sexual relations between parents and children or between siblings. Subsequently, he argued, restrictions upon promiscuity were introduced by the establishment of 'group marriage', in the first stage of which – the 'consanguine' family – parents and children were now excluded from sexual relations, but not brothers and sisters. In the second stage – 'punaluan' marriage – brothers and sisters were finally excluded from marriage. Whole generations were thus believed to have shared partners in common, even though Engels admitted that 'no verifiable example' of these 'extinct' forms of marriage now existed.

It was not these ideas about bygone stages of social organization that modern feminists have found exciting so much as Engels' ideas about the 'stages' *subsequent* to group marriage – the emergence of the 'pairing' and eventually the monogamous family, and the belief that there were still traces of 'group marriage' in contemporary primitive societies. In particular, the high status of women in cultures where descent was traced through the female and not the male line was seen as a survival of a time when women actually had been the dominant sex – the epoch of 'matriarchy'.

Engels had explained these changes in the family as part and parcel of a complex package – the emergence of private property, class society and the state. But even radical and socialist women, who thought of themselves as members of an oppressed class, also knew that the inferior place of women in the social division of labour was determined by sex as well as class, even for rich women. They therefore found Engels' analysis of patriarchy unsatisfactory, since it argued that the inferior position of women derived from differences in their 'relationship to the means of production'. To feminists, however, the inferior position of women in both the class structure and social life generally was to be explained by the way in which sexual differences, which were biological facts, had been converted into gender inequalities. But women were also attracted to Engels' argument because he provided them with a vision of liberation. Male domination, he asserted, was not eternal – there would be equality between the sexes in a future communist society, just as there had been in the primitive communism of the past.

Evolutionists pointed out that some Australian societies were matrilineal, others patrilineal; some societies had two marriage classes, others four and yet others eight. The main question, then, was how this had *come about*. But since there was no documentary evidence at all, and because the reports of researchers in the field were gradually shown to be full of errors and ill-founded inference, the view that became dominant was that these questions were simply unanswerable, or could be answered without using evolutionist ideas. By the 1930s, A. R. Radcliffe-Brown was demonstrating that the special authority of the mother's brother, even in very patriarchal societies – where he was a kind of 'male mother', with authority over his sister's children – did not have to be seen as a hangover from a supposed epoch of matriarchy, but could be explained in terms of contemporary relationships. In patriarchal societies, for instance, once marriage had been consolidated by a marriage payment, a woman's children became members of her husband's clan; *she*, though, remained a member of the clan she had been born into (her father's). The 'final test' was that 'their gods were not her gods'.[29] And in matrilineal societies, the mother's brother was important because, though the matrilineal group traced its descent through women, he exercised *authority* because he was the woman's senior *male* relative of her generation.

The Aborigines could be considered 'classless' according to economic criteria. The means of production – tools and the know-how for making and using them – were available to everybody: every man could make a spear-thrower, every woman a digging-stick. There were therefore no closed classes monopolizing the means of production, and no propertyless proletariat deprived of access to these things, no rich and no poor. Nor did individuals and families own land privately, although each clan had very special rights over its clan territories and usually hunted there more than anywhere else. On Mornington Island, clans even had rights over 'strips' of the sea.[30]

On Groote, David Turner writes:

the members of each local group, while residing primarily in their own country with their wives (from other local groups) and families, were nevertheless relatively mobile and would normally be allowed to travel through other territories, particularly within each island or mainland area, in search of food and water and for ceremonial purposes.[31]

At the individual level, a good hunter would produce more than his less competent or idler peers, sometimes more than he and his close kin could consume. But surpluses could not be converted into capital. They could not even be stored. What was possible was to convert economic surplus into social prestige.

In these societies of only a few hundred people, *everyone* was a close kinsman. But some, of course, were closer kin than others, and you had to behave very differently indeed to different categories of kin. The complexity of Aboriginal kinship structures, the key building block of their entire social organization, has fascinated anthropologists for a century and a half. Being intellectuals, they have struggled to reduce this apparently bewildering complication to a few basic principles.

Nineteenth-century researchers living with the Aborigines quickly discovered that their marriage system was far removed from 'primitive promiscuity'. Rather, it was regulated by the social divisions into which a person was born – moieties, sections and subsections – and marked by different terms for different categories of kin. In a society with four marriage classes, for example, people belonged to one or other of the four sections. A man from section A, belonging to one moiety, would marry a woman from section B, in the other moiety; their children, however, would belong to neither of the parents' sections, but to the second section, D, in the mother's moiety:

Moiety 1		Moiety 2
A	=	B ↓
C	=	D ↓

$$= marries$$
$$↓ children\ belong\ to$$

Marriage systems vary in different parts of Australia: on Groote, for example, there are no sections or subsections. Modern scholars, notably Radcliffe-Brown,[32] reduced all these systems to a few types, based on simple principles so schematic that this kind of study subsequently became sarcastically known as 'kinship algebra'. Not only the marriage classes but the kinship terms, Radcliffe-Brown argued, fitted together to form a closed system. How the differences arose – the question the evolutionists asked – was something the anthropologists could not answer.

In European and North American cultures, we, like the Aborigines, group relatives of different kinds under one label. Thus the brothers of both my mother and my father are called 'uncles'; the parents of both my mother and my father are 'grandparents' or, by sex, 'grandfathers' and grandmothers'. All these separate terms also fit together to form a *system* of kinship terminology – we trace our relationship to an 'uncle' by extension from the primary relationships of the nuclear family.

But Aboriginal systems are far more totalizing. Whereas we are related to only a handful of people out of millions, for them *all* relationships, over the whole of society, fit together into a system – not just a logical system, but one which governs behaviour in matters of sex and marriage, on which, in turn, the entire social structure is based. Further, in the schema developed by Radcliffe-Brown there appeared to be no anomalies, no nonconformity, no exceptions. It was a model in which there was not only no evolution but also no history.

It was not until Frederick Rose carried out his exceedingly detailed research on Groote Eylandt, just before the Second World War, that this model could be seriously challenged. Rose, a revolutionary if there ever was one, was sceptical of the idea that the Aborigines were any more conformist than he was. Using the methods he had absorbed in his training as a natural scientist – and which he used in his subsequent work as a meteorologist – he collected a vast amount of data on kinship terms, identifying no fewer than 25,000 used by Aborigines towards other people (out of a possible 50,000).[33] Some twenty years later, I collected another 11,000 – mainly for children born since Rose's time together with some he had not been able to record.[34]

Non-anthropologists generally think it unproblematic to translate the kinship terms used in other cultures into what they think is an English equivalent. Sometimes, indeed, there may be overlap, but more often this is not the case. Translating Aboriginal kinship terms into categories such as 'mother', 'father', 'elder brother', 'younger brother', 'mother-in-law', etc, however, creates new problems rather than making things clearer, because the Aborigines group together relatives whom we distinguish, and distinguish others we lump together under the same label. Obviously, a girl and her sisters and brothers may have several younger brothers. There is, therefore, no difficulty here in translating the Groote Eylandt term *nenigumandja* (I use the vocative form because it's shorter) as 'younger brother', both in the singular, or – in both languages – where there are several younger brothers, using the same term as a *category* of relationship too. But it is surprising to us – even shocking – to find the same principle applied to mothers, for if people can have a set of younger brothers, they can also have several people in a set of mothers – not just their biological mother but also sisters of their mother (though, of course, Aborigines are as capable as we are of distinguishing their own biological mothers from other, 'social' mothers).

The same applies to wives, though here – since we are used to the idea of polygyny (and remarriage) – we are less surprised to find that several women may be labelled by the term 'wife' (though in our culture only one *after* the other). But it *is* surprising to us to find that the term *dadinga*, which we translate as 'wife', is also applied to people to whom one is related *even before marriage*. It means 'marriageable female' and not just wife, and is thus a potential as well as an actual term, including women who will be called *dadinga* who are not yet born. The probability is that one or more of them will be marriage partners, but whether they are or not they are still called *dadinga*. So there are 'wives' one is not married to. Nor is this simply an individual, person-to-person relationship. Since a set of brothers will all call a whole set of women *dadinga*, a group of brothers has a group of *dadinga*.

In Britain, by contrast, though we practise what anthropologists call 'assortative homogamy' (which ordinary folk call 'like marrying like'), there is, in strictly legal terms at least, an open market for spouses – the general principle is that anyone can marry anyone. But for Aborigines, the market is segmented; there is only a limited set of women called *dadinga*.

These rules do influence actual choices of spouse. But rules do not explain, or guide, everything in social life. Marriage is also guided, as in other cultures, by further important considerations which exponents of kinship algebra do not take into account. These are (a) demographic factors, (b) the exercise of political power, (c) deviance (people break the rules) and (d) cumulative historical changes which result in contradictions and inconsistencies in the system as a whole (i.e. it becomes *unsystematic*). Let us look at each of these in turn.

The Politics of Bestowal

Traditionally, which *dadinga* one actually got to marry depended on agreements made between the senior male relatives of the two potential marriage partners, especially their fathers, often when the future spouses were only children, about six years old. When the deal was concluded, a boy came under the control of his future wife's father. Having control over marriageable children therefore gave these men enormous power, as it did to British aristocrats who had control over their 'wards'.

When Tindale landed on Groote in 1921, no women were ever seen except by accident. Even the missionaries who had preceded him a year or two earlier never actually got to see a woman until 1925, and women only came to live at the mission with their children as late as 1937. As he records:

There was general and strict enforcement of seclusion of the women ... No native, from the time of his initiation until he is of age to marry, and no stranger, is allowed to approach the women, who are compelled to live in camps guarded by the older men ... The women are ... monopolized by the older men, who each have two or more if possible ... The younger men are not allowed near places where the women were likely to be digging yams or gathering burrawang, or to look at them, under penalty of spearing. Few men under about thirty, unless of exceptional prowess ... are entitled to wives ... Old men are sometimes deprived of their wives, and it depends on their influence whether they are assisted to find their former wives or not ... Several solitary old men, practically hermits ... have lost and been unable to regain their women.[35]

When whites did encounter groups of women, an astonishing sight met their eyes, for the women were all wearing 'dresses' made of two pieces of paperbark stitched together – in Tindale's words, 'like so many giant "jacks in the box"'. On the move, these were folded and carried underarm or on top of the woman's head, but if a man other than her husband approached, she would stand her 'dress' on the ground and hide behind it, or open it to form a 'V' to cover her face and breasts. If the visitors stayed longer, the 'dress' was stiff enough to place on the ground in a wider 'V' and the woman would sit down behind it. On cold nights, the covering could be used as a blanket.[36] The modesty, though, was probably merely conventional, for when one visitor moved round to the side of a woman who had placed a sheet between herself and him, she made no attempt to move it, but merely looked at him. The next time he saw the women, they covered themselves only fore and aft.[37]

The older men also exercised tight control over the boys in everyday life. When a boy was circumcised, at between ten and thirteen years of age, he was removed from the women's camp and thereafter took his part in

paddling, firewood gathering, collecting fishbait, and generally waiting on his older companion. One such guardian ... had two boys under his care; they were never allowed out of his sight, followed him when hunting, and when in camp attended frequently to his person (combing his hair, delousing him, or, at times, painting his body with ochre).[38]

Ideally, the guardian should also have been a boy's sister's husband. But often he wasn't, because these valuable properties were commonly exchanged, whatever the relationship involved, between the older men. Release from their control came at about sixteen years of age, when a boy underwent a further stage of initiation into manhood by having a deep cicatrix cut into his chest. Later, further cicatrices – as many as six – were added. A boy was finally considered ready to marry only by his late twenties.

The power of the older men to dominate society by virtue of their control over the distribution of women has been called the 'politics of bestowal'. It may have been intensified once Aborigines came into contact with the Malays, and, in the Tiwi case, Portuguese from Timor, who even took some of the tribe away as slaves. Leaving it to the younger men to trade directly with the strangers for iron, the older men distanced themselves, thereby diminishing the risk of being taken as slaves themselves, but ensuring that it was they who monopolized the profits and power which ensued from such trading contacts.

This kind of domination by the older men was even more graphically elaborated among the Lardil, nearby Mornington Island. There, David McKnight has recorded, young men were also made to undergo elaborate initiation rituals. But though circumcision was the beginning of their transition to manhood, for at least a year afterwards they were forbidden to speak the normal Lardil language. Instead, they had to communicate exclusively by using a special sign language called Marlda Kangka. It was not widely used outside ritual contexts and in hunting (when silence is needed), and, indeed, had nearly died out, until there was a revival of interest in traditional culture. By then, the only adult male left who knew it was a white man, McKnight himself, who was able to save it from extinction by teaching it to the son of the man from whom he had learned it!

The sign language, not surprisingly, is much simpler than spoken Lardil. Since it is the men's language, there are more names for animals than plants, and no signs at all for many small organisms.

Some signs represent physical features, such as the large beak of the cockatoo, or an animal's behaviour, such as the hopping of a pigeon. Others allude to the uses made of them by human beings: for example, the sign for shark and stingray – one hand cupped and the fist of the other placed in it – imitates the kneading of the highly valued livers of these animals into a ball. Yet other signs refer to the place of animals in myths. Signs for human beings relate to circumcision (for males), to a girl's nipples or to the swaying motion of the bark container in which women carry their babies. But a lot of them, such as the sign for fish, in which the palm of the right hand strokes the palm of the left hand, away from the body, appear to be purely conventional. Marlda Kangka can handle quite complex matters: tenses can be indicated, and one can say, by means of signs alone, 'Last night, I saw my mother's brother and brother-in-law fighting in the bush.' But by and large, it is a much simpler language than the verbal Lardil used in everyday life.

Though some of the very same signs were also used in everyday hunting, or in telling stories, only the newly initiated boys had to use them as a complete language. Later, they went through the second phase of initiation, which involved not only subincision of the penis but also the learning of a further special language, this time a verbal one called Demiin, very different, again, from ordinary Lardil. It was taught in public sessions in which men shouted out the names, in this new language, for fish and other creatures, kinship terms and so on, and the initiates had to repeat them, being whistled and jeered at whenever they slipped up. It was used by initiated men on ritual occasions, and sometimes even on secular occasions when initiated men were together. It was, however, not wholly secret in so far as no attempt was made to prevent the uninitiated from overhearing it. Some women could therefore understand it, but only second-stage initiated men were allowed to speak it.

Though the grammar and vocabulary of ordinary Lardil and of Demiin overlap, Demiin is strikingly different not only from Lardil but also from any other Australian language, since it contains 'click' consonants, which are not found anywhere else in the world except southern Africa and which are known to most people only via Miriam Makeba's famous 'Click Song'. In addition, Demiin has its own system of biological classification (a similar version of which we will find later on Groote Eylandt). A mere glance at one or two of the names of some important words for plants and animals used in Lardil and in Demiin respectively makes the differences clear. Thus 'fish' are *yaka* in Lardil, but *l*i* in Demiin (* represents a click sound); 'man' is *ngaburr* in Demiin, but *dangka* in Lardil; 'tree' is *wijburr* in Demiin, but *thungall* in Lardil. And the commonest vowel in Lardil does not occur at all in Demiin.

Demiin is also simpler than Lardil in its grammar. There are only a few terms for parts of the body in Demiin, but roughly 100 in Lardil. In Demiin, only two personal pronouns (equivalent to '*ego*' and '*alter*') do service for the seventeen personal pronouns of Lardil. Lardil is also far richer in the categories available for plants and animals, having some 500 recognized taxa, whereas Demiin has only 200 and the Marlda Kangka sign language only 150.

There is some overlap, however, between Lardil and Demiin. In both, the basic division is into plants and animals, and the overall classification of key species is similar – in Demiin, eleven classes of animals, with sea creatures further distinguished from land animals. But there are divergences too. Whereas Demiin uses separate names for shellfish in general and domestic animals in general, Lardil does not, and Demiin also has a couple of special, but quite minor, classes which are completely lacking in Lardil. (One, for example, contains only a single species, the small brown flying fox.) Over and above differences in phonology and vocabulary, Demiin, it would seem, has gone out of its way to introduce minor distinctions simply in order to emphasize its identity as a language separate from everyday Lardil. Thus, while both Lardil and Demiin recognize and name 'fish' in general (*yaka/l*i*), each language has quite different names for various important *kinds* of fish. Moreover, Demiin insists on adding the generic word for 'fish' after the name of each separate species, whereas Lardil does not; it uses just the name of the species.

These differences suggest that the secret languages must have been developed as a deliberate exercise in social engineering. In McKnight's view, 'There is no doubt that long ago some Lardil elders *deliberately decided to devise an initiation language*'.[39] It was not, therefore, just some process of 'mindless' evolutionary emergence. And there is no doubt as to who engineered and managed all this – the very same people who managed society generally, the senior males whom Elkin has called 'Aboriginal Men of High Degree'.[40]

Whatever their individual abilities in terms of leadership or intellectually – and a 'big man' in Aboriginal society would pass his specialized knowledge, whether about hunting or ritual, to his sons – achievement was more important than inheritance. The two elders who were Waddy's principal consultants were specialists in the field of biology. Others were ritual experts; some both. Collectively, senior males shared a privileged status in society which was reinforced by the use of the secret languages. In class societies, on the other hand, though not all of those who inherit wealth or titles necessarily possess any remarkable personal qualities, not only are property and rank handed on from generation to generation but privileged control over material resources enables them to be converted into formal educational qualifications in institutions closed to others, such as 'public' (private) schools in England or 'preppy' institutions in the United States. Even more closed are those institutions where the rich socialize, such as clubs with high entrance or subscription fees and provision for 'blackballing' those not wanted.

Idealists treat language as a means of communicating with one's fellows; cynics as a means of manipulating or deceiving other people. All groups, from large ones like social classes to gangs in the school playground, use forms of language – slang, idioms, accents, trendy 'in-words' known only to members. Some of these conventions are traditional, others deliberately invented, yet others emerge from everyday group interactions. Such languages distinguish insiders from outsiders. The secret languages of Mornington Island fall into the latter category, for they have been designed not to improve human communication but to reinforce what Max Weber called 'closure', by excluding women and young men from admission to a charmed circle, and concentrating power and influence in the hands of an oligarchy, the older men.

The traditional Aboriginal society, then, was no simple 'communist' society. Though it was not a class society in terms of the private ownership of the means of production, socially it was profoundly inegalitarian, based as it was on two non-economic, primordial *cultural* forms of 'structured social inequality' – sex and age. Rose, an orthodox communist who adhered to the evolutionist ideas of Morgan and Engels, was scrupulously scientific when it came to his fieldwork. And he called Groote Eylandt society a 'gerontocracy' – a society dominated by old men – or, to be precise, men in the prime of life, since, as we have seen, *really* old men often had their wives, especially their younger wives, snatched from them. In some ways, marriage on Groote was almost a Hollywood caricature of primitive marriage, in which the fittest came out on top, or a kind of real-life confirmation of Freud's fantasies about the world-historic defeat of the fathers by the sons.

Thus when the whites called the groups of women hiding behind their paperbark dresses 'harems', they were not far off the mark. For while young males were unable to marry until their late twenties, senior males usually had two wives. A few were 'super-polygynists'; one of them, in my genealogies, had had thirteen wives, and another, still living, had had at least nine, from seven of whom thirty-two children had been born.

But not all of these wives were necessarily simultaneous partners, for wives changed hands at a considerable rate. Young men could not rely on success in winning the patronage of a senior male. So though students of 'kinship algebra' took it for granted that addressing a relative as 'mother's brother' involved the same kind of behaviour towards everyone to whom that label was applied, the reality was that young men's chances were very variable and depended on the pattern of obligations between them and their guardians. There were mother's brothers to whom you owed a lot, others who had given you wives or who had promised to do so, and mother's brothers who had given or promised nothing. So the illegal acquisition of women, which the whites called 'abduction' or 'elopement', was a national sport, particularly where very young girls were involved. Even such stringent social controls as the system of segregation and paperbark dresses and the use of secret languages could not deter virile young men from pursuing either the wives of their elders or unmarried girls. In my day, mirrors were used to signal where you were in the bush to your lover. Illicit sex involving married people – what we call 'affaires' – were inevitable when men as old as thirty were forbidden to marry.

The ideal of marrying the 'right' sort of woman – a *dadinga* – was still the 'preferred' (proper) kind of marriage. But it was often not followed (and on Groote, as we will see, often *could not* be followed) just as only 11 per cent of households in Britain correspond to the stereotypical nuclear family made up of the breadwinning husband, a full-time housewife and their children.

Kinship algebra simply omits the facts of demography – the distortions caused by the system of gerontocracy which prevented many young men from getting married when they wanted to to women in the 'correct' category of *dadinga*. So the rules codified in the diagrams of 'functionalist' anthropologists could not possibly have worked in practice. Though a man was supposed to marry his father's sister's daughter, and sisters were also supposed to be exchanged in marriage, this could not have happened when, in reality, the average difference in age between wife and husband was seventeen and a half to eighteen years, and, with younger women, even greater – for when the wife was no more than twenty years old, her husband could be as much as twenty-five years her senior.

Philandering inevitably became widespread. Given the intensity of competition for women in societies which, before the whites, were numbered in only a very few hundreds (in the case of Groote little more than 300), the chances of finding *any* woman in the 'correct' marriageable category were very uncertain and highly variable. Sometimes there would simply be too few *dadinga*, and quite often nobody at all in that category, or nobody who was not already married or betrothed to someone else. Thus in one Groote sample, I found boys with twenty-three, twenty, fourteen, ten, nine, eight, seven, five, four, three, and one potential legitimate marriage partners, and two with none at all. The problem was compounded, and made even more intolerable for young men, because of the monopolization of so many women by polygynous, even 'hyper-polygynous', older men. So young men could often get sexual partners, let alone wives, only by breaking the rules. Over time, it would seem, simply *taking* women might have become a cultural habit.

Not surprisingly, no less than three-quarters of the Groote women had been wives to two or three men; several had each passed through the hands of seven men. For many women, marriage was thus successive and fluid – what has been called, for Hollywood, 'serial monogamy'. Nor do these figures include casual sexual relationships, though it is often difficult to distinguish between 'affaires' which led to new permanent unions ('marriages') and those which did not. Even if we take the birth of children to be an indicator of a stable liaison, men would often take on the social fatherhood of children sired by other men, as they do in our culture.

On Bathurst and Meville Islands, off the western coast of Arnhem Land, a similar gerontocratic regime existed. There too gerontocrats had twenty, twenty-five, even twenty-nine wives, whose possession gave them 'wealth, power, prestige'; the surplus food and surplus daughters enabled them to increase that influence further.[41] Once again, young men were made to lead:

a monastic existence, speaking to no one (especially to females) and obtaining their own food ... The tutors guarded the boy as if he were literally a prisoner ... taught him ... things grown men should know and allowed him to go home ... at intervals ... But otherwise he was under a strict rule of obedience.[42]

The consequences of this situation were similar to those on Groote. The 'compulsory celibacy' imposed on them led to 'endless charges of seduction against younger men'. Young wives became pregnant 'with monotonous regularity . . . no matter how ancient and senile their husbands'. The result was an 'enormous frequency of disputes, fights, duels, and war parties [and] 90 per cent of legal affairs were matters in which women were in some way involved'.[43]

These fights, however, rarely resulted in deaths. Sometimes there were formal duels, in which men would throw spears at each other in turn. More often, as I witnessed on Groote on one occasion, 'fights' were public occasions for very loud and violent accusations, during which past offences between the same parties or their kin were raked up. Spears would be waved frighteningly, even thrown, but there were a remarkable number of near misses at close range by these expert spearsmen. Eventually, intermediaries related to the disputants would intervene to calm them down. The main purpose of all this *Sturm und Drang*, then, was not to kill or wound, but publicity – public moralizing and recrimination.

From Evolution to History
Though the evolution of Aboriginal society was one of the major preoccu-

pations of nineteenth-century thinkers, both they and their successors, the functionalists, treated the Aborigines as, in Eric Wolf's words, 'people without history'.[44] But the history of the peoples of northern Australia can be documented. Australia, of course, was discovered by their ancestors: 'Long before the rise of Babylon and Athens ... the Aborigines were the only people in the world's history to sail across the seas and discover an inhabitable continent.'[45] Until recently, however, their descendants were unaware of the fact.

Northern Australia, one of the first parts of the continent to be sighted by whites, was, paradoxically, one of the very last areas to come under white control. Dutch explorers, searching for a westward route to the Spice Islands, the source of the world's most valuable commodity,[46] had sailed through the Torres Strait between New Guinea and Australia as early as 1606 and recorded many topographical features, including, in 1623, the large island which still bears the name they gave it: Groote Eylandt. But Groote was not to be brought under white control for three centuries, because, unlike the Spice Islands to the north, there was nothing of value to the Europeans in the region: no spices, no gold, not even usable people. Though a handful of Aborigines may have been taken as slaves, they would doubtless have proved physically unsuitable for plantation labour, for their nomadic life style made them unamenable to the discipline of agriculture, especially plantation agriculture, which provided the prototype for the later organization of industry.

Northern Australia was not only a spatial frontier, beyond which lay the last major undiscovered continent, but the boundary of the technical system that had dominated the rest of the world for thousands of years – agriculture. At its northern tip, the Aborigines who lived on Cape York Peninsula (to the east of Groote) could actually see the gardens of their Papuan neighbours on Prince of Wales Island. Some of them even imitated the Papuans by sticking a few slips of plants into the rich soil and eating the resulting crop – but only as a fallback when other food was lacking. Neither Cape York Aborigines nor a single tribe in the whole of the rest of the continent ever took to agriculture. As an Australian historian has aptly observed, 'The worldwide advance of herds and gardens halted within sight of a strip of ... the northern Australian coast. Two different ways of making a living stood side by side: economic systems as different as communism and capitalism'[47] – though in so far as both capitalism and communism were based on industrialism, the differences between them are not as impressive as the gap between hunting and collecting and agriculture.

One hundred and eighty years passed before the first English explorers arrived in Australia. It never struck them, of course – nor those who have talked about the great 'voyages of discovery' ever since – that the continent had been discovered by Aborigines 40,000 years earlier. A sinologist has even argued that the Chinese might have discovered Australia, since a jade image of the Chinese god Shou Lao was discovered at Darwin in 1879, four feet underground, wedged in the roots of a banyan tree (a foreign tree). But the presence of a Chinese object does not necessarily mean that it had been brought there by the Chinese. It is far more likely that it was other Asians – Malays, the middlemen in a trade chain which ended in China – who had brought the image to Australia and left it there.[48]

The first whites, Dutchmen, had sailed through the gulf as early as 1603. A year later, they returned and seized natives in order to take them to Batavia. As a result, a Dutch sailor was killed. In 1623, several Aborigines were killed and one seized. There is no way of knowing whether a folk memory of these early fights with white men was passed on from generation to generation, though we do know from records of frontier warfare from southern Australia that intelligence about the coming of the white man preceded their actual arrival and spread with extraordinary speed.[49]

Relations with the Aborigines were thus poisoned from the beginning. Two centuries later, when Flinders landed on the Wellesley Islands, to the east of Groote, he found the Indians 'timid'. But on an island just off the coast of the Great Island, he clashed with the natives; one Aborigine was killed and the master's mate, Mr Whitewood, was wounded. There was further friction on the mainland, when Flinders took a native hostage.

For Flinders this hostility on the part of the ancestors of the Groote Eylandters seemed 'contrary to all I have known or heard from their countrymen'. He concluded that it was probably due to their experience not of whites – for they had never seen any before – but of Malay proas, traces of whose presence he had already found. They had been coming, he was told, for two centuries (though archaeologists now think they may have been coming for 800 years) from what is today Indonesia, mostly from Makassar (now Ujung Padang) in the Celebes (now Sulawesi) and Timor. And they continued to come until 1907, when the 'White Australia' policy put an end to this historic trade.

It was easy for the proas to reach Australia, for the north-west wind blew them there in ten to fifteen days, and the south-east trade winds took them back. Indonesia is so close, indeed, that even today small vessels are occasionally blown down by wind and currents to the coasts of Western Australia and the Northern Territory. What they were looking for was the sea cucumber (trepang or bêche-de-mer), which was traded right up to China as a gourmet delicacy and, some say, an aphrodisiac.

In a historic meeting, Flinders finally spoke with the 'Asiatics', part of a

fleet of no fewer than sixty proas manned by 1,000 men. Each proa carried a crew of around thirty, so the trading parties did not have much need
for local labour. But they did use Aborigines as divers and in other ancillary capacities, rewarding them with exotic luxuries – rice, tobacco and
alcohol. They also traded for pearls, pearlshell, turtleshell and other valued commodities which the Aborigines collected throughout the year.
Pobassoo, the commander of the fleet, warned Flinders to beware of the
Aborigines, telling him of numerous clashes, in one of which he himself
had been wounded, a legacy of violence which probably further condi-
tioned the way the Aborigines responded to the arrival of the Whites.

After Flinders, northern Australia remained free from whites for half a
century, until Leichhardt's expedition of 1879, engaged in erecting the
Overland Telegraph line, presaged the later arrival of parties of mining
prospectors and pastoral settlers. They came in ever-increasing numbers,
from the initial zones of white settlement in south-eastern Australia,
northwards into Queensland, then westwards across the continent into
new cattle and mining country in what was to become Western Australia.
Mary Durack's classic account, which celebrates these pioneers, also acknowledges that theirs was a story of continual bloody warfare with tribe
after tribe over land and access to water, of Aboriginal 'hunting' of the
white man's animals, of inevitable punitive expeditions against them and
of equally bitter Aboriginal resistance.[50]

Since no significant valuable minerals were found in the Gulf/Arnhem
Land area, the miners in the main simply passed through. Pastoral development in this remote tropical region proved equally difficult. But for
Aboriginal societies numbered only in hundreds, the effects were nevertheless catastrophic. According to Searcy, around Borroloola, on the mainland near Groote, in 1886:

for thousands of miles ... the district was in a state of terror ... the
crimes committed were beyond description. All the outlaws of
Queensland made for the Territory, for they had nothing to fear; [the
country] was a sanctuary for every ruffian in Australia.[51]

Yet much of the interior of Arnhem Land and the coastal areas of the
gulf remained free of white presence until the 1930s, and even later in
some areas. Being an island, Groote was virtually unvisited until well into
the twentieth century, occasional shipwrecks and other brief landings
apart. Control over the island was thus still only indirect. A government
attempt to encourage the establishment of a cattle station failed. But the
arrival of representatives from the Church Missionary Society, looking for

a suitable mission site, was to prove the turning point, culminating in the establishment of a station on the Emerald River in 1921.

The new mission station, though, was not established in order to proselytize the Aborigines, but for 'half-caste' children (i.e. of mixed Aboriginal-white parentage), 'wards of the state' who were brought to the island from the mainland. A decade was to elapse before the missionaries turned their attention to the Aboriginal inhabitants of the island, with the establishment, in 1943, of a new mission at Angurugu, where it remains.

The first white person to make a significant record of Groote Eylandt society and culture, in 1920–21, was not a missionary but an entomologist, Norman Tindale. He was in no doubt about the effects of Aboriginal contacts with the Makassarese:

The Malays whenever possible obtained possession of native women and took them away on their homeward journeys. The ... native[s] thus learnt that women should never be seen ... Being comparatively few, [they] were frightened by the Malays, who robbed them, enticed them with drink, and beat them when they would not work. Their attitude to the Malays was one of hate; sometimes they tried to kill them, and stories of ambushes and attacks are told in the camps.[52]

Yet by the 1950s, the Groote Aborigines were depicting the Makassarese epoch as a Golden Age. The Tiwi similarly remember nothing about slave raids carried out by Portuguese from Timor in the eighteenth century. These images so flatly contradicted Searcy's first-hand accounts of violent clashes at the turn of the century, and also Tindale's later observations, that I asked Tindale to comment on the apparent discrepancy. He not only reaffirmed what he had written but added that he had seen the remains of stingray-tail whips used on the Aborigines by the Makassarese, hanging from tamarind trees (which they had introduced).

Relations with the missionaries were much more harmonious, in part because the mission was initially concerned with the imported 'half-castes'. On the mainland, however, relations with whites, and with a new set of hitherto unknown Asians (Japanese) pearlers and trepangers operating off the coast – led to periodic violence right up to the 1930s.

In 1932, five of the six Japanese crewmen of two luggers fishing at Caledon Bay in Arnhem Land were killed by nomadic Aborigines. A year later, two whites were also killed on an island off Groote. The immediate response was the dispatch of an anthropologist to the area, the arrest and trial of three Aborigines in Darwin and their return home from prison after two years. The wider consequences were an increased governmental presence in Arnhem Land, the eventual establishment of a patrol service to penetrate into remote interior zones and to inspect the conditions of Aborigines working on cattle stations and the establishment of new mission stations. [53]

The prime concern of the missionaries was, of course, the making of Christians, not the making of profits. But because of the high cost and the logistic difficulties of bringing in supplies from outside, the mission started to produce vegetables, using the labour of the 'half-caste' children. The famous outback 'character' Bill Harney – in turn drover, stockman, trepanger and patrol officer – first met his future wife while she was harnessed to a plough on Groote. This introduction to modernity could not have been more unattractive to professional nomads. As late as the 1950s, the Aborigines I lived with still displayed a marked aversion to both agricultural labour and the Protestant ethic; the moment the white overseer went out of sight they downed tools and spent their time smoking and gossiping.

At first, though, the mission avoided any frontal attack on the Aborigines' nomadic way of life. Their main strategy was to try to induce them (first the men, then the women and children) to visit, and eventually to stay at the settlement by providing rations and bartering Western commodities such as tobacco, blankets and knives for indigenous goods like pearlshell, turtle and dugong. [54] Barter of this kind had been going on with the Makassarese for centuries, though as late as the 1940s it was still secondary to a subsistence economy based on hunting animals (including the abundant marine life) and collecting bush vegetables.

Slowly but inexorably, however, the Aborigines were weaned away from their nomadic existence. By 1949, 313 natives were in contact with the mission, although most of them still also went on 'walkabout' for a month or two during the year. [55] But by then, hardly any of them were full-time hunters and collectors. Economic dependence on whites for food, cash and tobacco led in turn to white social control – children were separated from their parents and lived in dormitories attached to the schools. The missionaries also proscribed traditional religious rituals and, most important, interfered in the marrige system. Infant betrothal was forbidden and wives were taken away from hyper-polygynists and redistributed to younger men, in accordance with white ideas of what constituted suitable marriage partners, though often flouting Aboriginal marriage rules in the process. Among the Tiwi, Father (later Bishop) Gsell – dubbed by the press 'the Bishop with 150 wives' – purchased infant widows for axes, flour, tobacco and cloth. Though he tolerated some large households of 'boss men', new marriages had to be monogamous, while marriages between partners of very different ages were no longer permitted. [56]

There is evidence, indeed, of substantial deviation from the rules supposedly governing marriage in other Aboriginal societies which had experienced no such external influence (whites apart). In the early 1930s, in the Kimberleys of Western Australia, in six different tribal groups between a third and two-thirds of marriages were either legal 'alternatives' to the preferred form of marriage or thoroughly 'wrong' marriages.[57]

Groote Eylandt and Tiwi society may have been only exaggerations of tendencies built into Australian kinship, resulting in part from the power of the old men and in part from a contradiction between the formal cultural rules and realities of demography. There were often in fact no women at all available in the 'cell' of the marriage-system matrix which marriageable women were supposed to come from, either because none had been born or because of the distortions which derived from the exercise of political power on the part of the older men. One outcome was massive deviation from the rules, including two cases I found where men had married women they called 'mother'. This, to put no fine point upon it, was incest, in their culture as in ours.

The result was that an already unstable marriage system became even more chaotic. The ideal pattern of marriage – that a man should marry his *dadinga*, already as honoured in the breach as in the observance – broke down. So, necessarily, did the ideal pattern of kinship in which everyone is related to every other person in such a way that the terms they use for each other fit together to form a perfect system – A is related to B, B to C, C to D and so on, just as 'uncle' fits with 'father' and 'brother' in English kinship terminology. Up to now, I have used the traditional term 'kinship algebra' to describe this interlocking system, but a jigsaw puzzle would perhaps be a better analogy.

When a man made a 'wrong' (illegitimate) marriage – to a woman he called, say, 'daughter' – he would resolve the contradictions that ensued by calling her and her full sisters *dadinga*. Her full brothers would likewise become *neninga* (which we translate as 'brother-in-law'). But theoretically in a society like his, he ought also to have changed the terms he used for *everybody* – which would have produced chaos. In any case, it would have been impossible, because lots of other people were also making wrong marriages, and because no individual or group of relatives could make such across-the-board changes on their own. So the changes were restricted to certain categories of very close kin within the new wife's nuclear family – full siblings were renamed, but half-sisters and half-brothers were not, nor were her mother and father. The husband continued using whatever term he was already using before for them and for other less close kin. As a consequence, though there was still strictly speaking an *ideal* pattern – the jigsaw in which every piece fitted together – it no longer conformed with reality. It was no longer a *system* of kinship termi-nology, no longer a jigsaw, but a situation in which there were only what I have called 'islands of order'.[58] Thus, when I reinterviewed twenty-eight people whom Rose had interviewed more than a decade earlier, I found that 648 out of the 5,589 kin terms he had recorded had changed – roughly, 11 per cent. More than 10 per cent of Bickerton Island men, Turner found, were actually married within *prohibited* degrees. Indeed, from time to time, they met to try to straighten out the mess, on one oc-casion with mainlanders.[59]

The direct intervention of the missionaries in marriage was thus the *coup de grâce* to the indigenous system of marriage. But although mission settlements might look like 'total institutions', there was a good deal of cultural resistance, reflected in the very low level of conversion – the first baptism at the mission was recorded only as late as 1951.

The mission also had competition from another white-controlled but secular settlement run by an Englishman who had first come to Groote as a pearler. Fred Gray employed Aborigines as divers, until the Second World War put an end to that industry. The settlement he founded, where less than half the population lived, was then reduced largely to subsistence horticulture. When food supplies from outside dried up from time to time, the Aborigines would be sent to the bush to fend for themselves – which many of them enjoyed as a kind of holiday and from which they usu-ally returned looking far glossier than they did when they were dependent upon a diet of 'damper', tea, sugar and other station food.

The outside world began to impinge on Gray's settlement in a novel and dramatic way when, in 1938, a flying-boat base was built for passenger planes on the England–Sydney route, just across the bay. At the outbreak of the Second World War, it was taken over by the RAAF. As well as pro-viding casual employment for some Aborigines, a new source of cash in-come also opened up: the sale of curios to the passengers and then to the RAAF personnel at the base.

When Gray was eventually recognized by the Australian government as a 'Protector' of the Aborigines, with administrative control over the wel-fare payments which the government paid for their support, the state was to become the crucial source of Aboriginal income, gradually exercising more and more control over the Groote settlements. But residents also produced their own food, both by continuing traditional hunting and fish-ing and collecting bush vegetables, and by growing food and raising ani-mals. After the war, a new and much bigger source of cash income opened up when the purely local and small-scale sale of curios was replaced by the export of bead necklaces and other shell goods to big department stores down south in Sydney. Yet from time to time, when financial problems or the logistics of getting supplies from outside became insuperable, the 'protector' would still have to send most of the Aborigines out to fend for themselves. One of the consequences of this intermittent if diminished time in the bush was that the younger generation still learned bush lore under the guidance of elders who had themselves been brought up as hunters and collectors.

The decisive penetration of the outside world came with the establishment on the island, in 1964, of a manganese mine by Gemco (Groote Eylandt Mining Company), a subsidiary of Australia's largest mining corporation, Broken Hill Proprietary Co. Ltd. Today, this mine produces nearly a tenth of the world's manganese. The island has been utterly transformed and Aborigines are now a minority. More than 1,000 white technicians and administrative staff live today in a modern township at Alyangula, near the mission but quite separate from it. Some Aborigines have also found employment there: by the end of the 1960s, around fifty of them, mostly doing unskilled work. None of them held staff positions.

This economic transformation coincided with another revolution, this time in the political sphere, when the constitutional disabilities Aborigines had laboured under as wards of the state were finally abolished. Thenceforth, they were to receive the same wages and working conditions as any other Australians and were admitted into trade unions. New local government councils in Aboriginal hands at each of the two Groote settlements have replaced the paternalistic control of missionaries and protectors, while the royalties paid by the mining company have provided ample funds for modern development, such as European-style housing. Increased individual earnings mean that Groote Eylandt Aborigines now purchase their own food from a store which has a turnover of more than 1 million Australian dollars, travel to other places in Australia and buy consumer goods such as record players, radios and even cars. As one archaeologist who worked there recently wrote to me:

The road between Umbakumba and Angurugu is like a race track, with four-wheel-drive vehicles hurtling past each other at 100 km an hour, and light aircraft constantly taking off from the Angurugu airstrip flying people to communities across eastern Arnhem Land. Television, videos and rock culture are all an integral part of modern Aboriginal culture. School kids go on trips to the major cities.

Groote Eylandters, then – largely owing to their remote location –

have been spared the genocide that had wiped out the great majority of Aborigines elsewhere in Australia by the turn of the century. Whereas there were only some 300 islanders after the First World War, there were half as many again by the 1950s, and there are now three times as many as there were when whites first arrived. This is mostly the result of better food, better medicine and fewer mortal dangers in everyday life. However, the downside of modernization, as nearly all observers lament, is the massive consumption of alcohol, which has become a very grave social problem for the islanders. The same archaeologist remarks:

One of the frustrations of working in the 1990s is the rapid loss of knowledge about the old days – a number of the older men told me how they didn't listen to their parents' stories about the history of the island because they were too interested in getting drunk when they were young men. Today, Umbakumba is a 'wet' town with lots of grog [alcohol] problems, Angurugu is dry, but has a fairly horrific petrol-sniffing problem amongst young men and some young women.

The extensive knowledge which we are now going to explore is thus not shared by a younger generation of islanders for whom, in Julie Waddy's words, 'hunting and gathering are almost entirely for recreation at weekends and in school holidays ... Bush and sea foods are still relished but normally they are no more than a supplement to what can be bought from the shop' True, in the new 'homeland' stations in the bush to which Aborigines, normally based on the settlements, go from time to time, there has been a largely seasonal revival of traditional ways of life, from hunting and collecting to periodic ritual gatherings not just of people from all over the island but also larger gatherings of more than 500 Aborigines from all over northern Australia.[60]

Nevertheless, Christianity has made real progress, while a new religion, more akin to Christian mythology than to totemism, has also emerged, based on the belief that a man called Nambirrirrma came down from the sky, proclaimed a new code of living, married, had a son, died and was buried.[61]

We have seen that outsiders afflicted with what the French call the *esprit de système* (and probably Aboriginal theorists too) have commonly imposed over-systematized and over-integrated models on Aboriginal marriage. It is, perhaps, an occupational disease of intellectuals, for their job is to bring order to complex masses of data in which order is not readily evident. The same tendency will appear when we turn to a different sphere – the ways in which Aborigines classify not people but plants and animals.

Food Classification

Aborigines live off the land in a different way from farmers. Farming is an interventionist activity, involving the *production* of food through the use of various inputs, notably seeds, fertilizers and petroleum. Hunters and collectors appropriate what nature provides. To survive, an accurate and comprehensive knowledge about which plants and animals can be eaten is vital. This does not mean, however, that Aborigines are incapable of thinking about these things in a wider, more abstract scientific way, any more than the fact that we eat food and write cookery books prevents our having a biology. Though I begin with the ways in which Aborigines classify plants and animals as food, this does not mean that I subscribe to the view that their interest in, or knowledge of, plants and animals is dictated primarily by, or limited to interest in things which are edible. Rather, the classification of foods is a stripped-down version of a wider biological system of classification which we will look at below.

But *pace* Lévi-Strauss, Aborigines *do* have a very special interest in food. To them, plants and animals are not just 'good to think with'; they are good to eat. White researchers have studied Aborigines' knowledge of edible things, though, while disregarding their biology. Thus only two of the natural scientists with the large and well-heeled National Geographic Expedition to Arnhem Land of 1948 thought it worthwhile to record Aboriginal names for the plants and animals they collected, or to note the ways the Aborigines classified them, even though, as Waddy notes, 'the great majority of edible plants [which the Aborigines recognize] have a one-to-one correspondence with [Western] scientific species'.[62]

The first thing to note is the large number of edible species recognized and used: no fewer than twenty-four kinds of land animals; forty-four kinds of birds (both sea and land birds); 127 kinds of marine animals; forty-four kinds of crabs and crustaceans; and ninety-three kinds of plants and trees. Waddy identifies 332 altogether. (I noted 315, but some of these later proved to be synonyms for the same fish, or names for particular parts of a plant. A few others I simply did not record, and I probably noted some which only the children eat.)

Food taboos today are quite limited. Waddy found only one case of an animal (the scrubfowl) not being eaten because of its totemic significance; a few cases of restrictions during religious rituals such as circumcision and during pregnancy; and some age-related cases where only older men could eat certain fish, or children were not allowed to eat turtle – possibly because it was believed that children could not stomach it rather than on religious or social grounds. But it is not the volume alone that is impressive, for just as we classify foods into fruit and nuts, berries, meat, fish, and so forth, so do the Aborigines.

Non-flesh Foods: Aninga
Non-flesh foods are divided into three major types: fruits, root vegetables and food derived from flowers. To begin with edible fruits, forty-two kinds are recognized. But seeds, eight of them, are also classed with fruits; so are the nuts from two kinds of palm tree, and the burrawang nut, which we have already talked about.

The logic underlying some of these distinctions is sometimes made explicit by Aboriginal specialists. In the case of nuts, for example, the coconut and the pandanus resemble each other because both have large woody outsides which are simply thrown away; what is important is the nut inside. It is the part which is edible that determines how it is classified. (The burrawang forms a separate group because it has no flowers before the nuts come, and also requires processing.)

Further light is shed upon the principles involved by the way Aborigines classify introduced foods. Some fall easily into existing categories: apples, pears, oranges, bananas and mangoes are obviously fruits; carrots and potatoes are root vegetables; beef, pork and lamb are animal meat; while soft drinks can be classified with water (though some think orange juice should be classed with fruits). But whereas we label both peas and beans as 'vegetables', the Aborigines classify them as fruit because they develop from flowers. Cereals prove more problematic. Rice is obviously a seed. But there is debate between those who have seen wheat being ground into flour on TV, and therefore classify flour with seeds, and those who argue that, once processed into a powder, it loses its seed-like character and should be put in a class of its own.

Tea presents a special problem, because though the Aborigines eat so many different things, no leafy green vegetables were eaten in the past apart from water-lily stems (though the term *aninga* could be used for grass, which was eaten by wallabies). Today, Aborigines know from TV that tea comes from leaves. A new category of leafy foods/foods from leaves has therefore now come into being which includes cabbage as well as tea.

The second major division of vegetable foods are the thirty-one recognised kinds of root vegetables. These are not further subclassified, as fruits are – why, I do not know. They *can* be subclassified – for example, those found in freshwater swamps or billabongs as opposed to dry places – but this is a distinction on the basis of the kind of habitat in which they are found, not on the types of *food* they are, and can be applied to any plant or tree, not just edible ones.

The third major group is made up of five foods derived from flowers. 'Bee bread', because it is dry, constitutes a class all of its own, whereas honey, plus three kinds of nectar, are all classed together as juices or liquids. This group, however, does not include the giant spear grass, because the food comes from the stem, which is sucked like sugar-cane, not from the flower.

Spear grass instead is classified with two kinds of edible gum to form a small fourth group. Three trees whose growing shoots are eaten form a fifth. Just how basic the division is between flesh and other foods is indicated by the classification of water and milk (and nowadays commercially available milk products) as *aninga*, because they are not flesh, though they are each treated as separate and unique *kinds* of food.

Flesh Foods: Akwalya

Akwalya, we saw, can mean 'flesh food'. By putting a qualifying word after it, one can distinguish whether it is the flesh of animals from the sea, from the air or from the land. Thus *eningumakardumandja akwalya* means flesh from animals belonging to the sea, of which fish are the most important. So the word *akwalya* is often used, on its own, to refer just to fish, not to all kinds of flesh. But turtle flesh and shellfish are also important, and we can distinguish these kinds of seafood simply by adding a qualifier which tells us what kind of *akwalya* it is. Thus *adidira akwalya* is our 'shellfish': edible flesh that comes from sea animals which live in shells.

The sea provides no fewer than 119 different kinds of fish; forty-two kinds of shellfish; five kinds of turtle; two other sea mammals, the dugong and the dolphin; as well as four kinds of edible crustaceans (crabs, lobsters, crayfish and yabbies), plus the squid, which is put into a class of its own. All these groupings are recognized by the Aborigines.

Dramatic as it is to watch the hazardous pursuit of a huge greenback or hawksbill turtle by a team of men highly skilled in handling their dugout canoes, and the precision with which they harpoon these well-armoured animals, and important and exciting as the outcome is when such a huge supply of meat is landed on the shore, the bulk of everyday food from the sea comes from the much less dramatic catching of fish. There is an extraordinary variety in these tropical seas: from the vividly striped parrotfish (now reaching English supermarkets) and the toothsome grey mullet – both major parts of the diet – to dozens of less important species such as stingrays and sharks, milkfish, bonefish, catfish, garfish, whiting, mackerel, the large barracudas and kingfish, darts, perch, barramundi, trevally, rockcod, sweetlips, jewfish, bass, emperors, angelfish, damsel-fish, batfish, herring and triggerfish, goby and catfish, to name but a few.

Then there are the shellfish – a rich variety ranging from the smaller whelks, drupes, cockles and scallops to the large bailer and the giant clams, delicious rock oysters on the roots of the mangroves, mussels and scores more – as well as the crustaceans and squids.

The Aborigines simplify this great variety by distinguishing between salty kinds of fish from the sea and freshwater fish, and by making a culinary distinction between bony and cartilaginous fish, because they are cooked in different ways. Normally, bony fish are simply baked in hot sand and then eaten, though if there are a lot of them, they may be cooked with hot stones in a simple earth oven. Cartilaginous fish, on the other hand, have to be turned into fishcakes by washing the flesh with salt water, chewing it and making it into balls, which are then covered with fat, then with leaves – to keep the food clean – and finally steamed.

Two special groups of cartilaginous fish are also classified as separate subgroups: sharks and then a group which has no overall name made up of stingrays, shovel-nosed rays and sawfish. Older stingrays are said to have 'black' fat and are not generally eaten, whereas young stingrays, which have white or 'clean' fat, are.

Wurrajija akwalya includes the flesh of birds and flying mammals (notably the tasty flying fox). But insects are also *wurrajija* – flying creatures – and provide food (such as the large abdomens of the green tree ant) or bees which are often mixed in with honey and get eaten.

The image of Australian Aborigines has always been that of men spearing kangaroos and wallabies. Wallabies (not kangaroos) are found on Groote and eaten. But they are not an important item of diet, and it is the women (not equipped with spears and spear-throwers) rather than the men who are more likely to catch small mammals, goannas or freshwater turtles, while only children bother to hunt smaller lizards.

From a classification point of view, eggs present an anomaly. Clearly, animals grow from them, so they should therefore be flesh food. But some assimilate them to *aninga*, non-flesh food. So the term for fruit, *amamuwa akwalya*, and the word for egg, *yinumamuwa*, both derive from the word *amamuwa* – small round thing. Waddy found that other Aboriginal tribes show similar variability as to whether they classify eggs as 'vegetable' or 'animal'.[63]

Turning to land animals, the twenty-seven kinds which are eaten by the Aborigines are grouped into four-footed mammals – such as wallabies, bandicoots, possums and echidnas – and reptiles – various kinds of goannas, large frilled lizards and smaller ones.

Freshwater turtles can also contribute to the diet, but crocodiles and grubs, though recognized as edible, are in fact rarely eaten, especially today. Similarly, though people may count the python as edible, it is rarely eaten.

Overall, then, the classification of foods looks like this:

Figure 2 **Groote Eylandt classification of vegetable foods**

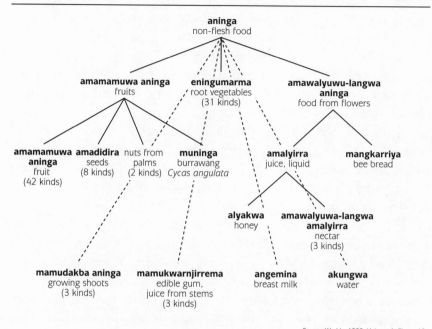

Source: Waddy, 1988, Volume 1, Figure 18.

Figure 3 **Groote Eylandt classification of flesh foods**

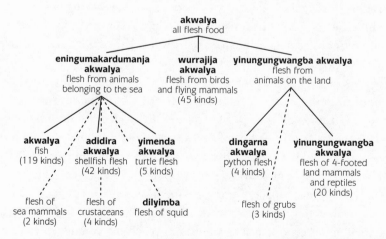

Source: Waddy, 1988, Volume 1, Figure 16.

Food, however important, is only one of the uses of plants and animals, which also have a part to play in the making of practical objects of many kinds. Bark and boughs were used to make shelters to protect people against the sun or the cold, and bark 'coolamons' to make watertight containers used to carry food and even babies. Paperbark was used for innumerable purposes, as was stringybark. Bark canoes – efficient enough, 60,000 years ago, to enable the ancestors of the Aborigines to hop the islands (then closer) of the Indonesian archipelago from South-East Asia – were the only type known before the Makassarese introduced the dugout. Stones were used as pestles and mortars. Fire could be quickly made by rapidly twirling a fire drill in a 'holder', using dry grass as tinder (even I became quite adept at it). The Aborigines also made string and rope; spears of various types, including pronged ones for fishing; harpoons and floats used in hunting turtle; spear-throwers; fighting-sticks; and didgeridoos; and women's digging-sticks and roasting-sticks.

For sickness, Levitt has listed an elaborate pharmacopoeia. Medicines were made from leaves, vines, roots, bulbs, berries, sapwood, bark, fruit pulp, the various parts of beehives, bark, young shoots, seeds, salt, seawater, powdered cuttlefish 'bone' and even dingo manure. For generalized aches and pains, vines and leaves were crushed, heated or soaked in water, then applied to the body. But there were special medicines for illnesses of the chest and of the ears; for headaches (one of which involved killing green tree ants in their nests, then steeping the lot in water, which was drunk, and the nest applied, like a plaster, to the forehead); for toothache; for snake-bite and for bites from spiders, sea-centipedes, cup-moth caterpillars, sea-wasps, stonefish and stingrays; for minor cuts and for more serious wounds; for boils, burns and sores; and for broken bones (including the making of stretchers for carrying people and the making of splints); to close up cicatrices; to cure constipation, coughs and colds; for diarrhoea; for difficulties in passing urine; for the eyes; for leprosy; for skin troubles; and for swellings.[64]

They also used contraceptives so powerful that they inhibited conception not just in the short term but for ever. After childbirth, women were treated for bleeding. If the mother had too little milk, wild plum leaves – also used for many other kinds of cures – were put on the breast to induce the milk to come. If a mother had too much milk, an old tree-snail shell was placed over the nipple to stop it dripping.

Finally, substances apart, there were medical practices such as the elaborate care taken to keep wounded people, and those attending to them, in the smoke of a fire, so that flies would not reach the wound. (Smoke was also used to 'cool down' over-excited children: soap bush leaves were thrown on the fire and the children held face down over it.)

The efficacy of most of these medicines – for example, the fruit of the quinine bush or the fruit and inner bark of the mistletoe tree, used as contraceptives – obviously depend upon their chemical constituents, only a few of which have been analysed. Some, however, such as water caught running down a tree, or eating the filings from a rusty metal axe, are probably wholly magical. The effect of others – for example, the eating of various kinds of clay by the women – is not certain.

There was a whole class of practices, though, not meant to cure people but to do them damage. An image of a person you wished to harm could be drawn on the bark of a tree or on a rock, and a spear inserted into the picture, or drawn on it, while singing special songs. Pieces of leftover food, or clothing, faeces or dirt from a person's sleeping place, could be put into a hollow log or other closed space, such as, today, a bottle, after which the victim would become ill and die. Poisons were also used, as were scrapings from the bones of dead people.[65] Otherwise, things known to be harmful would be avoided.

Western Food Classification: From Cooking to Cuisine

The categories Aborigines use in relation to plants and animals as food are cultural. Their counterparts in Western cultures are therefore not the taxonomies which biologists use but the practical domestic categories we use in cooking. If we look for advice, we usually get it not from nutritionists, who tell us about calories and vitamins, but from another kind of specialist, people who write cookery books telling us what tastes good or what is in 'good taste' – socially acceptable or fashionable.

As with the Aborigines, food is classified according to its raw materials – as meat, fish, vegetables and fruit. But in cooking, the basic element is the *dish*, and in social eating, a dish does not stand on its own. It is only one item – a course – in a sequence of dishes, the whole being designated a meal. The structure of the meal in Italian cooking, for instance, begins with *antipasti*: literally, things that come before the pasta, a course peculiar to Italy. Pasta constitutes the *primi piatti*. The *secondi piatti*, the main (usually meat or fish) dishes follow; then 'desserts', cheese and coffee.[66]

Modern cookery books take the dish as their main element, for dishes may be eaten on their own. They therefore give us the *recipe* for each dish, telling us how to make it from the ingredients listed. But they also advise us as to what kinds of things fit together best, and in what order, by including suggested 'menus' – sequences of dishes suitable for social eating, the whole constituting a 'proper' meal.

True, in her *Book of Household Management*, the Founding Mother of English cookery, Mrs Beeton, does have a section on 'The Natural History of Fishes' which includes a lot of quite scientific information – 'principal instruments employed by fishes to accelerate their motion'; 'how naturalists have divided fishes'; 'the organs of sense in fishes'; their food, fecundity and longevity; notes on the supply of fish in the ocean ('practically inexhaustible', she thought in those days, before the North Sea was fished out). It also provides historical information: the use of fish by the 'Ancients'; the Romans' love of fish; and the eating of fish in medieval France and ancient Britain. But, as with the Aborigines, the basic division is very simple and only implicit – meat, fish and vegetables.[67]

But her real focus is on 'Fish as an Article of Human Food' and 'Fish as an Article of Diet'. It is these practical sections, not her natural and social history (what biologists think or what the Romans did), which form the centrepiece and climax of this chapter – from her 'General Directions for Dressing Fish' and 'Table of Relative Prices' to the nearly 200 recipes she then gives us. It is the latter, of course, which brought her fame, both in her own generation and ever since.

So when she comes to meat, even though we are given a paragraph on prehistory in general (and not *just* about meat), anecdotes about 'the Croat mode' of tenderizing meat (cut off your steak and put it under your saddle), the reported absence of knowledge of fire in the Mariana Islands and its discovery in European antiquity, all of this is simply a lead-in to what really matters: how to *cook* meat by using fire, whether boiling, baking or roasting. The accent is overwhelmingly on the practical – on joints, cooking and prices.

A century later, Delia Smith has taken Mrs Beeton's place as the leading English authority. In her three-part *Cookery Course*, she starts with 'equipment'; then comes the cooking of eggs, bread and pastry, and only then of fish and meat. Part 2 covers scones and biscuits, stocks and soups, casseroles and braised dishes, rice and other grains, pastas and pancakes, poultry, vegetarian cooking, smoked fish and shellfish, and cheese. Part 3 is an even greater mixture, presumably of things left over from the first two parts: advanced pastry and cakes, offal, cream and yoghurt, salads and dressings, barbecues and picnics, herbs, summer vegetables, preserving, fruits and cold puddings, and leftovers.[68]

These headings are simply ways of organizing the material; there is no 'right' way and the subject can be entered by different doors – raw materials, dishes, courses. Each leads readers to what they are looking for – not intellectual purity, but practical advice about recipes – how to cook.

So, categories such as 'poultry' may be used because the animals in question resemble each other, even though, from a culinary point of view, the many ways of cooking chicken, duck, turkey and goose – from creamed chicken with avocado to roast stuffed goose with prune and apple sauce – are often elaborately different.

Lévi-Strauss' crude opposition between the raw and the cooked[69] completely fails to capture these crucial cultural distinctions. Instead, he tries to cram everything – not just cooking – within categories based only on pairs of inadequate polarities: particularly nature and culture, but also subsidiary polarities, such as cooking with hot air and with water, all of which are to him different manifestations of 'deep' categories of thought which all stem from an underlying duality – resemblance and difference – fundamental to human thinking and possibly even built into the brain.[70]

Yet his successive volumes on the subject of cooking, then, with all their piling-up of data, also fail, as Goody has pointed out, to capture a whole range of culinary practices, especially the variety of ways of producing, preparing and consuming food which different societies have developed throughout history. For though much has rightly been written about the 'conspicuous consumption' of food, it also entails elaborate (sometimes conspicuous, sometimes hidden) *production*. Today, the kitchen itself has become a major area for the display of expensive technology, from digital cookers to microwaves. Even post-consumption provides further evidence of wealth and status, especially in kitchen/dining rooms where cooking and eating take place. Where the servants once cleared up and washed up, today expensive dishwashers are used – and displayed.

Once *cuisine* replaces mere cooking, food marks the boundaries not just between cultures (as Lévi-Strauss assumes) but of class subcultures within them. In the past, armies of cultivators grew crops or reared animals on the land and in the greenhouses of aristocratic estates, providing meat, fish, vegetables and even exotic fruits every day of the year for the members of the household and their guests. A complex division of labour was involved. In the grounds of the great house, the 'outside' producers had their own hierarchy, leading up to head gardener. In the kitchen, there was another hierarchy of those who prepared and cooked the food, from scullery maids to specialist cooks. Upstairs, others, under the command of the head butler, served the food in special ways, for the upper classes ate elaborate, expensive kinds of food, served in fine public style. The presentation of the food became an art, which today has reached its logical absurdity, *nouvelle cuisine*, in which you may not get much to eat but it looks good.

This, then, was a *sub*culture of the ruling class, for the sheer cost of these sumptuary kinds of banquets meant that they could never be imitated by the lower orders. In the extreme, Islamic potentates practised not only conspicuous consumption but conspicuous *display*, on the table, of works of art sculpted out of one very expensive commodity – sugar. One caliph had a mosque built entirely of sugar – though, at the close of festivities, Muslim charity prevailed when beggars were invited to eat it.[71] European monarchs then imitated this cult of sugar, as did merchants by the sixteenth century.

Serving and eating food in this style calls for special accoutrements too, and these also became successively more expensive according to the occasion and as one moved up the social scale. Guests were seated by rank around large tables, and used different shapes and sizes of silver – knives, forks and spoons – for different courses, from soup to nuts; elegant napery; and ate off special 'china', not mere crockery. They were served from particular dishes, with different containers for different items. A range of glasses was required for the various fine wines which accompanied each course, leading up to port, liqueurs and brandy; then there would be coffee and, for the men, cigars. Though electricity eventually became available, antique silver candlesticks were still *de rigueur*.

The social inferiors of the upper classes might try to imitate them. Thus the waiter will light a candle at the table for an intimate *tête-à-tête* for two in a chic restaurant. But this is only a pale middle-class imitation of one item out of the culture of upper-class dining; the full repertoire of style and ritual remains beyond reach.

To separate their subculture further from that of their social inferiors, the upper classes borrow from the cuisines of other cultures in an unending drive for novelty, for the recherché and the exotic, which they have discovered on their world travels, and which they can afford to import or reproduce. For sheer luxury, nothing has subsequently outshone the *haute cuisine* of Apicius, who cooked for the Roman nobility recipes which called for ingredients brought from the corners of the world they ruled: 'boiled spiced ostrich, crane, parrot and flamingo, [or] a rich ragout *à la Baiae*, consisting of minced oysters, mussels, coriander, cumin, sweet cooking wine (*passum*), fish vinegar (*liquamen*), Jericho dates, and olive oil'.[72]

Cuisines of this kind, which go far beyond ethnic or national boundaries, cannot, then, be studied – as Lévi-Strauss assumes – as if cultural systems always had strict boundaries around them. Moreover, 'culture' is internally differentiated by class.

Cuisines, also, change over time. The study of how this happens, therefore, has to be *historical*, and this cannot be done simply by using not particularly well-selected pairs of polar opposites, since these fail to capture the richness of real life – for example, the astounding omission (for a Frenchman) of cooking by oil (especially frying).[73] Nor are subsequent attempts to prop up and repair Lévi-Strauss' model by introducing further sets of categories (resulting in a 'culinary tetrahedron' in place of his 'culinary triangle') much more successful.

A reading of a classic cookery book such as that by Fannie Farmer, the Founding Mother of American cooking, immediately calls into question the whole notion of an unproblematic 'national' culture. She initially based herself on WASP cooking (the original 1896 book was called The *Boston Cooking-School Cook Book*). But she was aware that, with the influx of millions of immigrants, what constituted 'American culture' was changing. A later edition was therefore specifically intended to cater for the 'cook or hired girl who didn't know English'.[74] Yet despite these qualifications, her book was, overall, very much part of a Western European, and in particular English, cultural tradition exported to the Eastern seaboard developed there during the colonial period. True, that epoch did see the introduction of new, American recipes into the cuisine, using Native American foods such as squashes and corn, and new ways of cooking them, such as hominy grits. But the dominant hegemonic cuisine was still that introduced during the long period of English rule.

The English upper classes themselves had for years absorbed cuisines from other Western European countries, especially France and Italy. Initially, only a handful of very rich 'milords' could afford the Grand Tour. But by the end of the nineteenth century, Thomas Cook was organizing tours of the Continent for the thousands of new middle classes, and the tastes they acquired were then transmitted to the United States via the Eastern seaboard as models for the new American bourgeoisie, for whom, in the epoch of Henry James, Europe was still the centre of the cultural universe. Increasingly, Americans themselves also visited Europe and other much more remote parts of the globe, and widened their cultural horizons. The tastes they imported were not just culinary; they included the arts and, above all, for the upper classes, the opera.

So Fannie Farmer's book, like Mrs Beeton's in England, had a distinctive class as well as an ethnic content and aimed at socializing an entire generation into 'cultured' ways of living. Mrs Beeton had gone much further than cuisine alone, advising women about household management in general. But as far as cooking is concerned, her readers got what they wanted: not impossibly expensive *haute cuisine* indulged in by the aristocracy, but affordable versions of upper-class recipes, plus some of humble lower-class origin, including regional dishes like Yorkshire pudding or Irish stew, nostalgically acceptable to people who, though upwardly mobile and aspiring to middle-class status, had nevetherless come from environments where they had eaten these things in their childhood. But, for them, a joint would still have to do for at least two meals, and probably provide cold cuts, 'mince' or sandwich fillings as well.

Fannie Farmer concentrated, then, on the production of 'good family foods', acceptable in middle class circles. Her book, we are told, was 'something which you could put confidently into the hands of a bride' (a middle class bride, of course). They needed guidance, though, not only about cooking but about staple foods, kitchen equipment and the planning of meals. They also needed to be told how to eat these foods, how to present them and what constituted 'correct' procedure, with regard not only to food but also to social behaviour – 'manners' and etiquette – generally. So, like Mrs Beeton, she provided advice to readers who were the counterparts of the upwardly mobile people today who turn to the book by 'Miss Manners' and her syndicated columns in American newspapers and magazines for advice on 'excruciatingly correct behavior'.[75] For all their ironic, arch, funny tone, these are actually deadly serious, for her readers need to be told everything, starting with the planning of meals and information about staple foods and kitchen equipment.

Since social eating involves the preparation and presentation of different kinds of meals, with different dishes, served at different times of the day, these are matters which vary greatly from culture to culture. Over most of the world, only one major meal, usually comprising one kind of staple – normally grain made into flour (wheat, maize, millet or bread), or a vegetable (rice, potatoes, manioc, etc.) – is eaten each day, apart from 'snacks' to top up energy. In the industrialized world, however, what constitutes a meal differs between classes – not only the number of dishes and the different kinds of dishes within the meal, but what meals are taken and when – breakfast, lunch and an evening dinner for the middle and upper classes; for the working classes, the main meal, dinner, is in the middle of the day, with a lighter 'tea' at the end of the working day and perhaps a light 'supper' later on.

Though neither Fannie Farmer or the successors to her literary estate (which became a corporation all of its own) grouped her chapters into parts, there is an underlying sequence. First come 'Appetizers and Hors D'Oeuvre' and 'Soups', which together make up what are nowadays called, appropriately, 'starters'. The conventional sequence then requires that 'Fish and Shellfish' come before 'Meat' and 'Poultry and Game-birds'. These are the building blocks. 'Sauces, Marinades, Stuffings and Quick Relishes' are things added to them. 'Filled Things', 'Cereals, Rice, Beans and Pasta' and 'Eggs and Cheese' are only ancillary to these main fish or meat dishes, with 'Vegetables' or 'Salad' as accompaniments to the fish or meat. 'Yeast Breads', 'Quick Breads', 'Cakes', 'Frostings and Fillings' and

– of course, in the USA – a whole chapter on 'Cookies and Cake Squares', plus 'Pies and Pastries', constitute a set of flour-based things, alternatively classed with 'Desserts and Dessert Sauces', 'Fruits and Fruit Desserts' and 'Candies and Confectioneries' as final courses. 'Preserves, Pickles and Canned Fruit and Vegetables' and 'Frozen Foods' are modern additions, with 'Beverages' bringing up the rear. Finally, there are suggested menus, and further concessions to modern ideas: a 'Pressure Cooking Chart for Dried Vegetables', a table of calories and metric measurements.

Today, the eighteenth and nineteenth century tropical exotics, from tea and sugar to oranges and bananas – once extremely expensive – have long been so familiar and cheap in the West that they now seem 'natural' components of the diet of ordinary people in the temperate North. Forests are cut down in Asia to enable the Japanese to throw away their chopsticks once they have eaten, and huge cattle ranches in the South supply meat for hamburgers as they once made corned beef a proletarian staple. Vegetables, likewise, are instantly brought by air to grace the shelves of supermarkets in the West: avocados have long been popular; now it is starfruit or passionfruit which consumers are being induced to 'want'.

The Third World itself has become not just a source of these commodities but also itself a new mass consumer market, a source of mega-profits for Western corporations which process food or set up branch plants in Third World countries. But whereas the tastes transmitted in the nineteenth century were those of the dominant power – Britain – many of these foods, now found in supermarkets and hypermarkets anywhere in the world, were pioneered in North America. The Third World masses assert their 'modernity' by eating not the foods of the Western élites but McDonald's hamburgers. They include ready-cooked meals for people who, unlike the Aborigines, have 'developed' – as Sahlins forecast, they now have 'no time'.

The tastes of the sole remaining superpower now dominate the global village not only in food but even in styles of dress. In Japan or Switzerland, Malaysia, Brazil or Russia, jeans are the ultimate symbol of modernity for young people, while the dream of the masses is to visit one of Disney's theme parks, preferably in the United States itself. The manufacture of these global wants, truly a revolution in taste and consumption, has been possible only because there has been a parallel technological global revolution in electronic communications. Where the cultural traffic once flowed from Europe to the rest of the world, including the USA, today the order is reversed.

Yet there is also both cultural resistance and conservatism. National and regional cultural differences still persist. Italian cuisine, for instance, follows the general pattern of the Western European meal, but also retains its own distinctive, idiosyncratic elements. Thus Marcella Hazan makes few concessions to modernity or to non-Italian ideas beyond calling *antipasti* 'starters', and insists fiercely on the *Italian-ness* of her cuisine, refusing such degenerate innovations as pre-grated Parmesan. Her defence of a national cuisine (actually composed of many regional dishes) thus constitutes a form of cultural resistance, a defiance of pretensions to global culinary superiority, whether on the part of America or any other power.

But Italian cuisine is celebrated, eaten and imitated by cooks and diners outside Italy who are not Italian at all. For there is a long-established, ever-growing and worldwide market for not just Italian but many other kinds of 'ethnic' cuisines, the market for which is not an ethnic group at all but a class: those who can afford to eat out and who demonstrate publicly their élite status by eating extraordinary (non-national) kinds of food – the more exotic, expensive and unknown to *hoi polloi* the better.

What Sharon Zukin has described as the 'gentrification of cuisine' has become a worldwide phenomenon. So when the English or American middle classes go out for a meal, they usually 'eat ethnic'; English or American cuisine are not *de rigueur*. Scotch whisky and French sauces, likewise, are what businessmen in Japan, Hong Kong and Singapore prefer. In the early nineteenth century, the cuisine we now think of as special to Paris (and as gastronomically wonderful) was not particularly well thought of. After the French Revolution, the best chefs had lost their aristocratic patrons; many of the greatest, like Escoffier and Alexis Soyer, eventually gravitated to the then centre of European prosperity, England. French cuisine revived only when the French economy began to grow, and Paris became the centre not just of economic and political life but of French culture. The newly rich of the Second Empire demanded good restaurants, so the cuisine we think of as 'Parisian' was created to meet that demand out of the innumerable regional recipes which provincial immigrants brought with them.

Likewise in the United States, local cuisines have been freely raided and combined in an often 'wildly incongrous' mix – Virginia ham, Maryland crab, Cajun, Creole, 'Tex-Mex', and so on, 'segmented vernacular cooking traditions melded into a homogeneous landscape of culinary power'. The rise of the USA to a position of world hegemony has further involved the appropriation of the regional cuisines of not just America but the whole world.[76] But appropriately the foodstyle which America has exported to the world has been not *haute cuisine* but fast food for the mass market – hamburgers.

Likewise, Chinese cuisines (whether Peking, Cantonese or Szech-wanese or quite new ways of coooking like chop suey, developed for igno-rant foreigners) and Indian restaurants are now common in British towns and cities, with cheap versions in the form of the 'take-away'. (They re-flect, of course, historic imperial connections.) So the race is on for more exclusive status symbols. Now the élites go for Thai, Vietnamese and Ko-rean food. Soon it will be Ethiopian or some other cuisine. Two paradoxes arise. First, the 'hot', really fashionable cuisines of the moment tend to come from very poor countries, sometimes places of endemic famine for the mass of the population, whose inhabitants have never eaten many of these foods, since they were available only to the aristocracy and the court and are now monopolized by the new élites and the growing middle classes. The second paradox is that the major market for ethnic foods is not indigenous at all; it is external – the bourgeoisie of the global village.

Both indigenous Third World élites and Western restaurant-goers are new classes. Like their nineteenth-century counterparts, Mrs Beeton's readers, they do not aspire to *haute cuisine*, which is still beyond their reach, because of both the cost of exotic materials and labour costs in the form of the salaries of highly paid chefs. As Goody has shown, a whole new industrial complex has been brought into being to serve the new mass market – a labour force to do the preparation (women for the mass mar-ket, men as chefs) and a literate, well-heeled food-consuming mass mar-ket who read the cookery books and eat the food. In Britain, where over 80,000 new titles are published every year, a new cookery book and a new gardening book – the twin principal cultural pursuits of the middle classes – are, it is said, published every day, rejigging for a mass market what was once exclusive *haute cuisine* now as *cuisine*.

What we have been talking about, then, has been cuisine, not cooking. The Aborigines have different ways of cooking, but they have virtually no cuisine – no repertoire of alternative ways of processing raw materials for human consumption. This is not to say there is *no* culturally determined processing of foodstuffs. A special range of easily digestible things is given to infants, for example—honey and water; powdered nuts; cooked fruit with the seeds removed; cooked crabs, snails and witchetty grubs; meat that has been premasticated for them; and fish that has had the bones re-moved.[77] For adults, flavourings, too, may be used to enhance (usually to sweeten) some dishes. They also like to have a gastronomic contrast be-tween flesh and non-flesh foods:

If there is plenty of fish they may be 'hungry' for 'sugar-bag'. If there are plenty of yams they may be 'hungry' for shellfish.[78] ['Hungry' is in inverted commas as it refers to cultural tastes, not nutritional needs. PW]

But by and large there is only one way of cooking a given kind of food. Thus cartilaginous fish are made into fishcakes and non-cartilaginous fish are baked; the difference is reflected in the use of the word *amadangkwa* for the latter, the same term that is used for animal and human flesh .[79] The methods of cooking are also limited, earth ovens and broiling on the fire being the main ways of cooking flesh. For vegetables, the only complex methods are dictated by the need to leach out poisons sometimes, rather than by the search for novelty. As Waddy perceptively observes, cooking was not a function of 'affluence':

In the past, the choice of food was generally limited by the success of the hunters and gatherers in finding what was seasonally available. They were not concerned about whether the food was raw or cooked, hot or cold or sweet or sour, as about what food was available ... They ate when they were hungry.[80]

Aboriginal cuisine, then, is a cultural process. But it is one that sticks close to nature. As Gertrude Stein would have put it, when it comes to cooking, a yam is a yam is a yam.

Aboriginal Biological Classification

We come now to the basic Aboriginal classification of plants and animals which underlies and is wider than the classification of things that serve as foods. Even allowing for species used for practical purposes other than as food, since the Aborigines recognize, and name, no fewer than 643 different species – nearly double the number of edible species (332) – the common belief that their knowledge is limited simply to the utilitarian – an argument which Sahlins calls 'practical reason'[81] – is not justified.

A pioneering study of the biological knowledge of an Aboriginal tribe, the Wik Monkan of Cape York Peninsula, by Donald Thomson, an anthropologist who was trained as a biologist, described their system as 'bearing some resemblance to a simple Linnaean classification'.[82] For, once more, it is not just the sheer *amount* of Aboriginal knowledge that is impressive. It is that, as with species used as foods, everything is classified within a *taxonomy*, the basic division being between plants (*amarda*) and animals (*akwalya*), which are then subdivided into lower-level sets.

Plants: Amarda

When they are looked at as food, plants are divided into fruits, root vegetables and food from flowers. But in Aboriginal biology they are divided
quite differently: into plants with woody stems (*eka*), such as trees and
shrubs, and non-woody plants, such as grasses, sedges, rushes, herbs,
vines, creepers, ferns, seaweed, etc. (One important species, the burrawang, is in a category all of its own because it is ambiguous, for although
it is deep-rooted like other trees, it has a soft rather than a woody stem.)
Altogether they distinguish no fewer than 114 kinds of woody plants and
eighty-four kinds of non-woody ones.

The term for non-woody plants – *amarda* – is also used for plants in
general, just as *akwalya* means both fish and flesh food in general.

One of Waddy's two chief informants, Nangurama, then divided woody
plants into eight categories and the non-woody plants into three main categories, 'partly on the basis of similarity in form, and partly on the basis of
shared habitat'.[83] 'Similarity in form' probably refers largely to leaf shape
and texture, plus the bark in the case of trees. Gula, Waddy's other chief
consultant, putting more weight on a different criterion, root form, split
up three of Nangurama's larger non-woody categories into seven. Not
surprisingly, given the importance of kinship in their culture, the Aborigines often phrase resemblances between one kind of plant and another in
the language of kinship, as when two or more kinds of animals are described as 'siblings' or 'friends', though this is usually when talking about
animals rather than plants.[84]

So though both of the sets of subcategories in the two different taxonomies of Nangurama and Gula were made up of combinations of the
same species, there were some differences in the way they were combined. More often than not, these subcategories do not have an explicit
name – those which biologists call 'covert' complexes. The same applies at
times to higher-level complexes – *akwalya*, we saw, can mean 'animals in
the sea', but can also be used for *all* animal life. It is sometimes argued that
where they do not have a specific *name* for a group of kinds of animal, it
might really be us doing the grouping – for example, with land birds, or
for the group of seven different kinds of bird which includes the orioles
and the cuckoo, which the Aborigines put together because, they claim,
these birds have similarities. The absence of a specific name, though, does
not mean that they don't recognize connections between the things they
group together. Europeans, Atran points out, name such life forms as
'trees', 'moss', 'quadrupeds', 'birds', etc. But they also have *unnamed* categories: they group 'trees' and 'plants' together, though there is no common name for 'things which grow out of the ground'.[85]

Thus for non-woody plants, though both Nangurama and Gula identified certain kinds of grasses and sedge rushes (which Western biologists also distinguish) and both put them in the same subcategory, Nangurama then proceeded to add in other rushes, bulrushes, ferns and cassia. Gula, on the other hand, considered that the latter constituted a separate subcategory, grouping them with water-lilies.

Nangurama and Gula thus represent different schools of taxonomy. This does not mean that either of them is lacking in scientific rigour, as the different criteria they employ make apparent. But Western taxonomy too has seen constant shuffling and reshuffling of the genera and species. Overall, there is a high degree of overlap between Groote categories and Western ones. Thus the Groote Eylandters classify twenty-three kinds of grasses by a single label, *dingadirungwena*, which Western biologists class as members of the *Poaceae* family. The Aborigines then recognize affinities between *dingadirungwena* and other kinds of grasses, as do Western botanists, who include another fifty grasses under the label *Poaceae*. But the Aboriginal classification is sometimes less elaborate: the single label *dingarrkwa*, for example, covers seven different kinds of grasses which Western biologists *distinguish* (as does popular Australian botany, under names like 'sugar grass' and 'native panic').

Of the woody plants, Nangurama's first group includes five kinds of figs, as well as nearly thirty other kinds of trees, bushes and shrubs – the wild prune, wild cherry, and various other berry-bearing trees, as well as some grevilleas, wattles, etc. His second group includes the wild plum, bush currant and half a dozen other trees, and most of the wattles, one which they label *mebina* covering five kinds we distinguish and give separate names to, in both popular and scientific usage. The third of Nangurama's groups includes the hibiscus, the red kurrajong, the wild kapok tree, the tulip tree and a dozen other kinds of trees. The fourth, a small group, contains some grevilleas and the native almond. The fifth covers the eucalypts – eight kinds – plus the milkwood and ironwood, though it further includes some plum trees, the wild apple and some mistletoes. Group six is mainly paperbarks (seven types), together with six types of mangroves, some of which we subdivide. Group seven includes the strychnine tree, the wild asparagus, the jasmine and the croton. Group eight includes palms and the coconut. Finally, there is the burrawang in its separate category, while the tamarind, which the Malays brought, is also in an exotic category of its own. Nangurama grouped non-woody plants into three large complexes and one small one (which includes seaweeds).

Animals: Akwalya

As we know, the word *akwalya* usually connotes 'fish', but can be applied more widely to mean all animals in the sea and, even more widely, all animal life. We also saw that sea animals which were important as food – fish, shellfish and turtles – were then divided into different groups.

As with food classification, animals are first divided into those from the sea (*akwalya*), winged and other creatures of the air (*wurrajija*) and land animals (*yinungungwangba*). Sea animals are divided into three named subdivisions: fish (137 kinds), shellfish (sixty-five kinds) and marine turtles (six); while cartilaginous fish (*aranjarra*) are distinguished from bony ones (*akwalya*). The twenty-three kinds of cartilaginous fish are then subdivided into sharks (nine kinds), with a second subdivision (with no overall name) made up of stingrays (eleven kinds), shovel-nosed rays and sawfish (three kinds) and suckerfish. The 113 kinds of bony fish they distinguish are divided into twelve categories. One of them contains freshwater fish, so in this respect the classification departs from the strict sea/land distinction. There is, though, only one deviation from the cartilaginous/bony division: suckerfish, which are actually bony, are grouped together with cartilaginous ones because their flesh is similar.

The second major division of sea animals, shellfish, includes almost all molluscs, as well as hermit crabs (though not squids, octopuses or cuttlefish). But whereas only forty-two kinds of shellfish are recognized as edible, no fewer than sixty-five kinds are distinguished in the biological classification.

Nangurama then divides this large complex (largely on the basis of form) into five 'covert' categories, with five or more divisions of each of them, and another fifteen categories with only one or two members. The strict opposition between land and sea is breached, however, since two kinds of land snails and one kind of freshwater mussel are included among all these hundreds of sea creatures.

Thirteen kinds of crustaceans comprise category number four. Next comes a category made up of two groups of marine mammals – the dugong and two kinds of whales in one group and five different kinds of dolphins in the second. Coelenterates constitute category number six, divided into three groups, made up of seven recognized kinds, the largest of which is based on the fact that they float on the surface of the sea, whereas another type of jellyfish is kept separate because it 'crawls', while sea anemones and soft corals, recognized as living creatures, form yet another group. When dead, they are considered to be akin to rock, covered with slime.

Nangurama had difficulty with squids, octopuses and cuttlefish, and in particular the problem of cuttlefish bones – were these animals like molluscs (as we think) or ought they to be kept on their own? He inclined to the latter view.

Of the smallest categories, the echinoderms, starfish and sea urchins, and the sea-cucumbers (bêche-de-mer), were also problematic. Eventually, because they live on the seabed, he placed them with starfish. Finally, two kinds of worm were thought of as constituting separate categories of their own.

Twenty-seven different kinds of land animals are recognized. Just as the word for 'fish', *akwalya*, is used in a wider sense to cover all marine life, the word for four-footed mammals and reptiles, *yinungungwangba*, is also used for land animals in general. There is debate among Aboriginal specialists as to whether these latter should all be grouped together or whether the differences between them are such as to justify subdividing them into three subcategories within the overall framework of 'land animals'. The preponderant view favours the latter – the first group includes nine kinds of marsupials and rodents (wallabies, rats and mice of various kinds, the possum, native cat and sugar glider, plus bandicoots). The second group is made up of eleven kinds of goannas, monitors and 'dragons', the frilled lizard and the crocodile (which, although it is the saltwater species, is reckoned as a land animal because it lays its eggs on land). The third group, though logically equivalent in status to the large group of land animals, covers only one kind of lizard and four kinds of skinks and geckos, while a fourth contains only one kind of animal: the freshwater turtle.

Snakes, together with legless lizards and eels, constitute a division of their own, one which, unusually, is not 'covert' but distinguished by being given a name, *yingarna*. These are divided into two sets, but just as we saw that the words *akwalya* and *amarda* can be used in both wide and narrow senses (to mean flesh or fish and vegetable or non-woody plants respectively), one and the same word, *yingarna*, is used of snakes in general and, in a narrower sense, to refer to only one particular set of snakes – poisonous ones – of which there are seven kinds. The second major set of snakes also has a generic name: *dingarna*. It includes nine kinds of pythons, tree snakes and sea snakes, thus breaching, once again, the strict sea/land division, as well as departing from biological criteria altogether by including a purely *mythical* snake.

Frogs are given a whole division of their own, but surprisingly a majority of the older people did not regard frogs and tadpoles as related, and so tadpoles form another category on their own. (It is similarly surprising to me that the development of grubs and caterpillars into adult insects is not recognized, though moths and butterflies are known to emerge from cocoons. Again, adult and young forms of certain fish are put into separate categories.)

Earthworms and blind snakes form another whole category, while seven kinds of grubs, leeches and caterpillars make up the last type of land animals recognized. Echidnas constitute a group on their own, as do dingoes.

Grubs are troublesome, borderline creatures. Some seem to have wings. Are they, then, to be classed as insects? But insects as a whole are even more troublesome. To start with, they are grouped with birds, quite rationally, since they have wings and inhabit the air. Flying foxes, again, are classified with birds and insects, because they too are creatures of the air. *Wurrajija*, therefore, at its widest, means 'winged creatures and other air-dwelling creatures'. But this introduces a third major habitat – the air – in addition to sea and land, the two that we have so far insisted on as cardinal in Aboriginal thinking. One logical way of handling this would be to stick to the sea/land dichotomy at all costs – which is what Nangurama proposed. Some *wurrajija* should then be classified as land creatures; others as sea creatures.

Gula, on the other hand, wanted to make *wurrajija* a third category of air-dwelling creatures, equal in status to sea and land animals. We would therefore have a trichotomy, not a dichotomy.[86]

Similar 'borderline' problems arise with insects which may be winged but live on the land, like green tree ants, and with animals which change their form, such as grubs or caterpillars.

Introduced animals, such as the horse and the cow, are kept apart from indigenous kinds of animals in Aboriginal classification.

Finally, one animal is not regarded purely as an animal: the dog (the domestic one, that is, not the wild dingo). Because of their close association with human beings, dogs are given personal names and the pronoun prefixes used for humans are used for them as well. All other animals fall into one or other of the noun classes applied to *non*-human phenomena (see Figure 4 overleaf).

Differences of opinion, and therefore of taxonomy, are sharpest in the field of plant classification, however, rather than that of animals (disagreement about *wurrajija* apart). In dealing with plants, as we saw, Gula came up with a different taxonomy from that used by Nangurama, because he had used root form as his main criterion, whereas Nangurama relied on form and habitat. Here we see a similar intellectual process to that which has marked the history of Western controversies – between 'splitters', who constantly seek to divide into ever finer categories – and 'lumpers', who try to manage with as few categories as possible.

As far as the basic kinds of animals recognized and named by the Aborigines are concerned, there is a remarkably high degree of correspondence between their basic categories (which biologists call 'folk taxa') and those (genera and species) used by our biologists. For four-footed land mammals and reptiles, it is as high as 86 per cent; for *wurrajija*, winged

Figure 4 **Groote Eylandt biological classification of animals**

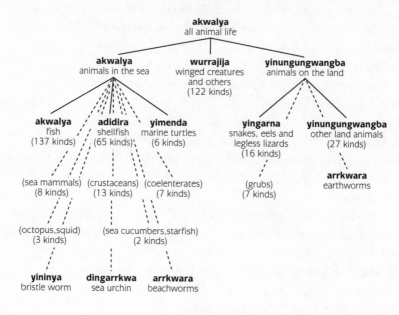

Source: Waddy, 1988, Volume 1, Figure 13.

creatures (both birds and insects), it is 79 per cent; and even for *akwalya,* animals in the sea, where there is least correspondence with Western scientific categories, it is still more than half (55 per cent). For animals as a whole, it is 69 per cent; for plants, it is 74 per cent. Using a different way of measuring the degree of overlap, the correspondence goes up to between 86 per cent and 90 per cent.

The higher-level grouping of these taxa, then, does not always overlap so neatly with those devised by Western scientists. They put together some species which we assign to different higher-level groupings and separate some kinds of plants and animals which we think belong together.

Two typical small excerpts from Waddy's second volume, which lists every kind of plant and animal recognized on Groote Eylandt, the popular names given them by whites and the Western scientific names, show the extent of overlap between Groote Eylandt biological classifications and both Western popular and scientific ones (see the table opposite).

Since Waddy's book appeared, there has been a dramatic reappropriation of their own culture, in modern form, by women of Groote Eylandt who have been working with Waddy and her colleague – though increasingly on their own – on a 350-page encyclopedia-cum-dictionary for secondary school students. While reordering more than 370 kinds of plants and animals for the encyclopedia, they arrived at what Waddy calls a 'beautiful affirmation' that, despite differences over plant classification between Nangurama and Gula, there does exist an overall Groote Eylandt system of classification, of which the two 'schools' are only variants. Though the finer details of how things were grouped *within* the major classes might vary with 'school of thought', there was agreement about the higher levels of classification. The only change was really 'presentational' – to put one kind of bird before another on the grounds that it was better known.

Groote Eylandt name	White Australian popular name	Western scientific name
A		
dilirrirnda	carpet python	*Python spilotus*
duwalja	water python	*Liaisis mackloti*
dumamungkwunamurra	children's python	*Liaisis childreni*
duwurrruruwilya	mythical python	–
daya	common tree snake	*Dendrelaphis*
dumurrengmurra	sea snake	*Hydrophis elegans*
		Lapemis hardwickii
B		
mebina	river wattle	*Acacia difficilis*
	ball wattle	*Acacia latescens*
	sand wattle	*Acacia loxocarpa*
	cream-coloured wattle	*Acacia oncinocarpa*
	deep-gold wattle	*Acacia torulosa*
yinungwaja	white pea bush	*Desmodium biarticulata*
	woolly pea bush	*Sophora tomentosa*
yinungwunya	small ball wattle	*Acacia multisiliqua*
	dwarf wattle	*Acacia yirrkalensis*
		Burtonia subulata
		Terminalia canescens

The Emergence of Western Science

Most people would think that there is an unbridgeable gap between Western scientists' thinking and Aboriginal thought. Yet four times out of five, the Groote Eylandt Aborigines recognize the same kinds of plants and animals as our scientists do. As Waddy remarks, there is 'a very high degree of correspondence with the [Western] scientific system as a whole'.[87]

There are some differences – they distinguish some taxa which we don't recognize and sometimes classify a land animal among sea animals. Very rarely do they separate a type of animal from its biological next-of-kin because of its special religious status. But even the great Linnaeus recognized the special *social*, not biological, connection between the domestic dog and humans, not, as the Aborigines do, by making the dog the only animal which belongs to the same noun class as human beings, but by making the domestic dog a separate species (*Canis familiaris*, the 'faithful' dog), together with the sheepdog (*Canis domesticus*) and the 'turnspit' dog (*Canis vertegus*), and separating all of them from the wolf and the wild dog.[88]

We have already seen that Aborigines have sophisticated taxonomies, based on empirical observation and careful thought. Later we will see not only that in reality there are *several* kinds of Aboriginal thought, rather than one, but that Western thought too is plural.

Scientific biology is only a very few centuries old, and had to compete both with older religious ideas and with popular conceptions which grew out of practical farming and animal-rearing. Even today, biology is by no means the usual framework within which people think about nature.

The sophisticated technology Western scientists have developed – the electron microscope, carbon-14 dating, DNA – does enable them to discern things which those who lack this technology cannot. And Groote Eylandters do not possess the comparative knowledge of the modern biologist who knows that invertebrates make up 95 per cent of the animal kingdom, vastly outnumbering vertebrates; or that there are over 35,000 species of gastropods (slugs, snails, limpets, etc.) or 300,000 species of Coleoptera (beetles).

Such highly developed taxonomies may provide materials for a better understanding of nature, but it is still a long way from explaining how the order people perceive in nature *works*; or how the natural world came into being; or where it is going; or even less, *why* all this happens. Explanations of those matters are therefore frequently provided by ideologies which are often quite independent of science, let alone taxonomy, so that it is perfectly possible to combine science with world-views which do purport to explain these 'first and last things'.

The popular image of Sir Isaac Newton, for instance, is still that of Pope's famous couplet (which Newton rejected as the inscription for his tomb):

Nature and Nature's laws lay hid in light.
God said, Let Newton be! and all was light.

But Newton believed in the Bible as the unique source of truth, and, at one and the same time, in alchemy as 'the heart of [his] system'.[89] His studies in astronomy, optics and mathematics, in fact, 'only occupied a small portion of his time ... Most of his great powers were poured out upon church history, theology, "the chronology of ancient kingdoms", prophecy, and alchemy'.[90]

Yet 'modern science denies [this] parentage'.[91] So learned men responsible for preserving Newton's scientific legacy actually *concealed* crucial evidence for centuries. After his death, his alchemical manuscripts were put into boxes marked 'not fit to be printed', while as late as 1936 they were sold at auction by Trinity College, Cambridge. His immersion in alchemy was only fully made public in 1946, by John Maynard Keynes, whose conclusion – that Newton was 'not the first of the age of reason' but 'the last of the magicians, the last of the Babylonians and the Sumerians' – created an intellectual scandal.

To Newton, the universe was a riddle whose 'secrets' could be decoded only by exercising the God-given faculty of reason. He believed, though, that meticulous experimental verification was necessary. But the techniques he used were the techniques that had been used by alchemists for centuries, focused upon the attempt to achieve the 'transmutation' of metals. This, in turn, demanded the identification of the fundamental particles of matter, a problem which the alchemists of antiquity had debated about, and carried out experimental research on, for centuries. Alchemical postulates, then, were 'perfectly compatible with modern science'.[92] There were, though, competing theories. Robert Boyle believed that certain 'noble and subtle' particles were the basic constituents of the universe. Newton, on the other hand, believed that there was only *one* 'Catholick Matter'. The new 'mechanical philosophy', though, also included a new and singularly radical idea: that all *events* could be explained in terms of matter in motion, 'by impact'.

Newton's scientific work went hand in hand with the study of mystical 'Hermetic' *religious* beliefs, which he studied obsessively, especially the writings of Jacob Boehme. The study of chemistry was, he thought, *necessarily* 'a study of God as He Himself had written out his word in the Book of Nature'.[93] Hence his searches in the Bible, and of the chronology of 'ancient kingdoms', because he was looking for clues – especially *numerical* clues – to the secrets of the universe.

As a final irony, Newton himself connived in keeping much of his alchemical research away from public scrutiny. When Boyle believed that he had finally discovered 'philosophical mercury' (mercury and antimony had always been key metals for alchemists), Newton urged him to keep it secret because it would cause 'immense dammage to ye world'.

William Harvey, who discovered the circulation of the blood, also be-lieved in astrology. And he also vacillated for decades over the disturb-ing social implications of the vascular system. Was the heart analogous to the sun in the solar system and therefore to the monarch in the body politic? For he lived at a time when to treat the heart as merely one major component of the body, together with the liver and the brain, was politically dangerous, tantamount to open support not only for re-publican ideas but also for the 'mortalist' heresy that the soul perished with the body.[94]

In the Middle Ages, science was not divided into the specialist 'disci-plines' recognized today. In Padua, the curator of the botanical gardens had also been the professor of pharmacology, for 'horticulture was for healing, as well as for food and beauty'.[95] This was still the case at Edin-burgh as late as 1760, when John Hope, professor in both medicine and botany, taught the former in the summer and the latter in the winter.

The ideas with which early modern scientists worked thus developed out of older frameworks. Aristotle, for instance, had used various criteria (animals with blood versus those without; the number of feet, etc.) to de-fine certain major divisions of the biological world still in use today – the distinction between birds, fish, whales and insects, for instance, as well as finer distinctions within each of these: the Coleoptera and the Diptera, or between winged and wingless, mandibulate and 'haustellate' insects.[96] Similarly, Pliny separated land animals from those inhabiting the water and the air, as the Aborigines do.[97]

But to Aristotle, all these forms of life were ranked on a unitary scale from the lowest to the highest – the *scala naturae*, a world-view which per-sisted throughout the Middle Ages. Even Linnaeus continued to use the Aristotelian system of logic, and adhered to the notion of the plan of cre-ation. But different philosophies could be attached to the same classifica-tory systems. To 'essentialists', the regularities of nature – 'the Great Chain of Being' – were evidence of a divine plan. Nominalists emphasized differences *between* species rather than common attributes. Increasingly they came to see those relationships in terms of differences in *descent*.

By Linnaeus' time, Aristotelianism had become an ossified dogma which impeded research and was often incompatible with modern find-ings. Most ancient classifications were based on single criteria, such as Pliny's distinction between water birds, with webbed feet, and wading birds, with long legs. But these were thoroughly mixed up with tax-onomies based on a number of criteria which resulted in very heteroge-neous groups indeed. Thus plants were divided into ferns, mosses, grasses, herbs, shrubs and trees, of which the first three are recognized as natural taxa today, but the second three are not. Aristotle's identifications of particular species, on inspection, were often proved accurate, but equally often they were not. Even Linnaeus' work, when subjected to verification, proved to be variable. His classification of insects, which he specialized in, was very good, and is still largely acceptable; on birds, amphibians and the lower invertebrates, however, he was 'very poor'.[98]

With the reorganization of taxonomy by Linnaeus in the eighteenth century, and the breaking-up by Cuvier of animals previously classified simply as 'bloodless' into vertebrates, molluscs, arthropods and radiates, new and better taxonomies were developed by empiricists like John Ray, who now classified species by looking at the attributes of whole populations rather than just the features of individual specimens.

But the status of science was still very insecure, and though the new scientists might dispense with 'ultimate' philosophies in their work, for all practical purposes, few (including Darwin) dared publicly admit that science might dispense with the divine altogether. Such was the institutionalized power of organized religion and its hold on people's minds that they feared the consequences of being branded as heretics here on earth and of eternal damnation in the afterlife.

It took many decades before a general theory emerged which could replace the 'Just So' story of Genesis, by showing that the present order of nature had not always been as it is today, coming into being only over vast stretches of time.

In 1859, Darwin provided precisely that – a *scientific*, as distinct from a theological/philosophical, theory, which challenged hitherto dominant philosophies since it not only provided an account of the order of nature but identified the mechanisms through which evolution had taken place: variation and natural selection.

The taxa could now be seen as related to each other not only horizontally, in terms of their contemporary resemblances, but also vertically, in terms of *descent*. Though Groote Eylandt biology is very hierarchical, in that it recognizes distinct levels into which animals and plants are classified, there is no counterpart to evolutionary theory. The only explanation of how all this came about is drawn from myths about the Dreamtime. As Waddy observes:

There is no overall theory which folk biologists can use to arrange folk taxa horizontally within the various superordinate taxa ... I was given no real guidelines by my Aboriginal assistants as to whether 'land animals', 'sea animals', or 'winged creatures' should be placed first, or as to the ordering of ... taxa within those categories'.[99]

So great has been the impact of evolutionism on modern thought, including thinking in the social sciences and on popular ideas about progress too, that it is now difficult to believe that scientific proof of the existence of sexuality in plants was not established definitively until as late as 1694, by Camererius, a German botanist, as a result of the development of magnifying glasses. Such revolutionary breakthroughs caused scientists to turn their backs on the knowledge of previous centuries.

Yet in its early phases, modern science had to coexist and contend with older systems of thought, enforced either by the Church or by potentates whose cynical slogan *cuius regio, eius religio* was used to justify the imposition of the ruler's religion on his subjects, including intellectuals like Galileo. But by the time of Darwin, it was no longer possible to do this; belief had become a matter for public debate, in which spokesmen like Bishop Wilberforce who made their stand on the basis of biblical literalism merely made fools of themselves.

But these were battles between intellectuals – the educated classes – over articulated ideologies. Popular or 'folk' thinking drew on other sources and was grounded in quite different, often unlettered, subcultures.

Nature: Biological versus Popular Knowledge

In anthropology, a whole literature has developed out of Robert Redfield's famous distinction between the 'Great Traditions' – Buddhism, Hinduism, Taoism, Islam, Confucianism, Christianity – developed and promulgated by an intelligentsia of monastic scholars and priests and encoded in great books, and the 'Little Traditions' – the 'folk' philosophies, at village level: the cults of the earth, of the lineage and of the local community. The two traditions are not entirely discrete; in Thailand, for instance, village boys used to spend part of their growing years in a monastery and therefore acted as transmission belts and reinforcements of Buddhist ideas at village level. Nor were the Little Traditions devoid of cosmic concepts, whether about first and last things or about basic ethical values. There was, rather, a constant interplay between the two kinds of tradition.

In medieval Europe, the main scientific heritages – those of ancient Greece and of Arab thought – were available to very few. Christian thought about the natural world was as obscurantist and devoid of scientific content as popular thinking, and the two commonly reinforced each other. One key distinction was between animals which were 'sweet' and those which were 'stenchy', including 'asses, beetles, bloodsuckers, bulls, caterpillars, cockchafers … cows, dogs, dolphins, eels, field mice, goats, horses, locusts, mice, moles, rats, serpents, sheep, slugs, snails, swine, ter-

mites, turtledoves, weevils, wolves, worms, and nondescript vermin'.[100]
But some could be 'tenderized'. Town rules often made it compulsory to
bait bulls and he-goats, not for sport but to make them tender. To make
them sweeter for human consumption, geese would be nailed to the floor
to bleed them.

Animals were also no less subject than humans to laws based on divine
authority and so universally applicable. Even the civil law accepted the reality of possession and of other forms of behaviour brought about by the
devil. A recent film, *The Hour of the Pig*, centres around the trial of one
such animal which broke the law. Court trials of pigs which attacked or
killed small children were not uncommon and often resulted in the exe-
cution of the offending animal. (In France in 1457, one sow was condemned to death, though her piglets got off on the grounds of their tender
age and because their mother had set them a bad example.) In Russia, the
sentence of banishment was, of course, imposed on animals – a billy-goat
was exiled to Siberia as late as the end of the seventeenth century.

Collective, sudden threats to the entire community, such as swarms of
noxious insects, were often dealt with by churchmen using formal adjura-
tions, anathemas and excommunication, as when the Archbishop of
Trèves, in the tenth century, roared an excommunication at a swallow
which shat on his head in church, or when St Bernard, tormented by flies
buzzing round his head, shouted, 'I excommunicate you!' (The flies there-
upon fell in heaps so high that shovels had to be used to get rid of them.)
As late as the sixteenth century, Bartholomew Chasseneux built up a reputation as one of the most distinguished jurists in France on the basis of his
expertise in these ritual procedures. In one famous case, he defended rats
accused of devouring the barley crop by arguing that they had been improperly summoned – how could they be expected to move away unless
given time to organize themselves? And they had not been given a safe-
conduct against their natural enemies, the cats, which were lying in wait
for them.[101]

Cases of transgressing the bounds of the normal order of nature – such
as cocks which laid eggs – induced 'sacred dread'. Such unnatural behaviour threatened the boundaries between human and animal life, and therefore invited judgement according to canon rather than civil law. There
were three possibilities – that the offenders were 'hungry creatures of
God, with neither reason nor responsibility, simply following the inclina-
tions given to them by nature'; that they might be 'instruments of God',
sent to punish a community for some sin committed by the inhabitants; or
that they were 'temporary vehicles of demons or instruments of the
Devil'.[102] Lawyers and judges then had to determine which category the

case fell into. During the witchcraft crazes of the sixteenth and seventeenth centuries, such cases multiplied, but from then onwards began to decline. (Racine's only comedy, *The Litigants*, is about the trial of a dog.) Yet even Kepler, the great astronomer, who replaced animism with mechanism ('*vis*', which means 'force', in place of '*anima*', soul) as an explanation of celestial movements, could not entirely rid himself of the legacy of millennia. When his own mother was charged with witchcraft, he presented a document of 128 pages, the fruit of a year's labour, to the court, in which he 'carefully accounted for every act for which his mother was being charged by referring it to a natural process' and thereby saved her life. But never once did he express any disbelief in the existence of witches. Einstein has argued, indeed, that Kepler 'never succeeded in entirely extricating himself from animistic thinking'.[103]

The Bible remained the most powerful authority right into the era of modern science. Popular thinking about the relationship between man and nature, Keith Thomas has shown, had its roots in the Good Book, which asserted that God had designed nature to serve man's interests:

O Lord our Governor, how excellent is thy name ...
What is man, that thou art mindful of him ...
Thou makest him to have dominion of the works of thy hands: and thou hast put all things in subjection under his feet;
All sheep and oxen; yea, and the beasts of the field;
The fowls of the air, and the fishes of the sea

Psalm 8

Animals, then, had been 'carefully designed and distributed with human needs in mind'.[104] (For the more scholarly, further validation of this was available from classical Greek writings.) Then came the Fall, after which some beasts became 'wild' and some plants became 'weeds'.

Such wildly anthropomorphic ideas did not flourish solely among the vulgar; they were still compatible with the new scientific humanism of the seventeenth-century intelligentsia. The destiny of man was to conquer, subdue and vanquish nature. The wild had to be cultivated and animals had no rights. (Reports that the Jains respected even the life of insects were received with incredulity.) The killing of wild animals therefore remained the central sport in the subculture of the ruling classes. In the Middle Ages, large tracts of land were preserved as royal forests, for hunting purposes only. Queen Elizabeth I's huntsmen would drive harts into corrals, where she could administer the royal kill with a crossbow to the accompaniment of music.[105] James I personally daubed the faces of his courtiers with the blood of the slaughtered beasts (as in today's 'blooding' of young children at English hunts) and the ladies of the court washed in it. The hunt validated both concepts of 'pedigree and breeding, and a taste for aggressive war'.[106] As late as the Second World War, as a young officer I was told that hunting was very good training for tank warfare since it gave you 'an eye for country'. Conversely, the unwashed were forbidden to hunt. One of the demands of the poor, historically, had been to be included among the animal-killing classes – to have access to 'game'.

Policing the borderline between the animal and the human was still needed, since 'animality', pollution and defilement[107] might appear anywhere. Even swimming was denounced as 'bestial', while working at night, being not part of the normal rhythms of nature, was therefore appropriate to people like burglars. Though incest was not made a crime until the twentieth century, bestiality had been an offence since the early sixteenth century and was only taken off the statute book in 1831. Becoming too familiar with animals, even pets, was disapproved of, while unconventional attachments – for example, to toads – were very suspect. The disciplining of animals through the use of halters, bridles, chains and cages was the model for the treatment of deviant humans too – lunatics, prisoners or children. To be labelled 'wild beasts' justified the use of the most ruthless sanctions – for example, the hunting-down of the Indians of New England like wolves. But contradictions began to multiply. By the eighteenth century, Abolitionists could attack slavery as a 'beast-like' institution; a century after that, imperialists might be compassionate towards animals – many, indeed, preferred 'black beetles' to 'black Zulus'. 'The line,' Thomas remarks, 'had to be drawn somewhere.' Today, the moral criteria have shifted again: some animals are now fed organically before being slaughtered.

Wider human moral values and categories have always been projected on to the natural world. Thus some birds pleased humans because they were melodious. Others, which had bad social habits, like birds which ate excrement or carrion, or which were insectivorous, were tabooed as food; those which ate a diet humans approved of, like rooks (which ate grain), could be 'baked in a pie'.

The cultural boundaries between humans and animals were drawn to avoid any ambiguity about the superiority of humankind. Aristotle had recognized three kinds of soul – the 'nutritive', shared by men and vegetables (!); the 'sensitive', shared with animals; and the 'intellectual/rational', peculiar to humans. Luther thought the institution of private property distinguished man from the beasts, though others thought the distinction derived from the transmission from generation to generation of a quite *im*material property – the faculty of reason. Animals, though, were mere machines, and wild ones were quite outside the moral order.

Some species passed into folklore as metaphors for human characteristics. Aesop's 'sly' fox and patient tortoise were still to be found in medieval bestiaries, while even those at the cutting edge of scientific advance commonly fell back on older folk categories. So it came naturally (i.e. culturally) to Linnaeus to divide the vegetable 'kingdom' into 'tribes' and 'nations', and to denote grasses as 'plebeian' ('the more they are taxed and trod upon the more they multiply'). Lilies, on the other hand, were 'patrician', because they 'amused the eye' and 'adorned the vegetable kingdom with the splendour of courts'. Mosses were 'servants', for the benefit of others; flags were 'slaves' and fungi 'vagabonds'! Even scientists found it difficult to disencumber themselves of pathetic fallacies: Benjamin Franklin objected to the use of the eagle as a symbol because the bird was a 'moral coward', while Ray and Willoughby stigmatized the partridge as 'obscene and salacious'.[108]

Animals also provided models of various kinds of human social organization projected on to nature. The larger 'monarchical' animals – lion, eagle, whale – were, of course, especially admired, plus the 'social' insects, with their bourgeois, domestic virtues of hard work, diligence and frugality. But because the social life of animals was so diverse, it was also morally ambiguous. Some species were culturally flawed, and provided negative role models – the 'lawless', 'thieving' magpies or the choughs. Others evinced more or less admirable forms of social structure: ants were 'monarchical'; bees had 'kings' and cranes 'captains'; but storks were 'republican' and rooks even had 'parliaments'. Sparrows, with their 'noise, squabbles, and ubiquity' were the 'Irishmen of birds'. These political values projected on to nature were to persist until monarchy gave way to parliamentarianism, and eventually to mass democratic society.

In Stuart times, deviant dogs were punished by being subjected to attack by a ram; not only bears and dogs, but even sharks could be tortured. Many of these older attitudes and practices, particularly the killing and torture of animals for sport, such as the ancient sports of bull- and bear-baiting, and cock-fighting, or the less well-known roasting and hunting of cats, still persisted into modern times.

Most of these were mainly wild animals. Working animals, serving man, were more privileged, while a third category – *non*-working animals, notably pets, especially cats and dogs – even more so. Though the medieval peasant family shared the same physical dwelling space with their animals, the latter had to be kept in their place and therefore had to observe the taboos humans imposed on them. At the same time, being both valuable commodities and personal companions, they had to be protected, and even in the Bible there were injunctions to take care of domesticated beasts, in particular working animals, which were not to be eaten. The cult of roast beef, for example, grew only as the working ox became less important as the principal means of traction in agriculture and meat was increasingly produced to meet new mass markets in the towns and cities. But once their working life was over, especially for cattle, sheep, draught- and racehorses, a 'ruthless eugenics' obtained, even for cats and dogs; individual animals which were physically abnormal or became unfit or just plain old were 'put down'. Favourite horses might be put out to pasture, or earn their oats as studs, but even animals close to man were abruptly terminated when their usefulness ended. Working dogs past their best were commonly hanged.

Nature Transfomed

Such thinking grew out of quite new ideas and cultural practices concerning the relationship of animals to humans, which involved nothing less than the transformation of nature itself. By the eighteenth century, Francis Bacon's categorical assertion that 'Man may be regarded as the centre of the world'[109] was being challenged. John Ray could adopt a much more relativistic view. In strict principle, he declared, naturalists should use in their work only 'what properly relates to natural history'. A parallel objectivism even came to penetrate the arts. Constable was to declare, 'I never saw an ugly thing in my life.' For many, this brought with it a new optimism – even weeds and lice had a positive purpose (as a stimulus to industry and an incentive to cleanliness respectively). And domestication was *good* for animals.

As agriculture gave way to urban and industrial life, and people became separated from farms where animals were part of everyday life, attitudes to nature changed. 'Country' comes from *contra*, that which lay outside the farm-homestead, the 'wild'. It was a local term. Now for the majority who lived in the new towns and cities, the world outside as a whole became the 'country*side*', whether cultivated or wild. The first immigrants to the cities, Engels recorded for Manchester, kept animals cheek by jowl, in their hovels. But by the end of the century, children grew up without ever having been to the countryside and without knowing that milk came from cows, not bottles. I know London youngsters today who were uneasy when they were first taken to dark villages where there were 'no people' and there was 'nothing to do'.

The new urban middle classes quickly absorbed new, unpractical and moral attitudes towards nature – the Romantic sensibility. Gradually, the cruelties of earlier centuries – where pigeons were torn apart and harts had their feet cut off, where dogs were set on ducks and geese, or were themselves hacked to pieces, or where geese were deliberately let into the pike pond for 'sport' – were now replaced by a new consideration for animals. The discovery of new exotic cultures in America, Asia and the Pacific, and of the remains of formerly great civilizations, induced a growing rejection of the notion not only that the earth was the centre of the universe, but that man was the centre of it too. This 'dethronement of man' – 'one of the great revolutions in modern Western thought', in Thomas' words – was further reinforced by the discovery of new realms of life and of new worlds outside our galaxy, revealed by the microscope and the telescope. By now the idea that everything was part of great chain of being brought into existence according to a Divine primordial agenda was increasingly being replaced by the idea that 'nature had no intention at all'. Coleridge could address a young ass as 'brother'; Byron could write about the pain felt by fish. We should not be asking the question, 'Can they *reason*?' or 'Can they *talk*?' Bentham said, but rather, 'Can they *suffer*?' A new generation influenced by Rousseau argued that 'pain is still pain whether it be inflicted on man or beast'. Animals could *learn*; they therefore had intellects, perhaps even souls. They could certainly feel – and men could be brutes. The more extreme extended this new sensitivity even to insects and plants;[110] vegetarians elaborated a new cult of tender-heartedness, arguing that 'beef tea had killed more people than had Napoleon'.[111] Less extreme expressions of the new mood were the introduction of close seasons during which shooting was forbidden (1883) and the enactment of legislation to control the slaughter of birds (after 1869) and the depredation of wildflowers (1888). New rules were introduced at Smithfield meat market in London in 1781, followed, five years later, by the licensing of slaughterhouses and public debate about humane methods of killing. Guilt at the shooting of an albatross became a symbol of an altogether novel mentality. In the wild, field glasses were to replace guns.

The old values did not disappear all at once. Gladstone could still cut down 30,000 trees as an expression of the ancient belief that the wildwood needed to be tidied up – 'savage', after all, came from *silva*, a wood. The axe also became the tool with which the American frontiersman 'tamed' the 'wilderness'. Distinctions were made between kinds of trees, as they had been with animals – 'wild' species were to be eliminated and replaced by useful, domesticated or decorative ones. Some, like 'Gospel oaks', might be grown because they had significance as symbols of 'eternity', or because they were appropriate sites for public rituals. Trees might even be punished for their social connotations – damaged as an act of protest against the tree's owner – and were also appropriate places for punishing people, notably by hanging.

They were also used to consolidate the social order. By the late eighteenth century, a quarter of the cultivated land in England was in the hands of 400 families. For miles around, vistas cut through the woods (even on land belonging to others) led the eye to the lord's mansion on the top of the hill – command of the 'prospect' was symbolic of command over society. One aristocrat even contemplated extending an avenue all the way to London, seventy miles away.

To make these vistas and parks, the populations of entire villages were removed, and brick walls, ha-has and other barriers established to keep out the dispossessed, who engaged in wholesale poaching. One or two might gain employment as decorative 'shepherds' and 'hermits' in artifically created Gothick landscapes – rural fictions reminiscent of Marie Antoinette's Trianon or the 'Potemkin villages' of Catherine the Great. 'No forest,' Oliver Rackham, the great specialist on English trees, has remarked, 'was complete without a resident hermit'[112] – although many succumbed to 'melancholy' and even committed suicide.

Parliament played its part in this rural civil war by providing penalties of transportation and worse.[113] The wives of two men caught raiding the deer park at Stowe and sentenced to death under the Black Act of 1723, pleaded for their husbands' lives. Viscount Cobham promised that their men would be returned and they were – after they had been hanged.[114]

On these newly enclosed giant estates, a new agriculture came into being. Enclosures necessitated new boundaries: 1,000 million plants, mainly hawthorn, for 200,000 miles of new hedges – more than had been planted in the previous 500 years.[115] Within these boundaries, an agricultural revolution took place. Perfect, vast lawns required the labour of three men with scythes, working all day, to cut a single acre, plus lawn-women who gathered up the cuttings. And the transformation of the landscape could combine profit with aesthetic pleasure. In a veritable mania of tree-planting, 14 million larches were planted on the Perthshire estates of the Dukes of Atholl alone between 1740 and 1830.[116]

At Fonthill Abbey, Mr Beckford had

relays of men working night and day on various projects ...When he wished a new walk to be cut in the woods, or any work of that kind ... he used to say nothing ... in the way of preparation, but merely gave orders, perhaps late in the afternoon, that it should be cleared out and in a perfect state by the following morning at the time he came out to take his ride. The whole strength of the village was then put in requisition, and employed during the night.[117]

Inside the 'big house', the labour of the villagers and the products of the estate provided not just food but visual gratification. At Akenfield, even as late as the eve of the First World War, the gardeners

had to creep in early in the morning before breakfast and replace great banks of flowers in the main rooms. Lordship and Ladyship must never hear or see you doing it; fresh flowers had just to be there, this was all there was to it … Work in front of the house had to be done secretly. About seven in the morning we would tiptoe about the terrace, sweeping the leaves, tidying things up, never making a sound, so that nobody in the bedrooms could hear the work being done.

Ladyship also regarded it as her prerogative to call upon any man or woman in the village to work in the house:

We were very happy. At first, that is. Until Ladyship said my wife must work in the big house. My wife … got migraine. The doctor told her she must leave her work … I told Ladyship, who said, 'But she must come'… She drove to the cottage and told my wife, 'You must come back to the kitchen – do you understand? You *must*' … Servants were just part of the machinery of the big house … If a maid was in a passage and Lordship or Ladyship happened to come along, she would have to face the wall and stand perfectly still till they had passed.'[118]

The landed aristocracy thus imposed its ideas on both the people and the countryside. The formal gardens of their parents and grandparents were now replaced by a new kind of landscape, in which 'parks' were built in accordance with the tenets of Romanticism – the celebration of the 'wild', 'Gothick' conceptions of the 'picturesque'. The Highlands, which Dr Johnson had denigrated as 'hopeless sterility', became for a later generation, 'sublime', a 'semi-religious' sentiment that made mountain-climbing a new activity for the educated classes. The untutored urban lower classes, though, needed to be *taught* how to appreciate this unfamiliar beauty, Wordsworth thought, and should be sent on *preparatory courses* before being let loose in the Lake District.[119]

Nature was also 'improved' by adding variety, so botanists were sent to the ends of the earth to bring back exotic trees and flowers. Botany had been an integral part of early colonial expansion in the mercantile epoch, when people like John Tradescant ('a superior form of pirate', Hoyles calls him), who had served on diplomatic and military missions to Russia, Algeria and elsewhere, now turned their hand to botanizing.

When Sir Joseph Banks sailed with Captain Cook to Otaheite, the result was a veritable botanic revolution, for he brought back 30,000 specimens (3,500 species) – more than half of them unknown in Europe, where Linnaeus had only listed 6,000 species altogether.[120] From Kew Gardens, seedlings of such valuable crops as rubber, tea, coffee and cinchona (for quinine) were sent out to colonial gardens in Singapore, Ceylon, South Africa, Australia and the West Indies as the basis for new kinds of plantation agriculture.[121]

At home, tropical fruits could now be grown, and gardeners could indulge new tastes for novelty. By the eighteenth century, 'crazes' broke out one after the other, for tulips, ferns, shells. By the nineteenth century, the revolution in gardening had become a mass phenomenon. Even wild flowers, despised for centuries as 'weeds' (except as 'simples'), now became objects of serious study and aesthetic appreciation. By the middle of the eighteenth century, natural history books had become best-sellers. By the 1850s, the flowers of most parts of England had been listed by naturalists, many of them middle class ladies or clergymen. But a century after 'natural history' had become a suitable, indeed fashionable, subject for the educated classes in the countryside, particularly young ladies and clergymen, eminent Victorians like Ruskin still considered the modern scientific focus upon the sexual parts of flowers rather indelicate for females.[122] Coarse names – mare's fart, ballocks, open arse – were now replaced by polite euphemisms, or by scientific labels.

New forms of cultivation and new forms of 'nature' were now also invented to meet the conditions of life in cities. From 1819 onwards, successive Acts encouraged a working class which still hankered after life in the countryside, allowing them to grow food on urban 'allotments' – big enough to grow vegetables and fruit to feed their families, but on the scale of horticulture rather than agriculture. The motives of the legislators varied – at first, it was to reduce the costs of the Poor Law (without reducing the supply of rural labour); then to improve public health; and finally came the moral, civic and aesthetic virtues of gardening, which would, for instance, counteract the pull of the public house. Today, there are still over half a million allotments in Britain,[123] sometimes on sites specially set aside, sometimes squeezed into unused land along railway lines.

John Loudon, the great pioneer of modern gardening, knew the new urban working class had not entirely lost either the utilitarian knowledge or the aesthetic values which they brought from the countryside. In the village cottage gardens their forefathers had cultivated, both men and women had grown vegetables and fruit and flowers side by side. In Britain's industrial North, back-to-back terraces were built without gardens. But in the South-East houses did have gardens attached, and over 10 million still have today,[124] in which both working- and middle-class people have developed a distinctive style of gardening, including reduced versions, on small lawns, of large country estates. Where wealthier gardeners were preoccupied with displaying the latest expensive exotic flowers, working-class gardeners kept alive the production of what came to be labelled 'mechanics' flowers'. In the 1850s, Lancashire textile workers were said to grow 'better specimens of flowers than anyone in the land'.

New public parks used masses of 'bedding-out' plants (2 million of them per annum in London) to form carpets and floral designs.[125] Urban pollution even led to the development of new species of trees. Over half the trees in London today are London planes, descendants of a hybrid between the oriental and the American plane which can stand the pollution because they shed their bark.

Gradually, a new division of labour grew up where vegetable-gardening was separated from flower-growing, and each confined to one sex. Women had long been confined to menial tasks in gardening, especially weeding. Now the production of vegetables became predominantly a male occupation, while working-class women absorbed the middle-class notion that growing flowers was a proper way for a lady to spend her time, in the garden and the borders immediately adjoining the house. In suburban gardening today, men do the heavy work, including anything involving machinery (especially mowing the lawn) and organizing the garden – for example, into industrial straight lines. But many women have internalized the gender division of labour so deeply that they leave everything outside the house to men, gardening included. Their sphere is the *inside* of the home (cooking, housekeeping and childcare). Now, it is being argued, women who no longer work outside the home, and whose children have grown up, devote more and more time to 'post-sexual' gardening to fill their lives.

The motivation for providing parks in the cities was the same as that which informed the provision of allotments. A visiting American farmer, Frederick Olmsted, the great designer of so many of America's finest parks, was inspired by one of Britain's earliest, Birkenhead Park, which he called 'The People's Garden', to replicate it when he got back home.

Civic gardens, though, were not exempt from class struggle. Landowners were only too ready to sell off land, whether for cheap 'spec' building or for elegant houses overlooking the new parks, and with privileged access to them or to private squares, so there was strong rearguard action over the provision of public parks for the inhabitants of the cities.

The urban working classes had to organize petition after petition over decades to have the new parks opened to the public and provision made for music, games, picnics, the selling of food, and other uses more in accordance with popular desires than the interests and tastes of the horse-riding and carriage classes. It was only mass protest that prevented the Lord of the Manor, Sir Spencer Maryon Wilson, from enclosing Hampstead Heath and developing housing on it. The parks, especially Hyde Park, became focal points for political protest, from the Chartists in 1848 to the Hyde Park agitation over the 1855 Sunday Trading Bill and the Reform agitation in 1866, the first May Day demonstration for the eight-hour working day in 1889 and, largest of all, the Votes for Women suffragette meeting of 1908, when thirty special trains brought more than half a million demonstrators to London from seventy towns, who then converged on the park in seven separate marches. The large London parks have remained venues for political demonstrations, recently against apartheid, nuclear weapons and pit closures, and for popular concerts, from Mick Jagger to Pavarotti.

Today, 'farming' is a mechanized operation, carried out on large fields by a small portion of the workforce, involving the destruction of thousands of miles of hedges and reliant on industrial 'inputs'. For the urban population, the countryside has become a place they visit to provide relief from the stresses of everyday life. Yet for some, what they find there often generates a new kind of depression. Long before the Green generation, W. G. Hoskins, the historian of the English countryside, expressed his horror at what industrialism and war were doing to his beloved England:

What ... has happened to the immemorial landscape of the English countryside? Airfields have flayed it bare wherever there are level, well-drained stretches of land, above all in eastern England. Poor devastated Lincolnshire and Suffolk! And those long gentle lines of the dip-slope of the Cotswolds, those misty uplands of the sheep-grey oolite, how they have lent themselves to the villainous requirements of the new age! Over them drones, day after day, the obscene shape of the atom-bomber, laying a trail like a filthy slug upon Constable's and Gainsborough's sky. England of the Nissen hut, the pre-fab, and the electric fence, of the high barbed wire round some unmentionable devilment; England of the arterial by-pass, treeless and stinking of diesel-oil, murderous with lorries; England of the bombing-range wherever there was once silence, as on Otmoor or the marshlands of Lincolnshire; England of the battle-training areas on

the Breckland heaths; England of high explosive falling upon the
prehistoric monuments of Dartmoor. Barbaric England of the scientists,
the military men, and the politicians; let us turn away and contemplate
the past before all is lost to the vandals.[126]

That poetic threnody, the backward-looking, gentlemanly and despair-
ing nostalgia of an isolated intellectual, was to be displaced by a newer,
much more widespread and activistic kind of protest in the 1960s, now on
a global level, with the rise of the anti-nuclear and Green movements.

Those who experienced the Second World War were horrified by genocide. Their children, though, grew up with an even greater fear, that of
ecocide. *All* life, it seemed, not just human, would be extinguished by nuclear, bacteriological and chemical warfare, reflected in the rise of two extraordinary cults among the young – vegetarianism, even among very
young schoolchildren, and 'Dinomania', a preoccupation with the major
instance of the global extinction of a once dominant biological species.

Popular Classification Today

All systems of naming living things have an implicit meta-logic. By this I
mean that they have not developed simply as a result of pure, abstract re-
flection – though this does happen too. They develop, rather, out of use,
which here means much more than merely the direct, practical exploitation of knowledge (Lévi-Strauss's 'good to eat'). Though both Aborigines
and Western scientists – in fact, people anywhere – do have inquiring
minds and pursue knowledge which they find interesting 'in itself', we
should not lose sight of the practical concerns that drove them to think
about these things in the first place. The modes of biological classification
developed by the Aborigines relate to their hunting-and-collecting existence. Western biology grew out of attempts to systematize knowledge
which would be of economic value in agriculture and animal-rearing. The
systems developed by scientists in the process, on the other hand, soon
lost direct touch with these practical concerns. Science developed its own
paradigms, rules and modes of organization.

The systems which we will look at now – popular knowledge about
plants and animals in the West – have yet a third, quite distinct rationale:
not practical-agrarian, but aesthetic and social, developed by city-dwellers
with gardens. In the case of plants, they mostly grow flowers, rather than
vegetables, in order to make a more attractive environment in a sea of
bricks and mortar, offering a quiet area free from vehicles which threaten
life and limb and poison the air. They also have animals, although these

(especially dogs) tend to be kept, not to be slaughtered and eaten, for security against burglars, muggers and rapists, especially by people living on their own (above all, old people and women). Other kinds of animals, especially cats (and dogs), help counter emotional alienation and are much more accurately described by the term 'animal companions' than the indulgent (aristocratic?) term 'pets'.

Popular systems for naming plants and animals have existed side by side with the scientific ones and been developed, over thousands of years, for quite different purposes from those which inform the work of scientists. But although they are distinct and separate, and much older, in modern times science has penetrated even popular biology. By popular biology I do not mean books such as the Reader's Digest *Classification of the Animal Kingdom*,[127] which aims at explaining the fundamentals of biological evolution and taxonomy to the lay reader. Most books written for amateurs are not of this kind. They are identification kits, written to be *used*, not explanation books. But although their primary purpose is to help non-scientists identify plants and animals, the identity they provide is one that scientists would endorse. And given the prestige of modern science, even the rankest amateurs want the handbooks they use to carry the authority of science. Most handbooks therefore contain lists of species, organized systematically, if not necessarily in the way biologists would present the same material when addressing their professional colleagues.

Usually, though, they do 'point' readers, if they are interested, to the underlying scientific taxonomies. But the connections between species, the underlying taxonomies themselves and the rationales for these are spelt out only very briefly. If readers do take the trouble to turn to more explicitly scientific works, they will find the classifications – into phylum, class, order, genus, species, etc. – into which a plant or animal species fits and the basis for these classifications. But most people do not do this – I certainly don't. All they want is a handbook, the smaller the better, which will tell them quickly what the thing *is*.

So 'twitchers', and mere dabblers like myself, can hardly do better than to use books such as Collins' *Birds of Britain and Europe*.[128] Here they will find all the birds they are likely to see (and many they won't). At the beginning of the book, the authors give us an admirably succinct account of how the classification process works:

Scientists classify all animals in a series of groupings, starting with 22 phyla and proceeding downwards through classes, orders, families (ending in -*idae*), subfamilies (ending in -*inae*) and genera to the actual species, below which there are sometimes subspecies or races based on geographical variation. Birds belong to the Phylum Cordata, along with the mammals, reptiles and fishes, and are themselves distinguished as the Class Aves. Within the Aves Class, there are 27 orders of living birds, much the largest of which is the Passeriformes, loosely known as song birds, perching birds, or Passerines. The passerines comprise more than half the known bird species of the world, and more than a third of the 154 bird families. They are all terrestrial and very diverse in shape and form, but generally adapted to perching in trees and often have a very well developed song. The Passeriformes in this book start with the larks … and end with the crows … The basic unit of classification used … is the family, of which 74 are represented.[129]

The reader is then referred to two standard scientific works and the system of naming in Latin is also explained.

All this is admirably lucid, scientific – and very brief. It occupies four paragraphs in a book of over 300 pages. This is not a criticism, for there is no call for more extended discussion. Users who wish to follow up the scientific taxonomy and its rationale are given a list of scientific works and a list of scientific names at the end.

The main body of the book consists of page-by-page classifications, beginning with 'Divers', plus their Latin name *Gaviidae*, then 'Grebes' (*Podicipiticadae*), then 'Albatrosses, Shearwaters, Petrels, etc.' (*Diomedeidae* and *Procellariidae*), 'Stormy Petrels' (*Hydrobatidae)* and so on, through more than sixty groupings. Some of these, like 'Albatrosses, Shearwaters and Petrels', cover several *different* species, for which the distinguishing scientific Latin names are given – for example, *Fulmarus glacialis* for the fulmars. Others, like the 'Divers', are made up of eleven different kinds of *Gavia* only. The reader is then given drawings and distribution maps, all of which are designed not to answer the question, 'Where does this species fit in the scheme of evolution?' but rather, simply, 'What is that bird?'

For plants, there are two quite different kinds of handbook: about cultivated plants – for the garden – and about wild flowers, the latter term being as anthropomorphic a distinction as the word 'weed', which means plants *we* don't want (though the only book on weeds that I've consulted doesn't even define them). Thus the authoritative *Dictionary of Garden Plants*[130] is for gardeners. In addition to 'What is it?' gardeners want to know 'How do I grow it?' So plants are grouped into 'Alpine and Rock Garden Plants', 'Annuals and Biennials', 'Greenhouse and House Plants', 'Perennials', and 'Trees and Shrubs' – popular, usable categories rather than scientific taxonomies, with 'cultural notes' on each and hints on photographing plants. Then come the 2,048 colour plates, followed by the dictionary of even more varieties, with the Latin names for each. The *Reader's Digest Encyclopaedia of Garden Plants and Flowers*[131] has a preface of two pages explaining how the scientific botanical names are used and a page of cultivation advice. Then come 735 pages, alphabetically listed, of individual plants, illustrated in colour. At the end is a further practical section covering pests, diseases, special-purpose plants, propagation, pruning, a glossary and conversion tables for length, volume, liquids and weight, in different systems of measurement. All extremely practical but not hard botany, even less taxonomy.

For wild plants, I use Collins' *The Wild Flowers of Britain and Northern Europe*. As with their *Birds of Britain and Europe*, there is a one-page discussion at the beginning of 'Classification and Scientific Nomenclature'. The layout for recognition purposes is different, though. Here the various species (identified by the popular and then the Latin name) are grouped into 'Trees and Tall Shrubs', 'Chickweeds and Allies', 'Peaflowers', 'Umbellifers', 'Two-lipped Flowers', 'Composites (Daisy Family)' and 'Waterweeds'; then, within each of these divisions, into families. The reader is also provided with notes on plant ecology, types of soil and basic botanical terms, plus names of plant societies and 'Further Reading'.

The hard botany is thus kept to a minimum, for again this is a book to help the person who wants to know 'What is it?' So readers are given a 'key', a second table at the front of the book, which leads them to the plant they want to identify by grouping trees according to leaf shape (shown in coloured drawings) and other plants according to the shape and colour of their flowers. The latter are grouped (with coloured drawings again) into 'Individual Flowers Large or Conspicuous', 'Individual Flowers Small, in Heads or Spikes' and 'Individual Flowers Small, in Clusters or Solitary'. The first of these is then subdivided into 'Open, Star-like or Saucer-shaped Flowers', 'Bell- and Cup-shaped Flowers', 'Lipped Flowers' and 'Two-lipped Flowers'. The first of *these* subdivisions is then divided into flowers with two, three, four, five and six or more petals respectively. Since there are plenty of quite different kinds of flowers with, say, five petals, they are further differentiated by small coloured drawings at the front of the book. These are what you should look at first. They will then direct you to the page on which the particular plant you want is to be found, grouped in its proper botanical family, with a coloured drawing. There you will discover that the snapdragon is actually a member of the figwort family (*Scrophulariaceae*) and is related to the toadflaxes, foxgloves, speedwells and others – which may surprise and illuminate the lay person.

This kind of book has always proved the most popular. It was the superb plates, rather than the 3,500 pages in the *Ornithological Biography, or an Account of the Birds of the United States of America*, by the great French-Creole naturalist Jean-Jacques Fougère Audubon, who attracted his rich patrons (some of whom might have been naturalists too) and which continue to attract subsequent generations. Though William McGillvray provided him with scientific identifications and Latin nomenclature, the book has always been seen primarily as a classic work of art rather than a scientific text.

Audubon himself had 'no formal·scientific training, no aptitude for books or taxonomy, nor cared particularly about describing new species of birds'. In the main he observed birds in life, out of doors, 'not stuffed in museum-cases', and had a special 'passion for representing birds in violent action'.[132] So rather than following a Linnaean classification, he uses habitat as the major way of grouping birds, into those which frequent the sea, the shore, the forest, meadows and upland, as well as behavioural characteristics such as aerialism, mimicry and diving. His artistic predilections are especially evident in the often poetic titles of some of the different sections: 'Divers of Lakes and Bays, Wanderers of Seas and Coasts'; 'Waterfowl'; 'Scavengers and Birds of Prey'; 'Upland Gamebirds and Marsh-dwellers'; 'Shorebirds'; 'Seabirds'; 'Showy Birds, Nocturnal Hunters and Superb Aerialists'; 'Gleaners of Forest and Meadow'; 'Songsters and Mimics'; 'Woodland Sprites'; 'Flockers and Songbirds'. Scientific and artistic qualities apart, these divisions are in the main frankly anthropomorphic, projecting our aesthetic interests in colour and song, and even the interest of humans as hunters, on to nature.[133]

The illustrations in modern handbooks do not pretend to be high art. They are tools, their central *raison d'être* that of recognition; the scientific concern is really subsidiary. Thus a book such as the *RSPB Guide to British Birds* [134] does provide a list of 'Information Books' (distinguished from 'Identification Books'), most of them fairly general and practical rather than strictly scientific, as well as other information of general interest – for example, on bird song, on conservation or on the exterior features of a bird. But the bulk of the text focuses – and rightly so – on information you need (especially visual) in order to identify that bird over there.

The smaller the book, the less room for science. The splendid *Collins Gem Guide: Trees*,[135] for instance, fits into the palm of the hand. After a few introductory paragraphs on what a 'tree' is (pointing out that it isn't an exact scientific category), on woodlands, etc. trees are then divided into 'Broad-leaved' and 'Conifers', with particular species described verbally, and both the popular and the Latin names are given. But the really important aids for recognition purposes are the excellent colour drawings, page by page, of the leaves, berries or other kinds of fruit, catkins, etc. with only small insets of the shape of the tree as a whole. 'Wandering around murmuring *Salix fragilis*' the authors rightly observe, is apt to be a little 'unnerving'. What we want, rather, is 'a process of quick categorization and elimination'.

The scientific information is thus very limited. But it is still there and constitutes an implicit basis of the classification used. This contrasts with the virtual omission of any discussion of scientific classification in older editions of recognition books such as *The Observer's Book of British Wild Flowers*,[136] which simply lists plants in alphabetical order, with nothing else other than drawings of the parts of a flower. Today, science is more obtrusive; there has to be *some* more overt connection to and basis in science, even though the handbooks are still constructed primarily as recognition kits – useful tools rather than theoretical studies.

We began with the discovery that Aborigines have more than one way of classifying plants and animals, and that these knowledges are also differentially distributed. What kinds of foodstuffs one gathers, for example, depends on one's sex, though we have little information about how food is cooked subsequently and who does the cooking.

This led us to look at Western food cultures, particularly in Britain and the United States, where we found, not surprisingly, in these much more differentiated societies, that there are many different kinds of cuisine. In the USA, we saw, immigrants from Europe brought many kinds of cooking with them; since then, foreign travel has become a mass phenomenon, so newer, alternative kinds of cuisine are now drawn upon.

When it comes to biological knowledge, we found everybody in Aboriginal society knows enough to enable them to contribute to the food supply, but only older people, particularly a few old men, possess specialized knowledge. In Britain and the United States, though everyone is exposed to some biology at school, scientific biological knowledge is still also the specialized province of professional biologists. Ordinary people use quite different, practical classifications of animal, bird and vegetable life.

We will soon be leaving the Aborigines for other, quite different cultures – those of Polynesia. But we have not exhausted the richness of their culture, so before we leave we need to look briefly at the last two kinds of ways in which they classify plants and animals: linguistic and totemic. We will then be able to pull together all these different kinds of knowledge in Groote Eylandt culture.

Linguistic Classification: Words and Numbers

As well as classifying plants and animals according to their use as food and in terms of a folk biology, the Groote Eylandters have a third mode of classification, built into the language itself. To be precise, there are two modes of linguistic classification.

The Anindilyakwa language and Nunggubuyu, spoken on the mainland opposite, are, in the words of a leading authority, 'by far the most complicated languages in north Australia, perhaps in the whole of Australia'.[137]

Structurally, the two languages are quite similar, but the vocabulary is utterly different, as is the phonology – the building blocks of basic sounds out of which all words are made – so that Nunggubuyu sounds as different from Anindilyakwa as, say, Spanish does from Russian. Why this should have come about, when the westernmost island of the Groote group is only a handful of miles from the mainland and there is plenty of traffic between them, I do not know (nor have I ever been given a satisfactory answer by a linguist).

Had I not known a couple of Bantu languages and had access to the manuscript of a splendid grammar written by a Groote Eylandt missionary, Mrs M. L. Short, I would have found Anindilyakwa an appalling language. One of its complexities was familiar, however, because, as in Bantu languages, all nouns are divided into one or other noun class, each of which is distinguished by a different prefix. Five of these cover non-human things: one, beginning with the prefix *d-*, is used for human females and for some non-human things; the remaining four are reserved for those supremely important things, human beings – *n-* for masculine singular and *d-* for feminine singular, as with *le* and *la* in French. But quite exquisite further distinctions are made about people. The pronouns for humans, for instance, go far beyond the simple English division into singular and plural, for what we call the plural is split up into the dual – 'you and I'; the trial – three or four persons; and thereafter, the plural English-speakers are familiar with. Anindilyakwa further distinguishes between the *exclusive* 'we', meaning 'you and I *only*' – 'we who are talking to each other' (forsaking all others, as it were) – and an *inclusive* 'we' when three or more people are involved – for example, the whole clan.

Altogether, there are no less than six pronouns for humans in the third person and another twelve for the first and second persons, making it possible to distinguish different combinations of person, gender, the number of persons and whether the speaker is included or not.

Not all of these fine distinctions are *necessarily* made. Where they don't matter, some can be omitted; nor are small children expected to get their tongues round these complexities. But many such distinctions *are* obligatory; they cannot be omitted. This elaboration of personal terms reflects the importance, in these tiny, person-centred, kinship-based cultures, of different kinds of *people*.

The existence of these noun classes has further consequences for the rest of the language, for verbs, pronouns, adjectives, etc. all have to be brought into agreement with the noun they relate to. Thus the adjective 'big' in 'a big snake' has a different prefix – the one appropriate to the noun class of which 'snake' is a member – from the one used when the adjective 'big' is being applied to, say, a crocodile, for crocodiles belong to a different noun class from snakes.

Then the verb has to be brought into line. The *subject* of the verb must belong to a particular noun class, so we have to have a different prefix to the verb too. For humans, 'he' and 'she' may present no problem to English speakers, and 'they' does for everything in what we call 'the plural', whereas in French, *ils* and *elles* are needed to distinguish gender. Anindilyakwa is far more complex – the existence of the dual, trial and *their* plural (as well as ways of indicating inclusion and exclusion) means that, over and above a single person, many different sets of humans have to be indicated – a system which is quite unfamiliar to English-speakers.

For the non-human classes too the verb has to have a prefix appropriate to the noun class to which the subject of the verb belongs. Thus in 'The dolphin saw the shark', the dolphin is the subject, so the verb has to have a subject prefix appropriate to the noun class that 'dolphin' belongs to. But if it was a wallaby that did the seeing, the prefix would be the one appropriate to the noun class 'wallaby' belongs to.

Then there are the *objects* of the verb. 'I see it' calls for different ways of indicating 'it', depending on whether the 'it' is a dolphin or a wallaby, since they belong to different noun classes.

I refrain from discussing the delights of the ten major kinds of verbs, or tenses, since this would take us beyond our primary concern with the linguistic classification of plants and animals, and it is the noun class system which is the main way in which they – and, indeed, all nouns – are classified in Anindilyakwa. But this results in a kind of classification quite different from those based on food and biology, for both of these, as we have seen, are *hierarchical*. The noun classes, on the other hand, are not ranked in any hierarchy at all.

A lot of ink has also been spilt trying to work out whether the different noun classes group together things with similar characteristics[138] – large animals in this noun class, fish in that, and so on. They are not, in fact, grouped in so systematic a way. In a sample of 560 nouns (mainly from stories), I found *some* clustering of kinds of species in certain noun classes

– land animals, for instance, fall mainly into classes *d*- and *y*-. But overall, natural species are widely distributed over the five different non-human noun classes. Thus, though the *general* word for 'fish', *akwalya*, belongs to class *a*-, my original finding that the ninety-six species of fish in my sample belonged to five *different* non-human noun classes, and that 117 species of plants and trees were similarly distributed across all these classes, has been more thoroughly confirmed by Waddy. So at the end of the day there is about as little semantic sense in the way things are distributed into different classes as there is in attributing femininity to a table but masculinity to a staircase in French, or making a girl neuter (*Mädchen*) in German but feminine (*devochka*) in Russian.

Since 357 out of the 560 nouns were names of animal and vegetable species, features of the environment, natural phenomena, parts of the body and objects made by humans, only just over 200 nouns covered all other aspects of everyday life, one might be tempted to conclude that Anindilyakwa is a singularly concrete language; or – more dangerously – to put it the other way round and infer that the Aborigines have a weakly developed capacity for abstraction.

To avoid making comparisons solely between their linguistic categories and those of European languages, such as English, let us compare Anindilyakwa with the Bantu language family, which, like Anindilyakwa, has noun classes. Bantu languages allocate an entire noun class to expressing abstract qualities. Thus from the root -*zuri*, in Swahili, we can not only make an adjective, *mzuri*, 'beautiful', when referring to a person (other prefixes are required where the noun the adjective describes belongs to another noun class), but also the abstract category *uzuri*, beauty, by putting the prefix *u*-, for abstract nouns, in front of -*zuri*. *U*- is thus a prefix which enables us to form a whole class of abstract nouns – evil, speed, length, etc.

Abstract concepts are expressed in other ways in Anindilyakwa, notably through inflections of the verb and through the subtle and complex distinctions of a battery of pronouns which – as we saw – enable its speakers to distinguish complexities of human relationships (inclusion and exclusion, number, gender, etc.) which languages such as English have to do in more roundabout ways.

Secondary Particles
Apart from the classes to which all nouns belong, some nouns are also classified in another way, for a second set of particles – around 100 of them – indicate that certain things have common properties.

These secondary particles do not cover all living creatures. They are also culturally peculiar to Groote Eylandt and a few other parts of Arnhem Land. They are used when referring not so much to particular kinds of creatures as to the particular *attributes* of those kinds of creatures – for example, animals with *feet* (which includes all winged creatures) or *marine* mammals. One such particle is *-akamungk(w)-*, which can be tacked on to the front of an adjective or immediately before the verb stem. Thus the ominous-looking phrase *yakamungkambilyuma yimuwarraka* is not as bad as it seems. It simply means 'two turtles', made up of the noun *yimuwarraka* (turtle) and the adjective *ambilyuma* (two), with the prefix *y-* (because turtles are in *y-* class) on the front of the particle *-akamungk-* and the resulting *-yakamungk-* then combined with *ambilyuma*. What the particle *-yakamungk-* indicates is 'animals with legs which live in a shell', which applies not only to turtles but also to crabs, hermit crabs etc. Similarly, *-rukw-* is used when talking about any animal with feet, including all winged creatures. A more esoteric case, I have been told, is the use of a secondary prefix which indicates the luminescence of the skin of certain kinds of fish.

Other secondary particles, however, do not necessarily relate only to living creatures but are used with reference to both living creatures *and* inanimate things with attributes in common. Thus I found *-ngarningk-* was used for what I thought of as stick-like things, from spears and clapping-sticks used in music to pencils, but Waddy has since discovered that what is implied is 'things that are pointed', which is also applied to lightning and the entrance to a wild bees' nest on a tree. Again, *-ngengk(w)-* is used when talking about sharp-edged bivalves, but also when referring to other kinds of sharp-edged objects than those which occur in nature; *milyurrk(w)-* refers primarily to mucus, but is also extended to squids; *-rrak(w)-* is used when referring to bony fish and sharks, root vegetables *and* hollow wooden objects. Again, I heard the particle *-embirrk(w)-* applied to kidneys, but also to stingrays, fruit and eggs – which share *roundness* in common – and further applied to pebbles and other *inanimate* objects such as stones and other natural phenomena, and to man-made things such as marbles, lollies and aspirins. (Waddy says it is used when talking about coins too.) Similarly, the particle *-rrek(w)-*, which connotes 'the properties of being flexible and able to be coiled', can be applied not only to snakes but also to rope and wire.[139] Waddy considers that many of these secondary particles are based on body parts (*-rukw-* on 'foot'; *-rrek-* on 'small intestine, and so on) and have then been extended to animals and other things. They thus constitute an additional way of classifying things – commonly, though not always, animals and plants – linguistically by emphasizing particular *aspects,* such as their roundness, their sharp-edgedness, their being kinds of clothing, their connection with voyaging, or with story-telling, with words or with songs, rather than – as with the main noun classes – classifying things as wholes, such as 'shellfish'.

This, then, is the third way of classifying plants and animals (and other things). It is not related, as the food classification is, to practical concerns, nor does it pretend to cover anything like the range of natural phenomena that the biological classification does.

The noun classes thus provide the general and comprehensive framework within which all nouns are classified; the secondary particles cover only a more limited range of things – as Waddy observes, they are 'neither exhaustive nor exclusive'. But not even the noun classes classify the natural world in a rigorously *systematic* way. Related natural species are distributed across the non-human noun classes; things unrelated in nature belong to the same noun class. But the significance of all of these linguistic classifications is not that they reflect some order in the world of nature or of human society *out there*; rather, they bring order into *language*.

If the meaning of a sentence is very clear, secondary particles need not necessarily be used. Alternatively, you can use them, and leave out the main noun if it has been referred to previously or is obvious from the context. But the use of either device avoids the kinds of ambiguity which occur in English when you are told, 'They're over there' and you do not know whether 'they' refers to the turtles we have been hunting but lost sight of, or the men we were talking about a minute ago. In Anindilyakwa, there is no such ambiguity, for 'they' will have appropriate linguistic indicators – prefixes, infixes, etc. – to tell you whether it is human beings we are talking about or turtles.

A further equally sophisticated capacity to abstract can also be seen, not just in names for things but in ways of indicating number, process and spatial relationships.

Groote Eylandt Mathematics

Few Australian Aboriginal societies have survived after two centuries of genocide. Groote is an exception, due largely to its remote location, and successive anthropologists and linguists have been able to study the culture in depth.

The Groote Eylandt missionary Judith Stokes has compiled a remarkable study of the 'ethno-mathematics' of the Groote people,[140] which is, moreover, 'the first substantial discussion of the mathematical concepts of an Aboriginal group which has ever been published'.[141]

We have already seen that pronouns in Anindilyakwa, besides allowing for distinctions of gender and of inclusiveness and exclusiveness, also indicate number, so that while the English 'We'll go hunting this afternoon' gives no indication of who exactly 'we' is, or their sex, in Anindilyakwa, by using the appropriate pronoun, we can indicate not only the number involved but also usually whether they are male or female and whether the person spoken to is included. To do the same in English would involve the use of many more words.

Though Anindilyakwa has a wider range of numbers than most Aboriginal languages, it may seem limited. There are number names up to five, but when combined with terms for five, ten, fifteen and twenty, numbers up to twenty-nine can be indicated. Beyond that, larger precise numbers were rarely required. The cardinal numbers can also be used to indicate ordinal sequences (first, second, third, etc.), the meaning being clear from the context or by using the prefix *arngk-* ('times').

There are words which make *sorting* possible. In the past these would have been used in dealing with, say, different kinds of berries or, in a more complex operation, in sorting things according not just to number but also to qualities. Again, in grouping things, togetherness and separateness could be indicated.

Yet because their needs and everyday activities were different from ours, some aspects of numbering were better developed than others. It was probable, for instance, when counting the total number of spears available, each man would have a different number, so addition was more likely to be used than multiplication, which would be called for only in the unusual situation that everyone had the same number and/or the same kind.

As Stokes points out, we are dealing with 'small numbers in concrete situations'[142] where objects were not as standardized as those in a mass-production culture. Spears were made one by one and each spear therefore had its individual, recognizably unique characteristics.

When a group of adults and children set off in canoes, each canoe would be different in size and each would contain different numbers of adults and children, with different bundles of possessions. Yet if they *did* want to, they could count small groups of equal numbers of things by using suffixes and prefixes for 'by ones', 'by twos' or 'times'. However, the numerical precision built into our quantitative operations was often lacking. *Ekwarra* meant not exactly a *half* full but a *partly* full container.

Cultural considerations also governed other aspects of their mathematics. Sharing and taking turns were fundamental forms of behaviour. But they were not totally egalitarian – shares were rarely absolutely equal and people got more according to their social status, notably the senior men. But though age-grading was central to the whole culture, with elaborate distinctions for the successive stages of social maturation, ages were not precisely measured.

Though what was being shared might sometimes be readily countable –
such as fish or portions of turtle meat – other things, like berries or small
shellfish, were too small to be individually counted and would be made instead into heaps. In such situations, division was more commonly used
than addition or subtraction.

Inequality ('more than', 'less than', 'fewer than') and equality ('same',
'as much', 'as many as', 'as little as', 'as few as') are expressed in ways
which differ from English usage, but they *can* all be expressed. An equal
score in a game is said to be the 'same'. (In the 1950s, when I ran Christmas sports for the children, such was their distaste for disgracing others
that the 'field', at first 'strung out' as better runners outpaced the less fleet
of foot, then closed up as the slow-coaches were allowed to catch up, so
that practically everyone came in more or less together). Other dimensions of identity can be indicated, as when a character recurs in a story but
in a different situation – where English would use the adjective 'self-
same'. The existence of the dual and the plural also makes it possible to indicate items which are not the same *in all respects* – where people or things
share only one or some characteristics ('those two men are the same
height').

The estimation of time depends upon their very accurate knowledge of
the movement of the sun. For 'What time is it?' one asks, 'How much
sun?', while the term for clock is the word for 'sun' with a different prefix. By observing the length and direction of the shadow cast by a stick
stuck in the sand, even I learned to estimate time to within about twenty
minutes, clock time. Duration of time can also be estimated by using the
yardstick of how long it takes to carry out familiar activities, such as travelling or gathering food.

The day (within which morning and afternoon are distinguished) starts
with dawn, not at the abstract European time of twelve midnight. The seasons are counted by reference to the two main winds, the south-east wind
of the Dry and the north-west wind of the Wet, a full year being one dry
season plus one wet season. There is an abundance of time suffixes and
time clauses to indicate past, future, or specific words which indicate our
'when', 'if' and 'before'; words for 'today', 'yesterday' and 'tomorrow', or
for more precise points in time – 'now', 'this very day', 'immediately',
'soon', 'recently', 'nearly' and 'for the first time'.

Apart from the subtleties of verb tenses, fine distinctions of time can
also be made by adding intensifiers – 'long ago' or 'much later', 'be-
forehand', 'afterwards', 'first', 'late', 'later' and 'last'. Some differ from
English usage: only one event can occur 'first' in English; the rest
occur 'afterwards'. But in Anindilyakwa, people can arrive 'afterwards'

(*arijilangwa*) – that is, after the arrival of the first *person* – but still be 'in time' for the *event*. And duration of time – 'for a little time', 'always', 'while', 'later', 'still' – repetitive or habitual action, continuous states and continuous action, extension of action and finality can all be conveyed.

Today, new words such as 'week' and 'Christmas' have been borrowed from English, while an older distinction between the 'big' days of the week – Monday, Tuesday and Wednesday – and the 'little' days – Thursday and Friday – has acquired added significance now that Thursday is pension day.

Distance and time are closely interconnected. As Stokes notes, 'Saying "As far as Darwin" is only another way of saying "Until one has reached Darwin."'[143] As we saw with their hundreds of variations for geographical place-names, the Aborigines have a highly developed sense of position, so when giving an account of a school camp they will indicate who slept next to whom.

'At', 'in', 'on', 'by', 'where' and 'here' are all indicated, plus much more precise indications of position. If you are asking where the tree is, Anindilyakwa enables you to indicate whether it is near the person answering the question or the person asking it, or, if they are close together, whether it is a short or long distance away from both of them, or even out of sight. The words corresponding to our 'inside' and 'outside' reflect ideas peculiar to their culture, for *arrawa* ('inside') also means 'below', 'low down', 'beneath' and 'underneath', since '*there was nothing a person could get inside as distinct from underneath*, like the buildings and vehicles of today.' Anything *arrawa* always had something over the top:

To sit inside and underneath a shelter were one and the same. To be inside a cave meant to be underneath the overhanging rock. People sit beneath the trees but not inside them. Eggs are always found inside the nest and not beneath. People are normally in a canoe and fish in the water below – unless the canoe is high and dry, in which case one does not expect to find either people or fish underneath![144]

Again, *errekba*, 'outside', carries a special cultural connotation – the clear area away from thick jungle. Anything *errekba* had nothing over the top. Today, by extension, it means outside *buildings*, etc. and the adjective *awurrekerrekba* means 'out in the open, on display'.

'Up high', 'on top', 'between', 'side by side', 'on each side', 'on this side' and 'on the other', 'beside', 'near', 'opposite', 'facing' and 'facing away', 'upside down' and 'head down' can all be specified. Motion *towards* – for example, 'where to?' and 'to where?' – and motion *from* – 'from', 'from where?', 'away' – as well as motion *along* a route – 'along', 'along where?' 'this way', 'that way', 'on the way' – and other refinements can all be expressed.

One cultural peculiarity is the use of the same verb for both 'to take' and 'to bring'. Likewise, the verb root -lik-, which probably originated from alika, 'foot', thus implying 'to walk', is used for both 'to come' and 'to go': the context indicates which direction is involved. Anindilyakwa-speakers also talk of a route they are following as coming from a certain direction rather than heading towards one. So English asks, 'Where to next?' where Anindilyakwa asks, 'Where from?' Is it, Stokes wonders, that in moving across difficult terrain, they are more interested not in the track immediately in front – which is easily seen – but in the potentially difficult areas out of sight which stand between them and their objective – say, an area where food is to be found?[145]

'Right' and 'left' and 'front' and 'back' relate to the body, but whereas we can have an 'impersonal', absolute right – as with road junctions, 'turn right' – on Groote 'right' always means 'to your right'. Direction is embedded. One directional term which English does not possess comes from climbing trees (usually to get honey), when a prefix derived from the word for 'groin' (yingamba) refers to using the front of the body (and hands and feet) to climb a tree. The body also provides the terms for 'front' and 'back', though these are used for non-human things as well, such as the front and back of a leaf. Within a canoe or a building, though, a different word has to be used for 'front' and the term for 'back' is literally 'tail'; alternatively, the back of the canoe may be referred to as the 'west' and the front as the 'east'.

Positions are ordered by using terms for 'first' and 'last', while the word for 'head' provides a prefix which indicates 'going first' – or, nowadays, coming first in a competition.

There is also a term for 'space', commonly used, for instance, to describe a strait between two islands or the space between objects such as rocks or houses. A confined space can also be indicated. Conceptions of line and area, however, were developed only in so far as they were needed, which was not a lot. Since an object like a spear could have a straight side, there is no problem in school with the concept of straightness, and there are also terms for something which has no obstruction or which carries on without interruption. But there was no term for 'line' in itself. 'Horizontal', 'vertical' and 'oblique' are expressed through verbs for 'lying', 'standing upright' and 'leaning', while the word for 'corner' (derived from 'crooked') derives from describing a curve (a bend in a river or a bay on the coast). A term for point 'in itself' was also lacking, though a spear has a point (its 'face'), as does a point of land or a pencil. 'Corner' also serves for 'angle' in English, though the kind of angle (right angle, obtuse or acute) has to be specified by context.

Flatness is not problematic, for there are plenty of flat objects in nature, but though the sails of canoes or pieces of bark for bark paintings were roughly rectangular, they were not precisely so. There were slightly concave traditional objects, such as bark containers for food or carrying babies, and deeper ones, such as Makassarese cooking pots in which bêche-de-mer were boiled, and the hulls of ships. *Convexity* can be indicated by a verb which describes the way the scrub turkey piles up leaves and earth when incubating its eggs or the shape of a turtle, a dugong or an island. *Round* and *ovoid* small objects were also indicated in several ways, such as the extension of words probably originally used to describe fingers and toes to eggs and parts of plants, and then to objects such as pebbles and introduced items. The respective shapes of turtles' and hens' eggs allow the distinction to be made between 'ovoid' and 'round'. *Collections* of round things can also be signalled, while the word for didgeridoo can be extended to all kinds of other round, hollow objects, such as bottles, tins, drums and pipes. Less obvious to English-speakers is the extension of the term for the trunk of the human body to other animals, such as dogs, which also possess large and solid bodies, and even to anthills! Again, the word for small joints of the body is extended to other 'knobbly' things such as seed pods and other parts of certain plants.

Size is covered by three adjectives, 'small', 'big' and 'huge', but the language, as Stokes observes, possesses a 'remarkable flexibility' in the use of qualifiers which indicate 'more' or 'very', or, for example, '*the* big one' out of several. *Height* and *length* are covered by the same words for 'tall (long)' and 'short', or by using secondary roots. 'Deep' and 'shallow' are, of course, available, while 'thick', 'thin', 'fat' and 'wide' (as well as 'spacious' and 'roomy'), plus 'narrow', can be indicated in various ways.

Mass is handled by the words for 'heavy' and 'light', plus a special term for things that are big but also hollow – and therefore light. Indications of *capacity* were needed when using bark containers, or bailer shells to get water out of canoes. An adjective probably derived from 'head' thus describes a container whose contents have reached the top, while there is also a verb meaning 'to be replete', used of a full stomach or a full bladder. The root *debirra* means 'empty' in more than a strictly spatial sense; the absence, rather, of what one might have *expected* to find.

Though long-range exchange was common in Australia – on Groote, in particular, the export of hooked wooden spears in return for ochres used in painting and for stone used to make spear-heads – money is, of course, a modern innovation. Yet it is easily coped with, either by borrowing the word *mani* from English or by calling coins 'stones'. But because the concept of the cash nexus was so new, and because two crucial terms in the process of commodity exchange in English – 'buy' and 'pay' – sound similar, a single verb *-bayindena* has developed which covers both operations. The context has to make it clear which is involved.

On the basis of this sort of evidence, Harris has argued vigorously that the capacity of Aboriginal cultures to handle numerical concepts has commonly been seriously underestimated, from the nineteenth century to the present day, not just by the general public but by mathematicians and even by anthropologists and linguists.[146]

Thus it is still commonly asserted that Aboriginal languages have no numbers beyond two, three or four; some even believe that they have no numbers at all! Underlying these claims, Harris suggests, is the 'social Darwinist' notion that the range and precision of number systems reflect the level of cultural evolution.

There is, in fact, considerable variation in Aboriginal number systems. Many languages, he points out, do have words for five, ten and even higher numbers. That 'five' is derived from the fingers of the hand for them is no different in kind from the etymological relation of the English word 'five' to 'fist' and 'finger'. And though higher numbers are often simply compounds of lower numbers – as when, in many Aboriginal languages, 'three' is a combination of the terms for 'two' and 'one', literally 'two-one' – this is no different in kind from terms like the French '*quatre vingt-dix*' (originally from an archaic number base of twenties) and the English 'seventy-two' from a combination of seven and ten, plus two.

Both Waddy and Stokes acknowledge that there are limits when it comes to quantification. Another writer, Barbara Sayers, remarks that 'height, length, breadth, etc. are not features that are abstracted. They are an inalienable part of the item under consideration' and 'there are almost no terms referring to ... areas of measurement', while 'terms used in applied mathematics are not usually abstracted'. She notes it is extremely difficult for Aboriginal schoolchildren to make the transition to thinking in terms of 'three-ness': 'they do not seem to grasp 'three' as something that can be instantly recognized, whether it be three blocks, three toy trucks, or three cans of soft drink – although the cans of soft drink would be recognized first!'[147]

Moving from this kind of cultural logic to that found in Western mathematics does create some problems. But this does not mean that their culture (including their language) inhibits Aborigines from either acquiring new mathematical concepts or extending their own systems if they need to. Thus Galarrwuy, a speaker of Gumatj, a language of north-eastern

Arnhem Land, has used existing numbers to count up to 20,000.[148]

It is necessary, in a world where people like the Aborigines are still thought of as inherently mentally inferior, to emphasize that these problems derive not from some innate, individual inadequacy of brain power, or from the intrinsic inferiority of one culture as against another, but from the interaction of two cultural systems, which anyone who has learned a foreign language will be familiar with. But languages can be learned, without losing one's mother tongue, and traditional cultural concepts can be replaced by new ones – or the old can continue to be used alongside the new, in different situations – doing school sums, say, as against counting wallabies or estimating the amount of time needed on a hunting-trip. We will see later that we too constantly use rough-and-ready 'social time' – concepts based on social activities, such as 'before going to bed', which are independent of clock time or any other kind of precise quantitative computation, but quite adequate for most purposes.

Conversely, Aborigines are perfectly capable of acquiring new categories of thought, especially forms of numeracy and literacy developed in the modern technical world. They have, in fact, been acquiring them for generations, nowadays normally beginning at school. But they do not need to use them all the time, or exclusively, any more than we do.

English as a Foreign Language

A final personal note about language. The logic which underlies these rules is not something Groote Eylandters have to think about. They do not analyse language; they use it – the noun classes with all their agreements, the secondary particles and the complex forms of the verb – with unerring accuracy. Only foreigners have to try to work out the principles underlying these usages. So they have to think hard, as I have to do when when I try to remember whether something is masculine or feminine in Spanish, while my mother-tongue-Spanish-speaking friends get the gender right, and all the agreements, without having to think about it at all.

Mother tongues, then, are special. Like the Aborigines, I do not have to think about grammar when I speak English, and I do not consciously think about the rules I know, or about the rules I don't know, which I use equally well. While writing this book, indeed, I discovered that the familiar allusion to M. Jourdain – Molière's 'bourgeois gentilhomme' who discovered that he had been speaking prose all his life – was not quite the cliché I thought it was, for I was M. Jourdain. Jet-lagged after flying from England to Perth in Australia, I couldn't sleep, so spent the night reading the nearest book to hand: my hostess' textbook on the teaching of English as a foreign language. I opened it, thinking I wouldn't learn anything I didn't know, for not only do I speak the language well but I had studied English grammar at school and had been taught there were different kinds of words – *parts of speech* – nouns, verbs, adjectives, pronouns, verbs, etc. all tied together by rules of *syntax*. I knew too that there were 'idioms' and 'expressions', though I would have found it difficult to define just what they were.

But I discovered, with a start, that there were all kinds of other linguistic conventions I was not aware of – to do not with parts of speech but with what I came to think of as 'usages', which convey very subtle but also importantly different shades of meaning. For example, when I say, 'I played squash with James every week and I could always beat him', I am aware that 'could' is a past tense of the verb 'to be able'. I know too that if I say, 'But one day, sneaky James, having practised hard in secret, *was able* to beat me', I am also using another form of a past tense of the verb 'to be able'. The differences between 'could' and 'was able to' – both past tense forms of the same verb – are the difference between implying (in the first sentence) that my beating him is *normal* and (in the second) that his being one day, suddenly, 'able to' beat *me* is something unusual, surprising, unexpected. Again, I discovered that there are rules which oblige me to use the definite article 'the' when I claim that I can 'play the piano' (American jazzmen can say 'I play piano', and in England we have imported that usage along with jazz, but the correct *English*, outside jazz, is 'I play *the* piano'). No article is used, though, when I say that 'I play tennis', for the rule is that you use the article when you are talking about playing an *instrument*; you do not when you are talking about a *sport*. Again, if I say, 'My daughter worked as a driver', I am describing a job she did (she actually did, too). And when I am asked, 'What do you do?' or 'What are you?' (which mean 'What's your *job*?'), the answer is, 'I'm an academic.' I do *not* say, 'I work *as* an academic.' But if I say, 'She looked like a film star', I imply that she wasn't *really* a film star at all. The difference between reality and hyperbole is all contained in the word 'like'.[149]

There are dozens of these rules. I discovered that when you use two adjectives, for instance, the one which expresses *opinion* comes before one which expresses *fact*: 'a lovely yellow primrose'. I found too that there are different forms of the possessive if the noun doing the possessing is a thing or a person: 'the roof of the building' but 'my brother's bike'.

As a native speaker, I use these modes of expression with unfailing accuracy, because I had acquired them as a child. Children also simply learn to speak foreign languages, for they are not encumbered with grammar. Adults might not necessarily have been aware that there were rules governing my 'usages', or, if they were aware, have been able to say what they were, or what the underlying logic was. If they were to think long and hard, they might be able to work out what the rules were, and the better-educated among them would probably also feel driven to find out, because they have been culturally deformed by our schooling to feel that they ought to speak 'grammatically'. Linguists, on the other hand, *do* have to work them out, so their grammars fit all the different facets of a language into a coherent overall framework which first identifies the major structural components (verbs, nouns, adjectives, prepositions etc.) and then analyzes the way sentences and noun phrases, grammar and syntax, are constructed out of these elements.[150]

Practical teachers of a language, on the other hand, do not need to know how everything relates to everything else in a philosophically ordered way. What they need is a book, like my book used for teaching English as a foreign language, which singles out a collection of the commonest constructions foreigners might have trouble with.

At first, I thought that my ability to speak without knowing the rules was similar to driving a car – when, thinking about a hundred and one things, you 'come to' and realize that you have been driving on 'automatic pilot' (perhaps listening to the radio) for hours – perfectly safely! But in driving you do at least 'come to' at times – you awake to consciousness and you do too drive in accordance with a Highway Code which you have had to learn and which is stored in your mental computer. In language, apart from what they teach you at school, you absorb most of it practically, not theoretically, with your mother's milk. It is use which is learned, reiterated, corrected by others and internalized, not rules, which are abstract statements about the implicit logic. As a foreigner, you are 'outside' the language, alienated from it, taught, often in high-pressure situations, by specialists in language, not your mother. Since you are taught the formal rules, you therefore become conscious of language as 'rules', which you think about before you dare speak.

In learning Anindilyakwa, I had used a grammar, which started with 'parts of speech': noun classes, forms of the verb, etc. I therefore learned the *rules* about many forms of that language where I had never learned similar rules about English 'usages', because I had been taught English grammar only up to the age of about fifteen, and most of that was *structure*. Thereafter I stopped being taught and never got beyond structure to the rules governing my 'usages'. But in learning a foreign language, I did have to figure them out – the principles underlying the use of the secondary particles, for instance.

My 'usages' (I still don't know what to label them, and I have given up trying to get linguists to tell me) were, of course, just as much rules as those I was conscious of up to the point at which my formal education in English had stopped. The 'basics' I had been taught; the 'advanced' subtleties which I do not 'know', but use so competently and confidently, I had not. These I picked up, informally, in infancy and childhood, in the playground and at home. Had I gone beyond school 'English language' classes to the more advanced work that linguists do, I would have learned these advanced rules too.

So though I speak English well today, I don't 'know' the 'advanced' rules at all. I did have to work out the rules of Anindilyakwa and Bantu, though, and I even dared to write articles in learned journals about them, despite speaking them much less fluently than native speakers. They, equally, would not even have been able to write the articles I wrote, because though they use their language far better than I do, they could not have readily brought the complicated rules they followed so precisely to the surface of consciousness without making the same kind of effort that I had to make in coming to terms with English 'usages'.

Totemic Classification

The Groote Eylandters, then, classify different kinds of plants and animals systematically as foods. They also have quite different biological (botanical and zoological) systems of classification and further ways of classifying certain natural phenomena are built into their language.

We now come to the fourth and final system they use, different in kind from any of the foregoing. It is not a practical-utilitarian system, like the classification of foods, or a scientific one, and nor is it built into linguistic structures. It is a religious association, both between certain animals and plants and between these and human social groups.

The traditional label used to describe this special relationship and the religious meaning that certain living creatures have for certain social groups is 'totemism'. The social groups to which the totems are attached vary in different parts of Australia: there are totems which 'belong' to individuals, to one or the other sex, to marriage classes and to sections and subsections (none of which are found on Groote), and so on.

On Groote the tribe is divided into two moieties. These contain a number of clans, each with their own clan territory and a set of myths which explain the place of the clan in not only the overall social order but also the entire cosmic order: how the world came into being; particular features of the landscape; the various species of plants and animals; and other natural phenomena, notably the winds. These are their myths of Genesis. In the traditional literature about Australian Aborigines, they are called myths of

the 'Dreamtime', so I will use that word (though the Groote Eylandters
don't).

During this time, when the cosmos began, great Creator Beings moved
around the earth. Since Aborigines are nomads, moving constantly because they will soon eat out the resources of any one area, so too were the
creatures of the Creation Time – though when they did stop, the order of
the world was frozen, as it were, once and for all. In the case of Groote,
they came from the mainland, stopping off at places which are known to
everyone as sacred today, usually marked by a natural feature: for example, coloured sand, a rocky outcrop or a water-feature such as a billabong,
a river or an inlet.

Though there is agreement between most researchers about most of
the sizeable main clans, there have been different views on where some of
the very small ones (which affiliate with other, larger ones in the same
moiety and historically have often been absorbed by bigger clans) fit in. It
may seem strange that the name for the Groote Eylandters as a whole has
been much more a subject of debate, though this is not uncommon in
studies among Aborigines elsewhere. Thus Waddy – to whose authority I
defer – considers it inadmissible to use 'Warnindilyakwa', the name of one
of the largest clans, as the name of the whole tribe also.

Nor did the islanders have a name for the island as a whole. People used
to refer to themselves as the people of a certain area, such as the Warnungwijarrakba clan, the name, literally, meaning no more than 'the people belonging to Jarrakba' (to the north-west of the Umbakumba
settlement). Or else they would describe themselves by the name of one
of their main totems. During the 1950s, however, the Australian government required people to have 'surnames', for State Welfare purposes, and,
though based on indigenous names, these resulted in a new set of labels.

Each clan has several totems, not just one. Altogether, there are over
200 clan totems, of which two-thirds are animals, one in ten is a plant
species and the remainder are natural features, natural phenomena and
manufactured items, such as hooked spears, coolamons (containers made
from stringy-bark), or canoe sails.

Nineteenth-century anthropologists espoused radically different theories about the distribution of totems. Idealists argued that virtually everything in the world of the Aborigines was a totem of one clan or another:
it was a kind of cosmic census. Materialists argued that the totems had
been taken as 'markers' of social identity because they were important
items of the diet. That argument collapses, however, since many plants
and animals which are larger, more common, visually more striking or
more important as food are not totems, whereas others less impressive in

such respects are. Second, quite inedible things – on Groote Eylandt, the winds and evil spirits; in other societies, vomit, diarrhoea or dysentery – have been reported as totems and it is difficult to argue that they were of 'social value' in the same sense as food.

Defenders of the idea that totems were necessarily things of social importance then stretched the notion of social importance beyond things which were of obvious *positive* value – like food – to anything of '*social* value'. But this is a circular argument: things of social value (totems) are important because they relate to important social matters.

Obviously, totems are going to be taken mainly from things in the natural environment, since there is very little that is man-made. But there are some other things in the environment which are not plants or animals, of which the most important, on Groote, are the seasonal winds we mentioned at the beginning. But the wind and the rain, monsoon forest, various stars and constellations, such as Orion's Belt, the Seven Sisters and the evening star (Venus), night (or sleep), mist, the tide, currents of the sea, different kinds of spears, 'warrior', cicatrices (such as were cut into the chests of young men at initiation), two kinds of stringy-bark, plus stringy-bark sheets and two kinds of coolamon made from stringy-bark, as well as the canoes made from these barks, calm sea, phosphorescence, harpoon float, fresh water, place (or land), stone, fire, smoke and ashes, rope or string, hollow log-coffins, falling star or fire are also all totems. Some are very important items, whether as food or not, and some are of quite minor or non-existent practical importance. Yet other things of considerable importance in everyday life are *not* totems: women's digging-sticks, for example, men's spear-throwers, the didgeridoo and the clapping-sticks used in music. Among major natural phenomena, the moon is not a totem, whereas the sun is.

The totems which are neither plants nor animals, not surprisingly, include Central Hill. Other natural features which are totems include a peninsula in the south-east of the island; Chasm Island, off the coast of the main island; Castle Rock, in the south-west of the island; a reef near the mouth of the Angurugu River, as well as an area of sediment flow between this river and the largest lake; and Malirrba, a large rocky outcrop on adjoining Bickerton Island. Some of these – like Chasm Island – are major features; others are fairly prominent; while others still are not outstanding at all. Even though the Aborigines were pointing to them for me, I had trouble picking out a pair of rocks on the east coast, identified with two totemic creatures, from a large number of others, some of which were much larger. (Turner reports the same difficulty.)

The major rivers and the largest lake are all totems. But particular places along the routes taken by creatures in the Dreamtime are also totems in their own right. Thus when the Sawfish was travelling to Groote, he arrived at the west coast and then cut his way through the island, thereby creating the Angurugu River and 'Salt Lake' on the eastern side of the island. But along this route, the area where the sediment flows down from Salt Lake to the sea on the west coast and another area of sediment on the *east* coast are emphasized, even though these two sediment areas are separated from each other by Central Hill itself. Physical facts, however, are often irrelevant, for we are dealing not with nature but with myth. In Groote mythology, both river and lake, despite their physical separation, are part of one (conceptual) river, called by a single name, Yinuma. What really links them together is not so much geography as the fact that they are all places along the track taken by Sawfish during its Dreamtime travels. Yet other spots where things happened in the Dreamtime myths are *not* themselves totems! (To make matters worse, there are places which mark the activity of totemic creatures, such as a small island considered to be Sea-eagle's nest, which are *not*, however, totems.) The myths thus contain complicated aggregations of things, many of which are otherwise quite insignificant.

These myths, then, may relate to things found in nature, but only certain natural phenomena are emphasized by the Aborigines *when they are thinking mythologically*. And the reason some relatively insignificant places are singled out and elevated to the status of totems is because they occur in a myth of origin. Their social importance is religious, not secular.

The same mythological logic explains something that I could not understand for some time (forty-odd years, to be honest!): how there were *human beings* in the Dreamtime. For among the creatures in the Dreamtime myths, you will find not only animals (some real, like dogs; others entirely mythological, like certain snakes) and plants, and natural phenomena such as rain and the winds, but also people. Dingirnarra was a *woman and* Jejabun, a *man*; another myth concerns two men, Nebiramurra and Ningayawuma;[151] and yet another, a couple called Neribuwa and Dumaringenduma. An 'old woman in the moon', a blind man and a Makassarese man (Neningumakaja: 'he belonging to Makassar') associated with various Makassarese objects also occur in the myths.

My difficulty was in grasping how humans could be thought of as coexisting with, and being the same kind of thing as, what I at that time thought of as entirely mythological animals and plants. Bruce Chatwin puts his finger on it when discussing the Yeti: 'The Yeti inhabits that nebulous area of zoology where the Beast of Linnaean classification meets the Beast of the Imagination.'[152] What he means (I think) is that, to people who believe in them, Yetis are real creatures in the world around us; to people who do not, they are purely mythological. This captures Aboriginal mythopoeic thought well, for in the Dreamtime things were not as they are today. Animals such as sawfish and stingrays did things that their descendants do not do nowadays. Equally, the human beings who travelled with them during the Dreamtime were *Dreamtime* human beings, part of a different cosmic order. In sum, none of them were animals or humans as we know them now; they were creatures of the Dreamtime, with the powers and activities of mythological not everyday beings. So the humans in these myths did the same sorts of things as their equally mythological animal companions, and both left the same sorts of traces behind them. (To further complicate the matter, most of these 'humans' – for example, the blind man – may belong to a clan but are *not* totems, and some totems do not occur in myths!) Finally, there are non-totemic stories such as the one concerning the old woman who lives in the moon or the one concerning the blue-tongued lizard and the crocodile in which personified creatures are used to teach appropriate behaviour, from not going off on your own and getting lost to reminders that 'your sins will find you out'.

Personification, whether in Dreamtime myths or moral stories, can be indicated by changing the noun class – in the case of the sea-eagle (*yinung-wakarrda*), for instance, replacing the prefix *yi-*, a non-human class prefix, by *n-*, used for humans. In English, we commonly make that distinction by using capital letters. In Kipling's creation myths, *The Just So Stories*, which explain, for instance, how the Leopard Got His Spots, the Leopard and his activities, are capitalized, like the Cat That Walked by Himself, for they were not everyday leopards and cats doing everyday things, but Dreamtime creatures doing wondrous things.

Kipling's stories were for children, but all cultures have myths which explain and legitimize the order of things. In Europe, some have come down from pagan times, though they have subsequently been overlaid by Christian mythology, notably Genesis. They survive today, though, not as religious myth but as art – transformed first into 'folk' literature, which, being the most ancient part of the cultural legacy and therefore specially revered, has become the basis of 'national' mythologies and has eventually been absorbed as part of 'high' culture.

The classical Greek myths thus describe a multi-'ethnic' mythological world in which heroes not only lived in intimate relations with nymphs, Titans, nereids, satyrs, sirens, centaurs and so on, but even interacted with the gods, who killed some humans, loved others and intervened regularly in their wars.

Like totemic myths, Greek legends explain how everything in nature came into existence: men, animals, trees, the stars, storms, earthquakes and so forth. Today, they are no longer seen as sacred accounts of the doings of gods that people actually believe in, but as 'poetry' and as theatrical statements about the 'human condition'.

Scandinavian sagas may concentrate more on the doings of humans – probably because they were brought into line with orthodox Christianity – but for the people who listened to them, humans, ghosts, prophecies, dreams, hallucinations, 'fetches' and portents were still quite real.[153] And the status of the central figures in *The Kalevala* still provokes scholarly debate: were the 'culture-heroes' gods or humans? The sacred Sampo they pursued remains as mysterious as the Grail or the Trojans' Palladium, its symbolic meanings as obscure as those of the Eleusinian mysteries.[154]

Whatever their original religious significance, nowadays these myths are known to us mainly as 'art'. Wagner's reworking of the ancient myths of a world in which dwarfs, giants, Nibelungs, humans, heroes and gods all coexist and interact is a major instance.

These European myths tell us about a world that was the same as that inhabited by the totemic creatures of the Dreamtime. For these are all myths of creation, of genesis and the continuing significance of the cosmos. The humans in that world are therefore aptly labelled 'heroes', a mysterious category of beings who seem at times to be like us, at others to partake of divinity, since they did things that humans beings today cannot do. The Aborigines, though, do not see them – as we do – just as 'art', because for them (or at least those among them who still cleave to the traditional world-view), by participating in totemic rituals, they themselves are contributing *now* to the perpetuation of a cosmic order laid down at the beginning of time. Their artistic representations of these beings, in bark paintings, songs and dances are not just aesthetic; they are also religious.

Lévi-Strauss has distinguished between cultures which are 'cool' in their attitude to history and those in which history is 'hot', where time and changes in time – chronology, continuity, discontinuity and development – are central to a people's consciousness of the world and of their place in it. Western cultures are 'hot'; traditional Aboriginal cultures are 'cold', and conservative in the extreme. For the order of the cosmos was laid down once and for all in the Dreamtime, as it was for orthodox Christians before Darwin.

There is, however, one Groote Eylandt totem which appears to flout these principles: Ship. It is actually a quite specific kind of ship, widely represented in Groote Eylandt cave and bark paintings – a Makassarese vessel. This is plainly a *historical* addition to the primordial myths of the Dreamtime, and Aborigines do recognize that the Makassarese were real people who had *not* been there since the beginning of time. Yet they have been absorbed into a framework which, being mythological, has room for such contradictions. Ship is associated with a clan and a territory which includes Chasm Island (a totem) and a myth of the Dreamtime which includes other totemic creatures such as bailer shell, dolphin and shark. The Ship myth is quite typically 'Dreamtime' in that it involves a travel route in which Makassarese sailors stopped at various spots marked by rocks and other natural features. A related clan, which shares these myths, has an even more modern totem, Aeroplane, which probably grew out of the coincidence of a large modern form of transport, flying boats on the pre-Second World War London–Sydney route in the late 1930s, which landed across the bay from where one of the two present-day Aboriginal settlements still is, adjoining the clan territory of the clan which already 'owned' the Ship totem. Later, a great song-maker composed a special song for its successor, the Catalina flying boat used by the RAAF.

Catalina seems to have died out (Waddy includes Aeroplane, but not Catalina). But creative song-men are still incorporating modern themes, even Ned Kelly and Captain Cook, into their myths. In one myth, Cook was 'around' at the time of Satan, *before* Adam and Eve.[155] In other versions, a distinction is drawn between the white man's Captain Cook and the *real*, earlier Captain Cook, who is identified with the Aborigines. Since federal legislation gives Aborigines in the Northern Territory the right to base claims for the restoration of their traditional lands on the grounds, *inter alia*, that Dreamtime myths constitute cultural evidence of the connection between particular clans and particular territories, totemic myths have become very important for land claims and cultural self-assertion. In Perth, Western Australia, for instance, the land on which the Swan Brewery stands (officially listed as a historic – but not mythological – building) is claimed on such grounds by one Aboriginal group; another has argued that it has rights over the site where a new tunnel has now been constructed under Sydney Harbour, where a mythological serpent travelled underneath the water and came out on the other side.

Any major myth involves the doings of a whole set of beings. To take one major Groote Eylandt mythological complex, Central Hill (Yandarrnga) came from the mainland, accompanied not only by Sawfish – as we saw – but also by Shovel-nosed ray and certain other stingrays, plus several other totems. His route took him to the north-east of Bickerton Island, which he found unsuitable. Then he carried on eastwards towards Winchelsea Island, but found it too soft. On the way, he dropped one of the rocks he was carrying – which is now Arrkarngka (Brady Rock). From there, he turned south-west and crossed Bartalumba Bay, making landfall on the main island, Groote, near Amalyikba. Moving inland, he dropped more rocks at places linked with the names of one of his companions, the red-winged parrot. He continued travelling south-east until he reached Salt Lake on the east coast. This was firm rocky country, so he decided to stay – he is there to this day.

Now comes a subsidiary story. When Yandarrnga and his companions left Bickerton, Sawfish and *his* companions decided to travel to what is now the Angurugu River – the story of which we have touched upon. Accompanied by them, he then cut out that river and went on until he arrived at the place which Central Hill (who had gone by another route, north-eastwards round the island) had reached. From there, Sawfish went on to Salt Lake.

What these travels explain – and legitimate – is the distribution of the present-day clan territories. Thus Arrkarngka, together with the spot where Yandarrnga first landed on Groote Eylandt after leaving the mainland, has a contemporary significance quite different from that of, say, Plymouth Rock in Massachusetts. Plymouth Rock is a real place, but it is also a place where real human people (however mythologized today), not mythological beings, are believed to have landed. Symbolically, it now stands for a very generalized myth: the beginning of white civilization in the USA (or of white domination and genocide if you are a Native American). The collection of Groote Eylandt myths, taken together, thus provides a generalized account of Genesis and of the culture of the Groote Eylandters. But the specific clan myths about the stopping places of the Creation-Time Beings on their travels are also more concrete, for they authorize the ownership of certain very specific tracts of land by certain clans and not others. Thus the myth of the travels of Yangdarrnga includes not just the rock in the sea dropped on his travels, plus the area where he landed on Groote, but several inland places where he dropped other rocks as well – a myth and totems, shared by three clans with adjoining territories along this track.

The sharing of some totems by several clans also explains the peculiar phenomenon of one clan's ownership of certain small pockets of land, sometimes very tiny, in the territory of another clan, often far removed from their main territory. This is because, during its travels, a totemic creature which finally stopped in a particular clan's territory (today its main territory and particularly identified with that clan) also stopped, *en route*, at various spots which are now in the territories of other clans, and often travelled along routes which are not at all obvious. Though the movements of the totemic creatures in the main follow major through-routes which anyone coming from the mainland by boat would follow today, some of the paths travelled in mythological times are far removed from real-life travel. Unless one knows the mythological link, for example, it is difficult to figure out why a clan whose main territory is in the north of the island also has a pocket of land in the south-east: the answer is that, in the Dreamtime, their totem, Dolphin, travelled *underground* and came out at a lake there.

Out of the one or two dozen totems which belong primarily to a person's clan, he or she will normally refer to the most prominent of these as the clan totem. Thus for the largest clan, the Warnindilyakwa, this is South-east Wind; for the Warnungawerrikba, it is Sea-eagle. The myths about these and all other totems which figure in the mythology of the Dreamtime are embodied in songs. Hence if you ask what clan a man belongs to, he may well reply 'the Warnungwijarrakba' – that is, 'The people of Jarrakba', his clan territory. But you can also uncover his identity by a different route – via mythology. You can ask 'What is your song (*emeba*)?' 'Song' here means the main totem of his clan, for songs are the most visible and public manifestations of totemic myths. They used to be heard most nights being played around the campfire, to the accompaniment of the didgeridoo and the clapping-sticks. As Waddy puts it, they are expressions of 'unity and identity'.[156] The performance of the songs does also have an element of what we would call the aesthetic, or, more simply, of 'recreation' or 'entertainment', just as religious people might sing hymns in their own homes for pleasure, both musical and in terms of sociability. Again, totems are symbolically represented in bark paintings. But the deep religious significance of the songs is most evident during important rituals, such as the initiation of young boys. Here, as the anthropologist R. R. Marett once put it, religion is 'danced out'.

Since clans commonly share at least some totems with certain other clans in the same moiety, and the same totems may occur in more than one myth, there are complex overlaps between totems, and therefore clans, which link them together in networks of social and religious identity.

The logic of totemism is thus quite different in kind from the logics which inform Aboriginal classifications of food, biology and language. The first two are based on common attributes. In the linguistic classifications, distinctions between animals and humans are built into the system of noun classes, or pronominal distinctions of sex and number, and via the secondary particles which highlight other attributes of living creatures (luminescence, roundness, etc.).

The classifications of plants and animals as food, as biological species and in linguistic terms use a classic algorithmic, branching logic. But with totemism we are in a different world, for the logic which connects totems

is not one established by the priorities of everyday living, as food classification is, or something to be found 'out there' in nature, like the biological classification, or built into language. The totems are related to each
other, and to the clans which 'own' them, because they coexist in a *myth*
and for no other reason. This, then, is a mythopoeic logic, a religious one,
different in kind from the other logics, and though totems are attached to
social units – the clans – as Durkheim said, the real links between them
are mystical ones. There is no natural or logical link between Ship, short
cut-leaf palm, long yam or dragonfly, all of which are totems of one clan –
the links between them, rather, are *mytho*-logical.

Over-integrated Anthropology: Durkheim and Lévi-Strauss

There is, then, no such thing as Aboriginal thought with a capital T, all of a
piece and based on a central unifying principle: in Durkheim's case, the elements of the social structure; in Lévi-Strauss', the categories built into
the human mind. Thinking, rather, is a plural, not a unitary phenomenon;
there are different modes of thought within any one culture. And the one
Durkheim took to be the basis for all systematic human thinking, including scientific thought – totemic thought – is the least scientific of all.

So when we compare different areas of thought – kinship, biology, religion, etc. – quite *different* categories of thought are involved. The 'same'
thing – a green turtle, for instance – therefore has a quite different significance when it occurs within different frameworks of thought. It is
not, as Gertrude Stein would have had it, that a fish is a fish is a fish;
rather, a fish has different meanings within each of the four separate systems of classifying animals. In the food classification, for instance, the
green turtle is classed together with other kinds of turtle, as it is also in
the biological classification. Linguistically, it is a noun in the class of
nouns which begin with *yi-*, together with lots of things quite unlike turtles. Totemically, it is one of the Dreamtime creatures found in a myth
belonging to a particular clan, together with three kinds of seaweed,
calm sea, phosphoresence, etc. and other things quite unlike turtles.
(The diagram on the following page will probably explain this more
clearly than further words.)

For Durkheim and his colleague Marcel Mauss, regularities in social organization provided a framework for thinking in general: 'The first logical
categories were social categories.'[157] But as we have seen, totemic classification is based on quite different principles from food, biological or linguistic classifications. Durkheim and Mauss did not, however, recognize

The four modes of classification

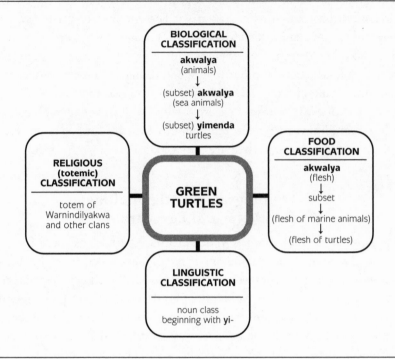

the existence of these classifications, which differ in kind from the logic of totemism; they simply lumped them all together as 'thinking'.

Durkheim was a rationalist, so he rejected the idea that the coherence of religious thought derived from any supernatural source. Like all systematic thinking, he considered, theirs must derive from the underlying order of society. In 'worshipping' supernatural beings and forces which, people believed, had created the order of the cosmos, they were really (unbeknownst to them) only worshipping society.

To be fair to Durkheim and Mauss, there is one sentence tucked away in a footnote at the end of their discussion, where they tremble on the brink of an idea which would have destroyed their entire general theory – where they recognize that, in addition to the totemic classification they have been talking about throughout (and no other), the Aborigines also had another mode of classification which, they disarmingly remark, 'we have not spoken of ... in this work'. This they call the 'technological' classification, linked to 'practical' concerns, such as the grouping of animals according to the means used to get them – for example, according to whether they live in the water or on the ground. If they had followed up this line of argument, it would have opened up the question of the existence of other modes of classification than the totemic – in particular, the possibility of a biological system, based on different premises (the observation of nature). But they simply swept the 'technological' classification under the carpet.

The Aborigines, though, are fully aware that they live in a physical world, different from the world that existed in the Dreamtime and which is invoked during rituals, and different too from life after death. As Turner notes, they distinguish stories which are true or real (*amamalya*), from stories of the Dreamtime (*alawudawarra*).[158] Though theirs is a religious culture, they recognize an interplay between the material and the ideal. So their ethno-biology, on which they depend in everyday life for finding plants and hunting animals, is based upon quite different principles from those which inform their totemic thinking. Which mode of thinking they use is situationally determined: whether they are hunting, say, or engaged in carrying out a religious ritual. This interplay between the material and the ideal, then, cannot be reduced to the simplistic opposition between nature and culture that Lévi-Strauss has proposed.

This plurality of modes of thought is no different in kind from our own, where scientific, religious and many other kinds of thinking coexist. Scientists and priests *claim* that theirs is the only authentic kind of thought – an issue we will come back to later. For now, it is enough to note not only that these different, theoretically incompatible ways of thinking flourish side by side but that one and the same individual can painlessly subscribe to more than one of them.

Both Durkheim and Lévi-Strauss are heirs to a great French cultural tradition, Cartesian thought, which, for all its strengths, is inimical to a pluralistic view of human thought and human society. Both were therefore drawn to seek a holistic model of human behaviour.

For Lévi-Strauss, the human propensity to think in terms of oppositions and resemblances is basic. Yet as Anderson has pointed out, there is a fatal defect in this whole intellectual strategy, for this model, borrowed from De Saussure's ideas about *language*, is '*no fitting model for any other human practice*'. Lévi-Strauss even got De Saussure wrong, for the latter insisted exchange of *words* is *not* a paradigm for other kinds of exchange – his model was valid for language, but was not to be used *beyond* it, in particular was not to be applied to kinship and economic relations. But these were the very spheres to which Lévi-Strauss proceeded to apply it, when he treated kinship systems as 'a kind of language' in which *women*, not words, are exchanged.

The language model is a false analogy, because, 'no speaker alienates vocabulary to any interlocutor [but] can freely reutilize every word "given" as many times as is wished thereafter, whereas marriages – unlike conversations – are usually binding: wives are not recuperable by their fathers after their weddings'.[159]

In writing about the evolution of human knowledge, Lévi-Strauss does recognize the massive technical contributions made by hunters and collectors over 95 per cent of recorded human history, which made possible the subsequent domestication of animals and the selection of the seeds of wild plants, which resulted eventually in agriculture.[160] He also recognizes that 'magic' is a 'well-articulated' mode of thought which, though 'complete in itself' and independent of 'empirical knowledge', involves the same sort of mental operations as science. Magic and science 'differ not so much in kind as in the different types of phenomena to which they are applied'. Yet the main foundations of his theory still rest upon the central assumption, as in Durkheim, that Aboriginal thinking possesses an overall character and is only an instance of a universal phenomenon – the primary attribute of human thinking, 'binary' opposition. At the end of the day, all this tells us is that they, like us, think in terms of resemblances and differences. It fails to tell us anything about differences in *kinds* of thinking.

Though both these writers were formidable scholars, well versed in the anthropological literature, including that on the Aborigines, neither of them did any fieldwork. Both suffer from that disease of theoreticians: the temptation to subsume everything under as few propositions as possible.

What even the briefest encounter with Aboriginal life would have shown them is that Aborigines no more spend all their time worshipping than they do eating, or thinking about the way their language works, or trying to improve their biology.

The influence of intellectuals such as Durkheim and Lévi-Strauss, especially on fellow intellectuals, has been considerable. But there are other sources of ideas than the academy. If the Aborigines were commonly regarded by settlers as vermin and their thinking as mumbo-jumbo, in our times young people, opposed to a more modern genocide, the Vietnam War, came to see it as part of Western materialism. In its place, many took to cult versions of Oriental mysticism, especially forms of Hinduism and Buddhism, which they (wrongly) thought were incompatible with war.

More recently, the Green movement, though very eclectic in its ideology, has developed a more secular critique of Western culture, focusing on hard scientific data about the destruction of the earth's resources (including its diverse human cultures). The celebration of non-Western cultures as being *inherently* superior to Western culture has become particularly common among intellectuals alienated from their own urban industrial societies. They turn instead to the Great Traditions of the East, also projecting their concerns on to Little Traditions, such as Amerindian belief systems or the tribal peoples of the 'Fourth World'.

Australian Aborigines, once seen simply as brute savages, are now more often celebrated as people who see better and further than Westerners, their minds not shackled and their vision not blinkered by Western materialism. There have been splendid films about Australian Aborigines: *Walkabout*, *Outback*, *The Chant of Jimmy Blacksmith* and so on. But there has also been a tendency to see them as mystics, as in Peter Weir's film *The Last Wave*, in which urban Aborigines are depicted as able not only to bring about paranormal tremblings in the city around them but also to perpetuate their traditional culture in caverns deep below the modern city of Sydney. In place of the nineteenth-century reduction of the Aborigines to a mere subhuman animalism, in which sheer material survival was the be all and end all of existence, Aborigines are now being seen as mystic visionaries.

In Aboriginal society, there are very few specialized roles. Technical equipment is limited, while, in social terms, as Nadel has observed, the 'role-inventory' does not run to much more than a few dozen roles, from mother to ritual specialist.[161] In industrial societies, conversely, official statistics about work roles alone divide people up into tens of thousands of different kinds of occupations – omitting even finer distinctions people in particular industries themselves recognize which are not listed in official statistics and leaving aside altogether non-work roles.

There is, however, a special class of people in their cultures who do spend more time than most in thinking. Some of them, the equivalents of Mrs Beeton or Fannie Farmer, apply their minds to practical concerns. Others – Elkins' 'Aboriginal Men of High Degree', people like Nangurama and Gula on Groote Eylandt, though they have to go out hunting like everyone else, spend a lot of time thinking about thinking. In our culture, some would be professors of biology, others of theology and yet others of linguistics, while many, being all-round intellectuals with expertise in more than one sphere, would hold several chairs at the same time.

In Aboriginal society, the experience of generations has been distilled, elaborated, codified and handed down from generation to generation by these part-time 'popular' intellectuals, working within an oral culture (until recently) in which knowledge is not stored or available to be studied in books and libraries. We do not know much about Nangurama and Gula, but we do know more about other such people, whom we will look at more closely later.

Apart – an important apart – from the products of their imagination, the raw materials they have available to think about are limited to what is given in the environment. For hunters and collectors, this means primarily plants and animals. But in other cultures, other domains of nature are quite as important, and therefore become the focus of intellectualization. For people who have to survive on tiny Pacific islands, the variability, unpredictability and contingency of the sea and the skies are sources of constant danger, so the mastery of elaborate, systematic knowledge about the cosmos, and of very sophisticated sailing techniques, has always been crucial.

Finding the Way: Navigating the Pacific

To the contemporary Western mind, the Pacific conjures up various images – sex, freedom, 'Robinsonades' of 'desert' islands, even Paradise. But the great pioneer explorers of the Pacific, whose voyages were to end in the creation of a single world, under European control, did not go there looking for freedom or sex, or scientific knowledge for its own sake, even if, as the scientific revolution in the West gained momentum, scientists from Sir Joseph Banks to Charles Darwin were carried on naval vessels which combined the virtues of 'a fortress and a travelling laboratory'.[1]

Though Cook's first voyage concentrated on scientific discovery, those who mounted his expeditions were primarily driven by quite material motivations – the twin desires for profit and power – and his second voyage was designed to capitalize on what he had found or might find. There had been no ambiguity in the mind of Cortés as to what he had gone to South America for: the Spanish lust for gold, he remarked, was an 'affliction of the heart'. The enormous effort Captain Bligh put into bringing breadfruit plants from the South Seas was equally material in purpose, and similarly breathtakingly global in scope: they were needed to feed slaves cheaply on the West Indian plantations. Though this strategy failed, with the disastrous voyage of the *Bounty*, a further expedition was mounted and this time he did succeed in bringing back the breadfruit. Ironically, though, after all this, the slaves refused to eat the new, unfamiliar food (at first). As he went from island to island, Bligh had also picked up another harvest – of mutineers – whom he took back to England to be hanged, for imperial policy also involved using colonies as dumping grounds for convicts from Britain. Once America became unavailable for this purpose, new convict settlements elsewhere had to be found, notably at Botany Bay, where Bligh now turned up once more, this time as Governor, and provoked yet another rising against his rule, the 'Rum Rebellion'.

Yet there were other, immaterial yearnings which were just as much part of European cultures – for the Spaniards, the dream of eternal youth; among millenarian friars, the dream of building new kinds of Christian communities in a New World, which they did in Paraguay. But those who dominated the Church, having extirpated Jewish and Muslim infidels in Spain, and then forced Christianity on to the Indians of America, had perfected the machinery for ruthlessly controlling any signs of heretical backsliding – a dry run for the Counter-Reformation their successors were to unleash in Europe.[2]

The European explorers of the Pacific, like the Spaniards in the Americas, brought with them the intellectual baggage of their times; this time, though, not the atavistic ideas of sixteenth-century Spain, but those of the Enlightenment, which they freely projected on to the inhabitants of the islands. As with Spanish churchmen, there were different schools of thought. The 'hard primitivists' stressed the ascetic, spartan lives of the islanders; the 'soft primitivists' saw Tahiti as an erotic Garden of Eden. Both schools believed their theories had been confirmed when they actually met real-life Noble Savages brought back as specimens to England: Prince Lee Boo, from the Palau Islands, and Omai, from Huahine, their faces and Augustan dress captured for ever in eighteenth-century paintings.

Their life back home and the plants and animals found on the islands were sometimes recorded quite naturalistically by the artists employed as human cameras on the voyages of discovery.[3] But not always:

Even Nature was seen through European eyes at times; the Australian eucalypt bush was often drawn with the soft foliage and outline of European woodland while when it came to representations of people ... Europe's spiritual search infused the vision of even the most scientific recorders. Bedraped Greeks disported themselves beneath the palm-trees in the grottoes and amphitheatres of the South Pacific.[4]

Reports by the first explorers of free and guiltless love as an integral part of the cultures of the Noble Savages beneath the Southern Cross were particularly exciting, but nor were they sheer fantasy. As Sahlins has remarked:

Almost anything could remind the Hawaiians of sex ... Sex was everything: rank, power, wealth, land. Happy society, perhaps, that could make the pursuit of the good things in life so enjoyable in itself ... It engaged men as well as women, chiefs as well as commoners. There was wife-capture as well as husband-capture, homosexuality as well as heterosexuality. Famous ruling chiefs were bisexual, but the preoccupation with sex was expressed as much in the virginity enjoined on certain young persons as in the liberties granted to others ... Love was a decisive principle of the form (or formlessness) of the family, as of its division of labour. It was a favoured means of access to power and property. Rank and taboo might be gained or lost by it ... Popular heterosexual games of chance were played for it. Children, at least of the

élite, were socialized in the arts of love. Girls were taught the *'amo'amo*,
the 'wink-wink' of the vulva, and the other techniques that 'make the
thighs rejoice'. Young chiefs were sexually initiated by older women,
preparing them for the sexual conquests that singularly mark a political
career; the capture of a senior ancestry. And all this ... was celebrated
not only in the flesh, but in dance, poetry and song.

What a place for puritanical American missionaries! One of them
complained that the Hawaiians had about twenty forms of what he
considered illicit intercourse, with as many different names in the
language: so that if any one term were selected to translate the Seventh
Commandment, it was bound to leave the impression that the other
nineteen activities were still permitted.[5]

But sex was not so central in the culture of mercantile capitalism. Most
of the Europeans who sought out these societies did so not in order to live
the simple life close to an abundant nature but to trade, and later to use
the labour of the inhabitants on plantations. Others wanted to harvest
souls for Christ. On the larger fertile tropical islands, such as Hawaii or
Tahiti, great kingdoms had developed, ready-made societies available to be
conquered. But on thinly populated, usually mountainous, islands, labour
forces had to be brought into being by raiding other islands. Only the tiny
atolls were 'desert' islands, in the Arabian sense of infinities of sand naturally devoid of people. But islands could be *made* 'desert' if it proved con-
venient to the colonizers – they could simply be depopulated, as the
Spaniards did in the Marianas, their populations relocated, concentrated
on chosen islands, with additional new labour brought in from other devastated islands. At the lowest level, dozens of white men, from buccaneers
to missionaries, could still find islands where they could create their own
– often very nasty – societies, right through the nineteenth century. It was
still possible, on Groote, only a generation ago.

These, though, were not the images of the Pacific that fermented in the
Western imagination. The idea of the Noble Savage had already become
suspect even in the time of its inventor. On hearing of the death of a
French explorer at the hands of the Maori, Jean-Jacques Rousseau had ex-
claimed, in horror, 'Can it be true that the good Children of Nature can
really be so wicked?' But the images he created live on even today. It is
sexual fantasy, not interest in coconut plantations, that draws millions to
the galleries to look at Gauguin's paintings. Few read his letters, which
chronicle the sordid reality of his wretched existence in the shanty area of
Papeete, ostracized by French colonial officialdom and respectable society, and dependent for his sexual gratifications on the cash nexus. For what

they want to hear (and see) is that the Pacific is still a sexual paradise. It is a dream which still powers not only fantasies but real-life sexual adventures: only recently, it induced two people, as the book and film of *Castaway* record, to leave London for an uninhabited Torres Strait island.

Though the image of the truly 'desert' (empty) island still persists – for example, in the Toshiro Mifune/Lee Marvin film *Hell in the Pacific* – in fact, most of the islands were inhabited by people, and had been first discovered and colonized not by Europeans but by the ancestors of the Australian Aborigines, the Polynesians, the Micronesians and the Melanesians. In Hawaiian cosmic myth and royal legend, they are traced back for 963 generations.[6] By contrast, the first European, Magellan, arrived only in 1521, on his circumnavigation of the globe. Nearly a century elapsed before the arrival of the next European, the Spaniard Quiros, while the French and British explorers that every schoolchild knows about, notably Bougainville and Cook, did not arrive until half-way through the eighteenth century.

The real pioneers of the Pacific, the non-Europeans, possessed extraordinary intellectual and moral qualities – courage, and the capacity to innovate. They developed a sophisticated technology of navigation and mastered the arts of survival on what nature provided on sometimes tiny atolls.

Even on the better-endowed, larger islands, the sea was as crucial as the land, not only in terms of food but because it constituted a lifeline to communities on other islands.

To us, the intervening ocean is a 'barrier', but to the islanders, as David Lewis, a leading authority on Pacific navigation, has written, the ocean is a 'highway'.[7] It could never have become one, though, were it not that they had developed a crucial piece of sophisticated technology – the outrigger sailing canoe.

The first Europeans to visit the islands were deeply impressed with the Pacific islanders' canoes everywhere they went. Pigafetta, who chronicled Magellan's voyage, 'marvelled' at those he saw. So did all who came after them. In 1774, Cook was 'perfectly lost in admiration' at the 'magnificent scene' during a 'grand and noble' naval review in Tahiti: 330 vessels with no fewer than 7,760 men. Five years later, in Hawaii, the *Resolution* was surrounded by 3,000 vessels, with 15,000 passengers on them.[8] And in nineteenth-century Fiji, Cakobau created an empire, based on the tiny off shore islet of Bau, which deployed such great naval power that his major war has been described by Sahlins as the largest fought in the Pacific until the Second World War.

The Europeans were particularly impressed by the large ocean-going vessels, and by the voyages accomplished in them. In the Santa Cruz group, they found that people sailed to the New Hebrides (Vanuatu) and the Solomons, much longer journeys than they made after the islands were finally brought under European control. Similarly, some refugees from the Spanish genocide on the Marianas were able to escape to the distant Carolines because they had traded there regularly in the past. The early Europeans believed that such long-distance voyages must have been accidental, not intentional. How could the islanders have *found* their way so far, by conscious navigation, lacking, as they did, charts, compasses, even writing? They must have simply *drifted* there, and this must have been the way that their ancestors had got there in the first place too. Cook was an exception, because, under the guidance of the Tahitian navigator Tupaia, he was able to have charts drawn which showed seventy-four islands.[9] Tupaia also guided him to Rurutu, an island 300 miles south of Tahiti, then unknown to Europeans. Cook was therefore persuaded that the islanders were perfectly capable of navigating for hundreds of miles, though he later changed his mind when he encountered castaways on the islands which today bear his name who had been blown there from Tahiti.

Most journeys, the Europeans thought, must have been short-range, and indeed they were. Although the Pacific covers a third of the surface of the globe, most islands and archipelagos are only about fifty to 200 miles apart. It is therefore possible to travel from South-East Asia to almost all the inhabited islands of Oceania (apart from New Zealand, Hawaii and Easter Island) without once making a sea crossing longer than 310 miles;[10] the islands between mainland Asia and the eastern end of the Solomon Islands are also 'intervisible'.[11]

Subsequent research by archaeologists and historians, and studies of the contemporary sailing techniques of Pacific islanders, suggest that, covering distances of 100–150 miles a day, voyages of 3,000–4,500 miles were not impossible,[12] including Tahiti to Hawaii (return journey 2,220 miles) and Eastern Polynesia to New Zealand (some forty days' journey). The first phase of that exploration and colonization occurred some 60,000 years ago, in the Pleistocene, carried out by ancestors of the Tasmanians and Australian Aborigines, in vessels (perhaps only rafts) which have not been preserved, from South-East Asia down through the islands of today's Indonesia to Australia, followed by the first colonization of Melanesia. The second phase was much more recent, about 3,500 years ago, when, in 'a burst of sophisticated maritime and neolithic settlement ... the first voyaging of its kind in the world', the ancestors of the Polynesians, in Irwin's words, 'virtually completed the human settlement of the world apart from its ice-caps'.[13]

Today, after reviewing a wide range of documentary and archaeological records, and deploying computer simulations, scholars have concluded that this world-historic exploration was not accidental but 'purposeful', 'systematic' and 'competent', and that though there may well have been high losses at sea, they were probably less than commonly believed in the past. Stephen Thomas records that a crew which struggled ashore after losing their vessel survived for several months, living on vegetables and turtles so successfully that, far from being emaciated, they could not fit into their loincloths when they returned seven months later; people who had given them up for lost thought that they were 'fat spirits'. Navigation methods too improved over time:

At a time when the Greeks were making short hops between intervisible islands in the Aegean … and Europeans still lived in rude huts scattered across … primeval forests Lapita navigators [the ancestors of today's islanders] were guiding long blue-water passages without charts, compasses, or instruments … in hand-hewn sailing canoes.[14]

To see how the world-historic exploration and colonization were possible, we need to look first at the technology of Oceanian seagoing craft and then at the navigational techniques employed by the descendants of the people whom the Maori scholar Te Rangi Hiroa (Sir Peter Buck) described as the 'Vikings of the Sunrise'.

The Canoes

Most of the canoes of Oceania were not used for long-distance voyaging at all but for offshore fishing, or for moving round lagoons. Travel further afield was done by much larger vessels, so large indeed that, as Lewis remarks, 'the word "canoe" is rather misleading … conjuring up as it does a picture of some tiny craft hollowed out from a tree trunk. The vessels we are here concerned with (and which have, in the main, long since vanished from Pacific seaways) deserve the appellation "ship" rather than "canoe".'[15]

In Polynesia, the larger vessels were generally double canoes; in Micronesia, they were single-hulled with an outrigger on one side. Tongan double-hulled canoes could carry eighty men. Some that Cook saw were longer than his own vessel, the *Endeavour*, while even today smaller vessels – pygmies compared with those of the past – can carry a ton of copra or, on short trips, fifty people.[16] In the past too there were very many more vessels of every kind. A canoe can easily last fifteen years. Especially well-made vessels, carefully protected from the sun's rays by sago leaves and coconut fronds when not in use, like the sacred canoe of the senior chief of

Anuta, can survive for the greater part of a century.[17]

The classic account of Micronesian boat design is Thomas Gladwin's description of indigenous boat-building on one Micronesian island, Puluwat, written a quarter of a century ago.[18] Gladwin, who is an anthropologist and ex-administrator in the Carolines, had the added advantage of being a former engineer, with considerable sailing experience. (Lewis similarly went to school as a small boy in a local school in the Cook Islands, became a medical doctor and has crossed the Atlantic single-handed no fewer than three times.)

Canoe-building techniques vary in different parts of Oceania. There are usually four crucial components: the hull, the outrigger, the lee platform, and the rigging and sail. Puluwat sailing canoes, far from being made from hollowed-out logs, are built from planks, stitched or lashed together with coconut fibre through holes drilled every few inches on either side of the joint. Where the planks meet, the joint, once smoothed down, 'resembles strongly a surgical incision after the stitches have been removed'. Coir lashings and knots almost never work loose, since the surface of coir bristles with stiff little fibres. Repairs similarly reduce leaks to a minumum, though bailing is a continuous chore in any canoe. Yet like boat-builders I have seen at work in coastal Tanzania, craftsmen first shape and then fit pieces of wood into damaged places entirely by eye, and then test the fit by smearing mud round the edges of the replacement part.

The hull is very narrow: these days, the average sailing canoe is about twenty-six feet long, though only about thirty-three inches at the waterline and three feet at the top of the hull. This means that there is very little 'drag': in Gladwin's words, the hull 'knifes its way through the water'. The length of the hull is determined largely by the size of the piece of timber available for the keel and the judgement of the builder, who has to balance greater speed against greater load-carrying capacity, as well as strength, stability and depth (since the canoe has to pass through shallow reefs). In section, the hull is a V, slightly flattened at the bottom. It is symmetrical from end to end, though some canoes curve sideways slightly, away from the outrigger, with the side of the hull higher where the outrigger is. The keel, though, is not very deep and heavy, as with European boats; stability is ensured by the outrigger, not by the lead keels which can make up 30 to 50 per cent of the weight of a Western racing sail-boat. Since these canoes ride less deep in the water, they can negotiate narrow passages through reefs and shallow lagoons where the heavy keels of Western vessels do not allow easy passage. There is also much more resistance to drifting, eliminating the need for sea anchors. Great care is nevertheless taken not to damage the keel when the canoe is dragged up the beach to the canoe-house, by using coconut midribs or pandanus logs as rollers. All this woodwork, it should be remembered, used to be done solely with stone tools. Today, modern materials and tools – paints which make the hull smoother, metal implements – have reduced, although by no means eliminated, the very hard work involved, making it possible to produce canoes that are in some respects better than those of the past. But traditional design still predominates. The outcome is vessels which are works of art as well as triumphs of engineering. When Feinberg asked Anutans – 'not,' he acknowledges, 'great sailors or navigators' – which was the best kind of boat design, they replied with a question: 'Do you mean best to look at or best on the ocean?' [19]

Measuring the midpoint of the hull is done by running a piece of cord the length of the hull, then folding it in two. Other measurements follow similar procedures. The outrigger consists of two heavy pieces of wood which arch upwards out of the hull, to which they are firmly lashed, and then curve downwards towards the float, in order to avoid waves splashing between the float and the hull in rough weather. But since the float constantly bangs on the surface of waves, it is made of heavy breadfruit wood, secured by short forked sticks and firmly lashed to the booms.

The platform (which can be removed) is made of heavy timbers laid on top of the outrigger. It extends outwards from the hull, with its base running along it. This provides a kind of box in the middle of the boat which gives it strength amidships. Standing a foot or so above the hull, the platform provides room for working, riding and stowing gear. A bench on its inner edge is the 'command centre' for the navigator, from which he holds the sheet, consults the compass and can see in every direction. Other crew members have the use of two other benches, and for those who have to stand up there are hand-rails against which to rest their backs.

Nowadays, the triangular sail is always made of cloth, replacing the old pandanus matting, which was not as flexible or durable, nor as good for holding the wind, and was very heavy, especially when soaked. It is a lateen rig, lashed at its upper front edge, not to the mast directly but to a yard which is suspended from the mast and, at its bottom edge, to an S-shaped boom. The lower end of the yard rests in a socket towards the front of the vessel, but the main weight is taken by the mast, which fits into a larger socket in the middle of the canoe. Among the many compromises which need to be made in designing a canoe, the sail must not be too big, because it has to stand up to the strains of the open ocean.

Sailing a canoe may sound vastly more clumsy than sailing a Western sailing boat, for every time the canoe tacks against the wind, the entire sail and rigging have to be moved from one end to the other. The vessel now faces in exactly the opposite direction. All of this is accomplished in scarcely a minute. Yet there are shortcomings when it comes to tacking: they cannot sail into the wind as well as Western fore-and-aft boats. Anutan navigators never sailed close-hauled to the wind and, if driven off course, paddled back until they picked up the original direction they had been sailing in.[20] But whereas Western boats have both permanent rigging (stays, for example) and adjustable 'running' rigging (such as halyards), virtually every component in the rigging of a Puluwat canoe can be adjusted – and has to be, since both the sail and the float, being asymmetrical, necessitate constant adjustments, mainly for the strength of the wind. With the further aid of a steering paddle and a Western-made pulley, and by moving a man to the stern when the sail alone cannot cope with keeping the canoe from turning, one man can control both the adjustments and the navigation, obviating the need for a steersman. Spiller lines can reduce the amount of wind entering a sail if strong winds make this necessary. Such vessels can keep going

in the face of virtually every challenge the Pacific Ocean can throw at them short of a full-scale typhoon – and even in a typhoon it is navigation which is more vulnerable and probably has accounted for more historically known canoe losses than has the failure of the canoes themselves.[21]

With a wind on the beam, the crew can relax.

Direction: Star Compasses

Western navigation is based on invisible abstractions: the magnetic North Pole, the parallels of latitude and longitude. Micronesians, Gladwin demonstrates, use visible natural phenomena, above all the stars, in a system of navigation called *etak*.

When leaving the home island, especially when the sky is overcast, the navigator can use what is called the '*etak* of sighting'. On Tikopia, for instance, there is a beach named 'Mataki Anuta', facing the island of Anuta. Leaving Tikopia, the navigator who is making for Anuta looks back, checks his direction against well-known landmarks and makes initial allowance for currents: 'At the back of this beach a gulley runs up the mountain side ... When setting out for Anuta the crew turn the stern of their canoe to this gulley and keep it in sight as long as they can'.[22] Thomas lists no fewer than twenty-six separate units of measurement within the '*etak* of sighting' between the canoe-house and the point at which the island is no longer visible.[23] As the navigators approach the target island, they switch to another 'etak of sighting'.

Western navigators have charts, hand-bearing and steering compasses, and sextants, which enable them to produce a dead reckoning of where they are. But once out of sight of land, Micronesian navigators using traditional methods have to depend upon a different kind of direction-finding: the 'etak of reference'. Now it is the stars which provide the right path.

Out of the myriad stars in the sky, they select about ten main ones as they rise or set close to the horizon. 'The foundation of any sailing plan,' Gladwin writes, 'is the star position which provides a bearing between the destination island and the island from which the journey began.'[24]

For a night voyage, then, a *succession* of stars, a 'star course' (*wofanu*), is needed, the whole set usually being named after one particular star in it. Some are actually constellations rather than single stars, though different stars within a constellation may be used at different times. Nor are they necessarily stars of the first magnitude; some of the biggest are not used and do not even have names, whereas quite small stars which are in the right place are given names and form part of a star course. Thus, on Anuta, some minor stars and constellations are dismissed as 'foolish', 'common' or 'undistinguished', but other, quite small ones are often the most important for navigational purposes because they enable the navigator to divide up the heavens into regular segments.[25]

Would-be navigators have to learn these star courses through memorizing the sequences of stars they need to follow in order to get to a given island – and the reciprocals which will get them back. Thomas lists no fewer than fifty-one of these seaways, some to islands as far away as Yap and the Philippines, plus 'brother seaways' – similarly aligned sequences of stars that a navigator can fall back on if he forgets the one he should be using.[26] He also gives more detailed sequences for fourteen voyages which are frequently made (Appendix 7). Stars can be used not only for long-distance navigation out at sea but for navigating through openings in a cluster of islands and reefs safely at night (Appendix 10).

Over the full year, of course, different stars are visible, and so the selection used changes from season to season. Large stars or parts of major constellations are commonly used in most of the region, and are often named after birds (like Gladwin's 'Big Bird', which we call Altair) or after fish, foods or material items like nets and adzes.

If you are travelling east, you aim for those which are rising; going westwards, you need the setting stars. After a while, a rising star moves overhead and slides across the sky rather than straight up from the horizon, thus providing a less clear directional guide. At this point, you change over to another star close to the horizon, and this can be used for a few hours, until it in turn needs replacing. It is possible to use stars even when they are at an angle to the course, or astern instead of straight ahead, by viewing them through the rigging, rather like a gun-sight, and thus keeping the canoe on course.

Figure 5 **Steering by keeping the rising Southern Cross behind the headsail**

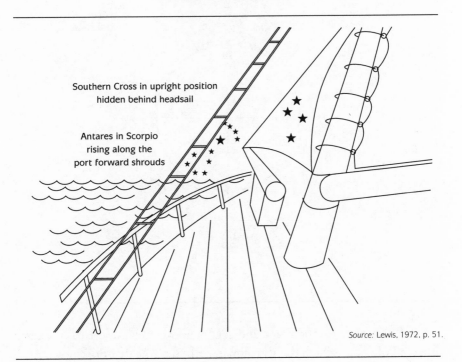

Southern Cross in upright position hidden behind headsail

Antares in Scorpio rising along the port forward shrouds

Source: Lewis, 1972, p. 51.

Not all Pacific islanders use these systems of navigation: Anutans, for instance, had no star compasses or *etak*, and only rudimentary knowledge of the winds.[27] Much knowledge once possessed in cultures with more sophisticated systems of navigation has also been lost in modern times: if a particular journey has not been made for many years, the names of individual stars and even of an entire star course are forgotten. But star courses to distant islands are often known, even where no journeys ever take place nowadays, and even for islands which no one has *ever* visited. But voyagers across the 1,800 miles of the Caroline archipelago still use the 'sidereal compass'. Like the thirty-two points on the card of the mariner's compass, there are thirty-two stars, but the system is far older than the European and evolved independently of it, so that the spaces between one star and its neighbour on either side may be unequal, whereas the European compass divides the heavens into equal intervals, measured in degrees. In the Puluwat star compass too, more stars are clustered around the western and eastern ends than at the north and south.

Figure 6 **Star Compass (Puluwat)**

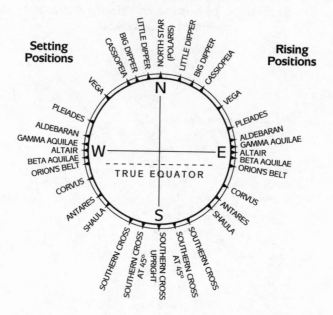

Source: reproduced in Gladwin, 1970, p. 149.

Each star rises in one place and sets in another, symmetrically, except for the Pole Star, which the Carolinians call 'the star that does not move'. North–south is therefore the same as in the European system, from Pole Star to the Southern Cross in its upright position. But in the Carolines, which lie along the Equator, east–west journeys are the ones that matter. So it is not the Pole Star but Altair, 'Big Bird' – which rises in the *east* – that constitutes 'the cardinal compass point and basis of their navigation'.[28]

As Figure 6 shows, the Carolinian star compass differs from the European in three ways: first because its star points are true points and not magnetic ones; second, because the selected stars are irregularly distributed around the horizon; and third, because their 'east–west' line is 8° out of line with European latitude. But the diagram is still a European construct, a *version* of their system, even to its circular shape.

Since their own system is accurate enough to take them anywhere, Gladwin remarks, 'they feel no intellectual need to maintain uniform standards of precision throughout the directional system ... It is least accurate

... where the least accuracy is needed.'[29] Nor do they need to undertake the difficult task of bringing their system into line with the European one, though they recognize the differences and can, if necessary, describe how the two systems overlap. Nevertheless, it is their own system that is uppermost in their minds. They therefore use their own names for the stars and their sequences when speaking about the points on the mariner's compass.

Using only these thirty-two key stars, a Puluwat navigator can work out sailing directions from every known place to every other known place – which filled several pages of print when one anthropologist wrote it all down. They do not rely on print, however; they memorize it all. Yet far from resisting Western methods of navigation, they have virtually abandoned their own.

Distance: The Moving Islands

Carolinian navigation is a system of 'dead reckoning': one's position at any time is determined solely on the basis of distance and direction travelled since leaving the last known location.[30]

In the mind of the navigator, the positions of the stars are fixed. Depending on the destination, one island is selected as a 'reference island' for the whole journey. A reference island need not be particularly valuable as a place to live on, or even as a refuge. Its importance, rather, derives from its place in navigation.

Ideally, it should be about fifty miles or so to one side of the line of travel, roughly half-way on the journey. The distance between the island of departure and the island of destination is then divided into segments, identified by other stars. The islands selected to mark these segments must not be too close or too far away, otherwise the segments will be unequal and will occur too frequently in some parts of the voyage and at too large intervals in others. As the canoe moves forward, the reference island is thought of as 'moving' backwards under each segment star in turn, from 'under' star X to 'under' star Y. The reference island is then said to have 'moved' one *etak*, the term being used, here, as a unit of measurement rather than for the system as a whole. The navigators are able to compensate for movements of swells and nightly shifts in the positions of the stars, in order to arrive at a dead reckoning of their position at sea.

The system is also used when they are driven off course, or deliberately leave it to follow shoals of fish, or when tacking. As Gladwin writes:

It is rather like sitting on a train and looking out of the window. In your little world you sit and talk while the scenery slips by. In the distance there are mountains which for long periods of time seem to pace the train. Looking at them you are distracted by nearby houses which flash backwards between you and the mountains. The mountains are the stars and the houses the islands below ... You may travel for days on the canoe but the stars will not go away or change their positions aside from their nightly trajectories from horizon to horizon ... Back along the wake, however, the island you left falls farther and farther behind, while the one toward which you are heading is hopefully drawing closer. You can see neither of them, but you know this is happening. You know too that there are islands on either side of you.[31]

Other Sea-lore

Navigators in other parts of Oceania use the winds rather than the stars as the basis of their systems of navigation. All of them also use other kinds of data: the sun, obviously, tells you where east is when it rises and west when it sets, while the shadow of the vessel's mast at noon tells you where north and south are. The sun, though, is less valuable than the stars: it is only in one position, whereas the stars provide thirty-two, and its movement over the course of the year makes it harder to use than the stars, which rise and set in the same places all year long. The year was divided into six lunar cycles, the twelve star months into two seasons of six months each, each with its sequences of vegetation, of plenty or shortage, of water supply on land and distinctive states of the sea. By observing certain 'fighting stars', which are said to control the weather, especially at dawn and sunset, and particularly at the beginning and end of the lunar month, a navigator can anticipate bad weather, especially during the five months when the storm stars rule.

The sea itself provides yet more information. Thus one shade of blue in the ocean indicates the likelihood of wind or squalls; another shade of blue, lighter than the sky, is benign. In a long journey, fluctuations of current tend to cancel each other out. But where currents intersect, sailors distinguish between 'swells', which have travelled a long way from the winds that produced them, and 'waves', which are produced by contemporary winds.[32] Swells have long wave lengths from crest to crest and pass slowly; waves produced nearby are shorter and steeper. The swells reach the Equator from major weather systems in distant parts of the Pacific, notably the trade winds, from the east, and the westerlies, which originate in the Southern Ocean. They can therefore be used for orientation. But these and other wave systems intersect in complex ways which vary in different parts of the region. In the Carolines, there are two major movements of water: the North Equatorial Current, running westward, and the Equatorial Countercurrent, which goes in the opposite direction.[33] But a master navigator such as Hipour, Gladwin's principal informant, knows that, for his area, *three* different swells have to be taken into account: the 'Big Wave' from due east; the 'North Wave', from the north-east; and the weaker 'South Wave', from the south-east. In the Santa Cruz Group, Lewis' great navigator, Tevake, also had to reckon with three major wave systems: the 'Long Swell' from the south-east; the 'Sea Swell' from the east-north-east; and the *Hoahuadelahu* from the north-west. Where two or three swells intersect, the navigator will steer by the 'knots', the peaks the swells make as they come together. At night, this may be all he has to go by, so navigators today nearly always use the magnetic compass instead. Interpreting the swells, then – 'wave-tying' the Satawalese call it – or the even less discernible ripples caused by the wind, is not always easy and is often a matter of personal judgement – sometimes, as Lewis remarks, 'a matter of feel rather than sight ... One might perhaps be tempted to refer to keeping one's course by the swells as "steering by the seat of one's pants".' An experienced European skipper told him that the most sensitive part of the anatomy, for this purpose, was a man's testicles.[34] Lest this be thought a merely frivolous remark, a colleague with long experience of Melanesia told me that a man would often slip over the side of the canoe with a rope tied round his waist and *feel* the movements of the currents. Some navigators are said to feel the water with their hand or 'taste' it.[35] The subtlety of these methods is indicated by Thomas' experience of being let down by a plastic sextant which gave him inaccurate readings and had to be corrected by the use of master navigator Piailug's traditional ways of estimating where they were.

Swells also indicate the presence of land. When a swell comes to an island, it is obviously forced to go round it, which slows the movement of the water and pushes the waves away from both sides of the island. But on the windward side, the waves are forced up against the coast with greater force and then pushed back into the ocean. When the swell reaches the end of the island and is no longer pushed up against the land, it moves round to the lee. On this side of the island, waves are similarly diverted, though with less force from the wind. The two sets of waves therefore meet on the lee side; the result is an area of turbulence, complicated by the fact that there is more than one swell system, and by the size and number of the islands. These disturbances can be felt out in the ocean and tell the navigator that there is land in the vicinity.

If it is too dark to see the stars or indications of land, canoes nearing their target will stop until daylight.

Reefs also break up the pattern of swells and waves. Though usually twenty or thirty feet below the surface of the water, some are 'shallow enough to make wicked waves, which would break up a canoe almost instantly'.[36] Their outlines were sometimes visible to Anutan sailors, but visible or not their location is well known to experienced navigators. Hence, like islands, they are invaluable navigational guides. Changes in colour obviously occur with changes in depth, as when passing over a reef.

Figure 7 **Swells deflected by land**

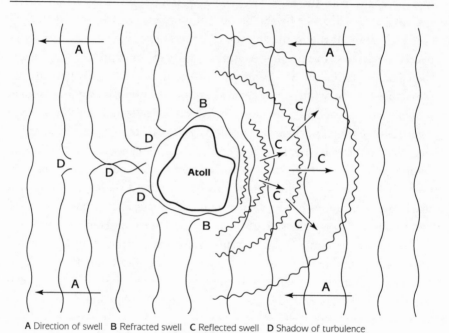

A Direction of swell   B Refracted swell   C Reflected swell   D Shadow of turbulence

Source: reproduced in Lewis, 1972, p. 181.

Even the light on the water can indicate that a certain kind of weather is coming. That there is phosphorescence on the surface of tropical seas is well known to most people. But there is also a less well-known kind, 'deep' phosphorescence, a good deal deeper, which Lewis describes as 'streaks, flashes, and momentarily glowing plaques of light' and which the master navigator Tevake likened to 'underwater lightning'.[37] It is best seen between eighty and 100 miles out at sea, when it flickers to and from the direction of land. As one moves nearer, it becomes scantier and finally disappears altogether.

'Birds,' a Gilbert Islander remarked, 'are the navigator's very best friends', not those which live out at sea but the land-based ones, especially terns and noddies, which fly out between twenty and twenty-five miles daily, going hither and thither while fishing, and make for land at dusk. Boobies fly further out – thirty to fifty miles. They tell the navigator, twice daily, that land which they cannot yet see is in fact nearby, and the direction in which it lies. Boobies are also nosy about strange vessels. So the islanders observe birds, hour after hour, far more consistently and acutely than Europeans. If a canoe is lost, all it has to do is wait for the birds' return flight home.

Clouds also indicate the position of islands. The Satawalese forecast weather by the 'talk of the skies' (*kapesani lang*): sensing the temperature of the air and analysing the shape and arrangement of clouds at sunrise and sunset, and, above all, the colour – thus deep red at either morning or evening warns of rain. Near the land too, one navigator said, clouds move slowly, 'as if stuck'; about seventeen miles away, when low-lying land is still out of sight, you can see a dark cloud. It indicates, though, not rain but land, and changes to a brighter colour fifteen miles from the land, while anything above fifty feet is visible from the deck of a canoe at about seventeen miles. This specialist looked for two particular formations: one when it is calm and no other clouds are to be seen, apart from a pair low on the horizon which look 'like a pair of eyebrows'; another, which is V-shaped, when it is windy and there are also other clouds about. Unlike the other clouds, V-shaped ones do not move. As you get closer to the shore, the colour of the clouds changes: over lagoons, the cloud 'roof' tends to be greenish; over extensive areas of white sand or surf, whiter than the rest; over a wooded green island, darker. Well beyond the range of sight, the white sand and the lagoon of atolls reflect the tropical sun's glare upwards, creating a 'pale, shimmering column', called 'loom', that can be seen even at night. 'Even Europeans', one navigator charitably remarked, could hardly fail to observe some of these things, though, as with birds, they are very elusive and cannot be treated like snapshots – clouds have to be watched intently, for hours on end, particularly for signs of change.

Not all of these aids are available everywhere, though. Driftwood and other flotsam are, of course, indicators at least of the direction they have come from, and freshly broken branches obviously must be fairly recent. Spanish explorers from Mexico, sailing northwards towards California, similarly used to note the *señas* (signs): various kinds of seaweed, seals and dogfish which appeared in a regular sequence.[38] There were, though, alternatives to doing one's own navigation. Vasco da Gama did not 'explore' the route from the Cape of Good Hope to Calicut; he was taken there, from Malindi, by the famous Arab pilot Ahmad ibn Madjid (who is still loathed for doing so in Calicut).[39] Drake's method was more direct: he simply kidnapped a local pilot.[40]

Given the vast expanse of ocean and the small size of the islands, it is not surprising that the land plays only an intermittent part in establishing positions and bearings. Six or seven miles out, navigators are dependent on other methods of orientation.

Learning

All this is only the barest outline of the very complex knowledge aspiring navigators have to acquire. It may seem unproblematic, but navigation in a real sea, with real typhoons, a broken mast out at sea, rain which obscures everything for days, exhaustion from freezing cold or total wreck can bring disaster upon even the most experienced navigator, while even on uneventful voyages there are constant changes of wind – sixty-four in a month's sailing on one voyage.[41]

Would-be drivers of London taxis have to spend two years studying the city's streets to get 'The Knowledge'. The knowledge Oceanian navigators have to absorb is every bit as voluminous, and much more demanding, for the navigator has no street signs or copy of an *A–Z* street guide with which to resolve doubts or refresh his memory. So although every boy grows up thoroughly at home with canoes, the acquisition of the huge masses of information a navigator has to remember requires formal training at the hands of senior navigators, who transmit their lifetime's experiences to the tyros. This training takes place both on land and at sea, for a young man may do well on shore but fail at sea.

In one lesson, the instructor places a toy canoe at the centre of a circle on the ground and asks each student to name the stars over the bow, stern, outrigger and platform. A full course will include all the elements we have discussed above – clouds, sea-lore, swells and waves, *etak*, navigating in storms, navigating when tacking upwind, weather-forecasting through observing the rising and setting of stars which are *not* the navigational stars used in navigation, and so on. But the stars and the star compass are the main subject matter to be learned. They are taught with the aid not of paper but of charts drawn in the sand, with stones for the stars. Such models used to be square in shape, but nowadays imitate the model of the European compass and are usually arranged in a circle. A student has to learn many sequences of stars. He may use such lists like a times-table to refresh his memory and as a quick reference system, but rote learning is not enough, so the teacher will start with any island and the student will have to 'rattle off the stars both going and returning between that island and all the others which might conceivably be reached directly from there'. Another teaching exercise requires the student to call out the *reciprocals* of stars the teacher names. Each item, Gladwin observes, is not just 'embedded in a long mnemonic chain' but is also 'discretely available'.[42]

On other islands, stone charts were used to teach swell patterns, a large stone representing an island or a canoe, surrounded by smaller ones representing the swells.[43] (See also the splendid colour photograph of a navigational training session in which Piailug is teaching his students by 'unfolding' the mat on which the stars are represented by lumps of coral.[44]) Ethnographic museums often contain examples of another kind of map used in teaching by master navigators in the Marshall Islands, in which the islands were represented by shells tied to sticks. Some of these maps were purely theoretical models used to teach about swell patterns in general. The points where the swells intersect are known as 'knots'; a line of 'knots' makes up a 'root'. Other charts represent actual islands or archipelagos. Straight sticks indicate that a journey can be made in a straight line, by steering between swells, but curved sticks indicate the way the swells are bent as they go around the north and south of islands.[45]

Such knowledge can be passed on to anyone who wants to learn it, though in such small societies the trainee and his teacher are usually relatives, and fathers are most likely to give their sons the best teaching. Non-relatives may have to pay 'a stiff price' for their course of instruction, while there are also forms of esoteric knowledge which master navigators would not pass on to everybody. The most secret of all would be passed on only at the end of a master's life, when the student himself was old. These days, though, many of the best navigators have never been formally initiated. So despite their great skills and knowledge, they are left off lists of senior navigators.

The borderline between esoteric lore and magic was often blurred. The recital of long sequences of names of star courses and of remote islands which people never actually used in real-life sailing and of purely mythological islands can be classed as 'esoteric'. So knowledge of magic – the observation by the initiated of special taboos, plus knowledge of techniques of divination – marked off 'graduates' and insiders from the uninstructed. In the past, magic could also be used as sorcery – to bring harm to others. With conversion to Christianity, the use of these kinds of knowledge has considerably declined. But some still know the secret names of seaways which, if recited, can do damage to others, and they will therefore lower their voices when speaking them.[46]

We saw that, on Groote, specialists such as Nangurama and Gula classified certain plants and animals in different ways. But these differences were not institutionalized: they did not represent different organized *schools* of thought. On Puluwat, there *are* two such schools (or 'masts'), two different 'intellectual corporations': one is Fanur, to which navigators from the chiefly clans belonged; the other, considered more formidable, is called Wareyang, to which Hipour, the principal informant of both Gladwin and Lewis, belonged. Some twenty years later, their work inspired another anthropologist and experienced navigator, Stephen Thomas, to visit another Carolinian island, Satawal, where he apprenticed himself to the master navigator Piailug, who belonged to Wareyang. It might have been thought that by this time nothing would have remained of indigenous navigational knowledge, and it had indeed become sadly reduced, but what he learned from Piailug over many months, during which he acquired a working knowledge of the Satawalese language, proved an invaluable fleshing-out of the information gathered by Gladwin and Lewis.

At one time, he discovered, there had been two other schools, Sapu and Fara, but these had died out.[47] The remaining ones, Fanur and Wareyang, in practice largely followed the same procedures, though there are some differences in their navigational procedures. Fanur is inclined to use only one reference island for one entire seaway; Warieng (Gladwin's spelling) uses two, shifting from one to the other half-way. Again, Fanur uses alternative reference islands, on either side of the seaway, one after the other. There is no great advantage or disadvantage in using either.

The training of navigators of both schools required them to learn another important kind of knowledge: knowledge of 'sealife' (*epar* in Satawalese) – not just general knowledge of the sea, but long 'inventories' of the particular swells, reefs, birds, fishes, whales, etc. found around particular islands. Navigating by using *epar* was called *pookof*. Thomas lists long sets of *epar* for different islands and seaways.[48]

Gladwin gives one such list: the name of the star Altair signifying a whirlpool at a specific bank in the sea; a white-tailed tropic bird, on its own; a frigate bird, alone; another white-tailed tropic bird, also alone (but which is given a different specific name); a large shark; a single white tern; and the large island of Truk. Each of the items in these inventories also had a specific name. He was unsure as to whether this kind of knowledge really had any practical value at all and, on the face of it, it seems unlikely that 'one green leaf of the *gool* tree' – an example cited by Thomas – is really to be found in the vicinity of Woleai island. But other such 'identifiers', especially in bulk, seem perfectly reasonable, as when navigators are told to look our for 'thirty or forty birds, brown, with black on their feathers' or a pod of small dolphins, since fish and birds do return to the same feeding grounds day in and day out. To Thomas, therefore, and to his informants, it was valid and useful knowledge, 'esoteric' perhaps in terms of everyday sailing, but though they didn't have sextants and charts, they did have this knowledge of *epar* to fall back on 'when they were lost'.[49]

The technical differences between Fanur and Warieng navigation, Gladwin concluded, are 'trifling'. Though treated as terribly important 'trade' secrets, so complicated that one man could never know it all for every possible island in the Carolines, there were in fact often no differences at all between the two schools: in two cases out of three, they use the same names (or agreed that there *was* no name) for particular kinds of sea-lore. Though star knowledge and knowledge of *epar* were highly utilitarian in general, the differences between the two *schools*, on most points, were largely 'non-functional' differences of 'absolutely no practical value', and of an esoteric kind only: 'In areas where practical [navigational] necessity demands accuracy, the two schools converge closely. Where this is not required there are considerable differences.'[50]

But these differences occurred largely in 'peripheral and non-practical' areas, 'generally greater the farther the subject matter is removed from practical techniques of actual navigation'. They were important, though, in so far as they were a body of secret lore known only to initiated professionals and unintelligible to outsiders or those who had merely *paid* for their training. The chants, in a 'formal and arcane dialect as similar to contemporary Satawalese as Middle English is to Modern English', had to be explained to young men, while even the elders who knew them by heart didn't understand all of them. As with the secret language of the Lardil Aborigines – or Western physicians who control patients' access to knowledge of what is being done to them by using bad writing and Latin when writing prescriptions, or technical medical terms for illnesses and parts and functions of the body when everyday well-known terms are available – their hidden significance was one of social *closure*: keeping out outsiders. The purpose, in Puluwat or London, is the same: they constitute what Nadel has called 'diacritical' markers, markers which 'signal the identity and unity of the ... group' and 'bemuse the uninitiated'.[51]

The secrecy surrounding various kinds of sea-lore did, however, restrict those who might have used it to harm canoes at sea,[52] though to do so could be a 'Faustian bargain', for on Satawal it was believed that if a sorcerer killed anyone, the god Anumwerici would take one of his relatives in exchange. Two cases in which canoes were bewitched occurred within living memory on Satawal and are held to be true. In the first, a man was seen performing magic as a canoe was being launched; it never returned. Later, he was seen kicking the skids on which a second canoe was being launched; it also disappeared at sea. He was then hunted down and killed. The second case involved rivalry between two men, one of whom used evil magic to drive the other mad. Rejecting his human wife, he is said to have replaced her by two sea spirits and finally killed himself by jumping from a breadfruit tree.[53]

In the past there was, however, one major occasion when secret lore *was* revealed to the uninitiated – during the great initiation ceremonies which took place when new members were admitted to the respective corporations – the ritual 'uncovering of the bowl', which admitted the neophytes, for the first time, to eat as fully fledged navigators in the company of their seniors. Then, in an act of catharsis, 'navigators of each school would vie with their rivals in their display of knowledge. All the pent-up secrets of navigation poured forth before laymen as well as fellow navigators.' There was no great danger, though, that this would become common knowledge, for 'the volume of information was so great it could not possibly be remembered'. Even today, although 'there is no longer any occasion of public rivalry, a real reluctance remains to pass along secret names and other esoterica if they might fall into the hands (or rather ears) of a navigator of the other school'.[54]

Navigation thus drew upon different kinds of knowledge: the *etak* of sighting, star courses, sea-life and knowledge of the winds. Together, they constituted 'the talk of sailing', which Thomas lists for the most commonly visited islands.[55] A final kind of knowledge, though, is thought of as the most important of all. It has little to do with navigation or the other practicalities of seafaring, and is never discussed with those who do not possess it, unless absolutely necessary, for 'to do so would be for self-aggrandisement and would therefore be a violation of the principles of wisdom'.[56] It is called *itang*: 'the talk of light' (or, as we might say, enlightenment). *Itang* is a collection of verses or poems which may be recited, in a 'remarkably involuted, circumlocutory, elliptical and metaphorical mode of speech' which constitutes a special form of oral literature, but whose meaning is secret, since it contains 'the wisdom and ethics of the culture'.[57] It can be used in various kinds of situation: in war, magic, meetings, navigation or for 'calling' breadfruit. It can also be used to solicit help when arriving at a strange island after having been lost at sea. But it differs radically from mere practical knowledge, whether of an everyday or esoteric kind, in that it involves *moral* values. The spirits, as we saw, might be associated with evil magic. But the spirit of wisdom, or some other spirits – 'She of the Meeting' or 'She of the Resolution' – might equally be invoked to restore order and beauty to the island and to bring people together after a dispute. *Itang* is used to expose and eliminate evil intent; to control the rebellious or those who threaten violence; and also to resolve conflicts. One Western scholar has described it as 'knowledge containing the wisdom of politics, diplomacy and human relations employed primarily to overcome troubles on the island or between islands and secondarily as a demonstration of a specialist's wisdom'.[58]

As with the classification systems of the Aborigines, then, several different modes of thought are involved: an ethno-scientific astronomy and knowledge of the sea and the things in it; magical ideas and practices resorted to when practical knowledge was limited in its efficacy or – in negative form – when magic was used to harm others; the use of language to mark boundaries between social groups; and an indigenous kind of moral philosophy. There is, once more, no unitary 'mode of thought'; instead, there are *several* modes which may overlap and be used at one and the same time, and may also be resorted to as discrete modes of thought in quite different situations.

The First Explorations

Although some of the routes would-be navigators study involve long and hazardous journeys along seaways unfamiliar to them, most of their practical studies take them along well-known routes near their home islands. Few of the larger ocean-going vessels which once travelled between, rather than within, archipelagos are now built, and on some islands are no longer built at all. So knowledge of these longer journeys has been forgotten or much of the detail lost. Since much navigational lore was secret, even, as on Tonga, monopolized by a navigator clan, the knowledge often dies with thse specialists. By 1922, only two generations removed from seagoing, though they know the names of the stars, Tongans had forgotten the star routes.[59]

Much of the knowledge described by Thomas, Gladwin and Lewis has probably been lost since they wrote. But knowledge can be preserved for surprisingly long periods of time: the journey between Puluwat, in the Carolines, and Saipan, in the Marianas, for example, had not been undertaken for two or three generations – over sixty-four years – until Lewis got Hipour to take him there, locking up the European instruments on board and relying only on Hipour's memory of the traditional sailing instructions handed down to him verbally.

Colonialism resulted in a serious loss of inter-island contacts. In fact inter-island travel was forbidden under the Germans and the Japanese in the Carolines, and inter-island commerce has long been carried mainly on European vessels. All of this has resulted in the loss of traditional knowledge. Even today, prohibitions remain in force in the Tahiti group, France's main nuclear testing ground. Though the peoples of the Carolines have not suffered as severely as those of the Marshall Islands – forever memorable for the nuclear explosions on Bikini and Eniwetok[60] – the inhabitants of Puluwat were removed by the Japanese to a nearby island and later had an American airbase installed on an adjoining island.

Foreign contact did introduce new kinds of knowledge and technology, notably European tools. Iron, first introduced by the Spaniards, made boat-building easier, while using sandpaper and rasps instead of sharkskin or coral made it easier to produce a smooth finish on hulls. Pandanus sails were replaced by cloth. But little other European technology was significant at first, apart from modern paints, steel axes, knives and adzes. On Anuta, in boat-building, nylon has also replaced sennit for lashings. European tapes and glues are used, while splash rails, introduced only in 1972, are now standard fittings on canoes, and European metal hooks and nylon lines are used in fishing.

New ideologies also have consequences, even for technology. Under the influence of the missionaries, the taboos which formerly surrounded canoe-building on Puluwat have long been dropped, so that today anyone, even if they lack the skills of master builders, can at least work with adze and plane, 'smoothing every tiny imperfection in the contour of the hull'.[61] The result is better and faster boats.

It might be thought that the European compass and charts would be far more important innovations. Yet, on Puluwat at least, they are used only for secondary purposes, notably to hold steady a course *after* it has been established by stars or other traditional means, and to keep track of the direction of drift when caught in a large storm.[62] True, with a compass on board, the navigator is relieved from having to continually monitor the waves; he can look at the compass from time to time, and if the canoe is heading off course can tell the steersman to watch the waves or keep an eye on a distant cloud. But they may have to fall back entirely on wave-lore at night, when pitch darkness means the compass cannot be seen. In a severe storm, conversely, they may depend entirely on the compass. So it is likely that the compass will eventually replace the star courses, and that these will go the way of the wind compasses the Polynesians used to use.

Most journeys today are made to known destinations along known routes. It might seem, therefore, that the motives which induced the ancestors of the present-day Polynesians, Micronesians and Melanesians to venture into completely unknown waters must have been quite different in kind. Yet they are probably not all that different from known historical instances where canoes have set off into the open seas for a variety of other reasons: 'Motives of Pacific expansion could have been as mixed as those of the later European maritime exploration.'[63] They include, Thomas suggests, the desire to prove themselves at sea or to escape from overcrowded islands, and attempts at political expansion.[64] Old men recall bloody wars of conquest, the devastation of whole islands by typhoons and wholesale flights to find a new home.

Sheer adventurousness was one driving force; even the Anutans, no great long-distance sailors, had 'extremely positive feelings towards the sea' and were 'fearless'. Even death at sea by drowning is looked on, in the famous phrase of their Tikopian neighbours, as 'sweet burial'. Though Anutan voyaging was small-scale, and usually only took people every now and then to the tiny islet of Patutaka, a mere thirty miles away, it still involved great risks, for Patutaka is 'the most inhospitable place imaginable', ringed with rock walls up to 500 feet high. To get through the four–six-foot waves offshore, they have to risk their lives. And though the rationale for the trip was supposed to be getting birds and bird's eggs, all they found on the trip Feinberg went on were a few dry coconuts and no yams or birds at all. In addition, the bow of one canoe broke off as it was being dragged on to the shore. 'We could all have died,' Feinberg remarks. But they had an exciting time – one of the highlights of his life, he says.[65]

On a more ambitious scale, in the past large expeditions would even set out to discover new lands, or to emulate spectacular voyages others had made, often over several years. 'Proud and arrogant' Carolinians would put to sea, 'regardless of storms or even certainty of disaster', when shame or honour was at stake: when, for instance, they were becoming a burden for their hosts to feed; or one of their number was involved in a fight with no apology offered; or a captain had decided that the weather was too bad to put to sea and local fishermen would confine themselves to offshore fishing only.[66] Today, navigators who are proud of their abilities still make long journeys, even when commercial inter-island vessels are available, just to get commodities like cigarettes.

In historical times, quite distant islands would be raided, particularly by the larger chiefdoms of the Society Islands and Tonga. The large wheel-shaped discs usually called 'Yap stone money', found in many a museum today, were in fact made of imported stone which neighbouring islands were forced to use in payment of tribute. Not just money but many items not available locally, such as special kinds of stone for making tools, were commonly obtained by trade, often accompanied by exchanges of objects like the highly valued armlets and necklaces described by Malinowski for the Trobriand Islands and nearby parts of New Guinea; their value did not derive from utility in everyday life but from the fact that they brought otherwise separate, and often hostile, peoples together.[67]

Other voyages were one-way, sometimes deliberately, as when youths put to sea to get away from intolerable parental control. After traumatic incidents, such as being accused of incest, some men would opt for virtual suicide; others would be sent into exile. Natural disasters resulted in other unintended long-distance voyages, such as the hurricanes which the anthropologists Firth and Spillius experienced on Tikopia in 1953–4, which reduced the food supply so severely that people were no longer willing to help their relatives, failed to pay customary dues to clan leaders and even stole from the gardens of the chiefs. When the chiefs themselves failed to observe the norms of *noblesse oblige* towards commoners, the notion that they were planning to force commoners to leave the island gained currency. Yet even then commoners did not challenge the chiefs' 'traditional privilege of survival, whoever else might have to die'.[68]

The most popular theories about the colonization of the Pacific are, unfortunately, almost certainly wrong. The best known, Thor Heyerdahl's argument that the islands were colonized from the Americas, was not a new idea but one which had long been dismissed by the great majority of Pacific scholars. Though he certainly proved that the journey was possible – by actually making his famous voyage on the *Kon-Tiki* – and followed it up with theoretical arguments in his book *American Indians in the Pacific* (1952), most scholars were no more impressed than they had been when writers had advanced the same theory in the last century, for the overwhelming weight of historical, archaeological, linguistic and physical anthropological evidence is still that the movement of colonization was from the mainland of South-East Asia eastwards.

A second book which influenced public opinion, Andrew Sharp's *Ancient Voyagers in the Pacific* (1957), accepted that the voyagers had indeed come from the west (as traditional stories recounted) but disputed oral tradition which had it that they had deliberately set out to explore and had returned successfully. By contrast, Sharp believed that the voyages had been neither deliberate, suicidal, irrational, nor made by people who were forced out – for example, into exile – but had been accidental – they had simply drifted there, mainly because of storms. Some of the archaeological evidence does confirm that accidental voyages – and tragic dramas – undoubtedly occurred. Thus the remains have been found of a group of men who lived for fifty years on Fanning Island, where they had probably been blown from the Marquesas – but since they had no women with them, when they died out, so did their culture.[69] John Updike's imaginative short story 'The Blessed Men of Boston' uses this incident, unfortunately, to denigrate Polynesian navigation ('The Polynesian islands were populated accidentally, as seed in nature is sown ... The stars are a far weaker guide than armchair theorists believe. Accident is the generative agency beneath the seemingly achieved surface of things') and to express a wider, bleak vision of 'life stripped of the progenitive illusion'.[70]

Many journeys *were* accidental, though, and Sharp was justified in discounting some of the arguments used to defend theories of purposive colonization – the notion, for instance, that navigators followed the flight of migrating birds, for though birds will eventually arrive at land, no one can know how far they are flying.

Yet even when crews were blown to remote and unknown parts of the ocean, they were still 'as much at ease and at home with the aquatic environment as the Australian Aboriginal is with his ... environment',[71] and could still often find their way back.

Some journeys were undoubtedly a deliberate search for new lands. This did not entail courting starvation. As well as knowing they would be able to catch fish, the crews would load their canoes with enough eating and drinking coconuts to last a month, plus fermented breadfruit, baked fish, baked sweet potato and breadfruit. Dried breadfruit 'chips', thick pastes or puddings of taro and banana in coconut oil, and nuts would last indefinitely, while, according to some accounts, the Tahitians carried water in bamboo containers.

Today these voyages are generally seen not as irrational or suicidal but as deliberate enterprises. If unsuccessful, they would often have meant death; expert opinion is divided on how many lives must have been lost. But many journeys did succeed, and many voyagers probably made the return journey too, after which further voyages with more colonists would have taken place.[72]

In addition to written and oral evidence, modern 'replica' voyages have been undertaken by people with sailing skills, such as Lewis and Gladwin, to test out indigenous crafts and indigenous sailing techniques, and there have been computer simulations of 'search and return' voyages, taking the distances between islands and the direction of voyages in relation to prevailing winds into account.

These researches suggest that sailing across large regions of the Pacific was not too problematic for highly skilled seafarers.[73] The usual image of seafaring in the Pacific is one of finding a speck in the ocean. But some islands were much more visible: the Hawaiian chain, for instance – which extends for more than 1,000 miles west-north-west to east-south-east – has mountains and volcanoes which rise to 13,000 feet. Most of the time the target was not an isolated island at all but an 'expanded island target', a *block* of islands. If we further allow thirty mile radii for the disturbed swell patterns and other land indications around each island, the overall effect is that of a 'screen' around whole archipelagos, in which islands are never more than sixty miles apart. A canoe passing between them can reasonably expect to be within thirty miles of land.[74]

Figure 8 **Island blocks**

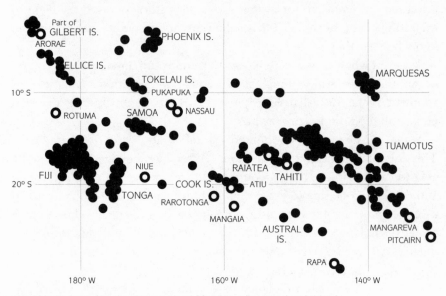

Island blocks formed by drawing a circle of 30 miles radius round each island; heights have been ignored.

Source: Lewis, 1972, p. 152.

Even when a navigator had lost track of his position altogether and was uncertain of the distance travelled, he had only to return downwind to the latitude he had started out from to be able to run down the wind into the 'safety net' of the home islands.

Outwards navigation was safer because it involved sailing east–west, *against* the prevailing winds – in the case of the original eastward voyages of exploration, against the trade winds. The very last voyages of exploration, however – to the most far-flung edges of Oceania – involved different winds and different swell patterns. Getting to Hawaii involved sailing *across* the wind, while New Zealand had to be eventually reached *down*wind.

Yet on the upwind voyages, when the time came to return, the winds blew you back far more quickly – an important consideration for exhausted sailors running out of food. Early European explorers similarly experienced shipboard conditions 'to which the only modern parallel would be the life in a concentration camp'.[75] Pigafetta, Magellan's chronicler, was one of only eighteen men who returned alive out of some 250.

During the original exodus of the ancestors of today's Oceanians from the Asian mainland – which took centuries, along the 'sea of islands' today called Indonesia – land would have been visible on more than one route all the way to the Bismarck Archipelago in Melanesia. Long periods must have been needed along the way, though, for developing new kinds of food production. The Bismarck Archipelago, the launching pad for the final phase of eastward colonization, was, Irwin says, the 'perfect nursery for learning [the] seagoing skills' needed, since the winds and the currents make it 'as easy to cross in one direction as another'. Voyages eastwards from there probably began earlier than 1500 BC; the last discoveries of isolated outlying islands such as Hawaii and Easter Island were not made until some time between AD 200 and 400; to New Zealand, not until some time between 900 and 1200.

Figure 9 **Islands between South-East Asia and Melanesia**

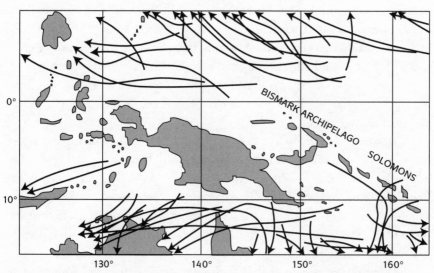

A corridor of large, often intervisible islands joins South-east Asia to Melanesia. Winds and currents reverse seasonally and the region lies between cyclone belts whose typical tracks are shown to the north and south. Conditions allowed Pleistocene settlement and, later, made an ideal 'voyaging nursery' for the first colonists of the Remote Pacific to the east.

Source: Irwin, 1989, p. 193.

Christianity has long been the dominant religion throughout the Pacific. On Anuta, for instance, much of indigenous cosmological belief, as well as the rituals of everyday life and those surrounding navigation, has disappeared. Today the spirits of senior chiefs are no longer the most important deities; the senior living chief is no longer also the high priest. The great deities, spirits of deceased chiefs, are no longer invoked when a new canoe is finished, while the ritual drinking of kava on such occasions has been banned by the Anglican priest. Nor are funerals held, as they once were, when canoes are lost or destroyed. The *vai pa* rituals – formerly held when a boy went on his first fishing expedition or his first inter-island voyage – are also no longer performed. The Anglican priest on Anuta has even banned inter-island sailing.

Given this loss of pre-European religious beliefs, but the persistence of much astronomical knowledge and of navigational skills, it is possible to present these maritime peoples as if, today, they were singularly secular in their thinking – scientists rather than believers in the supernatural.

Older accounts of Polynesian thinking, on the other hand, emphasized a very different perspective: the pre-eminence of religious belief. They focused upon the complex sets of indigenous myths: the origins of the universe out of primal nothingness; the coming into being of light, sound, life and stability; the emergence of the High Rocks, the Earth Rocks and their progeny, the Earth; the genesis of the gods and, eventually, of humans, who lived at the centre of the world the gods had created, shaped like a dish or a half-coconut shell, its edges the horizon, from whence the heavens – ten or more of them – could be reached and below which lay the Underworld.[76]

The potency of these myths is attested by singular historic events. During the long struggle between the British and the Maori, Maori military organization was so effective that the British had to fight four successive wars between 1845 and 1872 before finally triumphing. During the last of these, there was one peculiarly Maori revolt, led by Hone Heke. 'The whole revolt,' Sahlins writes, 'was about a certain pole' erected by the British at Korokareka, their most populous settlement.[77] Hone Heke mounted no fewer than four attacks on this flagpole; his attack on the settlement, on the other hand, was merely a *diversion* from his main objective – to cut down the British flagpole.

The British, equally, had their cultural peculiarities, and fought three major engagements over possession of this pole. In the first two, they were well and truly beaten and their flagpole was cut down. Every time, though, they restored it. To them, it was the *flag* that was the symbol of their dominion over the land. For the Maori, it was the *pole* that was important, for their relationship with the Earth had been established when the (female) earth had been separated from the (male) Heavens by the first parent, Tane, who 'pressed against the Earth, and, in an act likened to parricide, pushed the Sky Father from her embrace'.[78] He then propped up the sky with four poles, after which humans took possession of the earth.

Myth, then, informed practical action. For an older generation of ethnographers, on the other hand, Polynesian mythology was simply folklore. Williamson for example, acknowledged the Polynesians possessed 'considerable' empirical knowledge of the stars: the Tahitians, for example, divided the horizon into sixteen cardinal points, based on the rising and setting of the sun. By using these, plus their 'extensive' knowledge of the winds and the state of the weather, they could navigate and forecast the weather. But their astronomical knowledge, he nevertheless concluded, was 'confused' (they failed to distinguish Venus from Jupiter and the evening star from the morning star, while the constellations they recognized were not identical with those our astronomers use). In any case, he argued, only a few – the priests – possessed extended knowledge of the heavenly bodies and could use them when navigating out of sight of land.

The accent, then, is upon their 'confusions' and upon their religious beliefs, rather than their scientific knowledge of the heavenly bodies and the use of this knowledge in practical navigation. So whereas Williamson devoted nearly 140 pages to myths of the stars as the progeny of the sun and moon, to myths of 'matrimonial' relationships between certain winds and to the 'identity' of the name for a wind and a god, and so on, there are only a few sentences on Polynesian astronomical knowledge.

Those who, like Elsdon Best, did pay more attention to the empirical knowledge of 'bold sea-voyagers' like the Maori, still dismissed their mythology as 'puerile'. And though he acknowledged that Maori ideas about the heavenly bodies included 'a certain amount of genuine knowledge', this is greatly outweighed by 'many quaint concepts, many peculiar myths, [and] singular superstitions', the whole 'fouled by superstition and savage cruelty'.[79] Rather than undertaking ethnographic observation of Maori navigators in action, he therefore focused on 'star-worship' and 'the belief that the fortunes of men somehow depended upon signs in the heavens'.[80] The upshot is that, despite professing, in the subtitle of his study, to concentrate upon what he called the 'genuine and empirical' knowledge of the Maori, he greatly undervalued it.

Christianity, as we saw for Anuta, has greatly undermined or almost wholly replaced indigenous religion on all but a handful of outlying islands in the Carolines. But some pre-Christian ideas still persist, and they can be seen, for instance, in contemporary ideas about navigation and the sea.

Thomas, who developed a working knowledge of the Satawalese language, remarks that in the past:

the metaphysical world of the spirits was so integrated with the physical world of humans that scarcely a distinction could be made between them. Virtually all fields of human endeavor – navigation, canoe-building, cultivation, fishing, even birth and ageing – has associated magical rituals that were considered essential.[81]

Today, the Satawalese still retain a knowledge of the pagan deities, notably of Anumwerici, the 'spirit who wears flowers', who is manifest in the rainbow and is the patron saint and protector of navigators. But there was, as Thomas also discovered, no longer any 'fixed organizational chart of deities … only a collection of stories'.

It is doubtful whether there ever was such an 'organizational chart'. Nevertheless, pre-Christian religious ideas have been massively undermined and replaced by Christian ones, and people claim that they threw away their customs when the missionaries told them to. But spirits still abound, even in urban areas.[82] Old women, in particular, still fear their presence at night-time. Magical rituals too are still used to cure illness. But in the past the scope of magic was much wider: it could be used to 'call' things people wanted – tuna, floating logs, octopus, breadfruit and coconuts – to the island. Many taboos, appyling to everything from regulating the use of breadfruit, timber or bananas during certain seasons to the deference due from women to men and from commoners to chiefs, have disappeared. Yet during Thomas' stay, Piailug was able to pressurize the chiefs to use their authority to institute a new taboo on taking turtle eggs and small turtles from certain nearby islands.

Taboos also regulated the annual fishing cycle and every aspect of sailing activity. To gather his crew together, the expert navigator (palu) summoned up the spirit of gathering, Farepuey, with a great blast on his conch-shell trumpet ('like a walkie-talkie', according to one navigator). As the crew brought the mast and sail to the canoe, the navigator chanted to Anumwerici and the spirit of the mast. As they raised the sail, he chanted again to Anumwerici, asking for a clear head and protection for his crew while at sea. Sailing away from the island, he blew on the conch to greet the spirits of the four schools of navigation, the island's navigators and the island itself, and asked for protection from sorcery. Once at sea, no canoe should leave the fleet; if essential, a magic potion had to be drunk, accompanied by a chant to Anumwerici. If a mast was broken it could not be repaired on another island, since the spirit living inside it would be offended. At sea, there was a whole series of chants designed for various purposes: to protect the canoe against bad weather, waterspouts and swells, against the spirits of black clouds which presaged strong wind and a 'host of other spirits'; to remove certain taboos, such as stepping over anchor lines or having one canoe leave the fleet; to counteract sickness; to soothe whales which threatened to overturn the canoe; and even to call floating logs (as Western fishermen know, fish tend to congregate under them, so they use helicopters and sonar to mark floating logs). At their destination, further chants protected the crew against poisoning by their hosts or theft of their canoe. These taboos bound the crew together and to their leader. On return, they were ritually sequestered from the rest of the community in their canoe-house for four days. The *palu*, in particular, had to take special medicine if he was to meet women or children during that period, and was not allowed to visit the women's menstrual-house or to do any work on it.[83]

Not everyone, not even every navigator, still knows all this or observes all the taboos. Christian rituals are also intermixed with pagan ones: going to chapel (even during trips to other islands) is part of everyday life and the dominant modern form of insurance against misfortune and of ensuring good fortune. 'Before,' one chief remarked, 'we had magic to bring our fish; now we have just God.' So when the first satellite appeared, some people explained that, in Christian teaching, such a star meant that great changes were coming. People will spray holy water from plastic bottles to drive the spirits of illness away. According to Thomas, one pious master navigator, who would not cut timber on a Sunday – because 'God would get mad' – and who always went to church, seemed more concerned 'to cover all metaphysical contingencies than because he was a true believer'.[84] All gods, then, had to be placated, especially the Christian one, who claimed to be all-powerful.

Over-integrated Psychology: Piaget and Hallpike

Older ethnographers, we have seen, tended to emphasize the religious and mythological elements in the thinking of the Polynesians. The result was to present them as mystics. Modern researchers, on the other hand, by focusing on their empirical knowledge and navigational expertise, have converted them into 100 per cent scientists.

Given the evidence of these extensive observations of stars and winds by the islanders, and their capacity to transform these raw data into a coherent body of knowledge which formed the basis for outstanding feats of practical navigation, few would deny all this the title of 'science', though many would still want to place the qualifier 'ethno-' in front of the word, because they think our science is the most rigorous and therefore the most powerful of all.

However, the anthropologist C. R. Hallpike's major modern comparative study, *The Foundations of Primitive Thought,* concludes that 'primitive' thinking falls crucially short of being 'scientific'.[85]

He too discounts the theories of Durkheim and Lévi-Strauss. Thus he dismisses Durkheim's argument that the major categories of thought – the 'collective representations' of a society – could not have been worked out by even the most brilliant individuals but were *imposed* on the individual by society. Society, Hallpike objects, does not think; thinking is done by individuals who use their brains to produce thoughts, some of which others come to accept as convincing. These then become the 'collective representations' of society – the 'received' culture.

Conceptions of space, time, quantity, etc. could not have been developed solely out of categories provided by the framework of society, for they still involve an *individual* mental process: *thinking*. Durkheim's model also devalues non-verbal thought, particularly *imagining*, which may take place without necessarily being put into words at all and is not simply acquired from society or culture.

For Hallpike, Durkheim is also wrong to privilege society as being so paramount that the physical environment in which individuals and societies live is treated as irrelevant. Durkheim dismisses the relationship of hunters and gatherers to plants and animals as mere 'practical concerns'; the knowledge they develop in the process as merely 'technological'.

Hallpike's own approach is based on the analyses of the mental development of children carried out by the Swiss psychologist Jean Piaget. For Piaget, learning involves much more than the passive reception of impressions coming from the world outside the child's skin-boundary, or simply internalizing and reproducing the ideas of the culture, embodied in language and handed down by adults. Rather, *reasoning* is involved. Indeed, learning begins long *before* the acquisition of language: the child finds out about the world by looking, hearing and actively manipulating it (sucking, touching, etc.). But this is essentially a *private* phase. Exposure to socialized thought comes later and can conflict with both the child's biological drives and behaviour patterns it has already developed for itself. From the child's earliest days, then, learning is not a unitary process; later, its wants are increasingly likely to come into conflict with adults other than those belonging to the immediate family, who may expect different kinds of behaviour from the child.

So the child does not necessarily build up a unified, systematic picture of the world; it deals with one aspect of it at a time. Connecting up these different areas and replacing older, fixed categories by newer, more dynamic ones are particularly difficult.

Much in Piaget's work is both rigorous and impressive. I can still recall the excitement of first looking into *The Moral Judgment of the Child*[86] and admiring the ingenuity of a study which tackled the question of the genesis of ethical codes by watching children in a Swiss playground playing marbles. Playing games involves learning and conforming to *rules* based on strong moral principles; there are built-in rituals (taking turns, sharing, co-operating, not cheating, etc.), backed by sanctions used to enforce the rules (ostracism, physical punishment, etc.) – insights which Piaget then transformed into rigorous experiments, carried on over a lifetime.

A parallel body of ideas about the mental development of children, which helped me to understand the thinking of adult Australian Aborigines, was the work of the Soviet psychologist Lev Semenovich Vygotsky.[87]

Vygotsky found that children, in their progress towards adulthood, go through a succession of phases in their mental development, during which the kind of thinking they develop first is later displaced by other kinds. In the earliest stage, young infants group objects into 'heaps' (in more academic jargon, 'unorganized congeries') – 'inherently unrelated objects linked by chance in the child's perception'.[88] The child's thinking is thus *egocentric* and *incoherent*.

In the second stage (though, as with the first, there are actually a number of subphases), the child becomes capable of forming mental '*complexes*', which are not just arbitrary piles of things but are grouped according to some distinctive criterion: because they look alike, say, or are used in similar ways. Thus one child used the word *quah* to apply, first, to a duck swimming in a pond and then to any liquid, including the milk in his bottle. When he saw a coin with an eagle on it, the coin was also called *quah*; after that, so was any coin-like object. This was a *chain complex*: each new object had some attribute in common with another, but *different* attributes were involved, one after the other.

'*Any* factually present connection', then, 'may lead to the inclusion of a given element into a complex' (or 'collection'): because it has the same colour or the same shape, or because it is near another object – there is no *overall* coherence in the complex. Nor is there any stability: the type and nature of the connection which the child perceives between one object and another may change as successive objects come to its attention, and the order it sees in one particular set of toys applies only to that group at that moment in time; at another time, it may use different criteria to create a different set. There are, in fact, '*over*abundance [and] *over*production of connections' and, in consequence, 'weakness in abstraction'.[89] Complexes therefore often have 'a vague and floating quality'.

But the child is still incapable of reasoning either inductively – from a particular instance to a generalization – or in the opposite fashion, deductively – from a general category to a particular instance. Rather, it thinks only of *either* the parts *or* the whole. It is also unaware that its mental processes may or may not match up with those of other people, or that there might be differences in the way it perceives things and what the object's true properties actually are. For these reasons, 'A complex does rise

above its elements ... [It] is factually inseparable from the group of concrete objects that form it.'

The third stage is reached when the child can form *concepts*: when elements are *abstracted* according to a single principle and viewed 'apart from
the totality of concrete experiences in which they are embodied'.[90]

In developing concepts and skills of measurement, Piaget found, each
child progresses at different speeds but in a definite sequence. Thus children learn to conceptualize number before quantity, then area, while volume comes last. In the process, they have to manipulate objects, carry out
appropriate actions and co-ordinate them. By the third stage, they are able
to enter into communication with others and to develop the ability to
think about things not immediately in front of them, because they have developed the idea of the *symbol*: a generalized idea of things which exist
apart from any actual tangible things. Though they develop their own private symbols, the ones that come to matter more and more are those
which form part of a complex cultural system, encoded in language, that
everyone uses and which they are therefore obliged to learn.

Then comes the 'pre-operational' stage (from two to three for European children), when the child develops its own internal mental
categories for different kinds of things and actions; then the 'concrete-
operational' stage, when thought is focused upon concrete objects and the
classification of physical properties. The final stage is 'formal' thinking,
when the child develops the ability to operate with mental categories
based on abstract logic, independent of any direct connection with the external world.

This scheme depends upon the crucial assumption that 'operatory'
thinking is the 'normal intellectual attitude ... of educated members of
technologically advanced societies'[91] – people who have attended school
for many years, who are not only literate but also, in Piaget's words,
'steeped in the ideas of classical mechanics'. Even for them, though, earlier modes of thought do not completely vanish: while 'limited by ... later
additions, [they] still [remain] active within restricted domains' (which
implies that these atavistic modes of thought will be more common among
the less educated).

As Gell observes, Piaget's researches were in fact mainly concentrated
on people in institutions where they were being prepared for a future as
members of a technical élite. Yet scientists commonly think in quite non-
scientific ways even *inside* the laboratory. Thus in one study American students of physics were shown to hold quite scientifically fallacious ideas
about the behaviour of falling objects, despite what they had been taught
about Galilean principles: over a third of them believed that if a running

man dropped a ball, it would fall at the point below the runner's hand at the moment he had dropped it, an erroneous belief shared by nine out of ten non-physics students.

Moreover, 'the laboratory' is a shorthand for only one kind of scientific research, for meteorologists, palaeontologists and astronomers do not perform controlled experiments, which many assume to be typical of scientific work. In addition, as Yearley has written, 'Scientific knowledge [is still] the most authoritative account of the natural world we possess. But it is not absolute.'[92] Even when using the same criteria, he observes, scientists often come to *different* conclusions. Which theory or interpretation wins out depends on a complex set of social factors, including the power of competing groups and institutions, before one of them emerges as what Kuhn has called the 'dominant paradigm'.[93]

However, science is not all of a piece, Kuhn argues. Doing it involves quite different kinds of activities, many of which make no claim to be aiming at theoretical innovation. They are little more than what he calls 'five-finger exercises', such as routine 'quality control' experiments, which simply employ established procedures. Or people may drive cars, using what Berger and Luckmann call 'recipe knowledge', without knowing anything about the principles of internal combustion. I operate this word-processor, knowing virtually nothing about Boolean algebra or the theory on which the technology of semi-conductors is based.

Much science, Atran has argued, is an elaboration of common sense. Hence 'local folk' *can* 'provide a fairly accurate first approximation to the scientific distribution of the local fauna and flora'. Other kinds of science, though, such as genetics and molecular biology, are quite remote from common sense. Theoreticians at the frontiers of knowledge, in particular, are concerned not so much with the *objects* of knowledge as with the ways in which *thinking* about such objects is done – an objective, Atran remarks, which has been absent throughout most of human history and which only occurs in one culture, that of the 'West'. In that sense, then, Western science is 'a local phenomenon ... more or less restricted to one culture', that of the West. To that extent, it is an ethno-science. Yet in so far as it aims to establish propositions of universal validity, pretending to be timeless, universal and cumulative, and therefore to transcend Western culture.[94]

Garfinkel, though, has shown that 'science' itself, as a concept, is problematic: professional scientists have defined it in no less than fourteen major different ways.[95] Some emphasize the activity of taxonomizing. Others emphasize, the conception of a 'fit' between theory and observation. Yet others emphasize the criterion of regularly reviewed rules of theory; strategies of considering alternatives and their consequences; the *overall* strategy of research; concern for timing, prediction and predictability; the use of universalistic as against 'tribal' rules of procedure; adherence to rational rules of choice as between alternatives; the *grounds* of that rationality; the compatibility of procedures with the canons of formal logic; whether they are semantically unambiguous; whether this clarity is seen as something sought for its own sake ('pure' science), whatever the practical uses or non-uses; and whether the activity conforms with established patterns of scientific knowledge as distinct from common-sense feelings or beliefs.

Nor is the borderline between science and everyday thinking any less problematic. Ordinary people, Garfinkel argues, are no different from scientists in ten out of fourteen respects: they make comparisons, consider the consequences and the alternatives, inspect the criteria which influence choice, have intentions, assess predictability, choose between ends and means and use codified experience ('laws', etc.).

But they do *not* use four of the fourteen criteria rigorously. They do not adhere to a codified and consistent 'scientific grammar' of rules of procedure, in which there is a 'clear specification of the elements and of the rules for their combination'. Nor is the clarification of the body of knowledge a 'first priority project'. And they do not accept that only scientifically verifiable propositions are compatible with real knowledge.[96] Doing science thus *departs* from common sense in a number of crucial ways, the most important being 'the strange idea of doubt', which, if used in everyday life, would quickly lead to the consignment of its users to institutions for the mentally ill. Common sense, on the other hand, assumes that the world is 'as it naturally appears to be'.

Common sense also departs from science in a second way: it does not assume that time is a measureable standard phenomenon – 'One Big Time' or 'real' time – since in everyday life we use and experience multiple kinds of personal and social time.

The third special assumption of science which contradicts common sense is that, for scientists, events are 'matters of theoretical interest'. Science is concerned with models and the testing of models. The end to be pursued is the discovery of cause-and-effect solutions, not, as for most people in most situations, 'the mastery of practical affairs'.

The last difference is that, for scientists, their 'constituency' is not any real-life group or category of people but 'Universalized Anyman' – the scientific community of competent investigators. In some extremely idealized theoretical versions of this scientific community, Garfinkel writes, scientists are people who never forget, recall things properly at the proper time and always act to maximize desired effects – *never* on principle!

The knowledge a scientist uses, then, overlaps with common sense in ten respects out of fourteen. The other four-fourteenths constitute the special attributes of professional science – which are used, however, 'only in cases ... guided by ... scientific theorizing'.[97]

Thus 'clock-time' is particularly important for scientists. In industrial society, it is also important for everyone: the production and use of clocks on a mass scale began only with the Industrial Revolution.[98]

Yet even in the context of their work, scientists use *different* ways of reckoning time in different kinds of scientific operations. And for them, as for everyone else, the divisions of the working day are also symbolically structured: the approach of the end of the working day is both subjectively felt (tiredness, hunger, etc.) and socially marked (people start 'clearing up', slowing down, chatting, lighting up, etc.).

Outside the laboratory, even scientists handle time-reckoning in ways which are quite distinct from those they use when they are working as scientists. (Herbert Spencer classically described a religious physicist he knew as a man who, 'when he entered his oratory ... shut the door of his laboratory; and when he entered his laboratory ... shut the door of his oratory'.[99]) When, like everyone else, scientists are carrying out a hundred and one different kinds of activities in everyday life, they use the same ways of reckoning social time that everyone else uses, based on common cultural understandings and well-known social practices, which are *not* measured by using numbers. Thus even scientists talk about 'before' and 'after dinner' or 'when I get home', or, as Gell notes, use a variety of time-indications, ranging, at the short end of the spectrum, from 'in a jiffy', 'in a flash' or 'half a mo' to, at the long end, 'for ages', 'donkey's years', 'time out of mind' or 'for ever and a day'. If I complain, 'I've been waiting here for ages' or 'for hours', nobody thinks I mean that the time elapsed was actually precisely forty-seven minutes and forty seconds. A film can drag on 'for ever'; time spent with a loved one can be over 'in a flash'.[100]

So the logic that informs work, whether scientific work or other kinds, does not apply outside it. As Gell remarks, 'Work undertaken during non-working hours is not at all the same, for all that it may involve the same *activities*, as work undertaken in working hours.'[101] So the largely female activity of washing up, for instance, may be labelled 'house*work*', since for most people it is not a pleasurable routine but a chore, while the largely male activity of 'do-it-yourself' – home improvements – which may also involve physical or repetitive labour – will usually be regarded as a leisure-time 'hobby'.

Scientific Knowledge and Popular Knowledge

In the nineteenth century, theories about the mental inferiority of 'primitive' people were usually based on a comparison between their everyday folk knowledges and Western science. Yet we have seen that within all cultures different modes of thought coexist, and that even on Groote Eylandt there are specialists who know far more about important aspects of the world and think more systematically about them than most of their fellows, and also belong to different schools of thought. They do not, though, work full-time at thinking, nor do they work in institutions devoted to the pursuit of learning.

When we make comparisons between 'their society' and 'ours', then, we will come to very different conclusions if we do not make it clear not only which kind of thought we are talking about but also who, in the respective societies, we are dealing with.

Four different kinds of comparison are possible: between their specialists and our scientists; between their specialists and our non-scientists; between their non-specialists and our scientists; and between their 'folk' culture and our 'popular' culture.

Hallpike's study is mainly concerned with one of these: with comparing and contrasting their specialist knowledge and our science. True, he does also note that 'rather than contrasting primitive man with the European scientists and logician, it would be more to the point to contrast him with the garage mechanic, the plumber, and the housewife in her kitchen'.[102] This, however, he does not do.

Vygotsky, on the other hand, warned against assuming that 'our' thinking was always scientific:

even the normal [Russian] adult, [though] capable of forming and using concepts, does not consistently operate with concepts in his thinking. Apart from the primitive thought processes of dreams, the adult constantly shifts from conceptual to concrete, complex-like thinking ... transitional ... form[s] of thought [are] not confined to child thinking; we too resort to [them] very often in our daily life.[103]

Piaget's model is much more rigid. In Switzerland, fully developed 'operatory' thought was to be found only among an educated élite; in 'primitive' societies, adult thinking was limited to 'concrete' operations – only the third stage in his schema of mental development.

For Hallpike, similarly, cognitive growth is governed by '*laws general to human beings in all societies* such that all normal individuals will progress through a series of developmental stages'.[104] Primitive thought, then, can be 'practical, creative and wise' — but nevertheless normally gets only as far as the '*pre*-operatory' stage.

He does allow some qualifications to this model: even in our society most people capable of formal thought may 'operate on a number of different mental levels'; some cultures may progress further through the successive stages than others; while 'gifted individuals' may be able to transcend the collective representations of their society. But the great majority cannot.

This is a model based on only *one* out of Garfinkel's fourteen major kinds of definitions of science. It privileges abstraction — which the uneducated in Western society, as well as 'primitives', fail to develop adequately. Even in our own culture, 'It is ... possible that a significant section of the population ... does not advance to the stage of formal thought, which reinforces the probability that it will be even less frequent in nonliterate primitive populations.'[105] His general conclusion, then, is *not* that primitive thought is 'inherently different' from that of 'literate industrial man', 'totally alien' to our own; rather than it is 'more *elementary*, in developmental terms'.[106]

The prime focus of his book is on 'primitives', not industrial man. So he works through a vast amount of ethnographic material: about primitive classification, number, measurement, the analysis of dimensions and conceptions of time and space. He concludes that primitives, in dealing with nature, lack abstract conceptions such as 'hardness' or 'length'. They can measure things, but the scales they use are of a low order of generality and a low order of abstraction. Instead of relating objects to other objects, they relate objects to people, 'egocentrically'. And though there is experimentation in primitive society, it is not *controlled*. In consequence, children are able to *show* things in context, but have difficulty in 'telling' *out* of context. Their conceptual thinking is, in fact, 'retarded'.

Primitive mathematics, again, is mere 'tallying' — the adding together of concrete objects — rather than 'operational' thinking, which involves logical relations, notably ordination and co-ordination. Measurement is therefore concrete — different kinds of things (crops, distance, etc.) are measured in different units, not against an abstract, precise and quantitative standard, while operations like reversibility are ill-developed. So addition is often better developed than multiplication or division, since these involve abstract concepts — 'halves', 'quarters', 'eighths' — and different multiples. Abstract words for qualities — 'weight' or 'height' — are likewise absent. This does not mean that they *can't* think of such properties, or that they cannot measure them as relative amounts against a general scale; simply that as they don't normally *have* to, they don't do so easily.

Dealing with quantity, area, length, width and volume calls for 'conservation': concepts which make it possible to think in terms of co-variation – how, for instance, a given property may remain constant, even though other properties change, as when, if the same amount of water is poured into beakers of different shapes and sizes, the water level, the size and the shape of the beaker all vary *together*. In primitive thought, Hallpike concludes, such conceptions are weakly developed or absent and the categories of thought are inflexible; introducing something new into the middle of a series is therefore disturbing.

The order of their society and its culture, again, are fixed and taken for granted. The ambition of children, therefore, is simply to become an adult, not to ask why things are as they are. The experience of society is customary, the same for all, embodied in unchanging myths, in which events happen in a chronological not a logical order, and are simply *learned*. Likewise, even their languages do not help, because although they are organized according to highly structured rules, which can be abstracted and even written down, these are also just learned. They do not constitute objects of inquiry, nor are they a source of inquisitive habits of mind, and cannot, therefore, lead the user of a language to *hypotheses* about language, to develop ideas about possible alternative ways of thought or to raise questions of truth or falsity.

These are serious charges. Yet they do not seem to apply without considerable qualification to the cultures of Groote Eylandt or Polynesia. Thus Hallpike considers that primitive classification is generally weak: there may be *some*, but it is rarely consistent or exhaustive and is usually defined only by a single criterion; and if more than one criterion is used, 'no consistent logical principles' are involved.[107] As we have seen, in Groote Eylandt biology there *are* distinct hierarchies, involving criteria which make possible the coherent organization of a very considerable amount of knowledge, grouping different kinds of plants and animals at successively higher levels of generalization, as when types of fish are grouped together and then related to other types; all of these then being related to other, non-fish sea creatures, the larger marine mammals; the whole being treated as part of a highest-order grouping (all life in the sea) which, in its turn, constitutes one of the three basic life forms, the others being land animals and creatures of the air. Nor is scientific criticality absent – there are different schools of thought as to the best way of classifying certain species, depending on the criteria used.

All of this involves using *concepts*. True, a theory of *development*, such as the Western theory of evolution, is lacking, and the boundaries between biology and religion are – although only very occasionally – 'leaky', since

the odd mythological snake does wriggle its way into the biological classification – just as Linnaeus' 'faithful dog' found its way into his schema.

Precise quantification, as we have seen, is also absent, since it has no
utility. As Hallpike remarks, 'Ideas of number and measurement, like those
of space, time and causality ... depend for their development on the kinds
of problems that have to be solved [and] the means available for their solution'.[108]

Also, being

unfamiliar with machinery and lacking exact scales of measurement,
lacking writing, too (which obliges those who use it to develop the
ability to analyse grammar and to present ideas in sequence), they are
not able to provide precise, quantitative measures, for, say 'heat'.

Australian Aborigines, then, do not possess extended number systems
because they are not useful, not because they cannot think them. Results
from tests devised by and for Europeans, but tried out on 'primitives', are
singularly suspect. As we saw in the case of the footprint test in Chapter 1,
many tests assumed to measure mental ability in general are artificial, requiring the testee to imagine situations which *differ* from real-life. All they
tell us, in the end, is that people from other cultures often find it difficult
to do European tests.

Occasionally, though, their own culture can give them an advantage.
Thus Tiv peasants in West Africa performed *better* than comparable Europeans on one Piaget-type test because, in their own culture, they were expert at a board game which involved transferring pebbles between holes of
different shapes and sizes.

Again, as Gell observes, if peasants are unable to give a precise account
of the timetable of farming activities which they carry out very efficiently,
this is because they do not work according to clock-time: their farming activities are inherently irregular, depending as they do on variations such as
rainfall and temperature, from season to season and year to year. And
when children say that male adults are 'older' than female adults, this is
both statistically reasonable as a physical proposition, in so far as men are,
in general, bigger than women, but also reflects social differences of authority and power between the genders.

It is only when we turn to the totemic thinking of the Aborigines that
we find ourselves in a different logical universe, the furthest removed
from science (and thus the opposite of Durkheim's view of the matter), a
world not of conceptual thought but of complexive thinking *par excellence*.
Here the 'heroic' animals, plants and other things (humans, features of the

landscape, etc.) which figure in the Dreamtime myths are connected to each other only *through the myths*, rather than on the basis of real-life properties like those which form the basis of food classification (edibility, habitat) and biological taxonomy (the type of animal or plant and its habitat). The myths are thus the equivalent of the child's 'heaps', to use Vygotsky's term. Later we will see that this kind of thinking is characteristic of religious thinking in general, not just of Australian religious thought.

So far, we have confined ourselves to knowledge about what Westerners call the world of 'nature' – knowledge about plants and animals in the case of the Aborigines, and knowledge about the cosmos in the Oceanian case. In both these cultures there is profound knowledge of the natural environment in which people live. Their conception of what we call 'nature', though, differs from that of Western cultures, though Western ideas about nature are not all of one piece. On the one hand, nature is something 'out there'; on the other, we are part of it, like other animals. But we also think of ourselves as possessing attributes which give us a very special status.

So do the other cultures we have been looking at. They too possess a well-grounded understanding of the world in which they live. But in some situations they look at what happens to them in quite other ways than those based on their own, or anyone else's, biology or astronomy. For they see the world as also informed and affected by forces which Westerners would describe as supernatural.

In Western thinking, many people do not subscribe to the notion that there is any 'supernatural' at all. Others believe that there may be, but do not see it as impinging much upon our quotidian, mundane lives.

This dethronement of the supernatural, however, is not widely accepted in many cultures, for whatever people think about the world in which they live, they see humans (and, above all, their own culture) as special and distinct in ways that go far beyond Western conceptions of the place of human beings in the wider scheme of things. They therefore draw the boundaries between the social and the individual in different ways from those dominant in the West, and conceive of *super*natural forces as affecting human life. We now turn, therefore, to the (relatively recent) emergence of this way of thought in the West, with particular reference to one aspect of humanness: our ideas about the functioning of our bodies, the ailments that affect them and the therapies that we have developed to cure illness.

3

Sickness as a Way of Life

In Western cultures, health is usually thought of, especially by health professionals, simply as a physical state of the individual body. But to patients, being 'ill' (in Britain) or 'sick' (in the United States), usually implies a subjective element too — that the sick person *feels* distress. Both professionals and lay people also often recognize that there may be a social dimension to illness — that it may arise from an inappropriate lifestyle or bad living conditions, for example. But because people's social problems differ greatly in, say, Zaïre, and Western Europe, 'folk' ideas about health and illness necessarily differ from country to country.

The key elements of *official* Western medicine are '(1) scientific rationality (2) ... objective, numerical measurement (3) [an] emphasis on physico-chemical data (4) [on] mind–body dualism and (5) a view of "diseases" as entities'.[1]

These are only part of a much wider set of ideas: the belief that Man can control nature; the belief that this control is possible through knowledge; the belief that the scientific method is the only way of arriving at such knowledge; the assumption that understanding and controlling nature are good and desirable; the belief that progress depends upon scientific knowledge; and the ideal of dedicating one's life to understanding nature and to the pursuit of truth.[2] The distinction we make between 'physical' and 'mental' illnesses — based on the Cartesian opposition between mind and body (which underlies Lévi-Strauss' opposition between 'nature' and 'culture') — is not one most people in the world would recognize, for they explain a great deal of even individual illness, especially abnormal illness, not in terms of the world of nature but in terms of supernatural forces. They do not, though, regard all illness as solely or always due to such forces. Rather, there is an *interdependence* between nature, supernature, society and the person.

What we call nature — from the internal functioning of the human body to the influence of the natural environment (the kinds of foods available, say, or accidents which damage parts of the body) — is certainly seen as important in health and illness, and people accept that weakness of one part of the body sets limits upon human attempts to cope with disease.

Medical practitioners in other cultures do have systematic and remarkably detailed knowledge about the human body. In one city in Brazil, for instance, 'popular anatomists' (one of sixteen different types of non-Western specialists, many of whom are illiterate) distinguish four frontal regions of the body – the head, the chest, the stomach and intestinal region (which includes, for women, the reproductive organs), and the genital regions – and two dorsal ones, as well as the upper and lower limbs. They also have detailed knowledge of the internal layout of the organs of the body, of the vascular system and of differences in the genital regions of men and women. Their conceptions of the functions of these parts sometimes differ from those of Western medicine: thus the nose and the ears, in addition to their obvious functions, are said to 'ventilate' the head. The organs and the internal systems of the body provide it with 'filtration' as well as ventilation, with the co-ordination or integration *(composição)* of the different parts and the body's equilibrium and strength *(resistencia)*.[3]

But individuals are also subject to many kinds of influences other than the physical which affect their state of health. These include the need to be at ease – not *dis*ease – with those among whom they live their daily lives, in face-to-face groups, particularly kin and neighbours, as well as with supernatural forces, and – in the modern world – the effects on their lives of a wide range of modern institutions from hospitals to state agencies.

Official Western medicine, on the other hand – usually decribed nowadays as 'biomedicine' – operates within a theoretical framework which took a long time to come to terms with illness as a *social* phenomenon, initially with the recognition that epidemics were the outcome of poor sanitary conditions – in Britain, in the famous case of London's 'Broad Street pump', when it was found that 'black spots' of cholera clustered around water supplies.[4] Today the professional training of the doctor goes far beyond that kind of classic epidemiological study and includes exposure to the sociology, even the anthropology, of the social contexts in which illness occurs and in which it is treated, from the hospital to the home.

Yet the lengthy training of a doctor still also constitutes a 'deformation', since although the student acquires a formidable amount of knowledge, the basic framework is still a biomedical one. Patients too, even when told about social factors in illness, such as 'diseases of affluence' caused by irrational lifestyles (i.e. smoking or drinking onself to death), often ignore this advice, and doctors cannot *make* them change their ways. But neither patients nor doctors can do much about other social sources of illness, notably poverty, or change these social environments.

The incidence of illness is not only beyond their control; it is beyond their capacity to explain. In philosophical terms, doctors use 'meta-theoretical' conceptions like 'accident', 'chance' and 'disease', and effectively leave the entire subject to philosophers, theologians, psychologists or psychiatrists. In practical terms, they leave the handling of people with many chronic kinds of illness to psychiatrists, 'social' workers and the families of the afflicted.

Kongo Medicine: The Quest for Therapy

All cultures have their distinctive ideas and practices concerning illness. We will, however, take only one instance of a non-Western medical culture, a classic study of the Kongo of Zaïre by the anthropologist John Janzen and his medical colleague Dr William Arkinstall.[5]

During the centuries when it was the Kingdom of Kongo, then the Belgian Congo, the country today known as Zaïre suffered its own Holocaust – the loss of tens of millions of people as slaves. In the nineteenth century, when it was a personal possession of King Leopold of the Belgians, 10–20 millions more were killed in forced labour – those who failed to bring in rubber or ivory had their hands or feet chopped off.

It might be thought that after all this horror nothing would have remained of Kongo culture. Western ideas too had become deeply implanted long before the expansion of Christian missions in the nineteenth century – but so had a tradition of resistance. Not only did much of Kongo culture survive but new indigenous ideas and movements also arose. In the 1890s, a religious movement, Kimbanguism, named after the prophet Simon Kimbangu, combined Christian ideas with elements of indigenous religion to form a creed which nevertheless also rejected much of traditional belief.

A central aspect of the new religion was its attitude towards healing, interwined as it often was with conceptions of the supernatural. To most Europeans, curing involving magic was simply mumbo-jumbo. The missions, in particular, launched ferocious attacks on 'witchcraft' – a term they used indiscriminately for any of the many different kinds of indigenous belief in the supernatural.

The Belgian colonial authorities interfered with indigenous culture selectively and vigorously: in the political sphere, chiefs were deprived of their authority to judge and to sentence wrongdoers to death; in the medical sphere, indigenous 'doctors', the *banganga*, were refused the right to engage in ritual inquiry and accusation, especially trial by ordeal. But the attitude of adherents of the new cult towards 'tradition' was also ambiguous: on the one hand, they burned the cult paraphernalia used by the *banganga*; on the other, the equally traditional practice of curing at the hands of prophets (*bangunza*) was given a new prominence. By the 1930s, Kimbanguism had become a mass movement, its prophets hunted down 'with a paranoia unequalled in other colonial systems'. Virtually all *bangunza* the authorities could find were imprisoned, exiled or kept under surveillance until as late as 1958.[6] The Christ-like Kimbangu was himself sentenced to death, then kept in prison and finally died in 1951.

Medicine became a locus of political confrontation. The new sanitary laws, under which people were concentrated in larger villages in order to make improvements in hygiene easier, were resisted, as was the compulsory digging of pit latrines, even though the sanctions used included the destruction of houses or forced relocation. The Kimbanguists, then, were in religious conflict with the missions; in political conflict with the colonial government; and in cultural conflict with Western medicine.

There were, in fact, very few Western hospitals and doctors. In 1962, when Janzen began his researches, many villages were thirty miles from a hospital or dispensary which could only be reached on foot, on an infrequent passing vehicle or via a mission or government truck that had to be called by a messenger.[7]

The rigorous controls enforced during the colonial epoch did result in greater control of such endemic killers as sleeping sickness, yaws, leprosy, malaria, intestinal parasites and tuberculosis, though not their total elimination. Thus, though people may know very well that their water supplies are infested with bilharzia, if they have no alternative supply, 100 per cent of them will still suffer from it.

Western medicine remains thin on the ground, so respiratory infections kill from 25 to 75 per cent of those infected and diarrhoeas carry off from 10 to 50 per cent of children affected by them and by intestinal parasites. Sickle cell disease and whooping cough cause further casualties.

The Categories of Illness

At the turn of the century, the Kongo distinguished between three major categories of illness: illness of God, of the *nkisi* and of the *ndoki*.

The label 'illnesses of God', paradoxically, does not mean that they are seen as the result of divine intervention or retribution; rather, it refers to illnesses that are generally mild and in which no particular disturbance in immediate social relationships is entailed – illnesses we would call 'everyday' or 'natural', because we see them as part of the order of nature. They are 'natural' to the Kongo too. So illness or death among the very old and the very young is attributed to a variety of causes, ranging from poor diet to 'abuses', such as violating clan prohibitions and social laws.

The second category, *nkisi*, covers illnesses which were treated by specialists whose expertise derived from one of twelve cults which can trace their origins back to the twelve founding clans of the Kongo. Each cult has its special forms of sacred knowledge, the *nkisi*, and each has its own special medicines.

Two of these cults were oriented to the health of the community rather than that of the individual: one, *mpu*, was concerned with important rituals surrounding the consecration and inauguration of a chief; another, *lemba*, calmed the land and the villages. But the rest were linked with what both we and the Kongo would recognize as common problems: *mabola* with illnesses that affected young women; *muniangi* with cures for excessive menstrual bleeding; *mazinga* with measures to ensure the healthy birth of a child; *kilauki* with cures for skin diseases and eruptions; *mukoko* with cures for women's sterility; *mbola* with treatment for mouth diseases; *mpansu* with cures for insanity; *masekula* with measures to terminate a pregnancy; *mbwanga* with cures for headaches; while in *mpodi*, specialists used a cupping-horn to remove impurities from the body.[8] Some of these are areas we would label 'geriatrics' or 'obstetrics', while our practitioners would disclaim any use of *sacred* knowledge.

The third category of illness, *ndoki,* was brought about by witchcraft, though the supernatural powers witches used were often the same forms of sacred knowledge that *nkisi* practitioners used to cure rather than to harm people.

This division into three categories of illness, however, has changed over time. For indigenous culture was under a two-pronged attack – on the one hand, from the colonial authorities, and on the other, from the Kimbanguists. The Kimbanguists made people abandon or burn their *nkisi*. As a result, *nkisi* and *ndoki*, previously distinct, were collapsed into one category – 'illnesses of man' – while curing of illness shifted from the *banganga*, equipped with special ritual paraphernalia, to the *bangunza*, who had visionary powers.

Since independence, the state has formally backed Western medicine; traditional healers, of whatever variety, have no official status. Yet their activities are perfectly public. Officials recognize that they do cure people who would otherwise receive no treatment, though their cures often go far beyond physical illness – providing help to people who have been robbed, for example, helping them to get their property back, or dealing with cases of suspected incest. Even senior officials patronize traditional curers, much as members of the British Royal Family go to homoeopathic doctors and osteopaths, and provide testimonials to their efficacy. Many healers have a foot in both camps and use their experience of Western medicine, often as paramedicals or as ancillary staff in hospitals, clinics and dispensaries, to buttress their prestige when they perform as traditional healers. The one area of expertise of the indigenous medical practitioners almost universally approved of – and nowadays thought of as part of the 'authentic' cultural heritage of the country – is their knowledge of medicines, particularly medicinal plants. Magical devices and procedures, on the other hand, though equally part of indigenous therapeutic culture, do not receive official approval.

The Curing of Illness

Janzen and Arkinstall began by asking people what they *thought* about illness and its treatment. They found such inconsistencies between what people said they did and what they actually did that they shifted away from abstract questioning to following through actual cases of people engaged in the 'quest for therapy', sometimes walking with them for fifteen miles to watch a patient consult a diviner or, equally exhausting, driving over 'non-existent' roads which took their toll on their aged VW.

They soon found that illness was not perceived simply as something which happened to the individual. Social and supernatural factors were involved in the diagnosis, while the treatment of illness was managed by a *group*. It was not necessarily even the individual patient who consulted the doctor – they often played a very minor, passive part.

In other cultures, like that of the Gnau of New Guinea, studied by an anthropologist who is also a doctor, the sick person initiates the quest for therapy obliquely, by withdrawing from society. He 'shuns company and conversation, lies apart, miserable in the dirt or inside a dark hut, the door shut ... He eats alone [and] begrimes himself with dust and ashes.'[9] This is, of course, a highly public announcement that the individual is ill (which also serves to deceive the spirits who have caused the illness into believing that they have the sick person beaten), and is appealing to others to help the sick person get better, though thereafter he leaves it to them. The loosely organized Gnau have no illness specialists or expert healers; nobody examines the patient. Almost any adult will do to help the sick person – usually a senior man.

When people fall ill among the Kongo, they are usually able to doctor themselves. Mild illnesses, from which the patient usually recovers quickly, and which do not have major social consequences either for patients or for their kin, are thought of as unproblematic, and often correspond to our conception of diseases which are 'natural' in cause. Not many symptoms and diseases are attributed to social and mystical causes, though. They do not look for mystical explanations of the common cold, for instance, and treat most such illnesses simply with herbal remedies.

The body is thought of in ways quite different from those we use when thinking about the functions of the various organs. For the Kongo, just as each lineage has its own sphere of authority within the social order as a whole, each of the various organs has its special sphere. The abdomen – to us simply a place where food is processed – was, in the view of Nzoa-mambu, an important healer, specially linked to the vulva and the uterus, to pregnancy, to the mother's breast and lactation; it was the centre not just of material subsistence (milk), but also of descent, identity and repro-duction. The heart, the 'lord of the person', can be affected by factors out-side the body: because someone has been envious, has flouted certain moral codes or has practised witchcraft.

While Western doctors recognize that anger can raise blood-pressure, or that depression can be caused by feelings of guilt, Kongo doctors, when trying to find the *cause* of an illness, will consider a wider range of social and supernatural factors. Hernia, for instance, may be caused by lifting too hard, but might equally be due to bad moral behaviour. Blockages in the abdomen, from children's stomach complaints to appendicitis or sexual difficulties, even VD, may be attributed to the infringement of incest taboos or to human malevolence, from witchcraft to poisoning.

In his classic 1930s study of witchcraft among the Azande of the Sudan,[10] Evans-Pritchard showed that though witchcraft was part of the everyday environment, most people did not pass their days in constant fear of being bewitched. It was suspected only, rather, when something *ab-normal* happened. It was quite understandable that a hut should fall down when it had been built badly. But if a well-built hut fell and killed people sitting in its shade, this was an *extraordinary* event which must, therefore, be due to special factors – to witchcraft. We explain such events, statisti-cally, as the outcome of 'chance', though we may also introduce a moral element and describe them as 'misfortune'.

But the Azande think about causes more consistently. They observe that the collapse of the hut involves a remarkable *double* coincidence: the col-lapse of a soundly built hut and the death of someone who has done noth-ing to deserve dying in this way. Likewise, if a perfectly healthy person who has led a blameless life begins to suffer from chronic illness or sud-denly falls seriously ill, witchcraft will be suspected.

This is what is usually described, in most cultures, as 'witchcraft' – the deliberate use of magical powers to do harm to others. For the Azande, though, Evans-Pritchard calls it 'sorcery', in order to distinguish it from another kind of maleficent magic used in Zande culture, where a person can bring harm to others *unwittingly*, with no intention of deliberately hurting them, because he or she has witchcraft substances in his or her body. Deliberate or not, the use of magical powers is involved, and a par-ticular person is identified as the witch, the cause of the misfortune.

The arrival of the whites introduced a new kind of medicine, based on entirely different principles. As systems of ideas, the two were and are 'closed' off from one another. But when it comes to seeking a cure, especially for a serious condition, people move between both. They know that Western medicine may be efficacious. But it is not always so, nor does it provide an explanation of disease consonant with their conceptions of the connection between disease and misfortune and social and supernatural factors, and because Western medicine is not easily available and is expensive, most people use indigenous practitioners more often.

Most common illnesses simply involve a visit, perhaps accompanied by one or two relatives, to a herbalist, much as, in Western cultures, people take themselves off to the chemist or pharmacist, who prescribes a medicine, after which the illness usually goes away. Centuries of observation and thought, continuing experimentation and critical dissatisfaction with their own work provide Kongo healers, likewise, with an extensive pharmacopoeia of plant-derived medicines which are used not just for common minor complaints but also as tranquillizers, to cure snakebite or to bring about an abortion. A single Azande, Evans-Pritchard writes, may know more than 200 or 300 plants which yield drugs, and if all Zande knowledge were pooled, there would be well over 1,000. Nzoamambu cultivated no fewer than eighty-seven different kinds of herbs, trees and shrubs around his house.

Yet in a book of 544 pages, Evans-Pritchard devotes only one chapter to what he calls 'leechcraft', even though it is the humble 'leech' who treats toothaches, headaches, backaches, stiff necks, skin diseases, constipation, disease, pains in the abdomen or ears, drowsiness, poor sight and blepharoptosis.

Finding the *cause* of an illness, though, involves not just treatment but diagnosis. In Zande culture, this is done by divination, using oracles.

Anyone can carry out 'do-it-yourself' divinations because they call for only the simplest of techniques, such as putting sticks into termite mounds and observing if they have been eaten by insects. These inquiries are made in dealing not just with illness but with any kind of problem. The Azande, Evans-Pritchard writes, 'love to sit down in front of the oracle and think out every little problem which is troubling at the time and every possible misfortune which might assail them in the future'.[11]

Even women sometimes act as doctors and leeches, and operate simple oracles such as the termite oracle, especially in 'feminine' matters, from work-related activities to childbirth. But do-it-yourself medicine and do-it-yourself divination are ineffective when it comes to more serious illnesses: 'general and acute illnesses ... with sudden and severe symptoms and rapid course', and chronic illnesses which 'come on slowly, are protracted, and are not accompanied by violent symptoms or local sickness' – illnesses like those we call deep-intramuscular abscesses, pneumonia, epilepsy or cerebrospinal meningitis. When these strike, the Azande consult a specialist diviner.

Magical powers are an ambiguous asset, for those who possess them are open to the charge of using them for evil ends – practising witchcraft – for the same power can be used to cure or to harm. A person can be regarded as a diviner/magician, engaged in exposing and thwarting witches, but use the same techniques for evil ends. So though the common Western term 'witch-doctor' stigmatizes non-Western medical treatment, it does also express the two-sided, ambiguous nature of this kind of treatment.

The Azande avoid explicitly accusing their kinsmen of bewitching them, since this would make daily intercourse impossible. They are, however, perfectly prepared to accept the findings of an oracle when it seems to have come to the logical conclusion that an individual can be identified as the cause of the illness – for example, when a man against whom vengeance magic has been used actually dies, or when they put names of suspects to the oracle, until one, usually a known enemy, is selected.

But oracles can also be shown to have come to false conclusions. These shortcomings are sometimes accounted for as 'technical' failures – say, in the way the oracle has been operated. In the case of the poison oracle, for example, where poison is given to a chicken, it either dies (indicating a 'Yes' answer to the question put to it, such as 'Did so-and-so cause this illness?') or it survives (indicating a 'No' answer). We explain these varying outcomes in terms of *our* technical ideas – the chicken does or does not die because of biological factors (some chickens are stronger than others) or chemical ones (the amount or the strength of the poison). But to the Azande, failure can also happen because the proper *ritual* procedures have not been followed, or because some of those involved in the seance were in a state of ritual impurity, or had evil thoughts in their minds, or because people outside the oracle seance, probably the original witch, have used evil magic to distort the oracle's findings.

In any case, witchcraft accusations, like horoscopes in the West, are often couched in such general terms that they are difficult to falsify ('Something unusual is going to happen to you.'). And since knowledge about the verdicts of different oracles is neither pooled nor subjected to critical comparative analysis, people further afield may not be aware that a certain medicine or a particular healer has failed to cure someone. Though the Azande have prodigious memories, they lack any equivalent of the written case law or published scientific papers which our professionals look up when making systematic comparisons.

Evans-Pritchard identifies no fewer than twenty different types of explanation which the Azande use to explain such contradictions. Men of high rank, indeed, regard a lot of the magic that goes on as so much peasant, low-life activity (Evans-Pritchard calls it 'provincial'). But commoners too rank different kinds of oracles, and particular ones, as carrying more or less authority.

Superior diviners are able to arrive at more reliable verdicts because they use more powerful kinds of oracles, such as the 'rubbing-boards', which only older men own or can afford to consult. Even rubbing-boards, though, are not foolproof; those who operate them can fiddle the results by causing them to stick. So this kind of oracle may not convince everybody, and may be seen as no more than an 'inferior' and 'preliminary' step, a try-out. At this point, people turn to more reliable oracles.

The most authoritative oracle of all, the poison oracle, has an additional strength which lower-level ones lack, not because it draws upon some special mystical powers absent in the oracles operated by ordinary diviners, but because it is operated in the name of a prince. It therefore possesses *political* authority. Indeed, in very serious cases, such as killings or cases of adultery, the verdict of a prince's oracle is needed, and its findings may not be questioned. Finally, divinations carried out in the king's name carry the highest authority of all.

Within the terms of their belief system, then, Azande exercise considerable criticality. But oracles retain their credibility because they form part of a coherent intellectual system.

'Closed' ways of thought are by no means confined to Africa. In the West, they are characteristic of organizations based on ideological conformity, such as authoritarian political parties and religious sects. Thus in one such cult, in the American Midwest in the 1950s, it was prophesied that at midnight on 16 December a cosmic flood would overwhelm the earth, but that true believers would be saved by aliens from outer space who would take them to safety in their flying saucers. When the flood, the aliens and the spacecraft did not materialize, Festinger and his colleagues asked believers to explain this failure. Some did lose indeed faith as a result, but others were left unmoved, or explained it in terms of the cult's basic ideas. Thus perfectly ordinary phone calls were said to be 'really' messages from space, while anyone who came to visit cult members was declared to be 'really' a spaceman.[12]

The Therapy-managing Group

In the West, though, even in the epoch of Jamestown and Waco, these are the marginal, not mainstream, beliefs of people we denigrate as 'cultists'; nor, in our predominantly secular culture, do people who are ill usually seek treatment at the hands of curers who profess to rely on mystical powers. At first, like the Azande and the Kongo, we try to cure ourselves, taking advice from those around us, or ask the advice of a local chemist or pharmacist. If the illness persists, we then turn to doctors, and later to consultants and hospitals. Only when things get really desperate do we resort to non-medical help, including spiritual assistance.

The Kongo rely on much wider sets of kin and on fellow clan members from the beginning. Relatives suggest known competent healers and accompany patients on visits to consult them. If a cure does not result, they will help in the quest for a more highly skilled healer and other kinds of therapy.

The treatment of serious illness involves a succession of episodes, which Janzen and Arkinstall followed over time, as *historical* processes. Western doctors, of course, also keep case 'histories' — notes of physical symptoms, of medicines prescribed and of outcomes. But these are almost exclusively physical data. Kongo handling of serious disease involves a much wider and deeper investigation of the causes of the physical symptoms and the efficacy of the treatment.

Kongo society is neither as loose-knit as Gnau society nor as hierarchical as Zande society. Villages contain people belonging to different clans and lineages, so that only certain fellow villagers are likely to be called in, and only members of one's lineage or clan who are close neighbours.

But children of the same father and *his* matrilineage are also close kin and some time after getting married men can decide for themselves whether they will live with their father's or their mother's brother's people. So although matrilineal descent is the first principle of Kongo social organization, many different sets of kin are available and may be called upon for advice and help. This means that people can make choices as to whom they will involve, while kin themselves may or may not seek to intervene. All this makes for a good deal of what Janzen calls 'ambiguity and strain'. Like the Azande consulting oracles, then, the Kongo manipulate these alternatives.

As an illness continues, investigations become more elaborate, and more and more people get involved. In a serious illness, treatment goes through several stages of both diagnosis and treatment, in which different relatives become involved and different kinds of therapy.

In one case, a woman called Luzayadio had had a normal pregnancy and delivered her child safely. But she then began to suffer from swelling of the limbs, so she consulted a retired nurse (who gave her penicillin injections), while at the same time consulting a local curer. Dr Arkinstall diagnosed malarial parasites, but the treatment he recommended (emetine and chloraquin) was terminated by the family. Back in the village, representatives of the two clans involved were convened. They concluded that her illness derived from her intention to marry, improperly, a man from her father's clan. Though her father had approved the marriage and accepted a token payment, the full bride price had not been paid and her husband-to-be had gone off to town to earn the necessary money. Her mother, on the other hand, disapproved of a marriage which, to her, smacked of incest and was also akin to a kind of marriage contracted only by people of slave descent. These were the roots of the illness.

Western-trained staff at the local dispensary were unaware of (and uninterested in) these ideas, though one European nurse did note that Luzayadio's mother had said that the marriage was incestuous (a view disputed by an *African* male nurse!). At no point, though, did they communicate their (Western) diagnosis of the causes of the illness to the relatives.

Luzayadio then died and was buried in the graveyard of her matrilineage. Her mother took charge of the child. Yet the relatives displayed no uniformity as to what needed to be done. The two clans, even Luzayadio's father and mother, were at loggerheads over the bride price and the charge of incest – issues eventually resolved by the payment of ceremonial gifts.

In another case, a baby born to a woman who had already lost six out of ten children suffered head injury during delivery. Fearing another death, the mother removed the child from the hospital and went to see a prophet-diviner. Again, there was argument as to whether she had married a man from an acceptable social category, which threatened not only the life of her child but also the continuity of her lineage, as she was the only woman left. The healer treated the child with herbs, but also adjured the two clans to settle their differences. Finally, he urged that the child be taken back to hospital, where it died the next day.

In a third case, a woman was brought to a dispensary with no discernible physical symptoms. She refused to communicate either with her kinsmen or with hospital staff. With five children to bring up on her husband's wages as a doorman at a ministry in the capital, she had become a 'near-fanatic' member of a prophetic sect, and then became prone to psychotic episodes. But she also visited a Western-style dispensary, where she was given various medicines, after which she returned home. Insomnia and anorexia then followed. Finally, she was brought to the dispensary again by her husband, bound in the back of a truck. Though her kin were evasive about classifying her condition as madness (a disgrace in Kongo culture), this judgement was in fact implicit in the kind of healer her kin chose to treat her. She then attempted to escape and got kin to contact a prophetess for her. At the same time, her brother consulted a Protestant deaconess, who advised calling a clan reunion, though a senior Protestant pastor argued that this was sinful and that she should be taken to hospital. A clan reunion did then take place, at which it was decided to take her to a *nganga* who specialized in cases of madness. Without seeing her, he prescribed strong herbal medicines. She eventually arrived at the dispensary unconscious, though neither the *nganga* nor Dr Arkinstall could detect any physical symptoms of disease.

She then left the infirmary and was treated once more by the *nganga*, this time with a herbal meal. Gazing into her eyes, he 'saw' worms which were causing the trouble in her head. Making small incisions in her body, he applied plant juices and, after treating the eyes themselves, made her put her head into a bowl of water. In front of fifteen witnesses, worms appeared in the water. At this point, when Janzen and Arkinstall lost touch with her, the family was contemplating taking her to another prophet-diviner or taking the entire clan to the 'purification centre' of a modern sect.

In Kongo thinking, her condition was basically due to the deeply disturbing conditions of urban life, which had led, first, to her conversion to the sect, then to a love affair, resulting in profound feelings of guilt which, she felt, would be judged not only by her husband but also by God. In the cities, many women, dependent on their husband's small salaries, end up 'tilling the streets' – as prostitutes. Those who stay in the villages, separated from their husbands, have to feed their families on what they can grow, supplemented by small and irregular remittances from their absent spouses.

The Clan as Patient

Although these cases began because individuals were sick, not only were their immediate families drawn in but also wider networks of kin and members of their clans too. There are important differences, however, according to the sex of the patient. Those whom Janzen calls the 'subordinate' – young women generally, young wives and mothers (especially unmarried mothers) and the young – are more likely to come under the authority of the various sets of relatives who make up the therapy-managing group as the illness progresses. The group, which believes that it has a *duty* to take care of the patient, has what Janzen describes as virtually '*proprietary*' rights over treatment. It is *they* – whatever a consultant diviner may recommend – who choose a therapist, and, if dissatisfied with the treatment, will walk out on the healer and transfer the sick person to another healer or try a different kind of cure altogether.

Adult males, on the other hand, especially those who are able to walk and undertake journeys, who are adjudged capable of managing their own affairs and who have the financial means to pay for care, retain control over the treatment they seek and get. But as an illness continues, even they may become more passive and leave the treatment increasingly to the therapy-managing group.

In serious cases, as time goes on, more and more third parties become involved. This may even culminate in highly formal clan meetings, presided over by a ritual expert, following 'general rules of etiquette, debate, and public order', which Janzen likens to a court – no mere metaphor, since these meetings decide questions of guilt or innocence; possess powers to impose sanctions ranging from fines and compulsory marriage payments to demands that the parties bestow and receive blessings; and have the authority to decide who is to be responsible for a child's welfare and to make people reside where they tell them to.

At an even higher level, which Janzen terms 'grand kinship therapy', up to 1,000 people may be present. Such meetings are 'works of social art and organizational skill' in which hired speakers and prophets may participate in debates infused with litigiousness, with 'brilliant oratory, proverbs, enigmas, sanctions, songs, dancing, and hard rhetorical logic'.[13] There are sacrifices, blessings, gift exchanges and church services. When the prospect of an end to the tension is in sight, the occasion takes on the atmosphere of a 'festival' as the contestants regale the company with wines of different kinds, bottled beer or liqueurs, and feed them with garden produce, goats and pigs, and make gifts of bolts of store cloth, sugar, tea, coffee and cash.[14]

The therapy-managing group, then, is much more than another cultural variant of what in the context of the United States Freidson has called the 'lay referral group' – people in the patient's milieu, usually kin, who give advice (or help find good advice) about illness; who decide what issues are important and which are minor; and who 'exert ... pressure on the individual to behave accordingly'.[15] If they are educated 'WASPs', their ideas about illness may be consonant with those of doctors. But if they come from a different ethnic group or a different class, they may have different ideas and values.

The ranges of significant kin, though, are usually much less extensive than among the Kongo; nor are ethnic 'groups' in America anything like as highly structured as the Kongo clans. Though they may share similar cultural attributes, such as religion or language, they do not have anything like the same kind of authority over their relatives as the Kongo therapy-managing group does.

Since Kongo therapy is managed by the group, and strains in group relations underlie much illness, the logical extrapolation of this is that the clan itself is not just the agency which *handles* therapy but may also be the *object* of therapy: the clan, collectively, is the sick 'patient'. What may begin as individual illnesses can end by 'engulfing the entire clan, the local church organization within that clan ... non-kin prophet communities, and ... local government'.[16]

In one such case, a man named Mukala began to experience persistent pains in his back, neck and head; Mavungu, a fellow clansman, suffered from chronic stomach trouble; while Mbumba, a third clansman, was troubled by asthma. All of them were involved in a dispute over the ritual chiefship of the clan, which involved rivalry between senior and junior lineages. Traditionally, such roles used to be distributed over several lineages, but today – to the resentment of both junior and senior lineages – authority often becomes concentrated in lineages of middling status, a situation exacerbated now that educated young men leave for modern jobs, consigning leadership roles within the clan to minimally educated men.

Mbumba sought treatment for his asthma first at a local dispensary, then at a Catholic hospital and then at a Protestant hospital, and was finally X-rayed in a state hospital. None of them could establish the nature of his illness, or cure him, so he next went to a prophet. This man had originally been a catechist at the Swedish mission, had then joined the 1921–2 prophet movement, had been arrested and was able to return home only as late as 1959, after which he established a spiritual retreat centre to which many pilgrims came. He gave Mbumba holy water to drink; more importantly, he provided him with an interpretation of the true meaning of his illness. Before long, Mbumba was consecrated as a deacon of the church, along with others, in front of several thousand people, and began to work with the prophet. His asthmatic symptoms diminished and he returned home. Another prophetess then convinced him that all three men had fallen sick because of the irregularities in the way succession to the ritual clan offices had been handled. In addition, the pressures of his job as chief in a rural community, wages for which were continually frozen, led to new illnesses and this time he consulted both a French-trained psychiatrist and a prophetess.

The upshot was the convening of a general clan meeting, under the aegis of both the prophet and the prophetess, at which the clan was ritually reunified. The three patients knelt down while each of their kinsmen filed by and asked their forgiveness for a variety of shortcomings. They, in turn, were asked to acknowledge their own shortcomings, though some refused, demanding instead that past offences to *them*, over land and slave status, should be acknowledged.

This cleared the air. A year later, things had stabilized sufficiently for another meeting to be held without it being thought necessary to have ritual specialists present. The personal lives of the three men had also changed: Mbumba stayed with the prophet as his deacon; Mavungu, conversely, stayed at home and largely removed himself from public affairs; while Mukala also gave up the chiefship and occupied himself instead with clan affairs and cultivating his garden.

The Emergence of Biomedicine

Although it is individuals who fall ill, then, Kongo diagnosis and therapy see illness as supremely social; at the extreme, it is the clan which is the patient. It follows that the postulates and procedures of Kongo medicine differ radically from those of Western biomedicine, which focuses on the individual.

As we saw, all medicine operates within a set of ideas about the human body and its functioning which, in turn, rest upon a further set of *meta-medical* assumptions about the *meaning* of illness – the place both of human life and of medicine itself in the world as a whole.

The revolutionary assumption that began to gain ground in the West from the seventeenth century onwards was that the world we live in is a *natural* world. Everything in nature, including the human body, could therefore be studied using the same general assumptions and methods that are used in the study of rocks. This still left a place for the supernatural, though, and such was the persisting power of organized religion that the 'ultimate' questions – about the meaning of life, creation and the 'soul' – were still the special preserves of theologians, and the human mind was separated from the 'soul'. Eventually, though, even this terrain was contested by science, as physicians and psychologists tried to reduce the functioning of the mind to the functioning of the brain, and to treat mental malfunction by physical techniques, from surgery to drugs.

This separation of mind from body also penetrated deeply into the thinking of educated people. Philosophy now had to be based not on revelation but on scientific observation and the formulation of scientific laws. Yet Darwin still described his work as 'natural philosophy'; 'scientist' was a 'neologism that still seemed fairly foreign'.[17]

Before the revolution in science, medicine had been founded on the theory of the 'humours' and on astrology and alchemy. We saw in the case

of Newton that histories of medicine are teleological – they single out scientific elements in the genealogy of modern medicine which later became
dominant but in fact coexisted with older modes of thought for centuries.
These older frameworks, though, are ignored. Yet the theory of the humours began to be questioned only bit by bit, as it was seen to be incompatible with this or that new empirical finding, notably the anatomical
work of Andreas Vesalius (1514–64) and the later researches of William
Harvey (1578–1657) into the circulation of the blood. Even the discovery
of 'animalculi' as a result of the development of microscopes, by Leuwen-
hoek and Malpighi, did not undermine the medical profession's adherence
to Galenic medical theory, which dominated medical studies from the second century AD until well into the eighteenth century.

In the Middle Ages, the training of physicians took fourteen years and
included not just medicine but the classics, followed by study abroad at
distinguished centres like Paris, Salerno, Montpellier or Basle. As a result,
very few physicians emerged from this protracted and expensive training,
and most of them were scholars. When they did practise medicine, their
patients were kings and aristocrats.

Then, in 1518, the state awarded a charter giving monopolistic powers
to a new College of Physicians which would thenceforth control entry to
the profession and the training of entrants. Even so, they were licensed to
practise only in London, though Oxford and Cambridge universities and
bishops could also grant licences.

When the College was founded, there were fewer than threescore Fellows, and rarely more than fifteen over the next half-century. The physicians who were licensed wanted to *keep* it that way in order to recoup the
high cost of their education as fast as possible. But this social closure condemned them to a marginal role as far as the curing of illness in society as
a whole was concerned, for the poor could not afford their services.

For centuries, therefore, licensed physicians were only a tiny minority
among a vast range of curers who treated the ills of ordinary people in the
towns, cities and, above all, countryside.

None of them, licensed or otherwise, could do anything effective
against the big killers, smallpox, the ague (malaria), tuberculosis, the
plague, and syphilis, or for 'gout, dropsy, worms, rickets, spinal deformi-
ties, skin ulcerations, scurvy, repeated miscarriages, deteriorating sight
and hearing, gonorrhoea [and] depression', which did not necessarily kill
but made an active life impossible and daily existence a burden. So people
turned to other kinds of curers, of whom the barber-surgeons were most
numerous.[18]

Like the physicians, surgeons had been organized in guilds since the

Middle Ages, but their expertise, often developed out of dealing with wounds in wars, bore no resemblance to that of surgeons today, where 'brain surgeon' (like 'nuclear physicist') has become a popular shorthand for the ultimate in advanced science. Their social status, rather, was akin to that of other purveyors of quite mundane commodities and services, as indicated when they joined forces with the far more numerous barbers to form the Barber-Surgeons Company of London in 1520. Physicians, therefore, looked down on them.

Apothecaries, a much more numerous type of urban curer, were likewise of low status. The poor ones were little more than shopkeepers; indeed, they had been part of the Grocers' Guild since the fourteenth century and did not become independent of the grocers until 1617. In Norwich, the second city in England in Stuart times, with 17,000 people, there were only twenty-two formally qualified physicians. But for every one of them there were eight practitioners of many other kinds – forty-six barber-surgeons who were members of their Company, plus thirty-four others; thirty-six apothecaries; thirteen female practitioners, including midwives; three bone-setters employed by the city authorities; fourteen 'stranger' practitioners of various kinds, plus five 'itinerants'; and one 'astrologer, glover and empiric'. Their patients were 'critical, sceptical, and well informed' about the abilities of these different kinds of practitioner and about their individual skills, as were their families, kin and neighbours. They not only shopped around but bargained with practitioners in a way unknown today.[19] By 1775, surgeons, apothecaries and druggists outnumbered qualified physicians by more than eight to one, and provided treatments which today would be restricted to qualified doctors.[20]

Herbalism

In cultures dominated by print, we often assume that because we have a lot of documents we therefore necessarily know much more about our own medicine than we do about medical practices among peoples with merely oral cultures. In reality, the situation is the reverse: we know very little about the actual *practice* of medicine in the centuries before the rise of modern biomedicine, because there were no medical anthropologists or oral historians around to record how patients were actually treated.

Until the late eighteenth century, most people lived outside towns and cities. In the countryside, most illness had always been treated in the home – in the *domestic* rather than the public domain, as Stacey puts it [21] – and largely by the women of the household rather than during the more celebrated visits from the lady of the manor. Their main method of cure was the use of traditional herbal remedies.

The extent of illness has often been referred to as an 'iceberg of suffering', because most of it was (and is) not highly visible. But the *treatment* of illness also resembles an iceberg. Orthodox histories of medicine, which rely on documents, record only the one-seventh above the surface. The activities of thousands of unlettered 'folk' practitioners, such as the 'wise women' in the villages who treated their neighbours, are unrecorded. Documents, on the other hand, privilege those lettered ladies – the vicar's wife or the lady of the manor who took *noblesse oblige* seriously, or the more ordinary housewives for whom 'a good, reliable herbal, like a sound cookery book, was the first essential'.[22]

Such knowledge was shared, cumulative, collected together and handed down from generation to generation, like family Bibles. What got written down in these collections, though, was a mixture of culinary *and* medical plant-lore. In surviving copies, ladies wrote English equivalents of the Latin words and quantities in the margins, as well as their own favourite 'receipts'. Eventually, with the invention of printing, 'herbals' began to come off the printing presses, and in the vernacular. Gervase Markham's *The English Housewife* (1615) became the Mrs Beeton of its time. In later centuries, women curers kept up with newer medical developments; by the eighteenth century, medicine chests, complete with scales and other measuring devices, were to be found in many homes. By 1846, *Cox's Compendium to the Family Medical Chest and Compendium of Domestic Medicine* had gone into thirty-four editions.[23]

Herbalists, though, had long imported exotic drugs too. Mercury was known as 'Saracen's salve', while in 1597 'Joyeful Newes' was reported from South America: Spanish galleons were bringing back not only silver but also new drugs, above all guiac, as a cure for syphilis. Sarsaparilla was also first imported as a drug, 'China root', only later deteriorating into a mere popular drink, while in Britain a large trade developed with North America in cod liver oil. Such were the profits that some of the importing firms developed into major wholesale businesses and eventually into large pharmaceutical corporations.

The first printed 'herbals', though, were not derived from folk knowledge at all but were copies, in Latin, of venerated classical works such as Dioscorides' *De Materia Medica*. Even these fell into neglect for centuries, taking on a new lease of life only when a bridgehead was established at the medical school at Salerno between Arab and Western cultures. Greek and Roman writings which had been translated into Arabic were now retranslated back into Latin, together with translations of Arabic writings by Rhazes (Ar-Razi), Avicenna (Abu 'Ali Husain ibn Sina), Averroës (Abu-l Walid Mahammad ibn Ahmed ibn Rushd) and others.

This kind of intellectual traffic across what Charles Leslie has called the 'Oikumêne' of the world between Peking and Granada had gone on for centuries. Ayurvedic medicine, for instance, was known in the Mediterranean long before Greek medical texts were translated into Arabic and, in their turn, eventually reached India. (The Unani school of medicine in India today derives its name from 'Ionian'.)

Later, Europe imported medical knowledge from the great intellectual centres of the Muslim world such as Bokhara, Hamadan and Isfahan. In his *Qanun* (*Canon*), Avicenna alone wrote nearly a million words on philosophy, astronomy, physics, alchemy, geology and music, including five volumes on medicine which ranged from theoretical medicine to diseases and their treatment, including the uses of drugs; these writings became the most important source of medical knowledge for practitioners of medicine in *Europe* for the next half-millennium. Averroes' seven-volume *Kitab al Kulliyat* (translated into Latin as the *Colliget*) covered anatomy and physiology, pathology, general medicine, food, drugs and health regimens, and therapeutics, as well as commentaries on Avicenna and Aristotle (which, ironically, influenced the theology of St Thomas Aquinas).

Historical contacts like these may explain parallels found in the medical systems of countries very distant from each other. The conception of the 'humours', for instance – hot and cold, wet and dry – is found in cultures as far apart as China and medieval Europe, though the ancient Mediterranean Galenic medicine was based on only four humours, while Chinese medicine recognizes six and South Asian three. In the case of South America, where they are also found, some regard them as imported European ideas,[24] while others argue that they are indigenous concepts developed long before the Conquest.[25]

The first written description of herbal remedies in English dates as far back as 1260 but such herbals were normally written in Latin. There were none in vernacular Western languages until the publication of the German *Gart der Gezundheit* in 1485, and, in English, until the publication of the *Grete Herball* in 1526. Though they provided an abundance of information (John Parkinson's herbal of 1636 contained details about 3,800 plants), they still simply reproduced Greek, Latin and Arab authorities, and engaged in endless scholastic categorization rather than empirical observation. But all of them were driven by the search for medicines rather than by an abstract interest in botany for its own sake.

It took a social revolution before herbal knowledge became available in the vernacular, when Nicholas Culpeper translated the *London Pharmacopoeia* from Latin into English so that ordinary people could use it. A revolutionary in politics (he was wounded fighting for Parliament in the Civil

War), he was also the self-taught enemy of 'proud, insulting, domineering Doctors', who in turn accused him of everything from atheism to debased morals. But even his work was based on classical writings, and he also retained a strong commitment to astrology.

Folk herbal knowledge, on the other hand, was not based on Latin and Greek authors. People got most of the drugs they used out of their gardens and from the fields and woodland. Today, urban dwellers usually think about plants in aesthetic terms. They also distinguish 'wild flowers' – which we do not usually grow or collect – and 'weeds' – which we try to eradicate from our gardens – from the plants we deliberately grow simply because they delight the eye. But in past centuries virtually every plant, wild, weed or otherwise – acorns, aquilegia, irises, marguerites, feverfew, comfrey, cowslips, jasmine, mint, poppies, primulas, sage, raspberry leaves, oak bark, spurge, yarrow, verbena and literally many thousands of others – was not just as a source of colour but also of *medicine*. This knowledge was not derived from books or recorded in them; it was handed down by word of mouth.

Chemistry and Quackery

The stranglehold of classical learning was eventually broken not by the revival or extension of herbalism but via the emergence of a quite new kind of medicine: 'chemical' medicine. This revolution was led by an 'outcast' from orthodox medicine, Dr Theophrastus Bombastus von Hohenheim (mercifully more briefly known as Paracelsus). He had grown up in a mining centre in Carinthia, where he became familiar not only with minerals but with the occupational diseases of the miners. Later, he had wide experience as an army surgeon in Italy, Portugal, Prussia, Holland, Belgium and even in Scandinavia, Asia Minor and Tartary. Though widely read, he was highly contemptuous of the great medical authorities such as Hippocrates, Galen and Avicenna (he threw Avicenna's works on the fire in front of his students), excoriating the classic writers in such rumbustious style that the term 'bombast' is sometimes (probably wrongly) thought to be derived from his name.

To reach a popular audience, he lectured in German, not Latin. Publicly hostile to the Pope and Luther too, it is not surprising that he was driven out of Basle, and he spent the next thirteen years travelling, healing and lay-preaching.

'It is possible,' one writer has remarked, 'to prove almost anything by Paracelsus' writings.'[26] Another describes 'virtually everything' he wrote as 'enigmatic and unusual'. Only one of his books, indeed, was about medicine alone. The rest were mainly on cosmology and prophecy: 'magick,' he wrote, was a 'Great Hidden Wisdom', which is why he was widely accused of having 'intercourse with demons'.[27]

His botanical theories have proved to be equally unscientific, especially his belief in the 'doctrine of signatures': the notion that the physical structure of a plant gives a clue to its likely curative properties (thus the leaves of St John's wort have orifices which, he believed, indicate that they will be efficacious in curing diseases affecting the skin, because the skin too has holes in it).

But his belief that what he called 'ens' were the causes of illness represented a shift in thinking away from the whole patient, and even further away from the 'social' medical thinking of the Kongo, towards thinking of disease as caused by tiny entities, internal to the body, an approach which paved the way for the subsequent use of chemical substances in the treatment of disease, and for later biological ideas of germs, bacteria and viruses as causal agents.

Though his own knowledge of plants was very 'meagre' (not more than a couple of dozen plant names can be found in his works), he was not, as often thought, opposed to herbalism. Indeed, we could learn, he said, from 'old women, Egyptians [gypsies], and such-like persons, for they have greater expertise in such things than all the Academicians'. His chemical theories too, resting as they did upon the notion that sulphur, salt and mercury were the three 'principles' of all bodies, had little in common with modern chemistry. For him, 'mercury' represented fluidity; 'salt', stability and non-inflammability; and 'sulphur', change, combustibility, volatilization and growth.[28]

Despite these shortcomings, Paracelsus became the hero of the modernists, in part because of his demagogic attacks on authority, but mainly because he came to be seen as the founding father of modern, chemical pharmacology. For over subsequent centuries drugs produced from minerals slowly but inexorably were to drive out the older herbal remedies – the apothecary was to give way to the 'chemist'. For many people, though, either was preferable to orthodox medicine, which relied on purging by an 'evacuant' (emetic, diaphoretic, diuretic or purgative) and on bleeding – methods which condemned to agonizing death even the most eminent of their patients. Four of Louis XIV's heirs to the throne of France, three of them babies, were repeatedly bled, over weeks, until they died. Indeed, the House of Bourbon would have died out altogether had not their mother locked herself up with her last baby and refused to let the doctors near him. Charles II of England suffered the horrific torture of being blistered and bled for three days, until he expired.[29] The event was so horrific that it seared itself on the folk memory of people even in remote Devonshire, and found its way into R. D. Blackmore's *Lorna Doone* two centuries later:

'Dear Cousin, the doctor must know best … else what has he been brought up for?'
'Brought up for slaying, and murdering. Twenty doctors killed King Charles, in spite of all the women.'

The victory of the 'Paracelsians' ushered in a new epoch of 'heroic' chemical treatments, notably the use of 'herculean' quantities of calomel (mercurous oxide – long since abandoned because of its acute toxicity) and of antimony (tartar emetic). The latter caused massive salivation; extensive areas of facial flesh and bone became blackened, then mortified, then sloughed away, 'eye, cheek and all'. One eight-year-old boy in South Carolina had an incision made through the jawbone to remove eight to ten teeth, so that a 'Mott's dilator' could be inserted, enabling him to open his mouth. He was left with only three quarters of an inch between his incisors, the only teeth he had left.[30]

People in humbler walks of life were so terrified of the fate suffered by Louis and Charles at the hands of physicians that they preferred other kinds of practitioner. In any case, the only kind of full-time curer they were likely to come across was the 'quack' when he came round selling patent medicines on his circuits of the market towns or at periodic fairs.

Their huckstering style and vigorous self-advertisement was also entertaining, though it made them targets of abuse too. To Ben Jonson, a quack was a 'turdy-facey, nasty-pasty, lousy-fartical rogue'. Two centuries later, they were still classed with 'Highwaymen', 'Kidnappers', 'Pretended Friends', 'Bawds', 'Pimps', and 'Fortune-tellers'. But they were not in fact all charlatans. Like the women of the household, they employed traditional herbal and other remedies, also developing new ones (to the admiration of Francis Bacon), including mercury and antimony, and even pioneered inoculation. The most distinguished included men like Culpeper; the worst were killers rather than curers – like most licenced physicians.

The traditional quack was a true descendant of the Renaissance *ciarlatani*:

in eye-catching garb, sometimes exotic or hinting at an official uniform … generally accompanied by a stooge – a harlequin, clown or zany – whose job it was to draw a crowd and soften up the by-standers with fooling, dumb-show, doggerel, conjuring, and tumbling … backed by props such as cats, snakes, monkeys, skulls, stuffed alligators, alchemical apparatus, and surgical instruments,[31] he worked the crowd from a stage, or from his horse, surrounded by banners, bunting, music and testimonials from satisfied, especially distinguished clients. Some claimed to be able to preserve life for 'at least' 150 years. Flanked by bearded ladies and mummified giants, the charlatan put on a good show, full of patter, as he cried up his wares. What went into his remedies was usually a trade secret, though no less so than the remedies purveyed by physicians, who equally 'puffed up' 'proprietary' medicines, some of which bore their own names, or that of a colleague or a prestigious spa, like Dr Nehemiah Grew's Epsom Salts (which still sells today).

But in a new, increasingly urbanized mass market, curers were beginning to find their customers via a much more impersonal market-place. By the end of the eighteenth century, purveyors of patent medicines were using a new medium of mass communication: print. There were handbills in their hundreds of thousands and newspapers in their *millions*, while circulating libraries and bookshops were also often outlets for these medicines. In 1784, one Coventry bookshop listed over 100 of them, ending with:

Radcliffe's Purging Elixir
Ruston's Pills for Rheumatism
Royen's Ointment for the Itch
Spilsbury's Drops
Stoughton's Elixir
Swinfen's Electuary for the Stone and Gravel
Spirits of Scurvy Grass
Sans Pareille Powder
Storey's Worm Cakes
Smyth's Scouring Drops
Steel Preservative
Specific Purging Remedies for Veneral Diseases, by Wessels
Tasteless Ague and Fever Drops
Turtington's Balsam
Tincture of Centaury
Tincture of Valerian
Vandour's Pills, for Nervous Complaints
Velno's Vegetable Syrup
West's Elixir.[32]

Some quacks even got taken up in court circles, becoming very wealthy. 'Chevalier' Taylor, who 'dropped names like petals', described himself as 'Opthalmator Pontifical Imperial and Royal' at the courts of the

Kings of Poland, Denmark and Sweden, the Electors of the Holy Roman Empire, the Princes of Saxegotha, Mecklenberg, Anspach, Brunswick, Parme, Modena, Zerbst, Lovière, Liège, Bareith, Georgia, etc. and claimed to have treated Handel and to have restored Bach's sight. Despite this 'inordinate ... ballyhoo', he had received the finest surgical education available, with MDs from Basle, Liège and Cologne, and lectured in Latin as readily as in English or French.[33]

The Development of Scientific Medicine

But newer methods of treatment were increasingly being used. By the beginning of the eighteenth century, even so ancient a system as astrology had been abandoned by most quacks. The future of medicine lay with the emerging 'natural' sciences of chemistry and biology, and with empirical research rather than knowledge of classical texts. The elimination of scurvy from the British Navy, commonly attributed to the perspicacity of Captain Cook, had in fact been developed long before him and culminated in the work of a naval surgeon, James Lind, who, after reading everything in the medical literature, carried out clinical trials in which twelve patients were isolated and put on different diets for two weeks: cider; garlic and gum myrrh; elixir of vitriol; vinegar; and sea water. Meanwhile, the remaining two had two oranges and a lemon every day. Although the oranges and lemons ran out on the sixth day, the two who ate them were on their feet at the end of the fortnight; one had resumed his duties, while the other was nursing his comrades. All the rest showed little improvement.[34]

By the early nineteenth century, French researchers were isolating chemical causal agents of disease: Pelletier's work on ipecacuanha and quinine laid the foundations for the chemistry of alkaloids, followed by Magendie's isolation of strychnine. It was the latter's insistence on precise dosages and quality control, and his introduction of these methods into medical education, that paved the way for later breakthroughs, notably by Liebig, who laid the theoretical bases of both organic chemistry and biochemistry, disseminated through his *Pharmaceutical Journal*, which provided students with rigorous model procedures and guaranteed success even for the weakest of them. And by turning his research findings into mass-production businesses – including his famous meat extracts – Liebig laid the basis for the modern pharmaceutical industry.

Surgery also was transformed by the introduction of ether in 1847 and by the antiseptic techniques pioneered by Lister and Semmelweiss in obstetrics. These breakthroughs were so successful that chemistry now threatened to usurp the traditional leading role of medicine.[35]

Parallel breakthroughs came in the field of biology. After the development of vaccination by Jenner and the development of bacteriology by Bassi, Schonlein and Henle, culminating in the work of Pasteur and Koch, the body could now be thought of as a complex of cells. Contemporaries were so impressed that a proposal to inoculate all the youth of France with syphilis was once laid before the Paris Academy of Medicine.[36]

The introduction of the methods of natural science into medicine called for radical changes in the traditional organization and management of the professions which dominated medicine, for by the end of the eighteenth century London's Colleges of Surgeon and Physicians had degenerated into little more than 'exclusive gentlemen's clubs ... entrenched oligarchies, dominated by self-perpetuating cliques'.[37]

Socially, doctors were still treated with hauteur by their rich aristocratic patrons: on their visits to a castle or hall, they were likely to be given hospitality in the kitchen rather than in the drawing room, and were subject to the whims of people who might as readily turn to another physician or to other kinds of practitioner.

Such patronage, in any case, was becoming irrelevant in a new sort of urbanized society in which diseases did not recognize class boundaries. Scientific medicine now took place in the laboratory, and increasingly physicians and their patients met in a new kind of institution, the hospital, which was also the place where new generations of physicians received their training.

Medieval hospitals had been places not for the sick but for those – especially the elderly – needing shelter. Hospitals built after the Reformation were a mixture of prisons and reformatories, or housed children with no family side by side with lunatics and the helpless. In England, the 1720s saw the arrival of a new kind of hospital, the 'voluntary' hospital. 'Voluntary' reflects their funding, not by Church or state but by rich royal, aristocratic or civic patrons, who had the right to nominate themselves and others, including the 'sick poor', as patients. The senior posts in these hospitals were held by honorary 'consultants' who often carried out only a weekly ward round. Though they were unpaid, their posts were permanencies. As late as 1860, there were only 1,200 of them out of 15,000 doctors in 117 of the larger voluntary hospitals. Collectively, therefore, they occupied strategic positions which constituted an immensely profitable monopoly; within the hospital, posts could be bought and sold, or allotted to relatives.

It was the charity hospitals which became the crucial arenas for the development of advanced medicine. The consultants also controlled recruitment to the profession:

Teaching and examining were rapidly concentrated in [their] hands ...
[They] designed the curriculum, the syllabuses, and the examining; in
other words, they controlled the process of defining professional
competence. This gave them an exceptionally powerful position which
they have continued to defend.[38]

It was these hospitals, especially the teaching hospitals, which were to
'become the bastion from which the consultant surgeon and physician
could reach out to dominate the profession as a whole, as well as the auxiliary or para-medical occupations'.[39]

Most of the work was done by 'junior' doctors, all of whom, even the
most senior, were regarded as trainees and at first even had to pay consultants for their training. They were also forbidden to engage in private practice outside the hospital. Senior doctors, unable to become consultants,
often resorted to opening their own private hospitals. Consultants, on the
other hand, were able to cash in on reputations made in the hospital by
treating private patients outside.

Foucault has claimed that by the second half of the eighteenth century,
life as a whole had become increasingly 'medicalized'. But the small number of licensed physicians, restrictions on the kinds of illness treated in
hospital and the exclusion of children, pregnant women, the consumptive,
those who were dying, epileptics and those suffering from VD or infec-
tious diseases meant that sizeable sections of the population, and major
types of illness, were not catered for at all. Beneath these apparently diverse exclusions lay a clear economic rationale: only the 'useful classes'
were to be admitted. The rest had either to pay for private treatment or to
rely upon their relatives or the parish – a 'choice' which meant death or
destitution for most of them.

By 1834, the state had finally to accept the need to provide medical care
for the sick poor, under a new Poor Law which introduced a lower tier of
health provision. Even then, only the able-bodied were eligible for admission to these new, often unsanitary, hospitals, where most of the nursing
was done by people who were themselves paupers.

Professional medical treatment was provided by 'general practitioners',
who had emerged in the eighteenth century and provided what has been
called a 'one-man medical service' – medical, surgical and obstetric services, plus pharmacy – for the poor and middle classes. The doctors who
emerged from the new teaching hospitals found themselves, on graduation, treating the sick in patients' homes or as outpatients or longer-stay
patients in 'cottage' hospitals. Day-to-day treatment of the sick remained
at the level of the 'local state', where general practitioners, brought up to

think of themselves as gentlemen, now found themselves answerable to and paid by new patrons – not the rich (they were monopolized by the consultants) but penny-pinching Boards of Guardians, local authorities, sickness 'clubs' and eventually – horror of horrors! – trade unions.[40]

The appalling insanitary conditions of a new kind of urban 'mass' society also produced new epidemics, and therefore medical 'panics', such as the successive outbreaks of cholera which killed tens of thousands of people in London, culminating in the outbreak of 1854. Finally, the deployment of new statistical techniques – not laboratory research – tracked down the source of the disease to the water drawn from London's insanitary wells and in the process established a new, social branch of medicine, epidemiology.[41] Together with the need to control VD in the armed forces, these researches led to the establishment of special hospitals for the treatment of contagious diseases – notably scarlet fever, typhus, smallpox and enteric disease – and the enforcement of sanitary measures such as fumigation and ventilation. Like the Poor Law hospitals, the new 'fever' hospitals also provided 'good clinical material' for the training of new generations of doctors.

It was a profession, though, with many internal divisions of specialty and rank, and with powerful competitors from outside. Surgeons had long defended the independence of their profession from the physicians. Indeed, their college was upgraded to a *Royal* College in 1806, six years before the physicians' College achieved similar recognition. The position of the apothecaries, though, was much more insecure. Though they had been licensed to sell drugs since 1617, the drugs had to be prescribed first by a physician. Physicians used the law to get the shops of apothecaries suspected of breaching it raided or closed down; breaches were not difficult to prove, since nine out of ten apothecaries were still totally unqualified even in the late eighteenth century and many were undoubtedly dangerous prescribers (though no more so than most physicians). The medical profession's hostility to them was based on quite material grounds, for doctors made three-quarters of their income from dispensing themselves.[42] Even in 1815, when apothecaries finally got the legal right to practise, they could only *dispense* drugs; physicians alone could *prescribe* them.

Apothecaries eventually fought back by 'scientizing' their profession: embracing the new science of pharmacology and establishing a professional distance between themselves and the ever-growing numbers of untrained over-the-counter chemists and druggists by establishing the Royal Pharmaceutical Society in 1841.

The 'imperialists' among the physicians were determined to resist any expansion of the powers of other upstart specialisms and fought a protracted battle to control *all* types of medical practice. In the eighteenth century, apothecaries had to give up membership of Apothecary Hall before obtaining the licence of the Surgeons' Company, and as late as 1830 they had to give up membership of their own qualifying bodies before they could be admitted as licentiates of the Royal College of Physicians.[43] Despite the ancient lineage of predecessor bodies such as the 'Worshipful' Society of Apothecaries, and their new status as a 'Royal' Society, they were still not allowed to visit their predominantly poor and middle-class patients and prescribe for them. Not until 1907 did they secure recognition of their training as a complete medical qualification.[44]

The physicians fought a particularly ferocious campaign to protect and enhance their powers, led by the very unconventional Thomas Wakley, editor of the *Lancet* and later a Member of Parliament, who spoke not just for the consultants but for the GPs too, insisting on their kind of formal medical education as the prerequisite of eligibility to practise. He reserved his special fury for quacks, 'recklessly risking libel suits in order to expose them'.[45]

Demarcation disputes over the power to control the different fields of medicine continued to rage throughout the nineteenth century. The power of the state was the crucial resource. Parliament therefore became the main locus for these battles – no fewer than sixteen bills were introduced to reform medical practice before 1858 (Peel sardonically remarked that 'hardly a session passed without a Salmon Bill and it now seemed to be the case that the same was true of Medical Bills'), when the Medical Registration Act of that year finally 'sealed the process of professional closure and set up a single register of legally recognized practitioners with self-regulatory powers and a monopoly over not only the title of "doctor", but also state medical employment'.[46]

A massive expansion of the profession in order to service the new demands of mass medicine was, however, inevitable. The Colleges remained the bastions of the power of the hospital consultants, but the new race of GPs and the underpaid and overworked doctors who staffed the Poor Law hospitals began to organize themselves. By 1840, they had already established the Poor Law Medical Officers' Association. But they had no representatives on the General Medical Council, the key decision-making committee of the British Medical Association until 1886, and then they were not directly elected. (A College of General Practitioners – not 'Royal' – was established only in 1952!)

Though the GPs had absorbed much of the ideology of those who led the BMA and the Colleges – that it was 'not a pleasant matter' for educated gentlemen to serve under committees of working men[47] and that

the high status of medicine derived from its basis in scholarly knowledge –
this contradicted the market situation of the GP.

The situation of the specialists and consultants was equally contradictory. On the one hand, they continued to maintain the distance between
themselves and GPs and doctors who worked for Poor Law authorities or
trade unions and friendly societies, shamelessly manipulating constitu-
tions to ensure their control. As late as 1876, the Royal College of Surgeons refused to allow voting by ballot papers, thereby giving a crucial
advantage to those resident in London.[48] But the consultants, and the
BMA, needed the GPs as a mass base when dealing with government.
While continuing to cultivate the image of medicine as the epitome of
middle-class respectability, the dinosaurs in the Colleges now began to
look down on the BMA as a body now becoming swamped by GPs. The
physicians resisted attempts to undermine the pre-eminence of medicine
by having doctors qualify in surgery and pharmacy.

But differences between the GPs and the élite leaderships in the Colleges were not absolute. GPs were just as concerned to maintain the sanctity of private practice. Though the bulk of the patients they treated were
poor people, they fiercely maintained their right to charge fees to those
whom they considered *were* able to afford to pay. What constituted
'poverty' therefore became a central issue in the 'battle of the clubs', as
Poor Law doctors, with more and more patients on their hands, demanded from their employers more staff and improved working conditions, better pay, rights to superannuation and that drugs be paid for out
of the rates (local taxation), not out of their own pockets.

As the century wore on, GPs therefore began to use their numbers
within the BMA to put pressure on the leadership to campaign for *their* interests, not just those of a leadership primarily concerned with preserving
the privileges of the hospital consultants and their private practices.

Private Medicine and State Medicine
By the end of the nineteenth century, then, organized medicine had won
the decisive backing of the state. Yet there were still internal battles to be
fought between the physicians and their rivals. With the well-established
surgeons they had reached an accommodation in which each recognized
the other's expertise, the special place of medicine was still asserted: those
wanting to specialize as surgeons had first to be trained as physicians – a
path subsequently followed by anaesthetists, obstetricians and gynaecologists, pathologists and psychiatrists. The ancient struggle with the apothecaries, on the other hand, was brought to an end in a different way:
pharmacists could qualify without taking a full medical degree, while

pharmacology was given an important place in the training of doctors.

Other specialisms, though, were kept at a distance. Midwives succeeded in winning state recognition of their claim to be a profession in their own right as early as 1902, followed by dentists in 1921 and nurses in 1929. But as late as the Second World War, the BMA was still resisting attempts by opticians and chiropodists to achieve similar recognition, fearing that there would be no end to this proliferation of new classes of specialized practitioners outside their control. Despite the BMA's efforts to assert a 'sovereign' relationship to these upstart professions, the outcome was a compromise. Medicine needed their co-operation, so they were eventually recognized, in the words of the act of 1960, as professions 'supplementary to medicine'.[49] But they were still only the outworks of a medical system dominated by physicians and surgeons from their power base in the teaching hospitals and with direct lines to government.

With these limitations, the supplementary professions gradually achieved a recognized place and were conceded greater power and prestige. Degree-level qualifications for nurses, which had existed for decades in North America, were finally introduced in Britain, and most senior nurses became 'managers', theoretically equal in status to doctors and administrators in planning hospital services. The profession even got its own Royal College.

In reality, nurses were still dogged by their cultural origins as an extension of the domestic roles of housewife and mother, and so still 'trapped in a gender-subordination to doctors'.[50] In an overwhelmingly female profession, most of the managers in nursing were men; the women still did the bed-pan work.

The relationship of midwives to doctors took a different direction. After centuries of confrontation with doctors, they were finally able, in 1902, to be inscribed on a register if they met certain requirements. Although, to the chagrin of the medical profession, the board set up to control the profession did not contain a majority of medical practitioners, doctors were still able to ensure that in matters of professional practice and private morals, midwives remained subject to both local authority and medical control.[51]

The power of the doctors and the weakness of the midwives were exposed vividly in the 1960s, when 'painless childbirth' and home delivery had become a mass demand among women. I was one of a handful of men, among thousands of women who crowded to hear Dr Grantly Dick Read on one of his lecture tours; in France, Dr Lamaze had a similar following. But the medical profession had other ideas. In 1959, the Cranbrook Committee recommended 70 per cent of births should take place in hospitals within the next few years; by 1967, another committee set a target of 100 per cent. Midwives, now highly trained, had nevertheless been 'reduced to the status of technical nurses working under medical direction in the majority of cases'.[52]

A more combative stance was adopted by those who dominated medicine towards occupations in less central areas of health. Here the strategy was to deskill them, so as to nip any pretensions to professional status in the bud. The chiropodists, for example, went out of their way not to alienate the doctors, but it did not do them much good – they were made to accept a ban on any surgery under the surface of the skin and a limitation of their role to the care of 'superficial excrescences occurring on the feet'. One can see why: in a profession so *un*holistic that only paediatrics and geriatrics divide patients other than by a part of the body,[53] were physicians to lose control over special skills such as child delivery, or to allow new professions to appropriate one part of the body after another – the feet, the eyes, the spine and skeletal system – they would be left with only 'internal' medicine.

Such borderlines seemed arbitary to those who asked why illnesses of the ear, nose and throat are regarded as part of medicine and surgery – and therefore call for treatment by qualified doctors and surgeons – while teeth are not. Dentistry, for instance, like pharmacy, a long-established specialism outside the control of organized medicine, was a profession recognized by the state as long ago as 1858, when those who had been put on a register kept by the General Medical Council were to be recognized as qualified dentists. But the price paid for state recognition was a 'substantial degree of medical control and supervision'. By 1918, around 4,000 dentists had undergone a training recognized by the General Medical Council; but 9,000 still had not, and without this unqualified majority there would not have been enough dentists to serve the community. So, in 1921, there was a compromise: those who had been practising for five years would be put on to the new register – and thereby come under the control of organized medicine.

Ironically, the dentists then went on to introduce similar strategies of professional 'closure' to keep dental 'dressers' (auxiliaries), especially those in the school dental service, from threatening their new-found professional status by undertaking diagnosis and surgical treatment. Instead, they were restricted to cleaning, polishing, applying and removing dressings and temporary fillings, charting and recording. For what the doctors feared had actually happened in New Zealand, where, from the 1920s onwards, school dental nurses had undertaken local filtration anaesthesia, fillings, extractions and some preventive dentistry, without immediate supervision from qualified dentists, for almost all schoolchildren, a model whose success has led twenty-six other countries, mostly in the Third World, to follow suit. In Britain, conversely, with few such assistants, and those confined to strictly supervised routine work, surveys in the 1970s were still finding that 80 per cent of fifteen-year-olds needed treatment for both dental caries and for periodontal disease.[54]

But most medical occupations aspiring to professional status lacked the clout of pharmacists and dentists. In 1938, for instance, a board was established to license what were called 'auxiliary' occupations, whose members were required to work under medical direction and had to meet BMA requirements. Some paramedical occupations resisted: the ophthalmic opticians refused to join and the physiotherapists withdrew. The former, members of a profession which had produced significant scientific breakthroughs in the fields of both refraction and clinical optometry, put up a stout fight but still ended up with only a minority on the General Optical Council.

Concessions, then, were won by some of the paramedical professions, but overall they lost the battle, since they 'were not empowered to re-skill themselves'. On the contrary, by 1951, the boundaries of the previous decades were consolidated in law.[55]

Attempts by other specialties, even such an ancient one as herbalism – promised royal protection from 'all time from henceforth' four centuries earlier – to win recognition for themselves as autonomous health professions was given short shrift: they were contemptuously refused state recognition in 1923. The idea that chiropodists might go beyond their humble origins as itinerant corn-cutters and treat the joints of the foot too (and perhaps even the hands) was swiftly snuffed out by the doctors and orthopaedic surgeons.[56] The newer professions were left with varying degrees of autonomy, because they were useful, but only when 'subordinate to medicine's ascendency'.[57]

Those who dared to claim to be more than specialists in this or that illness or part of the body, and to possess a complete theoretical system, alternative to biomedicine, brought down upon themselves the wrath of organized medicine. In 1931, and again in 1933, 'the most jealous trade union in the world', as one member of the Lords described the BMA, backed by Ministry of Health officialdom, defeated the Osteopaths Registration Bill. During the Second World War, they were rejected as participants in the Emergency Medical Service. After the war, they were excluded from the new National Health Service.[58] Not until the Osteopathy Act of 1995 were osteopaths finally given control of their profession by the state.

These various struggles did enable many groups to achieve recognition by the medical profession and its ally, the state, as long as they met the educational requirements laid down by these two powerful institutions. Larkin has perceptively likened the outcome to the Indian caste system, in which what has been called 'Sanskritization' takes place, when whole castes succeed in achieving some degree of upwards collective mobility by imitating the behaviour of superior castes, but in so doing '*reproduce the overall hierarchy*'.[59]

In 1911, the relationship between the medical profession and the state entered a new phase: adaptation to mass medicine. Despite the BMA's last-ditch attempt to restrict the proposed National Health Service to those 'least able to pay', the act eventually gave access to medical treatment to those who paid National Insurance contributions. The most significant opposition came not from the consultants but from the GPs, 26,000 of whom, out of 32,000, refused to work within the new Act, a refusal which continued until 1913, with further wrangling over levels of remuneration. Differences of interest as between consultants and the GPs gave way to solidarity in the face of what both saw as a greater threat. Junior doctors finishing their training today still work inordinate hours (eighty hours a week or more is quite common), yet they offered no effective opposition until a strike in 1975. Despite public sympathy for them and the nurses, the situation is little improved.

By the outbreak of the Second World War, the doctors, despite their fears, had discovered that the new system was good for them. The poor practitioner had practially disappeared, the profession had become 'staunchly middle class' and the scheme proved far less expensive than initially feared. The BMA became a strong supporter, while 90 per cent of GPs were now participating in it:

The general practitioners, through the British Medical Association, had shown that they were able to use the private power generated by their well-organized and entrenched position to force the state to concede the profession's claims on almost all the key issues.[60]

If the profession had been satisfied, the scheme had not achieved its main social purpose – to bring medical care to everybody. As late as 1938, it still covered only 40 per cent of the population. The second major step in the extension of medical services to the population as a whole came with the establishment of the National Health Service in 1948, as a result of the new democratic mood and the positive experience of wartime medical services, including the 40 per cent of doctors who had served in the forces. The fears of Conservative physicians of what the left-wing Minister of Health Aneurin Bevan would do did not materialize, for he steered well clear of either a centralized state socialist medical service (as in the USSR) or a devolved form of co-operative medicine based on shared facilities in local health centres.

Organized medicine, in fact, was left in a stronger position than before. The inner committees of the BMA and of the Royal Colleges retained great powers and were strongly represented on the major bodies which determined national policy. Any potential opposition by senior members of the profession was silenced, in Bevan's own words, by 'stuffing their mouths with gold' – the teaching hospitals retained control of their (often extremely wealthy) endowments and enjoyed pay scales that made other professions jealous. GPs were more strongly represented on the new local health executives than they had been before on lower-level committees, while the powers of local authorities were actually diminished. Patients were the least well represented – they could not choose their own specialists but had to be 'referred' to them by their doctors. Overall, Parry and Parry conclude, organized medicine had carved out for itself 'a constitutional position in the realm matched only by the Church and the Law'.[61]

The Hegemony of Biomedicine

The consolidation of the power of the doctors within organized medicine was not just a structural process; it also involved establishing the cultural hegemony of biomedicine. Taken together, these developments gave the medical profession a degree of pre-eminence in the field of illness that constitutes an 'ideal type' of what Kuhn has called a 'dominant paradigm'. Despite the climactic public humiliation of religious orthodoxy in the person of Bishop 'Soapy Sam' Wilberforce by 'Darwin's bulldog', T. H. Huxley,[62] until quite late in the nineteenth century the reputation of the medical profession was anything but prestigious. In the 1840s:

medicine was often characterized as a profession filled with marginal men: drunken, randy medical students; half-caste army and navy surgeons; impecunious Scots with dubious medical degrees in their kits [kilts? PW]; and irreligious professors of anatomy who furtively purchased exhumed corpses from grave-robbers ... The line between the 'doctor' and the shopkeeper, at least in the eyes of the lay public, was very thin indeed.[63]

But as the century wore on, the new breakthroughs in chemical medicine strengthened the belief that disease could be licked by new kinds of 'magic bullet'. And the mid-century advances in pharmacology did indeed continue into the twentieth century: Ehrlich's '606' (Salvarsan), in 1910, to combat syphilis; insulin for treating diabetes in 1923; the development of penicillin from 1928 onwards; the first of the sulpha drugs in 1935. One of the fiercest critics of biomedicine has acknowledged that 'for the first time doctors could actually treat and cure meningitis, pneumonia, and other disorders, as distinct from helplessly observing their progress from the bedside'.[64] The Second World War stimulated the production of even more miracle drugs: streptomycin for use in TB; in the late 1940s, broad spectrum antibiotics – 'not so much bullets as grape-shot, lethal to a wide range of pathogenic bacteria'; later, the development of cortisone for treating rheumatoid arthritis, anti-malarial drugs, antihistamines, Beta-blockers and, eventually, mood-changing drugs and sex hormones.

But though the scientific community and the medical establishment were impressed with these achievements, public confidence in organized medicine was less wholehearted, since for ordinary people the major diseases they suffered from were diseases of poverty and the reorganized medical services still did not reach the majority of the population. Even after the 1911 Act, two out of five people were still not covered by National Insurance.

As for the advances in the efficacy of medicine itself, one noted authority has argued that social and economic changes, especially improved housing and education and family limitation, together with sanitary reform (sewage and drainage systems and the purification of water), were more important in reducing susceptibility to disease than prophylactics like vaccination or changes in the organization of medicine, particularly where diseases of childhood were concerned – diphtheria, measles, whooping-cough, tuberculosis and polio.[65] Despite the evident power of modern drugs, therefore, even many doctors, especially liberals, radicals and socialists – celebrated in literature from Dr Lydgate in George Eliot's *Middlemarch* (1871) to Dr Andrew Manson in A. J. Cronin's *The Citadel* (1927) – saw 'social' medicine, especially modern sanitation and improvements in living standards, as the best way of tackling diseases among the masses, rather than the development of more and more sophisticated chemical drugs.

Alternatives to Biomedicine

The Persistence of Popular Medicine
In Britain between the two world wars, doctors and nurses had moved to the top of ratings of occupations, though this did not manifest itself in the

salaries nurses were paid. The new-found public respect for medicine was consolidated after the Second World War, with the establishment of the National Health Service, the jewel in the crown of the new Welfare State.

For serious illnesses, the family doctor, to whom most people turned when they fell ill, referred them to specialists and clinics in hospitals. So in 1950 family practitioner services consumed only a third of NHS expenditure; by 1980, a fifth. By 1984, 80 per cent was being spent on hospitals, though 75 per cent of abnormal symptoms were treated not only outside hospitals but outside the professional health-care sector altogether.[66]

For minor illnesses too, even today, people consult their GPs only about once out of every five times they feel ill, though more frequently, of course, for conditions they fear might be serious. For common symptoms – including high temperature, arthritis, anaemia, bronchitis, backache, menstrual disorders and menopausal symptoms, nerves and neuritis, influenza and insomnia, headache, indigestion, sore throats, skin complaints, dental problems, vomiting and diarrhoea – they are as likely to turn to other people: to the chemist; to doctors' wives or husbands who may share some of their spouses' experience, if not training; to paramedical professions (nurses, pharmacists, physiotherapists, chiropodists); to individuals such as bank managers who interact frequently with the public and sometimes act as lay confessors or psychotherapists; to organizers of self-help groups; or to members or officiants of certain healing cults or churches. But health-seeking goes beyond consulting any kind of professional or person in public life; people may also seek advice from their hairdresser or the doctor's receptionist. Today the media have also become important providers of information for patients.

The main source of advice people draw on, in what has been called their 'hierarchy of resort', is their own past experience, or that of their parents, friends, neighbours, spouses or others with experience of certain illnesses and life events, such as women who have had children. Wives' advice is evaluated as being among the best; that from mothers and (less surprisingly) mothers-in-law among the worst.[67] On the other hand, people are remarkably critical of professional advice and treatment: for nearly half of the symptoms of illness people took no medicines at all, and even where they did get prescriptions from the doctor, nearly one in ten of these were not presented to the chemist.[68] The upshot is that two-thirds of the drugs used in the home are not prescribed by doctors at all but are self-prescribed and bought 'over the counter'.[69] When people do have confidence in a treatment, they are more likely to rely on the advice of 'over-the-fence physicians' – their friends, relatives and neighbours.[70]

Within Western societies, then, 'folk' medical subcultures based on the ideas about illness that differ from the dominant medical model have been remarkably persistent, particularly among immigrant ethnic groups – in Britain, among Indians, Chinese and West Indians, and in the United States among ethnic groups whose forebears came from the rural margins of Europe with a strong cultural identity which they preserved and passed on to their descendants who were born in the 'ghettos'. In one famous study in the early 1950s, Zborowski found marked differences in reactions to pain between Italian-Americans, Jewish-Americans and mainly Protestant 'Old Americans' in New York. The Italians, for instance, were particularly concerned with the immediacy of pain and expressed their discomfort by groaning, moaning, crying, and so on, though they stopped doing so once the pain had worn off. They were also particularly concerned about the effects of their illness on their immediate work situation. Jewish patients, by contrast, were much more 'future-oriented': more concerned with possible long-term consequences for themselves and their families; while 'Old Americans' tended to be stoical, to minimize the pain they felt, and were very co-operative with the professional medical staff who were treating them.[71] Likewise, in the 1960s in Boston, Zola found marked differences in ways of perceiving and communicating bodily complaints to the doctor between Irish, Italian and Anglo-Saxon patients respectively. The Irish focused on a specific physical problem, such as poor eyesight, and restricted themselves to its purely physical aspects, whereas the Italians were concerned about many more symptoms and about the effect of their physical problems on their work or their social life, and people other than the patient would take responsibility for getting the sick person to seek medical treatment.[72]

The persistence of 'folk' medical beliefs and practices is vividly illustrated by Helman's classic study of the archetypal British complaint, justly called the 'common' cold, which is the focus of a whole complex of beliefs including not only colds but also 'chills' and 'fevers'.[73] In lay belief, he shows, certain areas of skin – the top of the head, the back of the neck and the feet – are considered to be more vulnerable than other parts to penetration by environmental cold, damp or draughts. You can therefore 'catch' a cold if you go out into the rain without your hat on, or step into a puddle or walk barefoot on cold floors. Fevers, on the other hand, are believed to result from the penetration of 'germs', 'bugs' or 'viruses' through other breaks in the body's surface – the orifices, such as the anus, throat or nostrils. Germs are thought of as 'a cloud of tiny particles, or as a tiny, invisible single "insect"', while 'bugs' are more insect-like and larger. Germs are dealt with by expulsion – washing them out of the system (by 'coughing up the muck'), or via the bowels or through the skin (sweating). They can also be deprived of food – as in the old saying 'Feed a cold, starve a fever' – or killed, using modern drugs such as antibiotics and sulphonamides.

These beliefs reflect an underlying conception of two sets of *natural* factors, 'hot/cold' and 'wet/dry' conditions – categories commonly found in non-Western medical systems – which are probably 'folk' vestiges of ideas of the ancient theory of the 'humours' which dominated even official medical thought until only two centuries ago. And in popular thought, infection by germs also involves social relationships – they are transmitted by other people.

But since these popular ideas have a place for germs, viruses and antibiotics, they are not simply 'unchanging tradition'. Rather, there is an *interaction* between biomedical and folk ideas – germs and viruses, Helman insists, 'are easily incorporated *into* the folk model without challenging its basic premises'.[74] Doctors too adapt to the folk models their patients use ('I'll give you something to dry up that cold') or treat symptoms by referring to folk models of illness rather than medically recognized causes of 'disease'. They will thus often give antibiotics, appropriate to diseases caused by bacteria, for viral infections too – where they are inappropriate. For the majority of diseases, which cure themselves, it does not matter all that much which model they use.[75]

Culture and Illness in the West

There are also persisting cultural differences between countries which, theoretically, subscribe to the 'same' Western medical theory.

As in Britain, medicine in other Western countries is virtually monopolized, legally speaking, by organized biomedicine, endorsed by the state. Western medicine was highly international anyway, a convergence of the theory and practice which evolved in several countries. And in modern times, given commonalities of social organization, including rising living standards (with whatever inequalities), and the political and economic co-ordination of the industrialized countries of Western Europe, the United States and Japan, the eastern representative of 'the West', it is not surprising that there are close resemblances in health patterns too. Thus in four countries studied by Lynn Payer – England, (then) West Germany, the USA and France – men live to just over seventy-one on average and women to just under eighty. Only one in 100 infants out of every 1,000 born alive die before reaching their first birthday.[76]

Yet in each country differing historical legacies are also reflected in the different ways medicine is organized today. In a huge country like the United States, for example, the organization of the medical profession has been based on associations of doctors in individual states. However, the profession also needs the endorsement of central government and in turn can bring great pressure to bear on government, as the failure of Hillary Clinton's attempt to use the power of the state to take on the pharmaceutical corporations and organized medicine showed.

Despite the internationalism of Western medicine, marked cultural differences, subscribed to by patients and doctors alike, still persist in each country. In Payer's survey, the West German patient saw his doctor nearly twelve times a year; the French and English just over five. A British patient was half as likely to have surgery of any kind as an American and one-sixth as likely to undergo a coronary bypass. German doctors prescribed *combinations* of drugs more frequently (70 per cent of the time) and prescribed almost twice as many items as their British counterparts.

The Americans and the English, Payer found, were very anxious about high blood-pressure. Germans, on the other hand, worried about *low* blood-pressure. Though the death rate from heart diseases is pretty much the same in all three countries, Germans used six times more heart drugs than the French and the English, took eighty-five different drugs and were *more than 163 times* more likely to go to their doctors with this problem than were the English.[77] 'In England,' one British doctor remarked, 'we are taught that low blood-pressure may be unpleasant, but we should be happy to have it', while according to another British doctor working in the States, 'The analysis of low blood-pressure makes American doctors laugh. [They] think it is almost bad practice to treat low blood-pressure.'

The British also worry about their bowels and about 'catching a chill'; the Germans about poor circulation and *Herzinsuffizienz*, which accounted for the greatest number of visits to doctors in some surveys. Anglicized as 'congestive heart failure', it really cannot be translated, because it would not be considered to be a disease in England, France or America.

The French have the highest rates of cirrhosis of the liver in the world. They blame their livers (and their eating habits) for a whole range of what might more appropriately be labelled 'complaints' than 'illnesses': migraine, nervous depressions, faintness, insomnia, painful menstruation, paleness, yellowness and general fatigue, among others. By 1970, they were taking 300 different drugs for the liver – nearly 5 per cent of French drug consumption. But in 1976, in a culture where the Académie Française legislates which words are to be used and which are not, the liver was officially cleared by French hepatologists – after which the number of people saying they suffered from liver disease declined by a factor of four.

In France again, women take the threat to life presented by breast cancer as seriously as women anywhere else, but they are often reluctant to undergo radical mastectomy and opt instead for radiotherapy because they

attach great importance to the aesthetic, sexual and psychological consequences. Their images of the ideal body also differ from those of, say,
American women. So, at a time when American women were increasingly
demanding breast 'augmentation', surgeons in France were much more
likely to be asked to perform breast reductions. French doctors take tem-
peratures rectally rather than orally because it is more accurate, but English and American physicians think such a degree of accuracy unnecessary.

As with the common cold in Britain, many of these cultural differences
are by no means simply the 'folk' ideas of patients. Doctors often share
many of the same ideas, and treat illnesses and their patients in different
ways in different countries. In a thoroughly anthropological way, Payer attributes the persistence of such differences within Western medicine in
part to 'deep' differences of culture. The French, for example, 'value
thinking as an activity in itself',[78] especially Cartesian thinking, whose
prime concern is with logic and theory. In the past, anthropologists have
tended to think of primitive cultures as founded upon cultural values
which are simply 'givens' – immanent, eternal and unaffected by change.
Payer, on the other hand, sees cultural differences as products of history,
of major social and political events and movements in each society. Thus
French rationalism goes back to the Enlightenment, when in 1778 the Société Royale de Médecine, the voice of science, tried to outlaw any medical remedies of which it had not approved. Even though the 'freedom'
consolidated by the (bourgeois) Revolution included 'sacred and invio-
lable' rights in property, including medical remedies, these were to be
subjected to the scrutiny of science at the service of the state; the state was
also the main purchaser of all new drugs. Under Napoleon, medicine was
further rationalized: the old medical colleges and faculties were reorganized, culminating in an *étatisme* even more all-embracing than that exercised by the old Société Royale.[79]

In a society founded upon the worship of reason, nothing is more prestigious, even today, than to be an intellectual. The English, on the other
hand, in a country which does not even have a written constitution, have
no 'intellectuals'. They recognize 'academics', but denigrate people who
deal in ideas as the 'chattering classes'. What they value are *facts*; nothing
is more damaging than to be accused of dealing in 'mere' theory.

French doctors and patients are therefore more likely to take mental
and social factors into account. The concept of the *terrain*, for instance,
emphasizes the body's vulnerability to risk and its 'constitutional' powers
of resistance. Many diseases are thought of as resulting from 'a combination of some type of outside insult and the body's reaction to that insult ...
English and American doctors tend to focus on the insult, [while] the

French and Germans focus on the reaction'.[80]

So French medical treatments skew drug consumption away from antibiotics towards modifying the *terrain*. They are more prone to admit psychological factors and they opt for more limited operations, longer stays in hospital and a tolerance of dirt which would be unacceptable in America but which they think helps promote certain kinds of immunity.

The French also see rest, sick leaves and spas as health-giving and vacations as opportunities to rest or to 'change ideas', whereas Americans think of them as opportunities to 'charge their batteries'. In France 'fringe' medical treatments, notably homoeopathy, are accepted much more readily by doctors, because they are considered 'gentle' treatments which bolster the *terrain*. The drug dosages prescribed are usually smaller than in America, while tonics and other modifiers of the *terrain* constituted 10 per cent of drugs used in 1976 – as high a proportion as broad-spectrum penicillin. No other classes of antibiotics even made the Top Twenty. Conversely, no tonics were included in the British Top Twenty, and no antibiotics in the German Top Twenty.[81]

It is important, though, to distinguish between folk ideas about health and illness and the effects of Church and state controls over popular choice. Much of patient choice and of treatments favoured by doctors is not necessarily an expression of 'deep' cultural values so much as a response to and consequence of state and professional medical policies. Due to historic opposition from the Roman Catholic Church and the illegality in France of the diaphragm and, indeed, of all forms of contraception as late as 1977, only 2 per cent of French women of reproductive age used any female barrier method. 'The diaphragm,' Payer remarks, 'had no history in France.' A third of French women relied on their husbands to practise withdrawal as a method of contraception, at a time when only 3 per cent of American husbands and 6 per cent of British continued to do so. But when the ban was lifted and the pill became available, a third of French women readily took to using it.

Such changes are most obvious in revolutionary societies. In the United States, 'the first new nation',[82] for instance, it seemed to perspicacious foreign observers like de Tocqueville that the historical development of the New World was quite different from anything in European history – the colonization of a moving frontier in what was a continent rather than a mere state or 'country'. Once Indian resistance was broken, limitless land was available for the taking. Freed from foreign control and from the feudal heritage of rank and property which had shackled innovation in Europe, the United States became a land of opportunity, in which action and enterprise were rewarded above everything else.

On the frontier, the pioneers had to fend for themselves in health matters as in everything else and where European medicines were lacking, they borrowed from the Indians, whose remedies had found their way into works like Samuel Stearns' *American Herbal* by the end of the eighteenth century, though they were attributed to 'country people'.

American medicine had emerged during the colonial epoch and the Indians were barbarous enemies. To doctors, it was European not Indian medicine that was the most prestigious. Dr Benjamin Rush, not only a Founding Father of American medicine but also one of the signatories to the Declaration of Independence, declared that there were 'no discoveries to be hoped for from the Indians of North America'. So American doctors imported their drugs from Europe and relied on the same remedies as their European counterparts: opium, mercury and antimony. They also went to study in Europe – to Paris, Leiden and Edinburgh – and continued to do so for much of the next century. The first medical school in the United States was founded only in the late eighteenth century, in Philadelphia, by then the second city in the country.[83]

Yet in other respects American medicine was stamped with distinctively independent attitudes from the beginning. In particular, it was aggressive and interventionist. Rush, for instance, thought that European doctors relied too much on the powers of nature to cure disease. Americans were tougher than Europeans; so were American diseases: 'To cure [them, therefore], Americans would require uniquely powerful doses administered by heroic American physicians.'[84]

Foreign observers have always seen this positive, activistic, 'can-do' attitude as quintessentially American. Max Weber, for instance, considered it part of the legacy of Protestantism. In Payer's view, it is still 'as characteristic of American medicine as it is of the American character in general'. Americans , she remarks, 'regard [themselves] as naturally healthy. It therefore stands to reason that if [they] become ill,there must be a cause for the illness, preferably one that comes from without and can be quickly dealt with'.[85]

Problems are there to be solved; indeed, the main purpose of a person's life is the solution of problems. The very existence of problems is intolerable. They *must* they be solved and they *can* be solved. So it is always better to do *something* rather than nothing. Since Americans expect results, if they do not get them, they are much more likely than Europeans both to pay for them and to sue for malpractice, for large sums.

Rush believed in 'massive purging and bloodletting', and advocated bleeding off up to four-fifths of the body's blood. Americans who studied in Paris admired French diagnostic skills, but were impatient with their 'therapeutic nihilism': in American idiom, their 'do-nothing' attitudes.

This tradition of interventionism explains the performance in the United States today of twice as much surgery on patients as in Britain. A British patient is half as likely to undergo surgery of any kind as an American. For women, an American woman is two or three times more likely to have a hysterectomy than a woman in England, while episiotomy, on a wider scale and much earlier than in other Western countries, plus the use of forceps and the early removal of the placenta in childbirth, had already become so routine, so self-evident an improvement upon nature, that by the 1920s some obstetricians were advocating that childbirth by Caesarean section should become the norm. It is now the most commonly performed operation in the States.

American medicine also displays the same tendencies to specialization and the same reliance on advanced technology as American science in general. Technological innovation, ceaseless *improvement* upon nature, has therefore been as characteristic of American medicine as it has been of agriculture and industry. As with the armed forces, the ethos is one of knocking out the enemy with high-tech 'magic bullets', or, if this is not possible, of developing new man-made drugs which, like the 'Star Wars' defence initiative, will prevent the enemy from getting through. The linch-pin of the British system, on the other hand, has been the all-purpose GP, who is expected to know a good deal about not only the lives of the individuals he or she deals with but their families and communities too. Only when their problems exceed his or her professional competence are patients referred to specialists. In contrast, American families routinely consult a range of *specialists* directly, from gynaecologists to psychiatrists.

This kind of medicine, in which scientifically trained specialists 'knock out' 'killer diseases', has had its successes – for example, in cutting the rate of heart attacks and other serious illnesses such as strokes, though changes in diet and lifestyle are also involved. But it has been unable to eliminate or even significantly reduce others, notoriously cancer, or to eliminate many chronic illnesses, or to stem the rise of new 'diseases of civilization' and of lifestyle, such as obesity. So when medicine doesn't work in this activistic culture, patients search for other kinds of cure, from revived traditional 'folk' remedies to a never-ending succession of new and exotic kinds of 'health foods' and new lifestyles, from yoga and diet-fads to aerobics, a proclivity which, in the extreme, has been called 'healthism'.

The high value put upon the individual in the United States – which Christopher Lasch has called the 'culture of narcissism'[86] – plus what has been called 'the medicalization of everything', generates widespread expectations that doctors should be able to deal with not just their patients' physical problems but their personal and social problem too. There is therefore a very large population of therapists, medically trained and otherwise, who specialize in mental problems – twelve pages of listings of psychologists and psychotherapists in the Yellow Pages of the Manhattan telephone directory alone, as against a mere column and a half of psychoanalysts, psychologists and psychotherapists for the whole of Greater London.

Conversely, Payer considers, the most striking characteristic of British medicine is its economy: 'the British do less of nearly everything' – fewer visits to the doctor; less time spent by the physician when they do get there; fewer drugs prescribed; less high-tech medicine; smaller vitamin requirements; fewer screening examinations and less often – a level of 'under-doctoring' which reflects the lower proportion of GNP expended on health care (6 per cent as compared to 11 per cent in the States).

Though the patients of British GPs see them slightly more often than people in France or America, their visits typically last six minutes compared to fifteen or twenty minutes in the other two countries. The writer's experience in moving from a doctor's practice in north-west England to one in London is not untypical: my NHS card was inspected, and my pulse and blood-pressure checked (which had not been done for several years). Moving to the United States, I spent two hours (and several hundred dollars), gave blood and urine samples, and underwent a battery of tests in which I was festooned with electrodes before the physician would even accept me as a patient.

The legendary lack of criticality of British patients probably reflects both the social deference they accord to doctors and their sheer lack of knowledge about medical matters. Few know what their blood-pressure is, or their cholesterol level, even fewer where their heart or liver is, and only about one in five the correct location of their stomachs. Deference, ignorance and under-doctoring reflect the social prestige that the medical profession had achieved by the mid-twentieth century. That deference still persists: in one study, a third of British patients did not question their doctors because they thought he or she would think less of them, while 20 per cent were scared they would get a hostile reaction – even though four out of five of those who *did* ask questions were in fact given clear answers.[87]

These differences in cultural attitudes towards illness between Britain and the United States derive from overall differences in the ways in which the two societies developed. American medicine was stamped by its colonial political origins and by its development, even in the colonial period, as part of a rapidly growing capitalist market economy. In economic terms, so was medicine in Europe. Even after political control was broken by revolution, Europe remained for Americans the centre of civilization and culture. America was merely part of nature, a 'wilderness', awaiting the fertilizing influence of the pioneers. (The image of the West as a 'garden' only developed after the Plains had been covered with wheat.)

By the beginning of the nineteenth century, it had become illegal to practise medicine in cities like New York without a diploma. The frontier was a different matter, for the control the medical profession was able to exercise in the cities was absent there, so it became the perfect breeding ground for innovations and heresies.

Even in the cities, there was still a great popular demand for herbal knowledge, a demand met, in scientific circles, by the publication in the same year, 1817, of two works: a three-volume *Vegetable Materia Medica of the USA*, from within the medical profession, by a Harvard professor, James Bigelow; and a study of the same name by a Philadelphia botanist, William Barton. Yet Bigelow's study found room in its three volumes for only sixty *American* plants, and Barton's only fifty.

On the frontier, the demand for folk remedies was far greater. Peter Smith's *The Indian Doctor's Dispensatory* of 1813, crammed with herbal remedies, boldly asserted the superiority of *Indian* doctoring and was explicitly addressed to the 'Citizens of the *Western* Parts of the United States'. In the following year, the *New and Complete American Family Herbal*, by Samuel Henry – who had been a prisoner among the Creeks – contained much Indian medical lore.[88] Thereafter, medical publications such as *The North American Indian Doctor, or Nature's method of Curing and Preventing Disease According to the Indians* began to proliferate.[89]

By the end of the century, Indian medicine had become part of white popular culture. Travelling medicine hawkers often carried a living Indian with them as proof that what they were selling was genuine Indian medicine. By 1911, at least 150 'medicine shows' featured Indians – the most famous were the Kiowa Indian Medicine and Vaudeville Company and the Kickapoo Indian Medicine Company – compared to 180 stock companies playing Broadway shows around the country.[90]

The shortage of orthodox doctors on the frontier made space for unorthodox ones, such as Samuel Thompson, a poor farmer's son who had lost his mother in his youth and had witnessed the agonizing labour of his wife, as well as the illness of his two-year-old daughter which left her blind in one eye, plus the death of a neighbour's child poisoned by the mercury treatment given her by a doctor who got, Thompson said bitterly, '$25 for killing the child by inches'.[91] He, conversely, believed in raising the body's 'vital heat' and used a wide range of vegetable remedies, from bayberry and sumac to cayenne and myrrh, and, above all, lobelia. His success in preserving the lives of his patients during an epidemic in New Hampshire, in contrast to orthodox doctors, brought him the unremitting hatred of the medical profession and, eventually, a term in gaol.

Yet by 1835, the Governor of Mississippi could report that over half of the population of the state depended on Thompsonian practitioners; the figure was around a third in Ohio.[92] In these parts of America, then, the physician established himself as *qualified*, not by displaying diplomas, but by 'winning the confidence of his fellows in practice' in an open market.[93]

The Thompsonian movement was only one of the major unorthodoxies. Dr Albert Isaiah Coffin's unfortunate name did not prevent his movement – which had begun with his experience of being cured by a Seneca woman as a boy, after which he 'threw in [his] lot amongst these roving tribes'[94] – from 'spreading like a prairie fire' after the publication of his *Botanic Guide to Health*, which went into twenty reprints. Before long, there were Coffinite branches in every major city in America, and his *Journal* was claiming 10,000 readers. Thompsonianism and Coffinism even spread into Europe. Warfare between the new unorthodoxies and established medicine was, of course, inevitable, but it also developed between the various unorthodox movements themselves, and, as in most sectarian movements, internal schisms emerged. Heretics like John Skelton, who advocated using new drugs like aspirin, even though it had begun life as a plant extract before being synthesized in the laboratory, was denounced for his pains as a traitor to herbalism.

By the end of the century, there were five times as many doctors in the United States as in France, 15,000 of them 'Irregulars', as against 60,000 'Regulars'. America also proved to be highly receptive to foreign unorthodoxies such as Samuel Hahnemann's homoeopathy. A campaign to put up a statue to Hahnemann attracted more money than a similar proposal to honour Dr Rush! And organized medicine failed to overcome this growing competition until well into the twentieth century, when the Flexner Commission of 1910, backed by Carnegie and Rockefeller, finally recommended, and achieved, not the expansion of medicine but the closure of no less than a third of existing medical schools, many of them no doubt appalling, with ill-equipped and filthy 'laboratories'. They included nearly all the unorthodox institutions. By 1939, there was virtually no organized alternative medicine left.

In Britain as well there were two kinds of alternatives to orthodox medicine: persisting traditional herbalism and other kinds of treatment by the unlicensed, and a succession of new modes of curing – Mesmerism, spiritualism and homoeopathy – denounced by orthodox doctors as 'cults'.

Some of these, like medical hypnotism or hydrotherapy, were even acceptable to orthodox nineteenth-century practitioners, and to people like Darwin, who suffered agonies taking the waters, and whose daughter died when entrusted to the ministrations of his Malvern guru. In the twentieth century, other unorthodoxies, such as osteopathy, likewise won a great deal of acceptance even from orthodox doctors.

Despite the entrenched position of biomedicine, its hegemony was challenged after the Second World War by two developments: first, the undermining of the belief that Western medicine could do nothing but good; and second, an emerging awareness that there were other alternatives to Western medicine.

'Diseases' are not 'things-in-themselves' – only 55 per cent of the entries in the World Health Organization's International Classification of Diseases are reducible to 'single, universal, and duplicable sign-symptom complexes'.[95] So drugs 'targeted' at specific illnesses can have unintended consequences ('side-effects'). Public confidence in chemical drugs touched bottom in the early 1960s, when 8,000 mothers who had been prescribed the drug thalidomide gave birth to children who had shortened limbs or none at all. Their sufferings, and those of their parents, were made worse by the heartless resistance of the corporations which had produced the drug to demands for adequate compensation from the parents of the deformed children.

By now, criticism of drug-based therapy was not confined to this or that drug. It gave rise to a general critique of drug-based medicine and of the pharmaceutical industry. By the 1970s, for many, especially the young of the 'Vietnam generation' who had become alienated from Western culture generally, biomedicine was dethroned. A new word – 'iatrogenesis' – entered common parlance: doctors were now people who not only cured but also *killed*.[96]

The second challenge to biomedicine came after the 'opening-up' of China following President Nixon's visit in 1972. Americans found out that everyday illnesses were being treated on a gigantic scale not by people trained in Western medicine but by 'barefoot doctors' – medical assistants with a basic training mainly in traditional medicine – using herbal medicines grown in the commune hospital's grounds and processed in their laboratories in the form of pills and liquids. It was even more startling to find that 100,000 operations – often for life-threatening conditions – were being carried out annually, many without resort to Western anaesthetics, but using instead indigenous techniques such as acupuncture and moxibustion. In 1972, I myself witnessed a mastoidectomy – using acupuncture – and was able to talk to the patient, give him segments of oranges and watch him, at the end, swing his legs off the operating table and walk out on the arm of a nurse. The techniques, though, were not entirely traditional, for the acupuncture needles in the patient's skin were wired up to electrical equipment. A second operation I witnessed, a more serious case, involved open-heart surgery, also under acupuncture, though this time a Western oxygen mask was also used. The patient, nevertheless, was still wide awake. Chinese medicine, one could see with one's own eyes, did indeed draw upon both 'traditional' *and* modern Western biomedicine – in Chinese parlance, it 'walked on two legs'.

Just *how* these treatments worked was not clear, for Chinese explanations in terms of the traditional 'meridians' and the 'humours' did not satisfy Western scientists. Nevertheless, overnight acupuncture became a vogue. Many once highly prestigious and ancient 'alternative' medical systems like astrology and alchemy had fallen into oblivion, as had more recent ones like Mesmerism. Now ancient treatments were explored again and newer ones treated more open-mindedly. The superiority of Western medicine could no longer be taken for granted, as it had been a century earlier, when Macaulay had celebrated the occasion of the first dissection of a corpse by an Indian by ordering a salute to be fired from Fort William.[97]

Today Western medicine is a powerful and distinctive body of theory and therapy everywhere in the world, not just in the West. It is usually contrasted with something labelled 'non-Western' medicine. This, though, is only a *negative* category – it merely tells us that other kinds of medicine differ from the Western. There is, in fact, a *plurality* of very diverse non-Western medical systems: in India alone, for instance, there are not only two major kinds of non-Western medicine, Ayurveda and Unani, but also Siddh, Yoga and homoeopathic medicine, not to mention popular kinds and modern imports.

China and India, which contain a majority of the world's population, are not cultural exceptions or peculiarities, for '*most* societies,' Wallis and Morley observe, 'are and have been historically, medically pluralistic'.[98] Western biomedicine, by contrast, has been in existence for only two or three centuries.

So in the Third World today, traditional medicine is not confined to backward rural areas. The markets of the towns and cities are filled with traditional remedies. In one such market in Pátzcuaro, Mexico, I noted cures on sale for ordinary coughs, asthmatic coughs, varicose veins, phlebitis, rheumatism, diarrhoea, skin complaints, gastric ulcers and gastritis, wind, vomiting, allergies, diabetes, anaemia, kidney and urinary complaints, high and low tension, and nervous attacks. The illnesses were thus defined in Western terms, but most of the remedies were traditional: not just herbs, seeds, leaves and roots, but also snakeskins, coloured fluids, rubbing ointments for both head and chest, 'witches' brew' and foetuses, as well as holy pictures. Some, like Hare Krishna incense sticks and horse-shoes, were both modern and exotic. They were not necessarily cheap in relation to local incomes, and some *curanderos* who treat people with these medicines can make a lot of money, though earnings vary considerably – from a probable gross income of US$800 a week to a mere ten pesos charged by less prestigious practitioners.[99]

These remedies are mainly used for everyday illnesses, though you can buy medicines to 'tie and nail down' your lover or for success in exams. More serious illnesses may call for a visit to a personal curer. Thus high-land Indians in Colombia travel down to the jungle, where the medicine of the selvatic tribes is considered particularly powerful, or to the Pacific coast in search of the esoteric knowledge and curing skills of the blacks. One prestigious jungle curer counts among his clients a former president of Peru.[100] Really famous ones become practically saints, and attract clients from hundreds of miles, even across national boundaries.[101]

Pilgrimages to shrines in search of supernatural solutions is also very common, though by no means confined to the world outside Europe. If Brazilians visit Aparecida and Mexicans go to Chalma, Westerners in their hundreds of thousands also travel long distances to such world-renowned centres as Lourdes, Medjugorje, Fátima and Częstochowa. What they come for is plain to see, for it is physical illness that predominates. Racks of crutches discarded after miraculous cures far outnumber the *ex votos* after success in examinations or the victory of favoured football teams.

A variety of different medical therapies has always existed within any culture. The ancient Aztecs, for example, had a plethora of types of both 'empirical' and 'magical' doctors – no fewer than forty kinds of the latter – concerned with treating not only illness but other kinds of problems too, by a variety of methods, including divination.[102] Today, so great is the flow of people and ideas across the globe that cultural exchanges over-come political barriers. The notion that each culture possesses only one medical system – 'one culture, one medicine' – therefore becomes ever more outdated. Though Western remedies may diffuse particularly rapidly, the traffic is not all one way.

Most of the illnesses for which people seek cures are minor and do not call for intervention by supernatural forces. 'In practically every case which does not cause great pain or incapacitation' the Tzotzil Maya resort to the lowest category of healers, the *ts'ak bak*, and use *naturalistic* not su-pernatural explanations. Only for serious illnesses do they go to the more expert *ilol*, and to *me'santo* for persistent, life-threatening illnesses. It is here, at the edge of life, that magico-religious rituals become dominant. [103]

In African cultures, which most Westerners generally think of as 'underdeveloped', there is a similar plethora of specialists. The Urhobo of Nigeria, for instance, have indigenous 'general practitioners'. But they also have a whole range of specialists – herbalists, faith-healers, bone-setters, traditional midwives, 'reformed' witch-doctors (former witches), traditional surgeons and healers of the psychotic – whose methods run from herbal treatments, hydrotherapy, massage, cupping and faith-healing to surgery and heat therapy, some of whom are no longer allowed to practise their skills. [104] In other cultures, we find circumcisers, lead-pourers, umbilicus-setters and coccyx-pullers. [105]

Some specialists, like Man Aher, the most distinguished doctor among the Radjang of Sumatra, and a bard and historian into the bargain, refuse to treat cases of 'magical' poisoning, even though these constitute more than half the afflictions which patients bring to their doctors. The therapists who *did* treat such illnesses – by using 'psycho-magnetism' – were treated by Man Aher with the same kind of contempt that they would have received from a Western-trained physician. [106] Usually, though, indigenous doctors fully share their patients' ideas about magico-religious causation in illness.

Prins has likened studies of medical treatment in Africa to the three legs of an African cooking pot: first, there is the extent of actual illness; second, the concepts and methods used by indigenous curers; and third, the analysis of all this by Western doctors in the light of *their* own theoretical framework. [107]

Anthropologists concern themselves only with the second of these elements, neglecting the first and third, since they lack specialized medical knowledge. Thus, in Turner's classic study of the Ndembu, illness is a '*social* drama', not a biological phenomenon. But people like Lewis, one of a very select band who are both Western doctors *and* anthropologists, face an extra problem. For him *as a doctor*, illness has an independent biological reality. But for him *as an anthropologist*, Gnau beliefs about illness 'do *not* constitute a clearly bounded department of knowledge', a medical system, specifically concerned with the understanding and treatment of illness and separated off from supernatural beliefs. To make sense of illness as a *cultural* phenomenon, therefore, he had to take into account what it meant to the 'actors'. As for the Kongo, in Gnau culture illness is a consequence of disharmony in their social relations. [108]

As we saw for Britain, West Germany, France and America, each culture has its 'favourite' illnesses. In Sri Lanka, people worry about phlegm, caused by colds in the head, and loss of semen in the body, due to bad living, especially sexual excess, smoking marijuana and eating 'hot' foods.[109] But there is far more variation *within* a set of supposedly 'common' beliefs than formal accounts of 'the' belief system of this or that culture allow for. Thus Hindus everywhere are assumed to subscribe to the same religious beliefs and the same medical theories. According to the scholarly and priestly 'gatekeepers' of Hindu cosmology, there are five basic elements (fire, water, earth, wind and ether), together with three humours and seven body components (food juices, blood, flesh, bone, fat, marrow and semen). But Ayurveda in Sri Lanka differs from Ayurveda in India, and in any case the 'classical' texts cover only a few illnesses and provide only a few cures for them, though in real, everyday life people suffer from a much wider range of illnesses. So even physicians who purport to follow Hindu orthodoxy use only four of the five 'chief' elements, only three are generally recognized and peasants reduce the whole lot to two – fire and water. And in two Mysore villages, Beals found that there were many cures for the same disease, while different individuals attributed different causes and cures to the same disease.[110]

We also find a variety of beliefs about illness and about magic and witchcraft from one culture to another. Thus the Navajo distinguish witchcraft (where corpse poison is introduced into the victim's body during sleep) from sorcery (a branch of witchcraft which involves the use of spells and bodily exuviae) and both of these from 'wizardry' (where foreign substances are introduced into the body). The Lardil Aborigines of northern Australia, on the other hand, distinguish between purposeful evil magic (*puripuri*) and mystical punishments which occur when people break important taboos (*nganwi*).[111]

Finally, different cultures have distinctive ways of handling what Max Weber called 'theodicy': the problem of evil. Christianity has given rise to differing explanations as to why God created evil, so that vicious and amoral people flourish like bay trees, while the innocent and generous suffer in agony. The Azande, we saw, have a conception of responsibility and of probability in which a person can be a *carrier* of sorcery (which is a substance in the body), unbeknownst to him or her (and unintentionally). In Hinduism, conversely, Kali is the deity of death and destruction, one of whose manifestations is Devi, a terrifying goddess who can nevertheless also be tranquil and pacific in some forms. Somewhat differently, the Aztecs believed that the god Tezcalipoca represented *indeterminacy*: *undeserved* misfortune.[112]

Anthropologists have attempted to reduce this cultural variety, in various ways, to one or two basic categories. Horton, for example, has argued

there is a basic similarity in all African magico-religious thinking, any differences between Kalabari and Lugbara thought, say, being only 'surface'
differences.[113] Yet Kalabari theology is very different from Lugbara. The
former, for instance, distinguishes between the ancestors – who 'underpin
the life and strength of the lineages'; their 'heroes', who are 'the forces in-
forming the community's life and strength and its institutions'; and the
water spirits, who are 'patrons of human individualism' – a repertoire of
beliefs about the supernatural which differs from the beliefs of the
(equally African) Azande.

Horton also argues that African thinking lacks the 'critical attitude' that
characterizes Western science – putting basic assumptions 'up for grabs';
subjecting theories about cause and effect to *testing* – and therefore argues
that abstraction and probability are poorly developed (ideas which we saw
earlier in Hallpike).

More usefully, Foster and Anderson distinguish between *personalistic*
and *naturalistic* systems (though they say these categories are 'rarely if ever
mutually exclusive'). The former explain disease as 'due to the *purposeful
intervention* of an *agent*', who may be human (a witch or sorcerer), non-
human (a ghost, ancestor or evil spirit) or supernatural (a deity or other
very powerful being). While 'naturalistic' systems – such as theories of the
'humours' – attribute disease to 'natural forces or conditions' such 'cold,
heat, wind, dampness, and above all ... upset in the balance of the basic
body elements ... Health conforms to an equilibrium model'.[114]

Biomedicine has no theoretical place for illnesses which their patients
believe to be brought about by supernatural, not natural, forces and so
cannot deal with them. People therefore *have* to turn to other sources of
hope and comfort: to diviners, shamans, interpreters of oracles, religious
specialists and practitioners of magic of all kinds who *are* willing to tackle
disorders that are believed to arise when people's social relationships are
out of kilter – because of conflicts over land, money or inheritance; or
when they are trying to further their own political ambitions and frustrate
those of their rivals; or when they experience jealousy, hatred and suspicion because their marital and sexual relationships have gone wrong.

Those who are commonly labelled 'traditional' curers, then, actually
come in many different shapes and sizes, and different cultures have different repertoires for dealing with sickness. In Western thinking, however,
they are nevertheless commonly reduced to a lowest common denomina-
tor: a simple stereotype of 'the typical' curer.

The South American *curandero*, for example, is thought of as someone
who belongs to the same face-to-face network as his or her patients, and
who therefore knows them as total personalities. This familiarity, it is

often assumed, is the basis of the patient's trust in the curer and explains why cures work – a kind of 'faith-healing', using cultural 'placebos'. Given this special relationship of shared cultural ideas and mutual familiarity, the *curandero* is thought to treat his or her patients in an altruistic, Hippocratic way, helping people because they are in need, at minimal cost, not as a source of income. The relationship is not a 'cash nexus'; filthy lucre does not enter into it.

A moment's thought, though, will suggest that this cannot be the case in the exploding cities of the Third World. In the village, when a Tzotzil Maya curer asks his patients, 'Have you been angry lately?', 'Have you had any bad falls?', 'Any nasty arguments with anyone?', 'Have you been frightened by anyone or anything lately?', he may already know the likely answers to his questions,[115] and is therefore able to present the names of people mutually known both to the diviner and to the person consulting him, and therefore likely candidates as the cause of the trouble.

In urban consultations, the curer probably does not know the patient at all and may have to establish the cause of the illness without any clues from the patient. Nor does the patient know the doctor. The higher a practitioner's prestige, the greater the likelihood that he or she will be treating people they do not know. In Vellore (Madras), Taylor found that 47 per cent of the patients of *all* kinds of physicians – Western, Ayurvedic, Unani and mixed, received *no* physical examination at all.[116] And though it is commonly asserted that alternative medicine is less 'invasive' of the patient's body, this is by no means always so – acupuncture needles, for instance, are highly invasive!

Our doctors practise various kinds of impression management to emphasize their professional standing – for example, by displaying certificates written in (incomprehensible) Latin on their surgery walls. The presentation of the self and the management of impressions used by curers in the Third World are often much more sophisticated. Thus Colombian *curanderos* take pains to acquaint prospective patients at length with their good reputation, including their specialisms; the origins of their vocation (apprenticeship, dreams, visions, etc.); the source(s) of the cures they use (medicinal, supernatural, etc.); the cultural identity of the techniques they use (Indian, foreign, non-medical, etc.); and the skills of their assistants. Sometimes they appeal to tradition; at other times, to the exotic; at yet other times, to modern science. New patients coming to one eminent curer in Indonesia are greeted with a sales pitch like this:

Salaam aleikum salaam! I studied with my father, my father studied with my grandfather; my grandfather studied with a childless ancestral doctor;

the childless ancestral doctor studied with Doctor Bado; Doctor Bado studied with Doctor Tembukan; Doctor Tembukan studied with Doctor Muning Bueun; Bueun studied with Muning Mas; Muning Mas studied with Setangai Remas; Setangai Remas studied with Radjo Makubumai; Radjo Makubumai studied with Setangai Renyang. That is the pedigree of my learning which ultimately derives from the holy First Being. The holy First Being knew how to approach the Lord of Omnipotence. The Lord of Omnipotence communicated with ... [the] ... Archangel Gabriel. That is the pedigree of my learning. The holy First Being knew how to approach ... the Seven Deities, the Nine Custodians, the people who guard the Hall of Mists, the Abode of Winds, the men who guard the gold mines, the Four Gods who guard the village community and watch over it. The holy First Being has the power to grant wishes, for he knew how to address the Creator, and the Ancestral Spirits ... Help us, First Being, Ancestral Spirits, Beneficent God, and Nine Custodians.[117]

This 'collapsing' of the innumerable generations betweeen the beginning of time and the present consultation gives the patient the reassurance – much more impressive than a Latin certificate – not only that he has chosen a good doctor but that that doctor has divine endorsement. Nzoamambu, Janzen's great Kongo doctor, impressed his patients with his professional lineage by using special 'props' inherited from his grandmother: a spoon so powerful that it was not allowed to touch the ground; a flywhisk; a full-sized grandfather clock he had imported by mail order; and a crockery mug of eighteenth-century German provenance, filled with teeth he had extracted.[118] Urban *curanderos* in Bogotá impress their patients with both their knowledge of traditional medicine and their mastery of Western medicine too through the wearing of stethoscopes, the display of framed testimonials or the crutches of cured patients.[119]

In Bogotá, the range of possible 'alternative' curers from whom a person can choose is 'remarkably heterogeneous': specialists in herbalism, massage, illness-sucking, fallen fontanelle and witchcraft, as well as chiropractors and osteopaths. The techniques they use are naturally varied.

We are introduced to four of these curers. The first, Serafina, treats only ten patients a week, mainly for 'natural' problems such as grippe, abortions, pregnancy, childbirth, sinusitis and asthma, but also for an illness we do not regard as natural at all: *susto* (fright). All were treated in the same way. Her sister-in-law, with whom she works, has a much wider repertoire: she handles *all* illnesses, including some very serious conditions like cancer and tuberculosis, as well as ailments of more obviously social provenance like evil eye, sorcery and luck problems. After detailed

inquiries into the patient's ritual and social background, including information about their enemies, and a battery of techniques which include the
taking of urine specimens, she will recommend the use of home remedies
or give advice about better nutrition and the need for rest; for evil eye, she
recommends prayer, for only the Church can cure that.

A second *curandero*, known as 'The Bishop', was a lay friar for many
years and is also a licensed homoeopath. He examines his patients through
the iris of the eye. His office, with its diploma, his neat desk, a glass-
fronted bookcase, a filing cabinet full of charts and a dentist's chair, looks
'medical'. 'Seen through a 6-8" lens,' Press remarks, the Bishop's eye is
'omnipresent: huge, intimidating, invincible'. Treatment includes beef
broth, massage and medicines which have to be purchased at his pharmacy. As a result, he is much more prosperous than homoeopaths who restrict themselves to only that field of expertise.

Pablo Gato is so much in demand that his patients often have to wait all
night for his office to open on the two days a week when he treats more than
seventy patients a day. Each patient gets only between five and ten minutes;
verbal interchange is rarely for more than two or three minutes, and less on
subsequent occasions. The kinds of problems treated range from sorcery,
errant spouses, bad luck and the sending of evil against the patients' enemies by sticking pins in their photographs to cancer and obesity. Diagnosis
is carried out in a markedly 'bedside' manner and includes the taking of the
pulse and the examination of the urine, as well as laying hands on the wrist,
the temples, the back of the neck, the knees and the forehead. A quarter of
his patients are diagnosed as suffering from natural illnesses, yet the cures
may involve a mixture of Catholic prayers and 'obscure references', while
votive candles, altars, the cross, skulls and saints' portraits are also used.

Delfino Pacheco treats up to thirty patients a day. They travel daily to
wait in line all day for treatment. His wall bears a portrait of St Martin,
plus framed testimonials and the crutches of his cured patients. Though
dressed neatly and formally in 'Western' style (he always keeps his fedora
on in the office), he nevertheless professes to have learned much of his esoteric skill from Ecuadorean Indians. Yet he does *not* profess to cure supernatural illnesses or socially caused ones, apart from *susto* and *aire*
(illness cause by the 'air'). Eye, nose and ear drops, massage and a question
or two – rarely for more than a minute – enable him to call out the symptoms. His secretary then pulls out a slip of paper containing herbal directions from a box on the desk – usually between five and eight slips for each
case. Thirty symptoms constitute his entire repertoire, but it includes such
sure-fire winners as cures for illnesses which usually run their course anyhow, such as occasional dizziness, pains in the stomach and diarrhoea.

Medicine in the Plural

Plainly, these complex mixtures of beliefs and practices do not fit neatly into boxes labelled 'traditional' and 'Western'. Nor do they show that Western biomedicine is displacing traditional kinds in some kind of 'evolutionary' way.

In the West, biomedicine has registered many striking successes, not just in curing or counteracting particular diseases but in contributing towards a general rise in health. Of the leading causes of death in Britain in 1900, only heart disease and consumption remained by 1980. Much of this can be attributed to the efficacy of modern drugs. A second major strength of Western medicine is the expertise of its practitioners in surgery, including such modern refinements as microsurgery, ultrasound surgery, balloon angioplasty and keyhole surgery.

Its critics, though, have often denounced it as 'mechanistic'. The body, they insist, is not a machine. The skeletal system is perhaps the nearest approximation to the model of a machine, since its inter-related parts act upon each other like, say, pistons, camshafts and connecting rods in an engine. So surgeons and nurses often use the metaphor of a 'pump' to describe the circulatory system.

The validity of the machine analogy seemed perfectly self-evident to the Mexican health promoter who told his audience that the parts sometimes break down (*se rompen*) and 'when this happens, they have to be repaired immediately'.[120] The analogy is even stronger now that *spare* parts, from livers to hearts and hip joints, are being used to replace worn-out originals. Western medicine, indeed, is singularly unholistic. All but two of its specialties, as we saw – geriatrics and paediatrics – are based on *parts* of the body, although as osteopaths remind us, the skeletal system does not exist 'in itself', for blood vessels and nerves not only run through the bony framework but supply it with blood and relay messages between the brain and the different parts of the skeletal structure, and in turn are affected if bones malfunction.

The image of a machine, though, is scarcely applicable to the nervous system, or to areas like cytology, where through the use of electron microscopes, Western medicine has made fundamental major advances in studying cells, enabling biologists to identify disease-bearing agents, notably bacteria and viruses, and chemists to develop powerful drugs to counteract or destroy them.

Biomedicine has also registered a whole string of spectacular successes in countries outside the West – the elimination of smallpox, malaria, tuberculosis and yellow fever, and the likely elimination of yaws and Hansen's disease. Its prestige has therefore grown everywhere – one study in India showed that 82 per cent of physicians of *all* schools prescribed *only* Western medicines.[121] For high-status groups, Beals remarks, using Western medicine has become 'almost a caste obligation'.[122] In fanatically 'Westernizing' countries like Japan, traditional medicine had been virtually eliminated by the end of the last century;[123] in Taiwan, a later convert to across-the-board Westernization, traditional medicine has likewise steadily declined.[124]

But there are also considerable reservations about Western medicine in cultures which, for thousands of years, have concentrated more on maintaining health than on coping with illness once it has arrived. Since ancient times, the brilliant physician in China was one who could recognize the 'disease which is not yet a disease' – they favoured, that is, preventive rather than reactive medicine.[125] Western medicine has been singularly unholistic; it is also intolerant of medicines other than biomedicine. In ancient India, on the other hand, Buddhist medicine used 'everything useful', including the knowledge of 'hillmen, herdsmen, and forest-dwelling hermits',[126] while today Beals contrasts the 'asymmetrical' exclusivism of Western medicine with the 'almost spongelike readiness of ordinary people in India to accept other kinds of medicine'.[127] For Asia generally, Leslie finds no 'animosity' in Asian systems, no parallel to what Freidson has described as the 'authoritarian', 'definitive', 'subordinating' exclusiveness of Western medicine.[128]

So, while in general people are open-minded about Western medicine,[129] they are not uncritical. They accept that though it works well for some kinds of physical illness, for other common and serious conditions, such as arthritis, neuralgia, paralysis, rashes and haemorrhoids, it is less effective. It is especially useless in dealing with psychosomatic problems ranging from heartbreak (not heartburn) to witchcraft and malicious mothers-in-law. The mismatch between the biomedical and other cultural perspectives on illness can be seen when Western doctors are accused of refusing patients drugs to keep them awake, thereby allowing witches full rein to work on them while they are asleep.[130] Again, Melanesians find European thought contradictory. In the colonial epoch, white men told them that magic and witchcraft were just irrational delusions, yet took them so seriously that witches were brought to trial in the courts. And though they are accused of irrationality because they believe in spirits that cannot be seen, Europeans themselves believe in very powerful agents of disease called 'germs' – which cannot be seen!

Indigenous methods of treating mental illness have rarely been studied. Only in a very few countries, notably Nigeria and Senegal, have Western-trained psychiatrists tried using indigenous possession-techniques to treat mental illness.[131]

Western science prides itself on its 'openness', according to which new theories are constantly tested, some accepted and others, usually older ones, rejected. Yet, as one authority writes, 'In practice, the rise of scientific authority has meant a narrowing of the range of alternative systems of explanation or treatment'.[132]

The major exception has been in the field of pharmacology, where bodies like Mexico's IMEPLAM (the Mexican Institute for the Study of Indigenous Medical Plants) are systematically listing traditional herbal remedies used in the numerous indigenous cultures of that country on their computers, thereby attracting interest from Western pharmaceutical corporations on the lookout for cheap, effective and profitable latter-day equivalents of the most widely used drug of all, aspirin (developed from willow bark), or the heart drug, digoxin, developed from the foxglove. Over 7,000 medical compounds, with a retail value of US$43 billion in 1985, have been developed from plants.

The major effort of these corporations, however, is put into outflanking their rivals by marketing an ever-growing variety of new 'wonder drugs' with proprietary names. In 1988, the WHO, on the other hand, drew up a model list of only 270 *essential* 'generic' (non-brand-name) drugs which would cope with the main diseases encountered in poor countries. At the village dispensary level, only ten to fifteen are needed; at the health centre level, forty drugs can treat 80 to 90 per cent of complaints; and even at district hospital level only 100 are needed. Countries such as Bangladesh, Sri Lanka, Australia, India and Mexico, which introduced national drug policies of this kind, not only improved health provision to the poor but provided drugs more cheaply than the transnational pharmaceutical corporations. By the 1990s, however, they were being forced to turn their back on much of the progress they had made as free market policies were forced on them.[133]

Today, many of the striking successes usually credited to drugs are increasingly being seen as a consequence of preventive measures. The elimination of yellow fever (which had defeated even De Lesseps) during the building of the Panama Canal, for instance, was mainly due to the *sanitary* measures introduced by the US Army, notably control of the breeding grounds of the mosquito and improved housing conditions. Half a century later, the WHO's attempt to eradicate malaria in the 1960s by spraying insecticides did at first succeed in reducing cases in India alone from 100 million in 1952 to 50,000 by 1962. But by the 1970s, 5 million cases were being reported, while worldwide over a million were dying from malaria and another 1,000 million fell ill from it, a massive recrudescence which has been attributed to another Western spraying programme, not in med-

icine but in agriculture – the heavy use of chemical pesticides, to which insect strains have become resistant, and to large-scale population movements caused by plantation agriculture.[134]

Nature, it seems, still has a few surprises which Western science has not
been able to anticipate or deal with, the emergence of the Aids virus, the
spread of which is predominantly due to cultural and social changes, being
the most serious.

Wider contradictions exist too between the Hippocratic ideals of com-
bating illness and extending the human life span, and their unintended social consequences – new levels and kinds of geriatric illness – while new
technologies such as computer tomography or magnetic resonance carry
with them such snowballing costs that they have acquired a special label of
their own – '*expensive* medical techniques'.

In the Third World, where poverty is still the major cause of illness, that
kind of medicine is irrelevant. Some of their poverty is 'relative poverty',
the result of spending income unwisely. But in countries like Bolivia, there
is also persistent *absolute* poverty – sheer shortage of resources, a vivid
glimpse of which is provided by one anthropologist's study of the
Cochabamba Valley. As Cajka writes:

In a man's lifetime, he will buy one suit, one white shirt ... perhaps a hat
and one pair of shoes, and one of rubber boots. The only other things
which have to be purchased in the market are a small radio-record
player, the batteries to run it, plaster religious figures, a bicycle, a picture
of a popular ex-President, and some cutlery.[135]

The *medical* consequences of such low material levels are indicated by
Lewis' estimate that men in New Guinea lose almost ten times as much
time because of illness than Englishmen. Women, though, suffer even
more, because they are under pressure 'not to stop work for mild illness';[136] in southern India, there is a 'virtual absence of medical treatment
for late-born female children'.[137]

So while economic development can make improvements in the overall
health of the population, it does not do so unless there is, as in Japan, a narrowing of the gap between rich and poor and between the sexes. In Britain,
on the other hand, a liberal newspaper has concluded, 'The Thatcher years
have conspired to make the rich richer, and the poor sicker.'[138]

On top of endemic, poverty-driven ill-health, massive suffering has
been caused by scores of wars in the Third World since the Second World
War, exacerbated by the use of ever more lethal military technology. In a
single village in northern Uganda, every family lost at least one member

during the two years that the anthropologist Tim Allen spent among them. Mothers gave their new-born babies names like Kodri: all go to the grave; Amadrio: without successors; Via: in hunger; Izama: impoverished; Mzapke: without hope; Ambayo: without elders; Apidra: survived death; Tabu: all my children have died; and, simply, Draa: death.[139]

Low income, then, is not the only cause of illness. In the West, 'diseases of affluence' – of lifestyles and consumption patterns – are common, and growing. Obesity – even among children – has become a common phenomenon, while a thirty-five-year-old man in Edinburgh can expect to live twice as long after retirement as a man of the same age in Glasgow, because poor people spend less, on a worse-balanced diet, than the better off, and because of high levels of smoking and alcohol consumption. But diseases of affluence are now occurring in 'developing' countries. Where people have changed to Western customs, diets and lifestyles, increases in appendicitis, diverticular disease, benign colonic tumours, cancer of the large bowel, ulcerative colitis, varicose veins, deep-vein thrombosis, pulmonary embolism, haemorrhoids, coronary heart disease, gallstones, hiatus hernia and diabetes have all been found.[140] The irony is that it is the poor rather than the rich who are more likely to die from these diseases.

Because poor countries lack capital and trained personnel, the WHO has long recognized that Western medicine, which relies on expensive drugs and high-tech hospitals, is singularly ill-suited to dealing with illnesses generated by poverty. Yet people in the Third World are subjected to an unremitting barrage of adverts for Western drugs on TV and radio. There are weaker controls too over the availability and use of drugs, many of which are available over the counter, outdated and dangerous. Even so, for poor people, they are often simply too expensive. In the United States, between 1960 and 1983, the average rate of return on capital invested in the pharmaceutical industry was 18 per cent, compared to 11 per cent for all other types of manufacturing industry. But in the Third World, rates of return on capital of the order of 30 to 40 per cent are common. In India, 'foreign drug companies are not only the most profitable of manufacturers generally, but also of all foreign-controlled business'.[141]

As long ago as 1976, therefore, the WHO urged its member states to develop primary health programmes that included traditional medicine and curers. In reality, though, the WHO has backed training Third World doctors in Western-style, hospital-based, specialist medicine. Alternative policies have been used, though, in the two states with the largest populations on earth: China and India. In India, there was resistance to any mixture of traditional with Western medicine both from the pro-Western, 'modernist' lobby and from Ayurvedic purists. However, when the state

finally decided to support Ayurvedic and Unani medicine, in 1962, only
9.8 crores of rupees out of a total budget of 341.9 crores were spent on
indigenous systems of medicine. Not surprisingly, many students of
Ayurveda, who had really wanted to follow Western courses but couldn't
get in, felt themselves to be second-class doctors. Between 1958 and
1964, there were more than fifty-five strikes demanding more Western
content in Ayurvedic courses. On graduation too, their status and salaries
were inferior to those of doctors trained in allopathic (Western) medicine. Yet the 5,741 Ayurvedic hospitals turned out more trained practitioners than the 12,600 Western-style hospitals.[142]

In China, the liberal revolutionaries of 1919 had scorned traditional
medicine. When their communist successors took power in 1949, there
were only 29,000 Western-trained doctors in a country of 500 million
people. The solution adopted was that of 'walking on two legs' – using
'barefoot doctors' as well as Western-style doctors and hospitals. Indigenous medicine, which is cheap, is used mainly to cope with the bulk of illness at the lower levels of society. Traditional medicine is largely for
peasants: town and countryside are treated differently. It prevails, above
all, in the villages, where 85 per cent of the population live; Western medicine becomes increasingly dominant as one moves up the system. In the
famous *Barefoot Doctor's Manual*, from Hunan, the medical assistant is
taught a simple 'hierarchy of resort': first, use acupuncture; then traditional *materia medica*; then Western drugs; finally, refer the patient to a
local hospital. It begins with a thoroughly Western discussion of the body,
its organs and systems, hygiene and the treatment of disease, then
launches, with no transition, into a discussion of treatment and Chinese
herbs, acupuncture and moxibustion – with no explicit link to what went
before – and finally reverts to Western-style 'general treatment techniques'. There is no explicit discussion of the theoretical differences underlying each of the systems – the issue is simply evaded.[143]

But in most Third World countries the project of combining traditional
and Western medicine in state-sponsored medical programmes remains
largely rhetorical, since it still calls for considerable organization and investment, while most political and medical élites, fixated as they are upon
everything Western as the quintessence of 'modernity', lack the will to develop such programmes. Nigerian doctors, for instance, have put pressure
upon their governments to restrict the sphere of operations of indigenous
healers, while even in countries where governments have favoured
progammes of basic health care, like Panama, doctors, especially those
trained in the United States, have used their muscle to press for 'the best'
– that is, high-tech, hospital-based medicine. The inevitable outcome is

the situation reached in Dakar, where the imposition of French standards of education resulted in the production, in 1964, of only twenty-eight medical graduates, of whom only three were Senegalese.[144]

Two leading medical anthropologists have argued that *all* kinds of health-care systems that 'meet at least some of the needs and expectations of sufferers who seek them out' – be they spiritualist therapists, 'charlatans' who use pseudo X-rays or the 30,000 needlemen who fill the gap in Turkey's health services – should be supported.[145] Their general conclusion, though, is bleak: while 'a good deal of lip service will be paid to traditional therapies in future years ... the impact on the development of national health services will be minimal'.[146]

Conventional surveys, based on questionnaires administered by upperclass, university-educated and sometimes foreign researchers, working in a language ordinary people do not speak, are feeble measures of the true extent of the continuing use by the urban (or rural) poor of traditional medicine, for admitting that they do so is equivalent to stigmatizing themselves as backward and uneducated.

The 'micro' methods used by anthropologists, on the other hand – the following-through of single cases in the context of all a person's relationships, in detail and over time – have led to the application of the concept of the 'life cycle', developed in kinship studies, to medical studies too. Some, though, have argued that the idea of a cycle implies circularity and that the image of life as a *career* is a better one.[147] One sociologist, indeed, spent his time in hospital charting the ways in which the passage of time was structured according to different 'timetables' for different illness.[148] The conventional notes GPs make on their patients' medical records, in contrast, are abstracted from time and societal context.

Though the WHO defines health as not just 'the absence of disease or infirmity' but '*a state of complete physical, mental and social well-being*', the perfunctory consultations given by Western doctors do not permit the degree of understanding of a patient's total social situation and its history that the Kongo therapy-managing group can provide. Nor does the sick person have the social support which makes it possible for the Kongo patient to successively try out different kinds of therapy.

In the West, in the end, chronic and life-threatening illnesses do drive people to experiment with 'alternative' medicine, though. In a study of some 28,000 people, within a single year, one in seven of them, *after* consulting their own GP and feeling dissatisfied, or finding only temporary relief, or being told that the disease was not treatable, had recourse to alternative practitioners: in order of frequency, to acupuncturists, homoeopaths, herbalists and chiropractors.[149] Nevertheless, regular resort to alternative medicine is still very limited: only 1 per cent of the British population uses an acupuncturist; 2 per cent use homoeopathic physicians; 3 per cent practise meditation; 7 per cent use natural medicine; and 16 per cent buy health foods.[150] That said, in the early 1980s, non-biomedical consultations were increasing by 10 to 15 per cent every year, five times more rapidly than biomedicine. By 1981, there were over 30,000 'complementary' medical practitioners, less than 10 per cent of whom were qualified in orthodox medicine, and only a third of whom belonged to professional associations.[151] The great majority, though, *were* trained in their discipline; in a study of 137 of them only four were not. By 1986, some £150 million per annum was being spent on consultations, and another £100 million on vitamins, supplements, herbs, X-rays and mechanical aids – together with the £1 billion spent on drugs sold over the counter, half as much as National Health Service expenditure on drugs prescribed by doctors. While the NHS bill was going up by 11 per cent a year, the sale of herbal medicines and food supplements went up by 50 per cent in five years and the sale of homoeopathic remedies reached £16.3m worth.[152] Among young people, Anita Roddick's Body Shops became a cult.

By 1983, the rise of alternative medicines had induced some younger doctors in the West to begin to pay more attention to integrating biomedicine with alternative therapies, evidenced by the establishment of a new association for doctors – the British Holistic Medical Association. In 1986, the BMA itself established a working party to look into alternative medicine. It concluded that any benefits gained were largely due to the 'placebo effect' – people being *persuaded* that they were better – so, as usual, the report emphasized that alternative healers must follow strict standards laid down by practitioners of orthodox medicine. Yet by 1991 the Department of Health had announced that complementary medicine could be provided on the NHS and a second BMA report in 1993 not only welcomed the 'explosion' of complementary medicine but recommended that, where appropriate, doctors should refer their patients to complementary therapists.[153]

Labels like 'alternative' and 'complementary' lump together vastly different therapies. One writer has distinguished no fewer than sixty of them, which she subdivides into 'physical' therapies, such as naturopathy, herbal medicine, and manipulative therapies, such as osteopathy and chiropractic; 'Oriental' therapies, from acupuncture to exercise/movement therapies (T'ai chi, yoga, dance) and sensory therapies using music, art or colour; 'psychological' therapies, such as psychoanalysis, hypnotherapy and humanistic psychology of many kinds; and 'paranormal' healing, such as the laying-on of hands and exorcism, and diagnosis such as palmistry, astrology and iridology.[154]

At one level, the growth of alternative medicines may simply reflect patients' worries about the side-effects of Western pharmaceuticals. But it also says something about the difference in relations between alternative practitioners and their patients, for these consultations, in Britain at least, last on average six times longer than those with general practitioners.

Alternative curers in the Third World, whatever partisans of holistic medicine in the West may assert, do not necessarily spend much time with their patients. In urban Colombia, as we saw, consultations are usually very brief, and curers and patients often do *not* know each other – which precludes any deep, 'holistic' knowledge of the patient's personal and social circumstances.

The growing popularity of alternative medicine is certainly not merely a question of cost. People do not go to alternative practitioners to save money, but to ease their sufferings and even to save their lives. Consultations with alternative practitioners in Britain cost between £6 and £10 in 1981 – cheaper than the cost of going to a private specialist, but roughly twice the cost to the state of providing general practitioner services (to which taxpayers contribute), excluding the cost of drugs, for which the NHS makes a prescription charge for most people.[155]

In the Third World, as we saw, alternative medicine is not necessarily cheaper either. People expect to pay more for better treatment: if the treatment is any good, the logic runs, it *ought* to cost more. Conversely, one does not pay those who don't deliver the goods. And even those curers who profess to serve the sick, in a truly Hippocratic way, and who disdain payment, usually accept 'donations' and other expressions of gratitude which enable them to dedicate themselves to their calling. The urban curers studied by Press were *all*, unambiguously, 'professionals for hire'.

Mind, Body and Society

The 'iatrogenic' critique of biomedicine and the spread of knowledge about alternatives have led to a growing acceptance of the idea that people can contribute to taking care of their own well-being through adopting a healthy 'lifestyle'. Jogging became a cult, and US presidents strove to increase their 'street cred' by highly publicized jogging (even though President Carter collapsed during one run!). Likewise, aerobics and food fads succeeded each other with bewildering rapidity and became enormous sources of income for those who, like Jane Fonda, catered to the new market.

Doctors themselves were affected by these new moods, for the newly qualified ones still found themselves, as ever, thrown into the firing line, handling not just their patients' physical illnesses but the social problems that had often caused them. In addition, the through-put of patients in the hospitals was now being speeded up by governments and administrators seeking to cut patient-bed costs. Outside the hospital, doctors still had to deal with chronic illnesses, especially those of the elderly patients who increasingly filled their surgeries, where they acted as surrogates for the priest-confessor and the social worker – without either the spiritual authority of the former or the professional training of the latter. Like bank managers and solicitors, they were necessarily available to the public. They therefore had to develop their own, quite amateur skills in handling anxious people and their relatives, who, though not as well organized as Kongo therapy-managing groups, could still put pressure on doctors, even sue them, or alternatively help them by undertaking care in the home.

As Foucault has classically shown, historically one way of dealing with the mentally ill has been to treat them like criminals and the very poor: to control and punish them.[156] In Tudor times, beggars were flogged and driven from parish to parish; by the nineteenth century, prisoners were kept under total surveillance, night and day, in buildings modelled on Jeremy Bentham's ghastly 'Panopticons'; and the insane were chained up like animals. A century later, Erving Goffman caused an intellectual furore when he showed that mental asylums were still 'total institutions', with inmates living in conditions similar to those not just of prisoners but of the inmates of concentration camps.[157]

In the nineteenth century, phrenologists had argued that the external configurations of the skull reflected internal patternings of the brain and therefore mental functioning, a reductionism which orthodox medicine definitively defeated. Later, eugenicists, including leading *social* scientists, campaigned for the elimination of the 'unfit' by culling, an ideology also rejected by orthodox medicine, to its credit. But the attempt to control 'undesirable' kinds of thinking and expressions of emotionality by operating directly upon the seat of consciousness, the brain, had by no means been renounced and a new reductionism emerged. The brain, it postulates, is a material organ, in which chemical changes take place, as in any other organ. The proven power of chemical drugs in treating physical illness has therefore tempted many psychiatrists to see this as the principal way forward in the treatment of mental illness also.

Looking back at the 1930s, a British Emeritus consultant in psychiatry made an assessment of the regimen of drugs and electroconvulsive therapy (ECT), administered under conditions which resemble Goffman's view of US mental institutions. His remarkable testimony is worth quoting at length:

mental institutions ... were in effect closed institutions, as closed *vis-à-vis* ingress and egress as Her Majesty's prisons ... All members of staff were uniformed ... so that, unlike today when everyone is uniformly ill-dressed, their identity was immediately recognizable. Thus it was mandatory for all doctors – with the exception of the Medical Superintendent who, as befitted an autocrat, could please himself – to wear white coats.

The clothing of the patients, too, was uniform ... coarse, ill-fitting suits for the men and unimaginative sack-like dresses for the women ... Uniformity was equally to be seen in the decorative schemes of the wards and corridors which were confined to variations on two colours – dark chocolate and oleaginous greens. The hallmark of uniformity characterized the too-too solid furniture, built far less for comfort than for durability ...

Discipline for both patients and staff was tight; sanctions were plentiful and included arbitrary dismissal for offences committed by staff, some of which by today's standards would be considered trivial. Patients were subjected to interferences with their civil rights and liberties, some only minor and irritating, but others were major and calculated to offend against the dignity of the individual. One such was enforced idleness.[158]

Over time, patients became 'institutionalized', progressively less able to readapt to life in the normal community outside, if and when they were released.

The inpatient community was made up of those suffering from the major psychoses ... for the most part admitted under compulsory (statutory) orders. Because of the grave stigma which admission to a mental hospital carried, the less serious mental illnesses (the neuroses, for example) were treated elsewhere, if at all. Psychotherapy, as we know it today, was available only to a well-heeled minority ...

Schizophrenics ... [would] spend their entire day in assumed statuesque postures, or in carrying out strange rituals, or in rocking rhythmically and tirelessly backwards and forwards, or in ceaselessly twisting pieces of string or strands of their hair. Flexibilitas cerea, or waxy flexibility, which permitted limbs to be moulded into unnatural positions and ... maintained seemingly indefinitely, was fairly commonplace, [as were] grossly depraved behaviour, such as coprophagia and faeces smearing, and persistent and open masturbation ... Fewer in numbers were those patients deemed to be suffering from the affective psychoses whose major symptoms were to be seen in gross disturbances of mood ... patients could quite literally die from what was termed 'exhaustion of mania', a cause accepted in those days by the Registrar of Births and Deaths. At the other extreme ... were victims of psychomotor retardation in which depression reached such depths as to lead to stupor [which sometimes resulted in] starvation; forced feeding of these unfortunates was a well-practised technique which I have not only witnessed, but have been party to. More importantly, there was the danger of death by suicide. The attempt to prevent suicide, or self-mutilation, was a major preoccupation. Every member of staff was obliged to sign the infamous 'suicidal caution card'. Written large in red lettering on top of the card was the injunction that the patient 'must on no account be allowed out of observation, not even in the WCs'.[159]

With the introduction of treatment by the use of convulsants in the 1930s, a new, biomedical phase of therapy began. The side-effects of the first, injections of camphor in oil, though, were so 'unacceptable' that it was abandoned, to be followed by leptazol. 'Such was the state of terror induced during the preconvulsive period,' Rollin remarks, 'that it became a matter in many cases of "first catch your patient"' – though positive results were claimed in nearly three-quarters of cases. Insulin therapy, later, also resulted in remission in nearly half the cases of schizophrenia in which it was used.

Psychiatrists then turned to a newer, but equally physical method: operating upon the organ of thought and feeling itself, the brain, by prefrontal leucotomy (or lobotomy) – 'in my mind,' Rollin remarks, 'the most inhumane treatment to which the hapless schizophrenic has ever been subjected'. By 1963, more than 15,000 such operations were performed in Britain alone.

It seemed to many that the regime of incarceration could now be phased out:

The ethos in the mental hospitals underwent a dramatic metamorphosis. The interiors were transformed by the introduction of attractive decorative schemes, modern furniture and the like ... Creature comforts were vastly improved [and] the penurious prison-like atmosphere ... eradicated. Locked wards were unlocked; blocks were removed from windows.[160]

By the mid-1950s, cardiazol was abandoned completely; deep-insulin clinics were dismantled and the flood of prefrontal leucotomies was reduced to a trickle.

However, a third biomedical treatment, ECT, was not abandoned. In its early days, it was given 'straight', without anaesthesia and without muscle relaxants. The results included fractures of the spine and long bones and dislocation, particularly of the jaw; in one study, over a third of those treated suffered fractures, especially compressed fractures of the vertebrae. To avoid this, force was needed: a team of nurses was used, one to hold the patient's feet, another to bear down on the pelvis, and two more to keep the shoulders on the couch and control the arms and chest. Yet another nurse was entrusted with head and jaw movements, the patients having been instructed to bite hard on a rubber heel covered with gauze inserted between the teeth. Another method involved the use of a restraining sheet, developed from the strait-jacket. Later, anaesthesia and muscle relaxants removed the need for brute force.

Rollin does not reject the use of ECT in cases of schizophrenia. 'In some cases,' he records, '[it] worked like a charm', and the more severe the depression, the better the response. He does note, though, that 'even today a least one-third of all bona fide cases of schizophrenia become chronic'. At his hospital, patients would routinely get one ECT a week. By 1954, leaving aside private patients and outpatients, a third of all patients admitted into mental hospital per year, some 20,000 people, were having ECT at some time during their stay – not only schizophrenics but also those suffering from depression.

Today, ECT has been largely (though not entirely) replaced by new psychotropic drugs in the treatment of the affective psychoses. Within eight months of its introduction to the United States, Largactil was being prescribed for an estimated 2 million patients. Stays in mental hospitals were reduced from months to weeks. Yet a third of cases still become chronic, and the side-effects from drugs given either orally or by injection, can be 'pretty intolerable'. Outside hospital, patients asked their doctors for mood-changing drugs, notably Valium and Librium, on a massive scale.

Little wonder, then, that the iatrogenic mood of many young people causes them to look upon psychiatry with the deepest suspicion. *One Flew Over the Cuckoo's Nest* is the only film I have ever watched where the audience (largely students) gave a standing ovation before the end, as the Indian 'Chief' escaped from the mental hospital.

There seems to be little justification, therefore, for Western scientists to denounce the methods used by those they label 'witch-doctors' when their own are so unreliable and often harmful. As long as psychiatry remains only one minor specialty, studied for only a few weeks during the five years of a doctor's training, out of the many that they have to cover, especially the far longer periods they spend on anatomy and physiology, doctors will inevitably emerge from medical schools equipped with a less than adequate understanding of mental illness. Yet these are undoubtedly among the 'diseases of affluence'. Since the term 'stress' was first coined, as recently as 1936, 110,000 papers have been written on it.[161] In the hierarchy of prestige of the different specialties, psychiatry is pretty near the bottom. For there is no correlation between the *social* importance of different kinds of illness and the prestige accorded them by the medical profession; despite the growing proportion of old people in the West, geriatrics is a low-prestige specialty.

Mental illnesses are equally part and parcel of life in the Third World. Though romantics imagine that peasant or tribal life is a 'pastoral' idyll, 'a world peopled by vengeful deities and ghosts, witches and sorcerers, and angry neighbours and envious relations,' Foster and Anderson remark, 'is not less stressful than our own'.[162] In any case, the majority of people in the Third World, half of them now urbanized and often overworked in unhealthy environments or underemployed, live in poor housing with bad sanitation. Mental illness is therefore on the rise even among those whose incomes have improved, and the notion that they all have available networks of extended family and kin who can take care of them when they become old is no longer true.[163] One consequence is that they increasingly resort not to Western scientific medicine but, in South America, for instance, to religious cults such as Umbanda or Protestant evangelical movements which promise to alleviate miseries of all kinds.

Western psychology, on which psychiatric treatment rests, has taken many false turnings. But whatever doctors may have done, social scientists cannot be absolved of their share of responsibility either for some of their contributions to the misunderstanding of mental illness. Though it conceptualized such crucial mechanisms as repression and sublimation, and focused on social relationships, especially within the family, and on the hidden importance of sex drives, psychoanalysis by overemphasizing the latter, distorted the thinking of a whole generation and gave partisans of reductionist biomedicine grounds for arguing that only their kind of biomedical psychiatry was 'scientific'. As a result, behaviourists from Pavlov and Watson to Skinner thought themselves justified in attempting to develop a psychology grounded predominantly on attributes commmon to humans and other animals.

Yet disease, illness, cure and healing cannot be reduced to merely physical, behavioural or physiological concepts, since this takes as the model for medicine the natural sciences, whose subject matter lacks that which is distinctively human, consciousness, though, as a philosopher of science has remarked, 'Electrons do not get sick and a break in chemical compounds does not require "healing"'.[164]

A truly social psychiatry, in which human beings are seen both as actors endowed with consciousness and as persons involved in many levels and kinds of social relationships, has been slow to develop, in part because psychiatrists have been divided into rival theoretical schools, but more importantly because psychiatrists cannot alter social relations, whether at the macro level, in areas such as unemployment or racial prejudice, which generate mental strain, or at a lower level, notably the family and the home. Inevitably, then, psychiatrists have to try to cure their patients through face-to-face intensive interaction in the very special, artificial situation of small groups in *clinical* settings.

Given the structure and culture of Western society, in which mobility, alienation and isolation are endemic, and given also our cultural perceptions of illness, including mental illness, as largely an 'individual' phenomenon, our psychiatry cannot match the kind of involvement that the Kongo therapy-managing group makes possible in their culture. Instead, Western doctors turn to the use of drugs in dealing with mental as well as physical illness.

Hopes of a less traumatic biomedical outcome have been stimulated recently by the introduction of the new 'designer-drug' Prozac, which is claimed to be a 'clean' drug – no side-effects and not addictive.[165] Yet once the patient stops taking it, if there has been no improvement in the social situation (such as a broken marriage) which gave rise to depression in the first place, the depression returns. The Kongo too take all kinds of medicines. Their medicines, though, are buttressed by the social support of the therapy-managing group, which even our social psychiatry lacks.

There has always been a variety of ideas about ways of treating illness in every culture, then, though generally speaking the more complex societies have a greater number of alternative therapies available. But even the less differentiated societies contain within them a number of *sub*cultures – medical, scientific and other. On the other hand, ideas and practices overstep the boundaries of social groups, even polities.

Today, Western medicine has become the single most influential kind of medicine globally. It has achieved a degree of cultural hegemony which enables powerful states and corporations to extend their global reach and influence. At the same time, the new global movements of ideas and people, and global communications allow other kinds of movements and organizations to penetrate the boundaries of even the most 'closed' countries. In the case of medicine, traditional kinds not only continue to exist but have spread outside their areas of origin, and new ones are constantly developing and spreading. In the medical sphere, then, culture and structure are by no means simply congruent with the nation-state – a finding which, we will see, has implications for the theory of culture generally, not just the field of medicine.

But before we turn to the place of culture in social life, we need to follow up the last part of our discussion of medicine, which ended with mental illness, by examining not just ideas about the tangible world around us – as we have mainly done so far – but religious ideas that postulate another kind of 'otherworldly' existence.

Remembering the Past, Interpreting the Present, Imagining the Future

African Genesis

Up to modern times, all cultures have seen the earthly order of things as part of a wider, all-encompassing framework provided by religion. We will look, then, at one culture in particular which has been described as being totally permeated by religion: that of the Dogon of Mali, West Africa, about which we possess a singularly rich knowledge because of two life-times of work by the French missionary-ethnologist Marcel Griaule and his colleague Germaine Dieterlen.

Griaule began his work among the Dogon in 1931, and from 1946 on-wards among the neighbouring Bambara too. He continued to study them, together with Dieterlen, until his death in 1956.

They also attracted teams of ethnographers, linguists, historians of reli-gion, students of art, archaeologists, botanists and zoologists. As the years went by, they used tape-recordings, film and even aerial photography. In recognition of the uniqueness of this research, the Centre National de la Recherche Scientifique in Paris even provided a boat on the River Niger, specially equipped as a mobile study base.

Griaule alone produced more than 170 publications on every aspect of Dogon culture, from social organization, technology and medicine to their pharmacopoeia and their art and games. But it is the study of Dogon religion which has attracted most attention.[1] Over sixteen years, Griaule checked the information he was collecting with the Dogon. As a result, the Dogon took the decision that, in the light of Griaule's proven dedica-tion to understanding their culture, he had reached the point where they could no longer reasonably withhold from him the most esoteric aspects of their religion, which should at last be revealed.[2]

The Dogon distinguish four levels (or degrees) of religious knowledge. In the simplest, boys learn about the major mythical beings, though only their 'outward' activities: certain sacred texts and accompanying rituals. The second stage gives the initiate a deeper understanding of the meaning of the religious knowledge he has already learned, though other areas are still withheld, nor is he shown how they all link up to form an intellectual whole. The third introduces him to yet other areas, and to the connections between all these areas, though very secret knowledge is still withheld. Only in the fourth stage – that of 'deep knowledge' – are these remaining areas revealed, and the cosmology as a whole synthesized.[3]

As a result, Griaule found that everything he had discovered over sixteen years, which had given him a worldwide reputation as a specialist on the religion of the Dogon, had been merely their 'simple' knowledge. They now decided to assign as his teacher one of their best-informed members, Ogotemmêli, who would have to report every day to the council of elders and priests on the progress of the instruction he was to give Griaule. For thirty-three days, he poured out a 'meandering' flow of information. This proved to be only a precursor to instruction which went on for months, then stretched into years, during which time Ogotemmêli died. Others were then appointed to carry on his work.

What he taught Griaule was the story of the successive phases of creation, the three Words of Dogon Revelation. In the beginning, God – Amma – had created the stars from pellets of earth flung into space; the earth, likewise, was formed from a lump of clay. Though its body is feminine (it lies flat on its back, from north to south), it possesses both a male sexual organ (an ant hill) and a clitoris (a termite hill). Ogotemmêli gives this phase of creation, though, less attention than the linked movements of the stars, for it is these which determined creation, particularly one star which revolves around Sirius and which, although tiny, is regarded as the smallest and heaviest of all the stars. It is named after the smallest cultivated seed – which we call *Digitaria exilis* and the Dogon *fonio*, or 'little thing'. To them, it symbolizes the original germ of life.

Space and life are thus interlinked. Quickened by internal vibration, the original seed burst its sheath and emerged to reach the uttermost confines of the universe. This unfolding matter moved – or moves, for it still continues – along a path which forms a spiral or helix. This oscillatory side-to-side movement, combined with the forwards movement of matter, is represented on the walls of Dogon shrines by zigzag patterns, symbolizing further the concentration of matter and the alternation of opposites: right and left; high and low; odd and even; male and female – forms of the principle of twinness which ideally underlies the proliferation of life. These opposites work together to bring about an equilibrium within each individual living thing.

As matter moves, it generates life. Within the 'egg of the world', there are seven other principal seeds of cultivation, which are represented by dividing the diagram of an egg into seven segments of increasing length. Together with the original *Digitaria* seed, they constitute the Divine Octet, from which the entire organization of the cosmos, society and even the parts of the human body derive.

At the seventh vibration, the segment which is the Dogon symbol of life, and the ideal food, because it is immune from impurity – female sorghum – breaks its envelope.

Inside this seed, represented as a huge egg, was an oblong plate, divided into four sectors (called 'shoulder blades' by the Dogon), each with one of the four elements: water, air, fire and earth. Inside each of these were eight signs, and each of these was further divided into eight, giving a total of 256 signs, plus eight others for the axes and two for the centre: a total of 266. Two of these are the 'guiding signs'; the other 264 are divided into twenty-two groups of twelve signs each. Between them, they encompass everything significant in the Dogon universe, beginning with God and beings like Him, endowed with thought and feeling, called the Nommo; then there are the ancestors, as well as speech (or the Word), the rituals of the seasons, agriculture, iron-working, weaving and pot-making.

As the plates revolved, these signs were thrown into space. When they came to rest, they brought to life every kind of being, which up to then had existed only 'potentially'.

Next, God created the Nommo. Prior to this, all the creatures created had been 'twin' beings, equipped with the attributes of both sexes. Each was a pair. But Yurugu, the male half of one of the twins, had pretensions to make a world of his own and emerged prematurely, bursting out of the egg and taking with him part of the placenta – which became the earth – and the *fonio* seed. He then copulated with the earth – his mother – a primordial incestuous crime, which, like those of Eve and Cain, brought disorder into the world. The beings he created, therefore, were impure and incomplete – with a male soul only.

Yurugu then tried to go back to heaven to find the rest of the placenta and the other half of his twin soul. But by this time God had handed over his other half to the other twin. Unable to find her, Yurugu has continued the search ever since, in darkness, on a dry earth.

To re-establish His authority and to purify the earth, Amma punished this primal disobedience by sacrificing Yurugu, henceforward symbolized as the sly, treacherous Fox. Given Dogon binary proclivities, these sacrifices inevitably involved four of Fox's component souls, plus four supplementary ones, and took place over eight periods of creation time.[4]

On the positive side, He sent down other Nommo, who descended via the great arch. Two of them – the ancestors of the blacksmiths, a separate community from the agricultural Dogon – stopped off first. The other four, the ancestors of the four existing clans of the Dogon today, continued down the arch. Now the earth, which had been in darkness, was flooded with light and water; times and seasons came into being; and rain purified and fertilized the soil. Yurugu, therefore, is a being of night and a symbol of death; the Nommo are associated with the daytime, with the habitable, cultivated land, with sky, water and fertility.

The eight seeds which the ancestors brought with them now became human beings, animals and plants. They then gave birth to twelve off-spring, consisting of four pairs of twins – some mixed-sex, some male and some female – plus two males and two females, thereby bringing society into existence.

Like the biblical Genesis, this is what Henri Frankfort called 'mythopoeia': creations of the human imagination which explain the origins of the universe, the place of humanity in that universe and the coming of sin and death. People familiar with Christian mythology will see analogues with Dogon myths – with the revolt of Satan, the disobedience of Eve and Abraham's sacrifice – and with such obvious symbols of the universe and of life as the stars, the cosmic egg and the seeds. The obsession with binary numeration, on the other hand, is a cultural obsession peculiar to the Dogon (and Lévi-Strauss).

Dogon mythology, then, has the typically 'totalizing' quality of all religious thought, bringing *everything* within a single explanatory framework. And what has been outlined here is the merest thumbnail sketch of some parts of extremely complex myths, which, with the commentaries on them, run to thousands rather than hundreds of printed pages, as well as many 'iconic' signs.

All cultures have to come to terms with the three metaphysical questions Gauguin asked: 'Where do we come from?', 'Who are we?' and 'Where are we going?'. Religions tackle these 'ultimates' of human existence by providing an answer to the first in the form of a *cosmogony*, which explains creation at the beginning of time; an answer to the second by providing a *cosmology*, an account of the order of the universe now; and an answer to the third by providing an *eschatology*, which explains the fate of the human being in the afterlife.

Religion, then, deals in ultimates. But people do not have to confront the ultimates of life and death every day of the week. When they do, though, there is ample room for religious explanations, for the incidence of illness and death seems to be random, arbitary, and biomedicine and Western science in general usually couch their answers to the questions 'Why me?' and 'Why now?' in terms of 'statistical probabilities'.

Dogon religion goes out of its way to do precisely this. The very layout of their fields symbolizes the descent of their four constituent tribes from four mythical pairs of twins; the fields contain shrines to the female Nommo, built out of the stones in the fields, as well as other shrines in the uncultivated bush. At the centre of the farming area are three ritual fields identified with three mythical ancestors and the cults associated with them. Around this centre lie the fields cultivated by each family: ideally, they should have eight, each associated with one of the original ancestors and grouped in pairs, facing towards the cardinal points. These plots radiate outwards from the central area in a spiral which recalls the original spiral movement of creation, while even the shape of the plots and the positions people take up when working on them are dictated by religious tradition. The farmstead, then, is a 'world in miniature'.[5]

The village is laid out in the shape of a human body, with the smithy at the head (the north) and certain shrines at the feet (the south); the huts used by menstruating women, to the east and west, are the hands. The family homesteads occupy the chest. The unity of the whole group is symbolized by a male shrine, cone-shaped, and a female one, a hollowed stone. The pattern formed by the plots is recalled in the designs on Dogon baskets. Villages are also built in pairs, symbolizing heaven and earth.

The next highest level is the district, also in two parts, with an open space at the centre which serves as a public meeting place and also symbolizes the sky. The district chief and religious authority, the Hogon, lives here. His importance is symbolized by the shrine which stands in the centre of this space and represents the sun. Other shrines belonging to other cults are placed around the edges of this space and symbolize the stars, the eight seeds and the ancestors.

The Dogon granary too is built according to a cosmic plan: the square roof is the sky; the circular base, the sun; a circle in the centre of the roof represents the moon, and so on. The layout of the homestead is likewise based on the body of the Nommo: four towers symbolize the limbs; the kitchen, the head, with the hearthstones as the eyes; the central room, the belly; the storerooms are the arms; two jars of water symbolize the breasts, and so on. The theme of procreation is also elaborately built into the plan of the homestead. Not only structures but also behaviours conform to this basic design – even the position a man (as distinct from a woman) takes up while sleeping or when they are buried.

The Hogon is not merely a political authority; he is also seen as the successor of one of the founding ancestors, the personification of the universe and regent of the Nommo on earth. A complex web of symbols relating to the stars, the seeds and the rhythms of the cosmos surrounds him, even to his clothing.

Social organization is also closely related to this theology. The four

Dogon tribes share the universe between them. Within the tribe, they live in groups of agnatically related kin between whom marriage partners are exchanged in a pattern which derives from myths of the doings of the ancestors in creation times. Through the family, each individual is also attached to twenty-two categories into which everything in the universe is divided. The ongoing order of the universe, and particularly the well-being and growth not only of human beings but also of seeds and crops, are ensured by cult rituals which Griaule and Dieterlen label 'totemic'.

It would be hard, then, to imagine a society more thoroughly permeated by religious conceptions and practices. Thus the twenty-four categories into which all things in the world are divided, according to Dogon mythology, provide the framework within which they classify all natural species: there are twenty-four classes of plants and twenty-four classes of insects. Each of the twenty-four kinds of plants also corresponds to one of the insect groups.[6] Furthermore, their staple food (our *Digitaria*) is also linked, in mythology, with menstruation; water plants and water insects correspond to each other; a certain kind of tree which is important in house construction also symbolizes the skeleton of the human body. Other plant sets are associated with the Hogon chief priest, with indigo-dyeing (a female occupation) and with charcoal-burning (a male occupation), while certain kinds of animals, such as giant tortoises, are similarly associated with longevity and clanship.

We need now, for a moment, to revert to our earlier kind of analysis, our examination of Australian Aboriginal classification systems, for what we find is that the Dogon, like the Aborigines, are in fact not restricted to a single, religious system of classification.[7] The system of twenty-four basic categories is indeed a *religious* framework of classification, not only because that number of categories derives from religious mythology but also because the names of each of the twenty-four sets of insects and plants takes its name from the principal species in the set — and their importance derives from their place in myth. Thus the first set of plants takes its name from the *Digitaria*.

But this by no means exhausts their classification of plants. In fact, they also have a quite different kind of classification: not into twenty-four categories but into eight major classes (which Griaule calls *genres*), and a few smaller ones. Within each class, though the species contained are sometimes identified by their connections with religious myths, others are identified with specialized human groups such as the indigo-dyers, the blacksmiths or the charcoal-burners, while yet others are identified according to their everyday uses, such as medicines or ingredients for making soup or sauces. And yet by far the commonest basis for identifying a particular species and classing it with related ones is neither mythological nor human-related: it is on the basis of their natural attributes, notably the external features of the insect or plant and the habitat it is found in.

The largest of these *genres* is that of the insects the Dogon call *keke*, which Griaule translates simply as 'insects' – a 'vague' term, as he says, which covers a very varied range of insects, mainly of what our entomologists call Coleoptera and Hemiptera. The other *genres* are the grasshoppers; the butterflies and dragonflies; the mantises; water insects; spiders; flies (including mosquitoes, wasps and other kinds of insect); the ants and termites; the crickets; the worms and caterpillars. There are also smaller sets of fleas and ticks, myriapods and scorpions.

Just as the number of *genres* differs from the twenty-four sacred categories, so does the number of species classified *within* each *genre*. For whatever Dogon priests may say, nature does not fall neatly into twenty-four Procrustean boxes. They recognize, rather, 359 different kinds of *keke*, 127 kinds of grasshoppers, 140 kinds of butterflies and dragonflies, forty-eight kinds of mantises, sixteen kinds of water-insects, seventy-two kinds of spiders, twenty-six kinds of flies, thirty-one kinds of ants and termites, forty kinds of crickets, and a few odds and ends.

What we have, then, is a system of classification, with eight major and a number of minor classes, within which the Dogon arrange insects they identify predominantly on a 'naturalistic' basis, with highly uneven numbers of species within each category. However, this 'naturalistic' classification 'nests', as it were, *within* a schema based on religious dogma, in which only twenty-four categories are recognized.

Dogon religion, then, is singularly totalizing, though not as much as commonly assumed. It has nevertheless been taken as if it were a universal model of 'the religious society'. We need, therefore, to see if other religious cultures are as coherent as that of the Dogon is made out to be. In the process, we also need to look at the intellectuals whose predecessors constructed this intellectual system and who today are its interpreters.

The Limits of the Supernatural: Irreligion in an Age of Faith

Religious thought displays two divergent 'moments': *imagination* and *intellectuation*. The former involves reaching out to explore every aspect of existence: plants, animals, the heavenly bodies, the human body, human society and the human mind. It is also concerned with *meaning* of all this: with the place of humanity in the cosmos, and the meaning of what we call nature and a wider whole in which nature is only a part – the supernatural.

Intellectuation, on the other hand, attempts to reduce all this to a few principles, based on the observation of people and events. Religious thought involves intellectuation. But it further admits the non-observable, whereas though our science subjects the workings of the mind to analysis, notably in the form of psychology, it does not go beyond what can be shown to exist.

In cultures like that of the Dogon, explanations of the world have been produced by remarkable and unusual people like Ogotemmêli over dozens of generations and condensed as myth: rich collective, social products. The sheer size of the entirely oral literature which is produced is astounding. In 1891, Sibelius heard the Ingrian bard Larin Pataske, who had a repertoire of more than 11,000 lines.[8] A single Aboriginal sacred song-cycle from Arnhem Land – Djanggawul – contains 188 songs in one version and 264 in another.[9] A second sequence of many hundreds of songs, used in the sacred Kunapipi rituals (only one of the sacred ritual sequences) requires between two weeks and two months, sometimes even as long as two years, to sing.[10]

If myth-makers simply continued elaborating existing myths, let alone creating new ones, the whole business would be exponential – ever-growing, interminable and unmanageable – for mythopoeic thought is not limited, as scientific research is, to what can be observed and checked by others.

So thinkers strive to contain the built-in drive of mythopoeic thought towards spinning an 'expanding universe' of myth to a set of core stories. The one movement, that of the imagination, thus thrusts towards diversification; the other, intellectuation, to systematization and integration.

The Dogon, of course, are not typical of all cultures. According to their religious specialists, religion provides the overarching explanatory framework. But however powerful religion may be both as an intellectual explanation of existence and as a regulator of behaviour, in everyday life it is still only a part of the social order, and not necessarily always the most dominant part. As a specialist in religious thought has remarked, religious cognitive models are *tools* for making sense of the world. But people have *various* cognitive models available to them. They take all of them seriously, including religious ones, but 'more seriously in some contexts, for some purposes, and with some problems than ... others'.[11] So they distinguish ritual occasions from routine ones, and do not spend the entire day, even in cultures like that of the Dogon, praying or reflecting about first and last things; even the major rituals are punctuations of routine existence, most of which is spent in cultivating, hunting or catching fish. So when people came to consult Ogotemmêli, they did so mostly not about esoteric religious matters but when they needed help in two areas in which he was a specialist: about bad luck in hunting and about bad health.

We therefore need to resist the Great Temptation: the assumption that religion has the same salience and scope in all cultures. It might well be that some cultures, like that of the Dogon, *are* singularly informed and integrated by religion. A striking more recently studied instance is the culture of the Iqwaye of New Guinea, where even their system of counting – using arms and legs, fingers and toes – fits within and derives from their cosmological view of the entire universe.[12]

But if some cultures are saturated by religious ideas and practices, others are not preoccupied so totally by conceptions of the supernatural. Even fewer societies are actually controlled by people who specialize in religious knowledge – a priesthood. Theocracies are rare – Iran today, for instance, is an exception even in the Muslim world. And in cultures which *are* undoubtedly ideologically dominated by a unitary religion, deviation from orthodoxy is widespread.

Hindu India is usually seen as a culture in which the supremacy of the priesthood, the Brahmins, is unquestioned. According to the ancient, sacred Sanskrit texts, it is they who are the bearers of *dharma*: the values and norms which underlie universal order. Since they possess the highest degree of ritual purity, they can pollute nobody below them but can be polluted by all others. It is they, therefore, who not only officiate at religious events but are also the arbiters of proper standards of behaviour generally.

These pretensions, though, involve them in conflict with those whom Wolf has called the 'real linchpin of the system', the Kshatriya ('Warrior') caste, who command secular power and whose authority rested not on *dharma*, as with the Brahmins, but on *artha:* force, gain and self-interested advantage – which, in orthodox Hindu thought, are equally valid objects of human endeavour. Kshatriya kings, not Brahmin priests, controlled the central state, and Kshatriya lineages controlled the villages. Lower castes, jockeying to improve their position within what is usually seen as a quite immutable system of caste ranking, could do so by practising what Srinivas has called 'Sanskritization' – trying to acquire a higher degree of ritual purity by imitating the customs and ritual of the Brahmins, and by getting certification of their success from Brahmin priests.[13] Another route was to try to emulate the customs and behaviour of the Warriors and get accepted, if not by them at least by society generally. Acquiring wealth was a further alternative.[14]

Religion, then, was one of several routes to high status. But even *within* organized religion, deviation from orthodoxy is very common. In the West today, we assume that the Middle Ages were an 'Age of Faith', yet there was massive deviation from the rules of the Catholic Church which were supposed to govern the behaviour of the faithful, both laymen and clergy. We have three crucial pieces of evidence.

At the end of the thirteenth century, Eudes, Archbishop of Rouen in Normandy, carried out what we would today call a 'social survey'. He was charged by King Louis IX (a religious enthusiast who was to die on a Crusade which Eudes also went on) with carrying out inspections of all the monasteries and convents under his jurisdiction. His terms of reference meant that he was to focus not so much on the extent to which the inhabitants *were* keeping to the holy rule which was supposed to regulate their lives as on the extent to which they were *not*. As the modern editor of Eudes' *Register* – his report on what he found during the twenty-one years he spent on the task – remarks, since Eudes was primarily concerned with what was *wrong*, his report was akin to a 'police record'.[15]

Yet it is still a shocking account. The Archbishop needed the full range of vocabulary available in canon law to cover the deviations from pious behaviour he found. If a monk or nun was known to have a bad reputation in society at large, they were labelled as being *infammatus* – it was deviance 'of the fact', which might then be formally investigated before an ecclesiastical court. Where proved guilty, the accused was then said to be *infammatus* 'of the law'. A person who had been formally denounced to his or her ecclesiastical superiors was *diffamatus* (defamed). Public knowledge (*notatus*) was crucial, and character witnesses would be called either to confirm the accused's guilt or in their defence. (This may seem confusing, but Eudes himself uses all these terms pretty interchangeably.)

I will divide the deviations from the rule which Eudes discovered differently: into deviations in terms of personal behaviour; deviations from religious duties; and maladministration of the religious houses.

In terms of personal behaviour, the least of the common deviations from the rule of ascetic behaviour were relatively trivial matters such as indulging oneself by keeping birds, wearing ornaments or elaborately adorned dress, eating meat or sleeping on feather beds. At the other end of the scale were gambling, dancing, drunkenness, even 'incontinence' and fornication. Eudes had to take the veil away from the most scandalous of the nuns, such as those who had had abortions.

In terms of religious duties, some nuns had never taken their vows, or been trained, while some monks displayed a lamentable ignorance of Latin and of music. Other deviations included not just whispering in the choir but failing to observe the rule of silence generally. The injunction to fast was often ignored, while even confession and communion were often only intermittently observed. Monks and nuns also commonly failed in their duties to the community outside the walls: alms were not provided and there was often no infirmary or other provision for the sick.

As for the administration of the religious houses, many abbots and priests were absentees, while 'simony' (the buying or selling of ecclesiastical preferments, benefices or emoluments) and the holding of more than one office at the same time were widespread. Some monks and nuns lived luxuriously on private incomes; others used the wealth of the community. But avarice and greed extended beyond personal lifestyles or the abuse of communal resources, such as the keeping of the keys to the cellar to themselves by some abbots. Many even gave away property belonging to the monastery or convent (including that very rare and valuable commodity, books) to relatives, while laymen were not only admitted to the cloister or the choir but also lived in some of the houses. Many religious houses did not even possess chalices; very few had copies of the rule; and buildings were allowed to fall into disrepair, even ruin. More serious was the involvement in large-scale trade on the part of many abbots, or the investing of rents collected from tenants of church lands for private gain, thereby flouting prohibitions on usury. Accounts were not properly kept or presented to the community. Debt on a considerable scale was common.

A generation later, Eudes' findings in northern France were replicated, far to the south, on the borders of Spain. But where Eudes provides us with an extensive survey of religious institutions over many years, Le Roy Ladurie gives us a fine-grained picture of life in one rural community: Montaillou – a village of only 200–250 inhabitants.[16] Here, the Cathar (Albigensian) heresy was rampant – scarcely surprising considering the scandalous life of the clergy.

Three major powers controlled the lives of the villagers: the secular power of the Comte de Foix and the dual power of the two major religious authorities, the bishop of the see of Pamiers (who later became Pope Benedict XII) and the Dominican Inquisition, based in the nearby city of Carcassonne. Though they were often at loggerheads with each other, at the end of the day the Church not only exercised 'totalitarian' rule over the parishioners but joined forces with the lay power.

The Church, indeed, behaved more like a rich landowner – which it was – more concerned with extracting tithes from the peasants than with their spiritual welfare. It is hard, therefore, to distinguish the extent to which heresy was a response to this exploitation, as opposed to a more specifically religious phenomenon. Whatever the case, alienation from the Church was both spiritual and temporal. Failure to pay tithes was visited by ruthless repression: even the 'mendicant' monks in the nearby towns acted as accomplices of the bishop, despite the rule of poverty to which they were theoretically bound, and refused to admit the excommunicated to enter their churches. In 1308, *all* the inhabitants of Montaillou were arrested in a drive to wipe out the heresy.

Concubinage was normal among the clergy, though this scarcely constituted an affront to popular morality, since 10 per cent of all households lived in sin too. According to the troubadour poets of the time, it was 'bad taste' for a woman to love her husband; for men, the ideal was 'romantic' love (*fine amour*) – expressed as reverence, abasement and service – for a married woman, though platonic to the point of absurdity. Peasants, on the other hand, were more earthy, though permissive rather than promiscuous. They did not 'couple like rats in straw' and condemned incest, the deflowering of virgins and sex with a *married* woman, not so much because of abstract ideals about sexual morality as because such behaviour threatened the viability of the farming household.

The peasants were not legally serfs: they owned, bequeathed and sold land. But whatever their legal status, *de facto* one family, the Clergues, though neither noble nor possessing manorial rights, nevertheless dominated both the secular and the religious life of Montaillou. The Clergue family also supplied the priest, Pierre Clergue, described as a 'womanizer par excellence' and a 'great carnivore' who sat like a spider at the centre of the family web, coveting 'all women whether they belonged to his flock or not'. Only once had he been unsuccessful in love.

Half a century later, across the Channel, we have a different kind of evidence: not a survey or an inquisitorial record, but Chaucer's superb literary account, *The Canterbury Tales*, of a variegated band of people whom one might have expected to be supremely pious in their behaviour since they were all engaged in a religious pilgrimage. His evidence is, of course, skewed, for of the three 'estates' into which medieval society was divided, he avoids criticizing either the higher nobility (who were supposed to protect people's lives and property) or the higher clergy (whose duty it was to protect people's souls), while the largest of all – the peasantry, who 'worked for all' – are simply left out. It is a sample, then, of the 'middling' levels of society and is deferential to noblemen and churchmen. Thus the Knight, newly home from the Crusades, is notoriously idealized; the Parson is shown as the very model of a humble, holy shepherd to his flock; the Clerk, as a dedicated scholar. Chaucer's strongest satire is reserved for those who flout the traditional norms of medieval society; the secular *nouveaux riches*: the land-acquiring, usurious Lawyer and the sharp-dealing Merchant.

Yet few of the clergy are perfect: the Monk, for example, though bookish, still takes his two hunting dogs along with him; the Friar rides on a horse instead of walking like a true pilgrim, and wears a comfortably lined habit; while the gentle Prioress is still a lady who spends money on her wardrobe and gives her dogs titbits which most peasants would have relished. Two of the Church officials, the Summoner and the Pardoner, are 'damned souls ... despicable symbols of evil'.[17] By and large, then, the clergy are by no means necessarily any better than the laymen. (One is put in mind of those guardians of the social order and defenders of official ideology, the apparatchiks of the USSR, few of whom proved to have seriously internalized Marxist ideology about equality and serving the working class.)

Religion in the Modern State

Resistance to the authority of the Roman Catholic Church was not simply confined to the level of personal behaviour. It was also structural and societal, for there is an intrinsic contradiction between the pretensions of some religions to be 'world religions' – and thereby to possess an authority which transcends that of any secular society or state – and the determination of kings and governments to keep power in their hands within their domains – even over the Church.

The Church also faced a growing, purely religious challenge, since from the sixteenth century the status of Roman Catholicism as the sole religion was undermined by the rise of Protestantism, itself a plural phenomenon.

Religion was now replaced by religions, plural, which henceforth had to coexist, peaceably or otherwise. Kings fought ruthlessly to try to impose their authority – during the gruesome Thirty Years War in Europe, for instance – by adopting the doctrine of *cuius regio, eius religio*, under which *they* would determine what was to be the official religion of the state. But these potentates were fighting a losing battle. The outcomes were many and varied. In what were effectively multinational states like England or Austria-Hungary, the religion of the hegemonic classes and the ruling dynasty was the 'established' religion of the state. In the end – though only over centuries – pluralism triumphed and even in states with hegemonic religions, religious toleration became the norm. Thus in Central Europe, the killing fields of Reformation wars of religion, Protestantism and Catholicism came to coexist in Bohemia and Germany.

Religion, in any case, was becoming less central. By the time of the Enlightenment, the *separation* of Church and state had become a major index of any state's claim to 'modernity'. Henceforth, religions existed *within* the social order; they were not the major source of a person's political and civic identity.

In countries which had had to wage violent struggles against Catholi-

cism, the outcome was initially a much less tolerant one: the establishment of new, militantly Protestant national churches – the beginning of
what was to feed into the much wider modern ideology of nationalism.

With the rise of science, even religious belief itself eventually came into
question. By the nineteenth century, Nietzsche could assert that God was
dead. At the intellectual level, religion had been pushed back into those
domains where science could not provide answers. In terms of social behaviour, it became a matter of private belief and personal morality. Soci-
etally, no particular church, not even all of them taken together, provided
a single, all-encompassing framework.

What we call 'secular' societies are perhaps better termed 'non-confes-
sional', for religion has not disappeared; it has simply been disssociated
from the state. But in theUnited States, for example, though religion is not
the central dimension of life in the great cities – New York, Chicago and
Los Angeles – in middle-sized cities in much of the rest of the vast subcontinent – 'Middle America' – the majority of the population still go to
church on Sunday and churches of various denominations play a major
part in civic life – raising funds for public parks, doing charitable work in
a society with a weak provision of welfare, and so on. As a newcomer in a
Canadian Prairie city in the 1960s, I was visited by a succession of the
'welcome wagons' from various churches whose members hoped that I
was or would become a member of their community. (When they found
that I was not religious at all, some of them concluded that I could not be
a moral person.)

There are occasions, however, when even people who do not belong to
churches have to come to terms with the meaning of life: with 'ultimates',
'first and last things'. For the most part, these issues, great as they are, are
not so much confronted as avoided, except in those very special situations
where this is not possible: when people get married or become parents,
when illness threatens life itself or when, eventually, people do face death.
But in the very nature of things these life crises occur only at a few points
in a person's lifetime.

By the 1950s, an anthropologist found that three out of five people in
England did not believe in a future life or in hell.[18] All but 7 per cent of
them went to church only for weddings and funerals. In the part of London where I live, the average Sunday morning service of a church whose
title is the 'the Church *of England*' can today attract only congregations of
a couple of score people; nationally, official Church statistics put regular
Sunday churchgoers at a mere 2.3 per cent of the population, while a third
of the population describes itself in social surveys as having 'no religion'.
As Peter Berger has put it, competition in the market is not simply an eco-

nomic phenomenon; religion, too, is plural, as rival creeds, churches, denominations and sects compete, not so much for pre-eminence as for survival.[19] Even the Catholic Church, the Jewish community and the
Methodists, which all once held on to their children by requiring not only
attendance on the Sabbath but religious education as well, are losing their
grip on the younger generation.

As for the theological beliefs that are supposed to mark off one religion
from another, Protestant and Catholic believers would be hard put to explain the difference between transubstantiation and consubstantiation.
Though people such as the Armenians of the Caucasus cite religion as the
quintessence of their culture, when they are questioned about it, they
seem to know very little about 'their' religion's supposedly sacred tenets.
It is simply an ethnic marker, separating them off from Muslims and Orthodox Russians.

The Intellectuals

All cultures, including their religions, are presented to us after they have
been doubly systematized: first by 'emic' intellectuals within the culture,
who, unlike most of their fellows, are specially preoccupied with making
coherent sense of the universe; and second by 'etic' intellectuals from outside the culture – people such as anthropologists who are struggling to
create order out of the masses of field-notes they have accumulated. Taken
together, these two sets of intellectuals collaborate in an often unper-
ceived over-systematization of culture, including, within it, religion.

Yet knowledge is not distributed uniformly in any culture, as an ethno-
botanist who has worked in New Guinea reminds us:

Different people do not necessarily know exactly the same things, hold
the same beliefs, or share exactly the same values ... The assumption that
a 'key informant', or several of them, will possess the information an
ethnographer is seeking, or that his version of that information is
representative of anyone other than himself (let alone the whole
community), completely disregards this basic fact.[20]

There have always been thinkers, special people, in every culture. But
people like Gula and Nangurama on Groote Eylandt occupy a quite different position in their cultures from that of thinkers in more differentiated
societies, where 'intellectual' is a recognized social category; nor do they
form corporate groups such as professions. Rather, like everyone else,
they have to cultivate and fish in order to provide for their families. And in

industrial societies too, though everyone thinks, we do not call everyone an 'intellectual', any more, as Gramsci put it, than we call everyone who can fry an egg a cook or everyone who can mend a sock a tailor.[21]

Though it is from people like Gula and Nangurama that anthropologists get most of their knowledge of the cultures they study, only rarely are we ever told much about these 'key informants'. Fortunately, though, there are a few exceptions who do emerge as distinctive personalities, shaped by life experiences in very different cultures. They also seem to be, often, people who are *marginal* in their societies, sometimes even alienated or resentful of those who exercise political power.

Another set of people occupying a similarly 'distanced' position in society, I suspect, are those at the apex, where they occupy positions of power which give them a singularly 'global', and sometimes critical or inquiring attitude, towards their culture and institutions. In exceptional situations, they can use this power to *innovate* as well.

Kings can be privileged in this way. But people able to stand apart from society also exist in stateless societies built upon the observation of tradition. Thus Bantu Kavirondo 'dream prophets', who built up great reputations because they predicted droughts, disastrous raids and epidemics, and even the coming of the white man and of the railway and motor car, sometimes used their prestige to advise people to *abandon* customary behaviour and to experiment with the unusual. One prophet is said to have persuaded his people to migrate from the country where they lived. Another persuaded people to refrain from circumcising the young boys for a few generations, so the next six age-classes, who should have been circumcised, were not – after which the old men of several clans decided that they would go back to the old practices once more.[22]

Given the paucity of information about such people in general, we will look more closely at three of those we do know more about.

Ogotemmêli, the Blind Hunter

Considering his importance, we are told very little about the 'venerable' Ogotemmêli. But we do know that he was set apart from others from childhood because he had lost the sight of one eye as a result of smallpox. But, endowed with an 'eager mind and ... considerable shrewdness', he nevertheless became a 'mighty hunter', with a 'profound knowledge of nature, of animals, of men and of gods'. Then, a second disaster struck; after an accident when a gun exploded in his face, he became completely blind.

He was not only a hunter, though. From an early age, he had also been initiated into the mysteries of religion by his grandfather, and after the latter's death his father continued his instruction – for more than twenty years altogether. Through divination, he found out that the accident was, in fact, a mystical 'warning'. He had already lost sixteen of his twenty-one children. Now, if he was to protect those who remained, he had to give up hunting, because hunting was a work of death and attracted death.

'Thrown back on his own resources, on his altars, and on whatever he was able to hear', his name and character became famous throughout the country, known to the youngest boy. People came to his door for advice, medical or mystical, every day and even by night. Every part of Dogon country 'discharged [its] sick and their sportsmen, the latter eager to learn how to be sure of killing a bush-buck. Ogotemmêli gave them all advice or powders, and his reputation continued to spread ...'[23] A French linguist considered that he had the 'purest speech' of the people of the district in which he lived, whose dialect was itself regarded as the finest form of the Dogon language.[24] This is about all we know about Ogotemmêli as a person.

Piailug, the Last Navigator

By the late 1980s, when Stephen Thomas arrived in the Caroline Islands, only a handful of traditional navigators remained, on five remote islands. Satawal, where the master navigator Piailug lived was the most renowned of these last redoubts of navigational lore. He had become a *palu* – a fully initiated navigator – by going through the sacred *pwo* ritual, which marked both his passage into manhood and – by virtue of receiving the power of Anumwerici, the spirit of navigation – his entry into the select and privileged class of those who possessed secret, mystical navigational lore. This, however, had been a long time ago: though he was the youngest *palu*, he was now in his fifties. Since then, he had achieved a different kind of fame as a navigator among Westerners because of his expeditions to places as far away as Hawaii, recorded in a *National Geographic* documentary film.

Master navigator he might be, but he was not a member of one of the chiefly clans which could trace its lineage back to the ancestral seafarers who had first arrived in the Carolines from further south. On Satawal, *they* were regarded as the 'captains' of the canoe of society.

Nor could a man acquire prestige through accumulating private property, whether in the form of means of production or of material goods. In this matrilineal society, he lived on his *wife*'s land and cared for his *mother*'s people. Their canoes were owned in common, and each member of a canoe-house (women first, then men and children) claimed their share in the turtles, fish and even cigarettes distributed by the 'master of dividing'.

There were, though, other avenues of social mobility for ambitious but non-chiefly young men. They could acquire distinction by mastering the six 'arts'. One of them, *pwang*, included the repairing of canoes at sea, building houses and a form of judo; the others were fishing, medicine, canoe-construction, divining the future and becoming a master of navigation, a *palu*. It was this avenue that Piailug had chosen. 'A chief,' Thomas observes, 'was a chief because of his heredity; but a *palu* was a *palu* because he had the right stuff.'[25] Piailug's initiation, in the *pwo* ceremony, at the age of fifteen or sixteen had been the most important event of his life.

He was therefore extremely sensitive about the rights of a *palu*. Only the initiated, he insisted, bore the dignity of the name of *palu*; the uninitiated were merely *arreuw*. Only a *palu* could lead a flotilla of canoes or sit in the navigator's place in a canoe-house. He had to observe special taboos over and above those required of other voyagers. A navigator, Piailug declared, needed three qualities – fierceness, strength and wisdom; 'a *palu*' had to be 'a *man*'.

Except in his cups, he did not flout the authority of the chiefs – though he criticized them for their money-making activities, and they probably resented his fame and reputation on other islands and his contacts with Westerners. But he reminded Thomas that:

if a chief sails with me he is considered a member of the crew and not the leader. When we arrive at an island, *I* will go ashore first. The chief of that island will wait for *me* in their canoe-house, and will listen as *I* tell them of our voyage and give them news of other islands. Our chief must stay on the canoe … because the chief is of the *land*, but the *palu* is of the sea … The canoe is the mother: it holds the food; holds the crew. The navigator is the father because he distributes the food to his sons, the crew. At sea, the *palu* is the chief, the father, the elder.[26]

When in command or delivering his informed opinion on sea matters, he was 'firm and definitive'. At decisive moments, he simply assumed 'that one would do his bidding, or be passed over'.[27] He was therefore gratified that an American navigator had come to learn from him, a gratification heightened because his own sons, and the younger generation as a whole, were *not* interested in the traditional navigational lore he wanted them to learn. He exercised considerable control over Thomas, making him ask permission to leave the village and even to talk with other people, especially outside the clan and, above all, with other navigators.

The major force pulling sons and daughters away from their parents was obligatory schooling, which took them to Yap and Saipan, while some even went further, to Guam or even Hawaii. 'This year,' Piailug remarked, 'my sons are on Satawal, but next year they will return to high school [on another island]. Why is it,' he asked Thomas – 'his voice crack-ing' – 'that they want to learn your way of navigation but they *never*, *never* come to me to ask about mine?' The first group of Satawalese who went abroad to school, he said, learned some traditional navigation when they returned; the second, less; the third, none at all. When special classes in traditional navigation were provided for them, they simply ran off. Now, at night, when he wanted the young men to listen to him calling the star sequences and singing traditional songs and chants connected with navi-gation, they were more interested in drinking and in pop music. 'The young men say, "Oh why are we going to tell those stories? Now we want to sing and laugh. For now we are drunk." And the old men just nod. After this happens two or three times, they never bring it up again.'[28] An-other navigator attributed decreased catch rates to the non-observance of taboos by the young: wearing flowers and aftershave while fishing; taking limes and lemons with them to sea; eating fish and discarding their bones in the sea; or failing to abstain from intercourse or masturbation during the fishing season.

Drinking had traditionally been a part of ritual and of sociability when getting ready to go to sea, and had involved the reciting of sea-lore and songs about voyaging. In his blacker moods of frustration at the behaviour of the younger generation, Piailug could be violent and 'brooding', prone to drunken outbursts. Had Thomas been a young Satawalese boy, Piailug would have seen him as a future navigator – one who would preserve and transmit traditional knowledge to future generations. To that extent, Thomas took the place of the son Piailug should have had. Already edu-cated in Western navigational lore, he would now preserve – in the very culture which would supplant his own – the ancient secrets of Oceanian navigation otherwise doomed to oblivion.[29]

Like other navigators, Piailug was by no means a conservative: he ex-perimented with technological innovations, as long as they worked, from the sextant, chainsaws and outboard motors to new materials like poly-sulphides for caulking, or new kinds of reefing points in the sails. Other navigators were equally interested in devices like the sextant. Nor was Pi-ailug devoid of individualism: in 'revolutionary' style, he built a new canoe-house himself (canoe-houses should be built by the clan); he even had plans to dynamite a channel through the reef, to clear more land so that he could move the new canoe-house and replace it with a larger one, to build new outbuildings for storing tools and gear and a new cooking-shed with a veranda screened against flies, and so on.

Muchona, the Hornet

Walking back to his home village in Ndembuland, part of Northern Rhodesia (now Zambia) in Central Africa, full of millet beer and therefore feeling lively, the anthropologist Victor Turner and his companion Kasonda played a game popular among children: trying to spot first a particular shrub which indicated the beginning of the rainy season. They were joined by a 'swart elderly gnome … padding perkily besides [them]' who soon took the lead in the game. He was, it turned out, a 'doctor', learned in several kinds of curative ritual and in many kinds of medicine. His name was Kapaku, though he generally used his nickname, Muchona, which, he said wryly, reflected his fondness for honey beer, which bees clustered around, and had a tendency to sting those who annoyed them!

If he indulged in self-deprecation of this kind, others too frequently scoffed at him. But many also respected him, not just because he cured most illnesses but because he did so with compassion and bravery – by visiting graves at night, for example, to find medicines with which to exorcize evil spirits. His initiation as a diviner too had involved his biting the head off a cock, 'beating the bloody head on his heart to quieten his mind', and lapping up the blood of a slaughtered goat. The power of the diviner's spirit, Muchona frankly acknowledged,

makes a person a little mad … When he is shuddering he feels as though he were drunk or epileptic. He feels as though he were struck suddenly in his liver, as if by lightning, as if he were being beaten by a hoe-handle, as if his ears were completely closed, as if he could not breathe. He is stopped up. But he is opened when he kills the cock. From the animals he gets wakefulness, alertness, for he must be wide awake to become a diviner and seek out hidden things … The novice experiences a release, an access of heightened sensitivity.[30]

So the ritual of initiation calls for the would-be diviner to exercise intellectual initiative: to refuse to follow preordained paths; to find things that have been hidden in the bush (as a hunter does). A diviner's place in society, as we saw, is therefore very ambivalent: on the one hand, his powers expose him to the charge that he is using them for witchcraft purposes (such people would have been speared or shot in the past); on the other hand, the diviner helps bring the community together again by exposing evildoing, despite his lack of ordinary secular power. In his daily life, Muchona was 'meek and comical', often playing the 'timorous fool', and when faced with established authority, he tended to capitulate without a struggle: to run away and build his hut in a different area. But a diviner does have special protection in that he is 'fortified by ritual and protected by ferocious spirits that torment him while they endow him with insight to publicly expose the hates that simmer beneath the outward semblance of social peace'. So Muchona always rationalized his ritual tasks as being for the good of society. And in exposing evildoers, Turner speculates, there might have been a certain 'unconscious revenge' against the social order: 'Beneath the jester's mask, and under his apparent timidity, [he] may have cherished hatred against those more securely placed in the ordered groupings of society.'

It was this kind of position in society, therefore, which made Muchona something of an anthropologist himself. Like Turner, he was primarily interested in ritual symbolism. Inclined to give learned explanations – about the etymology of certain words, for example – his comments were also full of psychological insight. He was, it became clear, a 'marginal', 'abnormal' man. By his early thirties, when he had acquired a wife, was living among his stepfather's kin on the Angolan border and had succeeded in emancipating himself from slavery, he must already have been 'something of an intellectual prodigy ... half derided and half grudgingly admired' and 'entirely unable to belong'. He was also an 'enthusiast' – a 'minuscule fellow with a needle-sharp and pin-bright mind ... brisk, agile, full of pre-science and *élan*' – whose vivid mimicry was 'expressive as a comedian's', with a 'streak of buffoonery' which he probably acquired as a child in order to curry the favour of the 'bigger and better-born'. Once he got launched on his analyses, he did so with such animation people like Kasonda often laughed at the ritual speech mannerisms and technical jargon he used (which others often had to render more comprehensible to Turner) and his 'salty village argot', and at times slandered him behind his back.

Turner and he quickly developed what became a daily seminar on religion and ritual esoterics. The third member of the seminar was Windson Kashinakaji, a senior teacher at a local mission school – a position of no little importance, for he could block or facilitate a child's progress through the educational system, one of the few avenues of upwards mobility in those days. 'A man of independent mind, obsequious to no European, arrogant to no villager', he was 'gentle, earnest, and not unkindly', and did not use his authority in an arbitrary way. Though brought up on the Bible, his attitude towards it was critical and he was curious to learn more about Ndembu beliefs and practices, from which he had been shielded in his childhood. He was beginning to 'look askance at the privileged lives of certain of the white missionaries' and to wonder whether the religion of his beloved father was really such a 'farrago of deviltries as he had been led to believe'.

Kasonda was a much more worldly character than Muchona, 'a shade spiteful', even rancorous, and more interested in the 'seamier' side of village life – the endemic everyday struggles for power, prestige and money. He could even, at times, accuse Muchona of lying. Eventually, though, he grew to admire his intellect, and the 'richness and sonority of the symbolic system' he expounded to the other two members of the seminar, and he came to appreciate Muchona's humane understanding of the complexity of existence, chuckling affectionately at the witty style in which it was often expressed.

Muchona, though deeply involved in battling against witchcraft and the 'moody, punitive dead', had a 'curious innocence and objectivity of outlook', and came off better as a human being, Turner thought. Kasonda was the politician, Muchona the 'true philosopher'. He turned out to be a restless man, often absent on his curative expeditions, perhaps reflecting the instability of his upbringing, for he had been born not in Northern Rhodesia, where he now lived, but across the colonial border with the Belgian Congo, whence his mother had been taken as a slave in pre-colonial times. His kin too were scattered all across the region. He had thus been 'doomed to rootless wandering since early boyhood', first living in the village of his mother's captors and then, when that village split, going with his mother, who was transferred as a debt slave to yet another group, where she was married to one of her owners. Muchona, by now a famous hunter and a wealthy man, had later been able to purchase his freedom. But in one ritual curing session, in which patients brought into the open their hidden grudges and resentments, it emerged that because of his slave origin he felt deeply that he had never really belonged to any 'snug little village community'; 'a deep well of unconscious bitterness and a desire for revenge against a society that had no secular place for him compatible with his abilities' lay buried in his psyche.

Most Ndembu travelled widely during their lives, even in those days, being hunters and semi-nomadic cultivators of cassava, but Muchona's experience had been even richer and more varied than that of most of his fellows. The Ndembu normally live in villages, the core of which is a group of matrilineal kin, but not Muchona. He lived with his two wives in a couple of huts near the motor road. 'Living as he had done on the margins of many more structured groups and not being a member of any particular one of them,' Turner remarks, 'his loyalties could not be narrowly partisan, and his sympathies were broader than those of the majority of his fellow tribesmen.' His long 'reveries' about rituals he had taken part in reveal something of his 'inner biography', since he found his deepest satisfactions in them – as a poet does in his poems – with all the 'nuances of gesture,

expression, and phrase with which he embellished ... his accounts and in-
tepretations'. In a sense, therefore, Muchona's 'ritual history' was his
'inner biography'.

His special relationship with his mother, born of constant uprooting
and travel, had great consequences for his religious activities and ideas.
She became an adept in many kinds of ritual and encouraged her children
to acquire ritual skills too. Ndembu believe that you must have suffered an
illness yourself before learning how to cure it by ritual methods. When he
was only seven, he was inducted into the Nkula cult – normally reserved
for women, since it deals with reproductive disorders – as a 'spiritual mid-
wife', alongside his mother when she was herself inducted into the cult. In
general, he always seemed more at ease among women – especially elderly
women – than men, many of whom disliked him. Turner describes him as
a 'Tiresias figure', with 'considerable insight into feminine as well as masculine psychology', especially in the fields of sex and reproduction, and
thought that his manner of speaking – in an 'alto' voice – reflected his
identification with his mother. Later, when Muchona began to suffer from
(probably) psychosomatic illnesses, he dreamed of his mother and several
of her relatives, as a result of which he sought to be initiated as a diviner.
After his mother's death, she became for him his way of gaining access to
supernatural powers. Male relatives on her side also helped him acquire
expertise in a number of hunting and other rituals. Because of his slave
origins, and his not really 'belonging', he felt himself to be chronically afflicted. 'His illness,' Turner remarks, 'was himself.'

During eight months of 'exhilarating, quick-fire talk', the seminar
analysed the whole gamut of Ndembu rituals and ceremonies, some of
which Turner had seen, others of which he had only heard about. There
was even a historical dimension – when they discussed rituals now remembered only by old men – and a comparative dimension too, in that
Turner told Muchona how other Ndembu specialists had interpreted various rituals and asked for his comments, which, according to Turner, were
'always fuller and internally more consistent than theirs'. A further his-
torical-comparative dimension was introduced by Windson when he suggested they look at resemblances, such as blood symbolism, between
Hebrew and Ndembu observances.

Turner's classic work on Ndembu colour symbolism, involving red,
white and black, uncovered the very complex meanings of each.[31] But
where Griaule had treated Dogon symbolism primarily as an *intellectual*
ordering of the universe – a cosmology – Turner and Muchona focused on
the *moral* and social values embodied in these colours.

During many rituals, food and beer are offered not only to the ancestors but also to other spirits. Muchona's compassion was evident in his attitude to even 'delinquent' spirits. They were also entitled to be fed, he argued, for they had once been human beings, 'men and women like ourselves'; though their hearts could not be changed, he did not want them to harm the living. Turner found that Muchona, the homeless one, was peculiarly susceptible to nostalgia: 'Could it be,' he wondered, that because Muchona had 'had to wander round the margins of respectable society that he felt fellowship with the despised and the rejected?'

Turner also wondered later what had become of Muchona: 'Could he ever be the same man he was before he experienced the quenchless thirst for objective knowledge?' Through working as an Ndembu anthropologist, it seemed, Muchona had at least 'found some kind of home at last'.

Antonio Gramsci: Culture and Counterculture

In modern industrial societies there are innumerable 'autodidacts' – people like Ogotemmêli, Piailug and Muchona. Yet the title 'intellectual' is usually applied only to people whom society pays to think on its behalf. Being a modern intellectual is not only a full-time job – an *occupation*; it is a particular *kind* of job, which carries with it social prestige – a *profession*.

The most creative theoretical discussion about the distinctive attributes of the intelligentsia, and their rise to occupy a special place in modern society, is that pioneered by Antonio Gramsci. His ideas are not presented in any clear and worked-out form, but are scattered through the notebooks he kept and the letters he wrote from prison, where Mussolini had put him. Though a communist, official Stalinism also ignored him.

Since recent interpretations of Gramsci have concentrated mainly on his ideas about culture, it is important to stress that, in classic Marxist style, he did place very great emphasis indeed on the way that ownership of the means of production makes it possible for economically dominant classes to establish political control over the state and over society as a whole, using all those forms of power to reserve the lion's share of society's 'goods' for themselves and keep others out.

This does not mean that these 'others' necessarily become conscious that they are a disprivileged class. People acquire ideas about their place in society from a wide range of what Gramsci calls cultural 'apparatuses' – institutions, both public and private, from schools and churches to the newer media of communication – which disseminate and instil in them not just cognitive ideas but respect for customary forms of social behaviour and for the dominant moral codes. These become so much part of everyday life that they seem 'natural', 'common sense'. Even the names given to the streets, he suggests, communicate images of the social order or refer to matters of common interest known to most people.[32] Unfortunately, he failed to distinguish between common sense as mere uncritical absorption of stereotypes and common sense based on observation, which, as Atran observes, is *not* a pre-rational mode of thinking, opposed to scientific thought, but one particular *form* of rational thought, out of which science can develop. Common sense 'lights a world that is ... much the same for the scientist, layman and bushman' whereas science '*extends that world*'.[33]

For Gramsci, then, culture does not simply emerge or exist; it is produced, brought into being, by intellectuals, who formalize and codify religious and social ideas and make them into a hegemonic ideology which they communicate to society at large, elaborating and reinforcing it continuously, transmitting it from generation to generation.

As an Italian, he was inevitably conscious of the historic and continuing influence of the Roman Catholic Church in social life. So though he commonly used the older Marxist term 'ideology' to refer to ideas and values, he always emphasized that 'ideas' included not just concepts (the cognitive) but also norms and values, *all* of which were communicated in social life. He had a conception, that is, not just of 'ideology' but of *culture*.

A ruling class, he argued, has its own private lifestyle, an upper-class subculture which is meant to distinguish them from the masses. But the ruling class also brings into being, and sustains, a different kind of culture, designed for the masses, for though people can simply be forced to conform – to do and say what their rulers want – it is more effective to disseminate ideas and values and forms of behaviour which justify the divisions of society. This he calls a 'hegemonic' ideology. But an effective hegemonic ideology involves much more than a simple defence of naked inequality. It *mystifies* people, by obscuring the *causes* of inequalities: for example, by finding scapegoats, or by inventing links between things that are not really causally connected; by blaming forces 'beyond our control'; by obscuring conflicts of interest; by persuading people that rich and poor alike have common interests; and so on.[34] For a hegemonic ideology to be truly successful, people have to *internalize* these ideas – *really* believe in them. A successful hegemonic ideology, then, penetrates the dominated class; it is a *cross-class* phenomenon.

Such a culture, often labelled 'mass culture', is in fact not a culture *of* the masses but a culture manufactured *for* the masses. An authentic culture of the masses is something they have to generate for themselves. It is, inevitably, a '*counter*culture', opposed to the 'hegemonic' culture sold to them or imposed on them. In the long run, he believed, the workers' party, if it was to have any hope of taking power itself, would have to not only challenge the political and economic power of the ruling class but also to replace ruling-class hegemonic ideology by imposing its own *counter*-ideology on society as a whole.

Ruling classes, though, do not formulate hegemonic ideologies themselves. This is done for them, by a specialized category of people ('officers', Gramsci sometimes called them), the intellectuals, of whom there are two types: 'organic' and 'traditional'. Although both provide political, intellectual and moral leadership, *organic* intellectuals, whether consciously or unconsciously, reflect and express the ideas and values of the dominant social class. They are linked to a class: in the case of the bourgeoisie, for instance, they include economists and accountants. Some, like the editors of most tabloid newspapers, are little more than 'hired pens'. The working class too has its own organic intellectuals. *Traditional* intellectuals, on the other hand (such as lawyers or ecclesiastics), though they emerged originally as proponents of the interests of a landed aristocracy, have over the centuries evolved into bodies with their own identity. They are not, therefore, mere tools of the ruling class. Today, they would include individuals working in universities, or for some of the 'quality' broadsheet newspapers and on some TV programmes and channels.

For an Italian, religion was the obvious instance of this kind of cultural force in society, though one which was missing from most political and economic theory. The Church claimed universal hegemony. In reality, it was part of a system of states. The papacy itself was an Italian principality in political terms. It had also become a complex organization, with its own internal subcultures. Both the professional staff and its lay believers occupied different positions within the hierarchically ordered body of the Church. The Church was further segmented into different, often rival, orders, each with its particular interpretation of Christian thinking and its own organization, from schools to theological seminaries and universities, between which there was debate and even contention and rivalry. At times too these orders could even defy the Papacy. And there were always the unorthodox. Hedge priests coexisted with proud prelates. It was these rival intellectual groupings, not the bourgeoisie, which competed for the hearts, minds and souls of the masses. Though the latter suffered inequality and oppression, *how* they responded was not predetermined. Usually, they gave their 'spontaneous' consent to the prestigious, historically and cosmically awesome ideas priests conveyed to them. But the faithful were also exposed to alternative, even radical interpretations of Christianity, including heresies, formulated by deviant thinkers, which spoke to their social and not just their religious discontents.

In past centuries, priests and theologians were predominantly drawn from the leisured classes: in the Christian world, they lived in monasteries and theological seminaries; in the Muslim world, in *madrasahs*. Today, by contrast, intellectuals work in universities and in the laboratories of multinational corporations.

As an Italian, Gramsci was also the legatee of a quite different, secular tradition: that of Italian Renaissance thought and, in particular, the political ideas of Niccolò Machiavelli, author of *The Prince*. A prince, Machiavelli wrote (and he wrote as an organic intellectual, being an adviser to Piero de' Medici), could rule simply on the basis of naked *force*. A really clever and flexible prince, though, would be better advised to use both force and *fraud*. As Bismarck (never reluctant to base his policies on 'blood and iron') was later to put it, you can do anything with bayonets *'except sit on them'*. Far better to persuade people that things were the way they were, and to get them to *internalize* the belief that this was 'in the nature of things.' It was inevitable that they should be ruled by a government or a dominant class. Nor were they encouraged to find any contradiction between the ideal of democracy as 'one person, one vote' and the reality of parties financed by multimillionaires.

For Gramsci, the relationship between class and ideology was not a simple, direct one, for old ideas did not disappear to be replaced overnight by new ones, even though the social circumstances that had first given rise to them had passed away. In an Age of Faith, people had to be persuaded that the order of society was part of divine creation – God had ordained it so; in modern, scientific times, hegemonic ideologies claimed a 'scientific' basis for élite rule – eugenicists, for example, 'proved' that only a gifted few were endowed with the intellectual ability needed in order to rule.

In the work of Marx, who had taken the idea from the Hegelians, Gramsci found the key concept of 'civil society' that he was to develop into a wider, extra dimension to what had hitherto been political economy: the concept of culture.

Machiavelli's conception of 'fraud', for all its cynicism, sensitized Gramsci to the importance of culture. But living in Italy, it was hard for him to see that ruling classes in the leading capitalist countries (Italy lagged behind) were developing new ways of taking the sting out of revolution: through political concessions – the incorporation of the masses into the parliamentary system – and, in economic and social terms, the growth of elementary education and health services, which were to culminate in the Welfare State, which, though thought of in Britain as a quintessentially Liberal innovation, was in fact pioneered by Bismarck. Italy, a much less developed country both in economic terms and in terms of civil society, was fated to experience fascism before it caught up with advanced capitalist countries.

Theories of Nationalism

Given Gramsci's awareness that every society is made up of a variety of cultural groups, from village and province upwards, each with its own conception of the world, and often shaped as much by the 'local priest or the ageing patriarch whose wisdom is law, or the little old lady who has inherited the lore of the witches',[35] and given his stress upon the importance of civil society and culture at higher levels, it might have been expected that he would have paid a lot more attention than he did to the fact that the modern state emerged not simply as a centralized polity and an integrated market system but also with distinctive *cultural* features.

Gramsci did say that the workers' party would have to do more than challenge the economic and political power of the ruling classes, including their historical success in hijacking nationalism and patriotism and harnessing them to their own interests, by asserting its own *counter*-ideology: bourgeoisie. In other words it would have to 'nationalize itself'; to become a 'popular religion'.[36]

And as a Sardinian in a recently unified country, he was fully aware of ethnic differences within Italy – particularly the 'southern question' – and he also paid a lot of attention to the experience of the Risorgimento. But compared to class, nation-building and nationalism had a subsidiary place in his schema, while his thinking about the polity emphasized the *state*, rather than the nation.[37]

Following the defeat of Italy by Austrian armies in the First World War and the subsequent mass revolutionary upsurge which led to the occupation of the great factories in Turin by the workers, the priority Gramsci had given to class rather than to nation might have seemed obvious. It seemed that the next item on the historical agenda – and soon – was victory for the proletariat in the *class* struggle.

But another response was possible, and was to prove victorious. Gramsci's attempt to analyse the balance of opposed forces in terms of a conception of the 'historical bloc' proved unsatisfactory as both explanation and political project, for fascism mobilized other kinds of popular response to military defeat and social chaos – fear of socialism and the reassertion of a new kind of hyper-national pride in the nation.

He did, though, provide the intellectual tools – culture, counterculture and civil society – which made it possible for those who came after him to develop a general theory of nationalism.

In analysing the rise of the modern state in the West, where it first appeared, historians have usually focused upon the emergence of new kinds of political institutions: the wresting of state power and judicial authority from feudal lords, and their centralization in the hands of the monarch; the creation of standing armies under the king's control; and the creation of an administrative apparatus – a bureaucracy. Economists have focused upon the growth of the market and the establishment of systems of taxation which paid for all this. 'Modernity', then, has usually been defined in one or other of these ways, or using both, but the nation has been defined only in terms of political economy.[38]

A new breed of social scientists, sociologists, who emerged only late in the late nineteenth century, long after economists and political scientists, added another dimension to explanations of social solidarity – or lack of it. A whole range of *cultural* institutions and forms of association – non-economic and, as we would say today, 'non-governmental' – were also crucial: not just the state, the party and the market, but institutions which expressed a conception of society as a *cultural* community too.

Donald Horne, an Australian who knows more about European self-images than most Europeans, since he has visited virtually every significant European museum between Petersburg and Lisbon, has found one major theme in all of them: the emergence and identity of the *nation*.[39]

Yet despite the tremendous importance of nationalism in the nineteenth and twentieth centuries, remarkably little attention was given to it as a theoretical category by social scientists of any kind until the last decade or so. Apart from Friedrich Meinecke, before the First World War, and the writings of Hans Kohn more than a generation later, the number of academics engaged in *theorizing* about nationalism could be counted on one hand. Most of the theorizing, rather, was done mainly by nationalist ideologues themselves – in Gramsci's country, for instance, by activists like Mazzini and Cavour.

For them, the nation was based upon a shared cultural heritage and upon shared historical experiences, culminating in the *prise de conscience*, the establishment of an organized political movement and, eventually, the achievement of their own political nation-state. This has become the unquestioned model for nationalist movements ever since. They could, however, have adopted a more problematic one, for very few nation-states have ever developed in this way.

States have existed for millennia and ethnicity is as old as humanity. But the idea that an ethnic group should have its own territorial state is a notion that emerged only in the eighteenth century.

Nationalists assume that the nation is only the final transformation of what Anthony Smith has labelled the *ethnie* (for we lack a single word in English that would embrace tribe, ethnic group and cultural community). For them, *ethnies* are virtually natural phenomena: cultural groupings which have existed from the beginning of time, handed down from generation to generation, absorbed, one might say, with one's mother's milk. And though the transformation of the *ethnie* first into the nationalist movement and then into a successful nation-state might take centuries, even millennia, and though *will* and consciousness were necessary, it was, in the end, an ineluctable process. Not only is ethnicity immanent, then, but also the process by which the *ethnie* becomes transformed into the nation. Like murder, it will 'out', whether it results in full independence or the recognition of the *ethnie* as a component, together with other *ethnies*/nationalities, each with their own rights and distinctive culture, within the boundaries of some larger state.

The counterpart of this celebration of the *ethnie*/nation is the denigration of other peoples as inferior, either in purely physical terms or on cultural grounds. Of course, these ideas do not simply arise out of intellectual error; they grow out of unequal economic, political relationships – relationships of domination and exploitation. But the ideas acquire a life of their own, becoming 'stereotypes'. Though the slave trade has long ceased, it has left a lasting image of blacks as inferior. In Britain centuries of resistance to English rule in Ireland has left an image of the Irish as savages, an image confirmed by 'scientific' racists who 'proved' that the Irish were close to the apes – *Punch* cartoonists therefore drew them with prognathous, beetling brows. Being simian, they were naturally irrational (today's 'Irish' jokes are still about their illogicality, stupidity, etc.) and inherently pugnacious (the shillelagh). Even when Irish immigrants fleeing the potato famine arrived in vast numbers in the United States, they found themselves still despised as an impoverished, uncultured, slum underclass, with New York cartoonists taking up English images of the ape-like 'Paddy'.[40]

Racist imagery changes as the position of inferior groups alters. It may even disappear. But stigmatized groups are more often likely to find themselves still in positions of social inferiority, albeit in new ways – as poor immigrants speaking a different language and with different religious beliefs and practices.

Racist ideas are also subject to criticism as *ideas*. Today older, physical forms of racism, for instance, are now politically 'incorrect' in some countries. One result, Stolcke has shown, is they are now increasingly being replaced by what she calls 'cultural fundamentalism', which underpins recent anti-immigrant legislation in Western European countries. Prejudice against immigrants from Third World countries is now 'justified' not on the traditional grounds of believed genetic inferiority but on the basis of the alleged inferiority or incompatibility of *cultures*.[41]

This kind of theory is a form of what is now usually described as 'primordialism'. It comes, Smith shows, in two varieties. The first, 'strong' primordialism, sees identification with an ethnic or national community as 'universal, natural and given in all human association, as much as are speech or kinship'. Socio-biology, for instance, tells us that this kind of banding-together is not so much part of the human condition as of the animal condition – savagery writ large. Its modern manifestations lurk below the surface of civilization, like some social equivalent of the Freudian id in the individual, needing only some relaxation of social control for people to begin butchering their neighbours. 'Weak' primordialism, on the other hand, emphasizes not biological inheritance but social factors – feelings or beliefs that the *ethnie* or the nation has existed from time immemorial (whether true or not).[42]

When social scientists finally turned their attention to the theory of nationalism, they were scornful of either kind of primordialism. Historians pointed to the complete disappearance of peoples who had existed in antiquity, such as the Scythians, the Catevellauni and the Gauls. More recently, they derided ('deconstructed') nationalist interpretations of history as just so much romantic mythology. There were, they showed, no serious grounds for accepting the argument that nationalities which had succeeded in acquiring their own nation-state had been able to do so because they had always been singularly strong and coherent *ethnies*, while others had lacked this kind of consciousness. It was pretty arbitrary or random as to whether or not a given nationality embarked on the road to nationhood. All you *could* say, they argued, in Nietzschean style, was that *some* nationalist movements, especially their leaderships, had possessed the *will* to succeed and had carried their project through to a successful conclusion – the achievement of nation-statehood. As Hans Kohn put it, nationalism is 'first and foremost, a state of mind, an act of consciousness ... the most essential element of which is a living and active corporate will. Nationalism is formed by the decision to form a nationality.'[43]

More recently, Gellner has castigated primordialism as the '*myth*' of the nation. The reality is that nationalism 'sometimes takes pre-existing cultures and turns them into nations, sometimes invents them, and often obliterates pre-existing cultures. That is the reality.'[44]

Not all *ethnies*, then, become nation-states. Some, like the Armenians and the Kurds, remain 'failed' or 'submerged' nationalities. Others persist as nationalist *movements*, even as parties, while yet others persist merely as cultural organizations aiming at self-expression at the level of language, or religion, or the arts, but make no serious attempt to acquire states of their own. They do not even seriously *try* to become politically autonomous.

Political scientists have been equally sceptical about the idea of ethnicity as something innate and eternal. It was, rather, simply a *resource* used by particular groups in pursuit of their (usually economic and political) ends. Such theorists have therefore been labelled 'instrumentalists'. The outstanding expression of this view was provided by Tom Nairn, who, in a vivid image, has likened nationalism to the mask of the Roman god Janus, with his two faces: one face looks back, to an (often imaginary) past; the other looks forward, to a glorious future of freedom and unity.[45] Developing Trotsky's notion of 'uneven development', Nairn argued that in a world divided into advanced and less-advanced groups, the force driving them towards autonomy was the urge to '*catch up*' with both the hegemonic powers that dominated them and their nationalistically more successful neighbours. The inequalities they sought to redress might be economic, political, cultural or a mix of all three.

The three modes of inequality do not always overlap, however. A country is not necessarily unevenly developed across the board, in such a way that underdevelopment is total. There can be contradictions – high levels of economic development, for instance, combined with lack of political autonomy or cultural self-expression. Perhaps the most striking example is Catalonia. Long the most industrialized part of Spain, it was nevertheless rigidly controlled from Madrid, culminating under Franco in the abolition of the autonomy granted under the Republic and in cultural repression so severe that speaking Catalan on the street could land you in gaol. In the Basque country, and in Quebec likewise, high levels of economic development were not matched by political autonomy or cultural self-expression.

To right these inequalities, a nationalist movement tries to mobilize not just material but also immaterial resources, bringing into being a new kind of consciousness by creating a cultural myth of eternal ethnic identity from time immemorial, or a historical myth of the nation out of a history in which there had been no nation. The past was an inspiration either because the *ethnie* had once been free and powerful or because its failure to become a nation was due to the lack of will, on the part of the people, to gird their loins in the struggle against the oppressor.

The approach of sociologists and anthropologists, notably Anderson[46] and Gellner, was even wider. For them, nationalism was a particular kind of politics: part of a *development* strategy by those hitherto excluded from access to the world's goods – economic, political and social. As a doctrine, it *could* not have emerged in its homeland, Western Europe, before the six-teenth century, because agrarian society before then had been too divided for any sense of homogeneity characteristic of modern nations to emerge. Peasants did not share the 'high culture' of the élites: to a Croatian noble-man, for example, the idea that he shared a common nationality with his peasants was as preposterous as the idea that his horse was a member of the Croatian nation.[47]

But in modern times, Anderson and Gellner argue, the rise of national-ism has been part and parcel of modernization, since rapid capitalist eco-nomic growth and the high degree of social mobility it entails override older cultural divisions and unify many local cultures into a single high culture. One essential requirement for all this was not directly or solely economic – life in a modern, highly mobile society required universal lit-eracy, using the same shared and standardized script, plus a high level of numerical, technical and general sophistication, all of which could be brought about only via a modernized education system. Capitalism would not have been able to take off without what Marshall McLuhan had called the 'Gutenberg revolution' – the revolution in printing sparked off by the invention of movable type.[48] Less than 150 years after Gutenberg, 200 million books had been printed, and even though most of them had been printed only in small editions, printed books had brought into being a new kind of community – not of religious believers or political subjects, but a 'horizontal' community of fellow *readers*.[49]

The argument, however, is illogical and ahistoric. Protestant proto-na-tionalists in Bohemia might have translated the Bible into Czech, but any-one who wanted access to the world's scientific and technological know-how had still – like the Pole Copernicus – to acquire it and to com-municate with other scholars through Latin. Today, equally, Malaysian stu-dents have to use the language which has become the modern equivalent of Latin, English. And Gellner too, though a Czech by origin, wrote in English, not Czech.

Nationalism: Hegemony and Counterculture

The notion that the nation is the 'outcome of ethnicity', as Smith has put it, may sometimes be true. But in the vast majority of cases it is not, for throughout most of human history the majority of ethnic groups have never achieved, or aspired to, statehood, while today, as the American anthropologist Priscilla Reining has put it, 'ten thousand cultures are try-ing to live within the boundaries of 165 nation-states'. The search for a unitary theory of nationalism, in the singular, valid for all kinds of nations and *ethnies*, is therefore delusory. A more adequate approach has to start, with Gramsci, by recognizing that there are two kinds of nationalism: hegemonic and countercultural. Let us look first, then, at the continent where the idea of nationalism was born: Europe.

The earliest nation-states came into being as hegemonic structures, created through military conquest and forced cultural assimilation, or via dynastic marriages. As late as 1914, most of Europe was still divided into a few huge empires, each containing many different ethnic groups within its borders. These polities, then, were *not* founded on ethnicity. In the Middle Ages, the 'English', for example – descendants of Anglo-Saxon invaders – drove the original 'Britons' – the Celtic-speaking people we call 'Welsh' – into mountainous country in the west fit only for keeping sheep, not agriculture, and built a string of castles from Caernarfon, along Offa's Dyke, down to Chepstow to keep them under control. The best land, in the valleys, was kept for the conquerors.

In their turn, the Anglo-Saxons were defeated by the Normans, who similarly controlled the conquered English by building more castles, and used the Doomsday census to systematically distribute the land among the conquerors. (I still pay 'ground rent' as a result.)

Politico-military repression was further reinforced by cultural hegemony. From the very first decades of occupation, the Normans set about building new cathedrals, or adding to existing ones, in the architectural style called 'Romanesque' on the Continent but 'Norman' in Britain.

The union with Scotland, on the other hand, was the result of dynastic accretion: the accession of a Scottish king to the thone of England. Even so, this did not prevent two major attempts to restore an independent Scottish kingdom in the Jacobite Rebellions of 1715 and 1745. Both were brutally suppressed by military power and consolidated by ruthless social transformation – the Highland Clearances. In Ireland, the third Celtic country conquered and yoked to England, the struggle is only now entering its final phase.

The defeat of Scotland gave rise to a new state, the 'United Kingdom', cemented by a policy of rigorous cultural domination. In Scotland, the Gaelic tongue was wiped out, as it nearly was in Wales and Ireland. Once the conquered accepted defeat, and as a strategy for winning support among Scottish lords and merchants, some tactical concessions could be granted: the Scottish aristocracy was assimilated into the new British social structure, and Scottish Law and Presbyterianism were allowed, though Irish (and English) Catholics were denied access to religious self-expression and to public office until well into the nineteenth century.

Political and economic incorporation, and the deliberate imposition of the culture of the conqueror, were related processes. Later, economic integration into a common market with England, especially the large-scale labour migration entailed, undermined Scottish separatism as effectively as any policy of deliberate Anglicization.

Constitutionally, the identity of all these people within a new 'United Kingdom' was now 'British' – a new national identity which transcended older Welsh, Scottish, Irish and even English identities.

Whatever the ideology of common citizenship, the reality in fact was the ineffable superiority of the culture of the conquerors. It never crossed Nelson's mind to signal to the fleet at Trafalgar that 'Great Britain' or the 'United Kingdom' expected every man to do his duty, even though thousands of his sailors must have been Irish, Welsh or Scottish: it was *England* that expected them to risk death for 'their' country. (In my own youth, I still used 'England' and 'Britain' interchangeably, and as late as the soccer World Cup of 1984 I was surprised to see on television an unfamiliar flag – the Cross of St George – used as the emblem of England instead of the usual Union Jack.)

Resentment on the part of once independent nationalities therefore persisted and was to be the basis for new counter-hegemonic nationalist movements which usually began as movements of cultural self-expression but ultimately took political form.

In continental Europe and the Near East, far larger empires, made up of conquered ethnic segments, had long existed. The Ottoman Empire, which stretched from the Maghreb to Mesopotamia, was made up of many ethnic communities, called *millets*. The ruling Muslims, of course, did not belong to a *millet*; they were simply members of the universal (and superior) community of true believers, Islam. Even the cities were organized on the same plan. Overlooking Cairo, for example, is the Citadel. But lower down, in Ottoman times, the people, whether Muslims or religious/ethnic minorities, lived in walled ghettos where they practised their own trades and their own religions.

To the ruling élites who governed successive Muslim states of this kind in the Middle East – and in empires elsewhere from Zululand to China – ethnicity was a ready-made administrative mechanism for handling conquered groups, using co-opted traditional leaders. It was also a kind of safety valve, for as long as people paid their taxes, supplied sons to the army and never challenged the authority of their rulers and the superiority of their religion, talented young people of any ethnic background could be recruited to serve the state, indeed to move to the very top of society, via the army or the bureaucracy. Saladin was a Kurd; Mohammed Ali, a nineteenth-century ruler of Egypt, came from Albania. At the height of the Ottoman Empire, 'scarcely one vizier in nine was Turkish by birth'.[50]

Such ramshackle empires, then, were essentially *additive*. The Austro-Hungarian Empire, for instance, which stretched from Switzerland to Russia, was a typical collection of ethnic segments, constructed and assembled, in Anderson's words, as much via the 'sexual politics' of the Habsburg dynasty – the 'innumerable marriages, hucksterings, and captures' through which lands were accumulated over the centuries – as by military conquest, as the (abbreviated) roll call of the emperor's titles indicates:

Emperor of Austria, King of Hungary, of Bohemia, of Dalmatia, Croatia, Slavonia, Galicia, Lodomeria, and Illyria; King of Jerusalem, etc.; Archduke of Austria [*sic*], Grand Duke of Tuscany and Cracow; Duke of Loth[a]ringia, of Salzburg, Styria, Carinthia, Carniola, and Bukovina; Grand Duke of Transylvania, Margrave of Moravia; Duke of Upper and Lower Silesia, of Modena, Parma, Piacenza, and Guastella, of Ausschwitz and Sator, of Teschen, Friaul, Ragusa and Zara; Princely Count of Habsburg and Tyrol, of Kyburg, Görz, and Gradiska; Duke of Trent and Brizen; Margrave of Upper and Lower Lausitz and in Istria; Count of Hohenembs, Feldkirch, Bregenz, Sonnenburg, etc.; Lord of Trieste, of Cattaro, and above the Windisch Mark; Great Voyvod of the Voyvodina, Servia ... etc.[51]

The multi-ethnic composition of the empire extended to the ruling dynasty itself, not just to the absorbed peoples. Among 2,047 ancestors of the assassinated Archduke in 1918 were 1,486 Germans, 124 French, 196 Italians, eighty-nine Spaniards, fifty-two Poles, forty-seven Danes, twenty Englishmen/women, as well as four other nationalities.[52]

To the east lay the empire controlled by the Tsar of all the Russias, stretching from Poland to Kamchatka. By the mid-nineteenth century, less than half of the Tsar's subjects were Russians. It was a multinational state, but one where, unlike Austria-Hungary, hegemonic rule was more nakedly based on force. To nationalists, it was 'the prison-house of nations'.

The new countercultural nationalist movements – what we generally think of when we refer to 'nationalism' – were obviously bitterly opposed to the hegemonic model of the nation. But two different varieties emerged: the German and the French. Common to both was the notion that people with a common culture (especially language) – though the two do not always go together – should have their own centralized state with its own territory.

The German version was a spiritual one, developed by eighteenth-century idealist Romantic philosophers, notably Herder and Kant. The state, they believed, should express the culture of the people – an idea appropriate enough for what bcame 'Germany', since no such political entity existed at the time. There was, though, a German cultural community, whose boundaries did not correspond to those of any one state. German was spoken in what is now Austria, in Switzerland, western Poland and Bohemia, in states and mini-states scattered across Central and Eastern Europe, and in enclaves of many kinds where German-speakers lived within a mosaic of other cultures, even as far away from the German heartland as Russia. Politically, Germany was only, to use Anderson's term, an 'imagined' entity, an aspiration. So the idealist conception of the nation stressed the importance of the *Geist*, the spirit: nationhood was an *idea*, something in the mind.

When German national unification was consolidated in 1871, it was not as some 'natural' coming-together of people with a common cultural identity, but through Prussian military conquest of neighbouring states where there were other people who might speak German (and many who did not) but who did not necessarily think of themselves as Germans at all. The second, virulent phase of German nationalism, following military and political defeat in the First World War, bore even less resemblance to the Enlightenment values of Herder and Kant. It was a nationalism born of smouldering resentment at their punishment by the victorious Allies: occupation, reparations, the exile of the Kaiser and loss of the Rhineland and the Saar. And there were still very large numbers outside the borders of Germany – a situation not resolved until 1945, when reality was made to conform with the model of the nation-state through massive population exchange with Poland and the USSR, and the redrawing of boundaries.

The French model was to prove far more attractive to subsequent generations of nationalists, in Europe and outside it, for the French Revolution involved not just an abstract philosophy of the nation but a practical model of how to achieve it. Just as the common people in France had seized power from their feudal rulers and then gone on to defend the new state against foreign intervention and restoration, the throwing-off of oppressive foreign (including colonial) rule, if necessary by the use of violence, was both justifiable and desirable. Nor had the French Revolution been simply political; it had also been a social revolution, involving the construction of both a new nation and a new kind of society based on the ideals of liberty, equality and fraternity. These provided guidelines for the root-and-branch transformation of the whole of civil society, from the legal system (the Code Napoléon) to the names of the months and new metric systems of numbering and counting. It was a praxis of both the total reconstruction of society and the creation of a counter-culture too, right across the board.

The central concepts were those of the nation and of citizenship. The key unit of political society now was not, as in feudal times, the estate, or the ethnic group, but the individual citizen, who was equal, in principle, to everyone else. The state, then, was made up of millions of these social atoms, and the job of those who ran the state was to ascertain what the *general will* of the citizenry was, through the ballot box or the referendum. Group particularism, on the other hand, had to be eliminated, so political integration was accompanied by cultural uniformity. The Napoleonic ideal, it has been said, was that every schoolchild would be turning over the same page in the same textbook – in French, of course – at the same hour of the day in every school.[53] In the economic sphere, the new individualism expressed itself in the unleashing of entrepreneurial capitalism: any interference with the freedom of the market, in particular the formation of trade unions by workers, was strongly resisted by a state firmly under the control of the new bourgeoisie.

These political and economic structures left no room for conceptions of community *below* the level of the state: 'intermediate' levels, whether reactionary nostalgia for bygone ethnic identities or newer sentiments of class identity, were impermissible threats to a still precarious 'national' solidarity. Ethnic identities other than those of the nation-state were discouraged, especially on the frontiers, where cultural borderlines did not necessarily coincide even with such major geographical barriers as the Pyrenees or the Rhine. In Brittany, people still spoke Breton, while even in the heartlands French was a foreign language for a substantial number of Frenchmen as late as the 1860s and remained so for half those who reached adulthood even as late as the last quarter of the century. But the vigorous inculcation of nationalist cultural values via the school system ensured that a strong sense of a unitary French identity finally triumphed: loyalties wider than the state were, at best, unpatriotic and, at worst, treachery. The universalistic ideal of the brotherhood of man became intermixed with the national ideal of the unity of all Frenchmen. Nationalism and patriotism could all too easily shade into chauvinism.

New nationalist movements outside Europe, then, had a variety of models to choose from. The hegemonic, the policy of their colonial rulers, was unacceptable, as were pre-colonial ethnic identities. In South America, for instance, there were too many of them, and no single one could provide a viable basis for the new, united people who had co-operated in the struggle to throw off the Spanish yoke. What they opted for, instead, was a new kind of national identity, proudly expressed by San Martín in 1831: 'From now on, the indigenous people are not to be called Indians or natives. They are sons and daughters of Peru and should be known as Peruvians.'

By the end of the century, a further social dimension had been added to mere political independence. In Mexico, following a social revolution in which Indians like Zapata had played a major part, there was a new pride in Indianness (*indigenismo*). Leading revolutionaries took Aztec names. But the dominant conception of Mexican national identity to emerge was that Mexicans were neither Indian nor Spanish. On the walls of the church in Mexico City where Cortés is buried, a plaque announces: 'On the 13th August 1521, heroically defended by Cuauhtémoc [the Aztec emperor], Tlatelolco fell to Hernán Cortés. It was neither a defeat nor a victory, but the painful birth of the mixed people of contemporary Mexico.'

None of the remaining great empires disintegrated before the First World War. The first European revolutionary nationalist movements, in Hungary and Poland, had been ruthlessly repressed by the Habsburgs, but they had been unable to crush the Italian Risorgimento. Thereafter, they cautiously developed a more flexible policy towards minority nationalities, abandoning the attempt to enforce Austrian political and German cultural hegemony across the board. Eventually, a degree of recognition was given to the component nationalities. By 1907, national quotas were provided for in the Parliament: out of 519 seats, 241 were to be for Germans, ninety-seven Czech, eighty for Poles, thirty-four for the Ruthenes, twenty-three for the Slovenes, nineteen for the Italians, thirteen for the Croats, plus five for the Romanians and three for the Serbs.[54] Nine main languages (Czech, Hungarian, Slovene, Croat, Serb, Ruthenian, Italian, Polish and Romanian), plus ten lesser ones, were recognized even in the army.[55] When the defeated nationalist movements resurfaced, they too were cautious, wary of inviting repression once more, and bore little resemblance to modern 'movements of national liberation', especially armed ones. Rather, they were movements of 'national awakening', led by disaffected intellectuals whose mobility was blocked because of their second-class civic status, and were usually expressed in cultural terms – through philology, with the production of grammars and dictionaries, and through opera, newspapers, poetry and museums – rather than by the building of barricades.

But the long-term dream of political autonomy was not, of course, abandoned. The moment came with the collapse of the three great empires in 1918. At Versailles, the real losers were not the Germans but Germany's allies: the Austro-Hungarian and Turkish empires were dismembered by the victorious Allies – a fate only narrowly escaped by China and Russia. Austria-Hungary was reduced to Austria and the Ottoman Empire to Anatolia, with a small European rump in Thrace and Istanbul.

The Tsarist empire, a conglomeration of even more nationalities and tribes, was still expanding into Central Asia and the Caucasus right to the end. But by 1917, there were eleven foreign armies (British, French, Italian, Czech, Romanian, Serb, Japanese, Latvian, Baltic German, Slovene and Croat) operating on former Tsarist territory, with the fiercely nationalistic Czech Legion rampaging like a loose cannon across Siberia, as well as anti-Bolshevik Russian forces and Cossacks. At this point, the empire might well have broken up. The Bolsheviks vacillated between opting for a Habsburg policy – accepting Finland's independence, for instance – but acceded to Poland's independence and the loss of the Baltic states only under military duress. Once the borders in Central Asia and the Caucasus had been secured by force of arms, the outcome in such a vast conglomeration of nationalities and tribes could only be multinational, though decisive power was in Russian hands and Russian culture was the model for civilization.

Constitutionally, the component *ethnies* now all had a place in the political system; culturally, the language of the local *ethnie* was used in administration and at lower levels of education. At the same time, *ethnies* were ranked according to a Marxist evolutionary schema of 'levels' of development which classified them into nations, nationalities and autonomous polities down to the level of the tribe. Those regarded as most highly developed had their own full republics; others were (in descending order) Autonomous Soviet Socialist Republics, Autonomous Regions and Autonomous Districts. There were, in effect, two levels of nationality: the official 'Soviet citizen' and the 'ethnic' 'Uzbek' or 'Estonian' or 'Jew', for example – a distinction stamped on the passport.

The idea that each nationality should have its own nation-state also received a shot in the arm in the West at Versailles, where President Wilson's war aims – the 'Twelve Points' – included the right to self-determination. But the reality was that most of the states constructed out of the defeated empires were not nation-states; they were *multi*national entities formed by combining previously several *ethnies*/nationalities which had never had their own separate states, in modern times at least. Nor were they to get them now. Instead, Bohemians and Slovaks, Serbs, Croats, Slovenes and other nationalities were joined together to form states whose artificiality was indicated by their compound names: 'Czechoslovakia' and 'Yugoslavia'. Even within these, there were still minorities.

There was, however, one way of bringing about the one-*ethnie* nation-state: what has come to be called 'ethnic cleansing' and 'population exchange'. Ideal-typically, it might be called the 'Turkish solution'. In place of the ramshackle multinational Ottoman Empire, Ataturk set out to construct a purely Turkish state in the Anatolian heartland. But since there were still very large minority populations in Anatolia, reality was brought into line with ideology by the Procrustean procedure of cutting off the parts that did not fit. Turkey was made fit for Turks – only. After centuries of lesser massacres, 1 million Armenians were killed and whole cities (Erzurum, Trabzon, Van) cleared of Armenians. Then it was the turn of the Greeks, who, when war did not solve the problem, were dealt with by 'population exchange' (which Greeks call the Katastrophē) between Greece and Turkey, in 1923. Nearly half a million Muslims, many of them Greeks in all but religion, were removed to Turkey where they then found themselves classified as Greeks; while a million Christians who were expelled from Turkey (mainly to Crete) found themselves regarded as Turks. The last remaining large minority, the Kurds, are still being dealt with by similar methods, including the denial of their cultural as well as their political existence: Kurds, Turkish nationalists insist, are really only 'Mountain Turks', despite great differences in language and culture.

To some nationalists, then, the idea that the population of the state should be restricted to a single nationality seemed the only answer. The presence of an intransigent culturally German population in the Sudetenland, for instance, brought down Czechoslovakia. As early as 1918, the Sudetenlanders had voted to stay with their fellow Germans in a *Deutsch-Böhmen* government, which failed. A quarter of a century later, when 60 per cent of them voted to join Hitler's Third Reich, they got what they wanted. Even such a tolerant and quietist political culture as that of interwar Czechoslovakia found its generosity strained; in 1947, it resorted to ethnic cleansing, with Allied support, as did the Poles in what became their new 'Western territories'. Some 2.5 million Sudetenlanders were put on the same rations that Jewish concentration camp victims had received; then they were expelled. The main strategy used to bring about the purity of the Czech lands, though, has not been ethnic cleasing but the reduction of the nation-state to Bohemia/Moravia. But neither this, nor the earlier destruction of Jewry in Central Europe, has entirely eliminated racial/ethnic problems, for the pariah gypsy community remains as loathed and socially discriminated against in the new republic today as it has always been across Central Europe.

Ethnic cleansing does not necessarily always occur when multinational states break up. In Czechoslovakia, a generation later, the 'velvet revolution' was accomplished without violence, and the drive towards ethnic/national purity also took place peaceably. Though President Havel retrospectively denounced the deportation of the Sudetenlanders as immoral, as well as the notion of the collective guilt of the Germans, these were deeply unpopular sentiments. Czechs who had lost their property under communism were eligible for compensation, but not the Sudeten Germans.

The notion that ethnic/national 'purification' would solve the problem of national minorities, popular for over a century, received a series of shattering blows, however, in the 1990s. Primordialism was now given a new shot in the arm, for Bosnia, Groznyy and, in Africa, Rwanda were widely seen as evidence that peoples of different cultures *cannot* live peaceably side by side. The reality was that these were the exceptions, for in every European state ethnic populations, often of considerable size, with different languages and religions – Orthodox, Catholic, Protestant, Uniate, Muslim – live cheek by jowl. The revolution in Romania, for instance, began among the Hungarian minority and was led by a Protestant pastor. But it did *not* result in a demand for the secession of Transylvania. It is not, therefore, 'natural', or inevitable, that ethnic groups will necessarily seek autonomy, even less that they will resort to mutual genocide. Post-Soviet Russia survived the (peaceable) secession of even very large territories such as Belarus and the Ukraine, plus the Baltic states, without bloodshed, even though the impetus to segmentation and secession continues. Yet zones like the Caucasus, with a heritage of political segmentation and ethnic multiplicity (Dagestan contains forty-seven different *ethnies*), are part of 'Russia'; the 'Confederation of Independent States', likewise, is a variegated collection of nationalities.

Russia also still intervenes in technically independent mini-states from Tadjikistan to Georgia. Russian political leaders and Russian generals, humiliated by the reduced military capability of once world-class armed forces and by their deteriorating social status and living conditions, are still a powerful pressure group for a 'forward' policy in Russia's 'near abroad' – to them the equivalent of America's 'backyard'. Where they see Russia's strategic interests as threatened, they have not hesitated to resort to the extremes of repression. Fear of Islam has deep historical roots in Russia, while racism is also widespread. The peoples of the Caucasus, in particular – Russia's 'blacks' – are blamed for corruption and for the rise of the 'Mafia' and the black market. But the special brutality visited upon Chechenya is not simply the outcome of such prejudices. Groznyy was obliterated because, although Russia has other sources of oil, that city is the hub of the pipeline from the Caspian to the Black Sea, and therefore threatens Russia's crucial trade in petroleum with the hard-currency outside world.

The governments of new mini-states in Russia's 'near abroad', with no real popular base, are therefore exhibiting a cautious pragmatism and are inhibited from making any moves towards real independence. They have no option but to accept their continuing political, military and economic dependence upon Russia, whatever their reservations, for embarking on the road to separatism would invite the fate of Groznyy. They also fear the rise of Islamism in neighbouring countries. From Uzbekistan, their Russian mentors remind them, there are only two roads out of the country: one leads to Russia, the other to Afghanistan.

The dangers of trying to build a state on any kind of ethnic dominance – the 'Turkish solution' – was horrendously demonstrated by the deaths of tens of millions during the Hindu–Muslim massacres in the Indian subcontinent in 1947, and deep religious and linguistic divisions of religion and language still persist, for India is the second-largest Muslim state in the world, and also contains tens of millions of Sikhs, Parsees and tribal peoples. The new state was therefore consciously established as a secular one and the working language was not to be Hindi. Instead, English, the language of the former imperial power, was adopted as the modern medium of communication in higher education, business and government, even though only a tiny handful of Westernized élites used it in their homes and the vast majority of other Indians used it only when at work – in schools, colleges and universities, in business and in the Civil Service. English, though, was still only the language of the state (as Urdu and Hindi had been earlier); indigenous tongues – Malayalam, Tamil, Gujerati, Bengali, etc. – are the languages of civil society, the languages used in the home, the languages in which cultures evolved over thousands of years are passed on to new generations.

In countries such as Tanzania where there were hundreds of *ethnies*, new identities had to be created, based not on pre-colonial ethnicity but on boundaries inherited from colonialism. People were now 'Nigerians', 'Kenyans' or 'Malaysians'.

In the nineteenth and twentieth centuries, countercultural nationalism has had a very good press, among liberals and radicals first, then among socialists and communists, for from Byron's time onwards, it has been seen as *liberation* – the nationalism of the conquered, of oppressed 'minority' ethnicities. In Europe, Hungarians, Bohemians, Poles, Serbs and others aspired to get out from under Turkish, Russian or Habsburg domination. In other continents too, newer nationalisms were seen as 'progressive'.

Outside Europe, nationalist movements, even armed ones, commanded widespread and popular support both within and outside the colonies, culminating in the watershed in anti-colonial struggle at the end of the Second World War, especially in Indonesia, Algeria and Vietnam. Once in power, the new independent governments were very wary about trying to build a state on any kind of ethnic foundation.

The progressive image of nationalism, however, has been severely dented in the last decade, above all in Europe. Even in the nineteenth century, many European liberals by no means necessarily approved of nationalism; they denigrated the proliferation of mutually antagonistic and economically unviable statelets as 'Balkanization', and feared the all too easy degeneration of nationalism into what they labelled 'chauvinism'. Ethnically 'pure' micro-statelets, they forecast, would be at best parochial and at worst hostile to their neighbours. They looked forward, instead, to a world which would be unified economically by the market and politically by international institutions. Socialists dreamed of a world in which the working class would 'have no country' but would bring into being a new 'proletarian internationalism' which would end war and usher in a new epoch of development oriented not to making profits but to raising the living standards of the masses.

The two world wars, which began in Europe, destroyed that dream. Today, the long peace enjoyed by two generations has been shattered by Bosnia. Burundi and Rwanda, ruled by the Tutsi in a totalitarian way for centuries,[56] descended into mutual genocide once that domination was lifted. Both nationalism and ethnicity now seemed no longer liberatory but the very source of genocide.

Primordialism has therefore undergone something of a revival, not as a policy but as an explanation. However, there is no reason to assume that the national and ethnic conflicts in former Yugoslavia and in the Caucasus, or in Burundi/Rwanda, are natural and universal consequences whenever peoples of different cultures have to live side by side. Sarajevo, Rwanda and Groznyy, rather, are exceptions that prove the rule, for whole regions of the globe, from the Balkans to Central Asia (to name no others), inhabited by innumerable nationalities and cultures, have not descended into such chaos. According to 'primordialist' theory, these things should have happened *everywhere*.

Instead most *ethnies*, including peoples who see themselves as distinct nationalities, neither seek full political independence nor try to massacre their neighbours. But is there necessarily any shift from cultural self-expression to fully fledged political nationalism? Many movements, rather, have settled realistically for what they can get – the use of their language in schools, representation at the level of the state and a limited degree of administrative power within their ethnic/national territory.

Democracy has always had two 'faces': the rights of the majority and the rights of minorities. The precondition for non-violent coexistence is the acceptance of a transcendent national identity that overrides any particular *ethnie*/nationality but which recognizes the rights of all of them. Early attempts to create multinational states – such as the 'United Kingdom' – were based on the imposition of new structures and hegemonic cultures on conquered peoples. Since then, there have been many attempts to create multi-ethnic and multinational polities out of very varied cultural components. The most dramatic recent example has been South Africa's attempt to create a 'Rainbow Nation', out of extremely unpromising materials, in a country where the major cultural/racial groups – African and white – were only yesterday engaged in very violent total hostility. Though the country was integrated as a single market and economy over a century ago, and as a single polity in 1910, only whites – even the conquered Boers – got the vote. Serious nation-building began only in 1994, when the vote was extended to Africans.

South Africa, indeed, illustrates the futility of trying to develop a single theory of nationalism, for three kinds of relationship between ethnicity and nationalism need to be distinguished. The most important is the attempt to create a new, over-arching 'South African' identity, while recognizing the cultural variety of the country: the proceedings of Parliament are therefore now published not just in English and Afrikaans but in nine Bantu languages too.

Under apartheid, ethnic identities were *forced* on peoples as 'racial groups'. Although individuals valued some aspects of their own cultures, they resented *having* to be Tswana, Zulu or Xhosa and being allocated artificial 'homelands' (Bantustans), when what they wanted was to be full citizens of the state which was actively denying them any other civic identity and any significant participation in public life except as workers. Benedict Anderson's designation of the nation as an 'imagined' community, then, does not mean that it is *imaginary*, for the labels applied to people by the state and by their neighbours are, in W. I. Thomas' famous phrase, very 'real in their consequences'. Being classified as a 'Jew' in Tsarist Russia or Nazi Germany, or as 'White', 'Coloured' or 'African' in apartheid South Africa, was fateful in the extreme, for it affected people's rights and social position in every area of life – their choice of school (if they went to any), where they might live, whom they could marry and so on.

'Rainbow' identity, though, is only one version of nationalism. It still has to compete with the racist white nationalism which dominated political life for half a century and with its obverse, 'Pan-Africanism', which, despite its name, aims not at uniting blacks across the continent but at uniting Africans of all ethnicities, within South Africa, in a racial 'front' against whites (Afrikaners and English).

Finally, there is the attempt by Chief Buthelezi's Nkatha Party to mobilize the country's largest black ethnic group, the Zulu (using a good deal of violence against both Zulu and other Africans in the process), into a new kind of ethnic-nationalist force, with the ultimate threat of sparking off civil war.

These last two kinds of nationalism are at present insignificant. But they do appeal, as does the militancy mobilized by Winnie Mandela, to those who feel left out of civil society, especially the 'lost generation' of youngsters who boycotted township schools during the 'Black Consciousness' period, and who are therefore now severely disadvantaged in competing for jobs and for access to housing, education and health services.

Nationalism as Hegemony

Uniting a Kingdom: British Myths of King and Empire
Given the diversity of peoples within their boundaries, empires face a singularly difficult task when they set about integrating the lands they have conquered, for they have to create not only new political institutions and new forms of economic organization but also new forms of cultural domination. It is with no intention of underestimating the importance of the first two that I deliberately concentrate on what has been least adequately theoretized: the establishment of cultural hegemony. I take as my case study the creation of the 'United Kingdom' of Great Britain, and then look at the imagery of empire outside the British Isles.

The English have not been ruled by a native English dynasty since the early eleventh century: 'Since then, a motley parade of Normans (Plantagenets), Welsh (Tudors), Scots (Stuarts), Dutch (House of Orange), and Germans (Hanoverians) have squatted on the imperial throne.'[57]

Foreign dynasties, especially the Tudors and the Stuarts, Cannadine has shown, often went to great lengths to establish their legitimacy. On his procession down to London, James Stuart handed out titles in abundance. He also took pains to create a 'theatre of power'.[58] Later dynasties which neglected these symbolic displays, as in the later Hanoverian and and early Victorian periods, did so at their peril. Well into the nineteenth century, the pageantry centred on the monarchy had long become 'conspicuous for its ineptitude rather than its splendour'.[59] By 1821, scandals involving George IV and Queen Caroline, far more disgraceful even than those of the 1990s, had made the Royal Family the 'most unloved royal generation in English history'.[60] While the funerals of Nelson and Wellington were spectacular occasions of mourning for the general population, commemorated in pottery, the Royal Family did not generate such consumer demand. Royal ceremonies were 'not so much a jamboree to delight the masses, but a group rite in which the aristocracy, the church and the royal family corporately re-affirmed their solidarity behind closed doors'.[61] Where royal pageants were staged, they 'oscillated between fiasco and farce'. During George IV's funeral, William IV talked incessantly and walked out early. Queen Victoria's coronation was so badly organized that Palmerston had to travel back by third class train and Disraeli had to sit on his wife's lap. The 'invisible' Queen even refused to open Parliament. By this time, the monarchy had become positively *un*popular: republicanism was rife.

All this was to change, for the growth of mass society required a *popular* monarchy. The 'preservation of anachronism' now became a central theme for those who set about creating to a new kind of hegemony. Ritual was crucial. In London, the Lord Mayor's Show was revived. Though it still proved impossible to drag the monarch herself, the 'widow of Windsor', into the public arena – she sent a telegram instead of appearing personally at the great Imperial Assembly at Delhi in 1877, and other members of the Royal Family had to be drafted in to take her place on visits to Canada and India – the ritual surrounding the monarchy as an institution nevertheless now became central in creating a new popular culture of the state.

The coronations of Queen Victoria's successors were major theatrical productions, beginning with that of Edward VII, which was stage-managed and highly rehearsed by the royal impresario Viscount Esher, with the enthusiastic co-operation of Elgar and the future king. Victoria herself had virtually deified Albert but a new cult of the Royal *Family* as a whole was now developed. On occasions such as the lying-in-state of Alexandra, the Queen Consort, royals other than the monarch were also given massive public veneration, while wider sets of kin were drawn upon to perform royal functions, such as opening new public buildings, from bridges to universities and hospitals. The new bourgeoisie were also incorporated into a modernized aristocracy via a greatly enlarged honours system. The role of the masses was to cheer royal processions in the street.

Participation in King George V's Jubilee on 6 May 1935 was extended even to the author, who, as a schoolboy born on that day eleven years earlier, was given 11d. in stamps and two free tickets to the local cinema. But by the 1930s, a new technology made royal broadcasts to the entire nation possible. At three p.m., people stopped eating their Christmas dinner and listened to the King (some families even stood). With the advent of TV, viewers were given direct access to the quintessentially middle-class life of a hard-working Royal Family, whom they had hitherto been able to see only as members of a necessarily limited crowd at public ceremonies. The highpoint of this modern popular cult of the monarchy was reached in 1953, with the lying-in-state of the Dowager Queen Mary and that supreme TV event, the coronation of Elizabeth II. Royal weddings, long occasions for ever more costly popular celebrations, were to climax in the weddings – possibly the last royal weddings – of Diana Spencer and Sarah Ferguson.

This experience in creating sentiments of solidarity despite vertical divisions of nationality and horizontal divisions of class was invaluable when it came to the far more difficult task of consolidating India as a major component of the Empire, only decades after the Great Rebellion (the 'Mutiny') of 1857, out of a quarter of a billion subjects who did not share the culture of their conquerors or even an older common culture.

The conquest of India, Cohn writes, was first justified by a theory that Indians had lost their right to self-rule through their own weakness, most recently at the hands of the Moguls, a supine record which English historians and administrators saw as stretching back as far as the Aryan invasions. Indians were simply too *incompetent* to rule themselves.[62]

A second theme was the bewildering diversity of Indian cultures, especially in religion. To avoid any repetition of 1857, social as well as political stability was vital. The key integrating institutions could not be based on any one, even the biggest, of the numerous cultures to be found in the subcontinent. Rather, India could be unified only by the state, notably the Indian Army and the Indian Civil Service. The co-operation of indigenous authorities was also required, so the native princes were assured of their position, though they were now co-opted as part of a new imperial system of control. The dilemma for the British was that, in the economic sphere, capitalism had long penetrated agriculture and was now developing industry. This, they were well aware would in the long run undermine traditional institutions. More than that, despite the desire to preserve ancient tradition, Indian society *needed* to be modernized.

New traditions therefore had to be invented. Only a year after the Rebellion, the Viceroy therefore began making tours, holding durbars at which honours and rewards were distributed to Indian princes and notables who had stayed loyal and to British officials. An elaborate, eclectic mixture of Mogul rituals of investiture and British feudal ones was now devised, with exquisitely grading of clothes, medals, insignia, gun salutes and other symbols of rank. Given the Victorian business mentality, presents from subjects were recycled and handed on to others, or sold at auction, while the recipients of these favours were carefully informed of the cash value of what they received.

Places which had been scenes of martyrdom or victory during the Rebellion now became centres of pilgrimage for the British. Mogul rule was degraded: the Mogul palace was desacralized when British officers drank wine and ate pork there as part of the crushing of the Rebellion. With the trial and exiling of the Emperor, the Mogul period was definitively brought to an end. The new capital could now be safely located at Delhi. Conversely, Hindu culture was favoured: even before the Rebellion, the gates of the famous Hindu temple of Somnath, taken to Afghanistan by Muslims, were brought back by a British Governor-General.

By 1877, the time was ripe for the symbolic consolidation of British rule, the Imperial Assemblage, at which Queen Victoria was proclaimed Empress of India. The invitees were the Indian princes, landowners and a variety of other notables (even a professor of mathematics), plus key British officials. The princes were carefully ranked according to the size of their state, the amount of their revenue, the date at which they had become allies of the British, and so on. After they had given proof of sustained loyalty, they might then be recommended for new titles and rewards, even 'knights' of a new royal order, the Star of India. The cultural synthesis of India and Britain was symbolized, on the one hand, by tours of India by members of the British Royal Family and, on the other, by a wave of 'Orientalism' − scholarly research and publications about the pre-British cultures of India. The title eventually invented for the new Empress (by a linguist of Hungarian origin) was neither Hindu nor Muslim, but pseudo-Sanskritic: 'Kaiser-i-Hind'.

Wholesale symbolic reconstruction was now the order of the day. The new Viceroy, Lord Lytton, replaced what had been a direct personal and very varied political relationship between Indian princes of various kinds and the Mogul Emperor with a graded, linear hierarchy of ranks, with the Empress at its apex. Indians, Lytton thought, loved hierarchy and ritual. They were given plenty of it at the Delhi Imperial Assemblage of 1877.

There, the princes were presented by the Viceroy with large European-style, shield-shaped banners bearing (again European-style) coats of arms, devised by Robert Taylor, a Bengal civil servant and amateur heraldist. These were partly based on selected themes taken from the history of the particular princely house − for example, the mythic origins of Rajput ruling families were represented by the sun, symbolizing their descent from Rama − and partly on new symbols − the recently-created state of Kashmir, for example, by three wavy lines (the Himalayas), plus three roses for the beauty of the country. But, above all, the key symbols were those associated with British rule.

Lord Lytton, who was the only one to arrive by that most modern symbol of British technology the steam train, then transferred to a quintessential symbol of royal might in Asia and processed around the city on the back of the largest elephant in India. The notables and their attendants, 84,000 of them, were arranged in camps in over 8,000 tents in a five mile semicircle, in accordance with a well-worn British theme: the *diversity* of India, which, the British believed, had had no 'coherent communality except that given by British rule'.[63] At the centre was the enormous pavilion of the Viceroy, with the Governor of Bombay and the Governor of Madras to his right and left; behind him the key civilian administrators, with the camps of the commander-in-chief of the Indian Army and the commanders of the Bombay and Madras armies nearby. Closest to the imperial camp were the camps of the great potentates: the Nizam of Hyderabad, the Gaekwar of Baroda and the Maharaja of Mysore. The rest of the princes were organized regionally, with the European officials attached to each region who controlled the princes sitting among them. Everything was planned so that questions of precedence did not arise: all were equidistant from the Viceroy, to whom each prince was presented at a protracted series of audiences. (At the Durbar of 1911 staged by Lord Curzon, princes even had to *kneel* to George V.)

Rudyard Kipling's father, a minor Pre-Raphaelite painter and director of the Lahore Art School, was in charge of designing the uniforms and decorations. One artist hired to paint the scene recorded his dismay at the Viceroy's dais, festooned as it was with laurel wreaths, imperial crowns, gargoyle-like eagles, banners displaying the Cross of St George and the Union Jack, and a frieze carrying English, Scottish, Irish and even Indian motifs (the lotus): 'Oh Horror! What have I to paint? A kind of thing ... in atrocious taste ... [with] decorations in keeping, that out does the Crystal Palace in hideosity.'[64] Vast numbers of new titles and honours were handed out; only with the first Non-Co-operation Movement in 1920–21 would Indians be urged, by the rising nationalist movement, to return them.

Europe: The Great Museum

Such ceremonials, symbols and insignia, Morgan has observed,[65] have a 'great healing function' which is of exceptional importance in building up a sense of nationhood. They have their counterparts in every other conquered or submerged country too.

They are often especially visible to outsiders. Tourists, for example, are not necessarily, to use a phrase coined by American sociologists, 'cultural dopes'. When white Australians, whose man-made history goes back only a couple of centuries, visit Europe, where the majority of their ancestors came from, in order to explore their roots, the perspectives they bring with them ensure a certain criticality of the images which Europeans seek to project of themselves.

To Australians, as to North Americans, Europe is not particularly interesting in terms of modernity; if you want modernity, you stay in Sydney or San Francisco. But the eastern seaboard and the Old South apart, there isn't much history in the United States, or in Australia. So what Americans go to Europe for is to see the past. Donald Horne concludes that the great buildings they visit, and the things in them are not so much a presentation of history as a re-presentation. Most of the historic buildings now used as museums or treated as 'monuments' had quite different functions when they were first built. They were certainly not built to 'commemorate' the things they have since come to symbolize:

The Parthenon was not built as a ruin celebrating Western civilization; the aqueduct at Segovia was not built as a monument to Roman power any more than Haghia Sophia [ex-cathedral, in Istanbul] was erected to commemorate Byzantine culture; the Palazzo Medici-Riccardi was not built to commemorate the Renaissance; the Winter Palace was not built to commemorate the Baroque; London's Trooping the Colour ceremony was not invented for tourist 'pageantry'.[66]

Achievements by individuals deemed to be 'nationals', in any field – science, the arts, war – are drawn upon as the achievements of the *nation*, even if the nation in question did not exist when the achieving was being done. When reburied in shrines like the Panthéon in Paris, these become collective monuments to the nation's genius.

Even the sheer physical landscape of the country, such as the mountains of Switzerland or Scotland, is considered to have put a particular stamp upon the national character. In Norway, for instance, the Ski Museum at Holmenkollen postulates a continuity of tradition from what was once a quite utilitarian technology developed by the Stone Age ancestors of the Norwegians to enable them to travel about in a harsh mountain environment but has now become simply a sport, participated in by all (including the Royal Family).

Cultural achievements of any kind in the past, from musical compositions to scientific discoveries, by people who can be claimed to belong to what has become, in modern times, a nation, are used by myth-makers as evidence not just of the richness of the national culture but of the country's contribution to world culture too. For maritime powers, for instance, the sea, though it does not lend itself to being parcelled up and appropriated by any one country, is assimilated to the national myth, in the museums of former imperial powers in London, Paris and Brussels, via the celebration of voyages of discovery and the establishment of colonies. Anthropology itself, in the shape of the 'ethnographic' museum, has been a major contributor to myths of exploration and expansion. Helsinki's National Museum, for instance, acknowledges, in a stained-glass window, the three major components of nineteenth-century Finnish nationalism: ethnography, archaeology and history. In St Petersburg's Ethnographic Museum, it is not the contributions of nineteenth-century revolutionaries exiled to Siberia to early Russian ethnography that are given pride of place but the accumulated material culture of the innumerable peoples subjugated during the extraordinary drive of Russian trading adventurers who crossed Siberia and reached the Pacific Ocean in only half a century – half as far again, and at the same time, as the distance between the American Atlantic and Pacific coasts when the English colonists had penetrated only a few hundred miles inland.

Countries which have lost global empires usually remain fixated on the imperial past. In Portugal, the national monuments that still matter most are those to the Discoverers and to Henry the Navigator. At Belém, the Discoverers are shown with their instruments of navigation and the friars, but not the muskets and manacles which they used to capture slaves and to control them on colonial plantations. Other diminished once imperial powers like Denmark, whose overseas ventures included slave-trading in West Africa, now use the vestiges of formerly serious military forces – the 'toy soldiers' outside the Royal Palace in Copenhagen – as a mere tourist spectacle, like the Horse Guards in London. Only the Tropical Museum in another ex-imperial city, Amsterdam, makes any effort to demystify the nakedly economic impulses which powered colonialism and to relate it to the present-day underdevelopment of the South.

Explorers, even when not necessarily involved directly in political expansion or in trade, are nevertheless taken as evidence that the country they came from breeds adventurers, people of a special stamp of whom we should all still be proud today. The Royal Geographical Society in London, thus displays a section of the tree under which Livingstone's heart was buried.

The heart and the brain of Ivan Vasov, on the other hand, preserved in the house in Sofia where he died, are not used to symbolize imperial expansion but national awakening, since this novelist was the inspirer of modern Bulgarian nationalism.[67] Language is another key element used in the celebration of the rise of the modern nation: intellectuals like the philologist Lönnrot in Norway, who recorded the oral literature of the 'folk', or those in many countries who converted one of many dialects into what was to become the official form of the national language. In nationalist myth, St Cyril and St Methodius, who in medieval Bulgaria translated the Bible into Slavonic characters, are now perceived as pioneers of cultural nationalism rather than as evangelists of Christianity.

The attempt to create new languages or scripts does not always succeed. *Ny Norsk* (New Norwegian), created in the nineteenth century, has not in fact displaced existing forms of Norwegian. But in many countries new forms of language created by intellectuals, were eagerly seized on by growing nationalist movements. Commonly, they drew upon forms of the language as spoken by peasants. But in Greece a quite new form of Greek was invented by an intellectual living in Paris who wanted to get back to the ancient classical civilization of Attica, rather than identifying Hellenic culture with what had been, for centuries, the real heartland of Greek civilization, Constantinople, in Asia Minor (now part of Turkey). He therefore turned his back on the demotic language spoken in the streets and produced an artificial language which he called Katharevousa, midway between classical Greek (which nobody spoke) and demotic. The opposite occurred in Bulgaria, where a new one *was* based on the language spoken by the people, in a script developed during the Middle Ages by St Cyril and St Methodius which replaced the Old Slavonic writing by Cyrillic characters used phonetically.

In the twentieth century, the new nation of Israel, its population boosted by the arrival of tens of thousands of immigrants from countries as diverse as Germany, Russia and Morocco – in Zionist ideology, the 'ingathering' from the Diaspora – to Palestine, where no Jewish state had existed since the destruction of the Temple 2,000 years earlier, opted for Hebrew as the language of the country, even though it was a religious language which, like Latin in the Roman Catholic Church, was not spoken in the homes the immigrants had come from.

The myth of a shared common culture never went unchallenged. Ancient 'folk' countercultural alternative identities and ideologies persisted which expressed social opposition to hegemonic cultures, old and new, and were likely to surface at times of overt social conflict. As late as the nineteenth century, the common people in England identified themselves not as Englishmen but as 'Saxons', and their rulers as 'Normans', rather than using 'English' (even less 'British') as the common identity of both.

Many of those seen today as forerunners of modern were very unlikely proto-nationalists (including one quite fictitious figure, William Tell). Spain's national hero, El Cid – whose very title is Arabic ('Sayyidi': Lord) – spent much of his life fighting for a Moorish ruler both in internecine wars and against Christian enemies, notably the Count of Barcelona. Only at the end of his life, with the capture of Valencia, did he play the role for which he is remembered in nationalist mythology. Others, like the *hajduks* of Serbia and their Greek counterparts, the *klephtes* – denigrated by their Ottoman rulers as 'bandits' or 'robbers' (in the way that peasant revolutionaries from Malaya to Algeria and Vietnam were more recently described as 'terrorists') – did actually fight the Turks, though they were not driven simply by ethnic hatred, even less by the notion that, in common with other people who spoke Serbo-Croat or Greek, they were engaged in a common struggle for a future state of their own, but fought, rather, whoever offered the best returns in terms of plunder. Gellner recalls singing songs around the campfire in holiday camps in pre-war Czechoslovakia which celebrated 'social bandits' who killed a shepherd boy when he refused to hand over his overcoat.[68]

Myth-makers not only reinterpret the past and invent new myths; they are also victims of what anthropologists call 'structural amnesia'. 'Studying the *absence* of monuments,' Horne remarks, 'can be as significant as studying what is celebrated.'[69] The relationship of class to nation is one such particularly sensitive matter, for popular uprisings are less celebrated the more recently they occurred and the more relevant their bearing upon modern political divisions. Thus, in Britain, only a plaque and a painting in Manchester's Free Trade Hall commemorates the ruling-class violence used at the Peterloo massacre in 1819; only a few score members of the Labour movement pay annual tribute to the Tolpuddle martyrs; while nobody celebrates the greatest mass movement of the nineteenth century, Chartism. Even radical reform is voided of content: young people come from all over the world to sit on the steps of the Eros monument in Piccadilly Circus which they think was meant to symbolize love, but actually pays tribute to the crusading reforms of Lord Shaftesbury, including his very unromantic campaigns to abolish child labour. The ultimate, and commonest, way of handling the brutality of the past is to dehumanize history, removing the human agent and ascribing progress instead to *things*, as when the grim history of enforced social change is attributed to impersonal forces: to changes in *technology* such as the spinning jenny or the motor car. What most museums of technology depict, therefore, is 'the industrial revolution without the revolution'.[70]

Symbols of modernity inevitably date. No one now bothers to look at the symbols of nineteenth-century American capitalism on the Custom House (where Herman Melville worked) in the financial district of Manhattan. Likewise, one of the greatest monuments to the Victorian age in Britain, the Albert Memorial, is at the time of writing wrapped up like some piece of avant-garde sculpture, its symbols of imperial trade hidden from view, because after nearly twenty years in power no Conservative administration had been willing to pay for its refurbishment. It is ironic, and unintendedly symbolic, that the decay is due to the rusting of that archetypical Victorian material, iron. Now, in a further ironic twist, we are promised that the state lottery may pay for the needed restoration of what has become an important tourist attraction.

Nationalism as Counterculture

Kilts, Druids and Vikings
When nationalists want to challenge imperial power, then, they look back, Janus-like, at the pre-colonial past in order to construct a new alternative identity for the future.

The materials they have drawn upon are often of the most improbable kind, ranging from cultural forms such as the tango to achievements in football. Those who created them were often equally bizarre. In museums of 'folklore', even class – which for socialists was not only the key category used in analysing society but something that challenged ruling-class myths of vertical national solidarity *across* classes – was pressed into service: on the one hand, luxurious objects once owned and used exclusively by the nobility, and unaffordable or often rigorously forbidden to those they ruled, are displayed as 'national' culture; on the other, the costumes and handicrafts of the peasantry; who were often quite devoid of *national* consciousness, which is an invention of city intellectuals.

National symbols become so familiar, over time, that their authenticity is never questioned. The Scottish kilt, for instance, universally and unquestioningly accepted as the symbol of the Scottish clans, is in fact relatively recent. Before the late seventeenth century, the Highlanders of Scotland did not form a distinct people.[71] Culturally they were 'simply the overflow of Ireland' and politically Scots had founded kingdoms in Ulster for centuries; the two Celtic societies simply merged into each other.

The creation of an independent Highland tradition, Trevor-Roper has shown in his classic study, developed only in reaction to the union with England, mainly in the late eighteenth and early nineteenth centuries. First came the cultural revolt against the idea that the Scots could be seen as descendants of Irish colonizers with the assertion of the counterclaim that Celtic Scotland was really the 'mother-nation'. Next there was the creation of new, artificial Highland traditions, which were presented as ancient and authentic; and finally the absorption of these notions in Eastern and Lowland Scotland, the most anglicized parts of Scotland.

Intellectuals were the leading force in this process, nowadays usually described as the 'invention of tradition'. In the case of James and John Macpherson, it is literally true, for between them they created an indigenous literature for Celtic Scotland by faking 'translations' of Ossian. Irish ballads found in Scotland, they said, were really Scottish; conversely, native Irish literature had been stolen from the Scots. Between them, these two 'insolent pretenders' put the Scottish Highlanders on the map.

The transformation of the kilt and the bagpipes into the archetypal material symbols of Scottish culture, though, was the work of later intellectuals. Far from being the aboriginal Highland dress, the kilt was invented by an Englishman after the union of 1707, while the differentiated clan 'tartans' were an even later invention.[72]

Brutal repression had followed the defeat of the second Jacobite Rebellion of 1745. A network of new military roads, the political incorporation of Scottish landed and business élites and the Highland Clearances ensured that there would be no third instalment of rebellion.

But cultural repression, involving the skilful selective incorporation of Scottish symbols, was more subtle. Just as Henry VIII had banned native dress in Ireland centuries earlier, the kilt was at first banned. By 1780, it seemed that the Highland dress was dying out in the countryside. At this point, though, it suddenly *did* become a national symbol. It had been revived, in a modernized form, by an English Quaker, Thomas Rawlinson, not out of any enthusiasm for nationalism but as a practical dress which could be worn by the workers in his factories. But it then got taken up, paradoxically, by urban, Anglicized Scottish peers, 'improving gentry, well-educated Edinburgh lawyers and prudent merchants of Aberdeen'.[73]

The next step came with the incorporation of these symbols into the British imperial system. Before the eighteenth century, each clan did not have its own distinctive pattern of tartan, while Highland regiments wore the belted plaid, not the kilt. Now the kilt became standard regimental uniform, though many leaders of Scottish society resisted this innovation. Yet by the 1820s, 'the Highland takeover had begun', with the foundation of the Celtic Society in Edinburgh, dedicated to promoting the wearing of the kilt. Sir Walter Scott presented one to George IV when he visited Scotland. Pattern books specifying the correct tartans for each clan were now written, while the manufacture of the appropriate cloths became a growth industry. One tartan design, previously sold in bulk to a West Indian slave-owner who used it to clothe his slaves, was now designated the 'Macpherson' tartan.

In 1842, the brothers Allen – whose pretensions included claims that they were descendants of the Stuarts – 'discovered' an ancient work, lost for generations, the *Vestiarium Scoticum*, which showed that the tartan had formerly existed in Lowland Scotland as well. This was followed by their lavish *The Costume of the Clans* — a book which Trevor-Roper describes as 'shot through with pure fantasy and barefaced forgery' — which even argued that Highland Scottish dress had formerly been worn everywhere in Europe. Nobody took much notice of them, but the publication in 1843 of James Logan's *Clans of the Scottish Highlands*, which won him the election as President of the Scottish Society of London, could not have been more timely, for it coincided with a new impulse given to the cult of the Highlands by Queen Victoria, who, under the malign influence of her ghillie, John Brown, had purchased Balmoral Castle. Highland scenery, Highland cattle and Landseer's paintings of the Highlands now became extremely fashionable. Books on the Scottish tartans began to multiply. One of them, General James Brown's *History of the Highlands and the Highland Clans*, became the standard work. Henceforth, Scottish tartans were to be worn by 'Scots and supposed Scots from Texas to Tokyo'.[74] More importantly, cultural nationalism was eventually to give birth to political nationalism.

The history of the revival of Welsh cultural nationalism is no less bizarre. By the eighteenth century, Morgan shows, it seemed that the minority of Welsh people who could still speak Welsh would soon lose it, like the Scots and the Irish. Not only the language but the entire Welsh way of life, observers in the early nineteenth century concluded, were doomed to disappear. The native culture, once Catholic, had already disappeared, to be replaced by the sixteenth century by Protestantism; the native legal system had been abolished and the Welsh language outlawed. (A Welsh vice-chancellor of an English university told me that using Welsh was forbidden in schools in Wales, even in the playground, as late as the 1930s; children found speaking Welsh were punished by being made to wear a stick round their necks.)

The rescue of Welsh culture, especially the Welsh language, began innocently enough with books on Welsh music.[75] Scholars emphasized that the Welsh were the earliest inhabitants of the British Isles, that they had later defended Christianity, introduced by the Romans, against the pagan Saxons, as the existence of many churches with holy wells indicated, while the Welsh aristocracy were descendants of tribal or Roman leaders. The very name 'Britain' was claimed to have come from Brutus; some Romantic nationalists even awaited the return of King Arthur. Myths about the second coming of the Welsh hero Owain Glyndwr who centuries before had risen against the English and then ruled his country, only to disappear mysteriously, were used by Henry Tudor, later Henry VII, to claim overlordship of the whole of Britain.

Bards – historians, copyists, librarians, heralds and musicians – dominated Welsh letters, but popular culture was being eroded away. Even Welsh baptismal names, formerly very varied, were beginning to give way to stereotyped names like Jones or Williams, and the upper classes were adopting names that emphasized their distinguished genealogy rather than using ones common in the local community. The old culture had included wakes, Maypole dancing, fortune-telling, even violent sport and drunken orgies of drinking. Now the 'sour spirit of Methodism' drove all this away. The stairways connecting the chancels of the churches to local taverns and the ball courts in the churchyards were removed, while popular plays and lyric ballads were discouraged.

The eisteddfod, a bardic competition, was not an invention, but it had practically disappeared by the seventeenth century. Then it began to experience something of a revival, often in taverns. By the 1780s, the first Welsh Society was established, in London, helping Welshmen visiting the capital and providing charity for those in difficulties. When the society began to attract even grandees, the common people started to organize more informal meetings in alehouses; the London Welsh also helped organize eisteddfods in Wales itself.

By 1819, Iolo Morganwg organized the first Gorsedd (throne) of Bards. Soon there were cells of bards all over Wales, using rituals and symbols created by Iolo, from crowns and chairs to a mystic sign. During the nineteenth century alone, 500 important ceremonial eisteddfods were held. Iolo also forged love poems supposedly written by Ifor Hael centuries earlier. Before long, local stories about highwaymen, incorporated in a novel by T. J. Llewllyn Pritchard, in which he created a Robin Hood, or Till Eulenspiegel-like character, Twm Sion Catti, were being taken as true.

The next stage was the rediscovery of the druids, holy prophet figures who had led the resistance to the Romans both in Britain and Gaul and were now said to be connected with sacrificial altars (which started an enthusiasm for cremation), megalithic monuments ('Druid Stones', including Stonehenge) and even a secret written language. Wales' cultural tradition, it could now be claimed, was 'older than any other in Western Europe, and it made the scholar or poet or teacher central to that culture. To some extent it restored the bard to his primary place in Welsh culture.'[76]

Though the Celts had never been associated with the British Isles, Welsh scholars soon began discovering their connections with Celts in other countries, notably the Bretons. A marked increase in books in Welsh had begun before the turn of the eighteenth century. Dictionaries then began to get larger, and the Welsh language, once derided as ugly and primitive, was soon declared to be superior to English. William Owen (Pughe) – 'the greatest and most effective of the language mythologists' – improved the orthography and 'found a Welsh word for every possible nuance in any language'. As a result, his dictionary contained 40,000 more words than Dr Johnson's.

It was at this time that Wales also became the 'Land of Song'. *Penillion* singing, in which the singer chimes in with either his own, sometimes extempore, verses or others of medieval origin, using large numbers of stanzas with highly elaborate alliterative schemes, to the accompaniment of the harp, now took on a new lease of life. The harp itself, now developed as an instrument with three strings, made possible styles which were often probably modern but soon became thought of as very ancient. 'Authentic' Welsh airs (in fact taken from English ballads and hymn tunes and given Welsh words) were supplemented by others written by Welsh poets. Finally, in 1856, Wales got its national anthem, 'Hen Wlad Fy Nadhau' ('Land of My Fathers'), while Lady Llanover turned what had been surviving forms of a countrywoman's style of dress (equally to be found in the past in England) into a national costume.

By the 1770s, Wales had already acquired a national hero, Owain Glyndwr. More bizarre was the legend of Madoc, son of a Welsh prince, who had discovered America about 1170 and whose descendants were said to be still living among the Mandan Indians. Explorers who went to see if the Mandan still spoke Welsh were disappointed.

By the end of the eighteenth century, the landscape of Wales, once considered to be a horrid, mountainous country, like Dr Johnson's view of Scotland, had become one of great beauty. Heraldry was developed to adorn Welsh ceremonies and to express national identity; the ostrich feathers of the Prince of Wales, for example, adopted in 1751, were actually of continental origin, via the Black Prince's mother. Radicals, liberals and socialists preferred the red dragon, which had been used as a Welsh symbol under the Tudors and was therefore considered to be less deferential. (The daffodil became a Welsh symbol only as late as 1907.)

By the end of the nineteenth century, a puritanical culture of nonconformist dissent was to emerge as a new expression of Welsh cultural separateness. Before long, Welsh nationalism acquired its own political party, Plaid Cymru.

Scottish and Welsh nationalism, according to these accounts, are tissues of delusion, illusion, fantasy and deliberate, often dishonest fabrication. To positivists, of course, all myths are unscientific; to Marxists, they are 'ideology'; to defenders of hegemonic cultures they are powered by emotion rather than logic (socialism, Durkheim once remarked, was not 'scientific'; it was a 'cry of pain'). A newer, more phenomenological generation seeks to 'deconstruct' everything: since reality can be perceived only through the screen of the human mind, they argue, there can be no such thing as history, only views of history. The application of this approach to nationalism resulted in charges levelled against nationalist myth-making that the 'traditions' they peddled were simply 'inventions'. Since *all* tradition is invented, this was a powerful kind of analysis which could be used to denigrate both imperialist myth-making and countercultural nationalism alike.

A lower level of criticism questions the honesty, even the mental stability of myth-makers. Trevor-Roper tells us that James Logan had been severely injured when a hammer smashed his skull during the Highland Games; Prys Morgan writes that Iolo Morganwg was a 'wild dreamer [and] a lifelong addict to laudanum'. Both he and the Allen brothers faked 'ancient' documents.

Myth-makers like these were able to deceive people not just because people were credulous but because they had genuine grievances. Moreover, however reinterpreted and developed, the existence of bards, druids and kilts in the days before Wales and Scotland became part of Britain was not just pure myth.

Our third case study from the British Isles is by Bronwen Cohen of a much less well-known culture, that of the Shetland Islands, and describes the rise of a very similar kind of Romantic nationalism in that remote part of Britain in the nineteenth century.[77] She, however, takes particular pains to show how these ideas were a reaction to the political, economic and cultural incorporation of the Shetlands into Scottish, and thereby British, society. With this, she shows, Shetland society underwent changes of many kinds: the displacement of the crofting system of farming and the traditional *udal* system of land tenure by farms owned by foreign aristocrats; the rise of commercial herring fisheries owned by a new class of merchants; improved communications with the outside world; the establishment of newspapers; the arrival of nonconformist and even socialist ideas; and the introduction of a modern education system.

The Shetlands were colonized by settlers from Norway from the eighth century AD, were brought under Norwegian political control a century later and then, following a dynastic marriage, passed to Scotland in 1471, and thereafter eventually to Britain. Half a millennium later, it might reasonably have been expected that, as in Wales and Scotland, any sense of a distinct national identity would have disappeared. In fact, a cultural renaissance began, though at first only among a few intellectuals. There was not even any consensus among them, though, as to the ethnic origins of the islanders: some emphasized Norwegian (or Danish) descent, others, resenting the domination of the English and the Scots — peoples they labelled 'Normans' — identified themselves as 'Saxons' (or, later, 'Teutons', 'Aryans' or even 'Goths'). Ethnologists like A. H. Keane devised racist family trees, based on those in Darwin's *The Origin of Species*, in which the main line of social evolution was shown as leading to the Norsemen and the Anglo-Saxons, and thereafter subdividing into Anglo-Americans, Anglo-Africans and Anglo-Australians. Such notions also found their way into the writings of distinguished pioneers of linguistics. Even today, I meet many otherwise utterly politically correct people who, though they would be horrified at any notion of *physical* racism, accept uncritically ideas developed by nineteenth-century linguists such as Jespersen and Jakobsen which are thoroughly *cultural*-racist: the belief that English is the most 'flexible' language of all, or that it possesses the richest vocabulary, or that it is superior because it is an 'inflecting' language, not a mere 'agglutinating' one.

Early Church chroniclers represented the Norsemen as barbarous, ruthless raiders who had descended on the islands 'like bees out of an hive', robbing and pillaging and even destroying churches. (The persisting ambiguity of Anglo-Scottish attitudes towards them is reflected in a recent advertising campaign featuring a Viking in a horned helmet with the slogan, 'They took our money, they took our women — but they left their beer.') By the early nineteenth century, though, Viking raids were being explained either in economic terms — the flight of poor people from a life which, though simple and idyllic, was still hard — or in political terms — they were freedom-loving people trying to escape from the harsh rule of lords and kings. Whether Shetland intellectuals thought of them as coming from the German forests or having arrived by Viking longboat, they were mainly agreed on one thing: that their forebears had lived in a free society and brought democratic institutions with them. It was the Vikings, for instance, who had introduced the jury system. They were also a cultured race, as the Scandinavian sagas and the fairy-tales of the Grimm brothers showed. Scholars now embarked on the study of the saga: it was there and not in Tacitus, one writer said, that we should look to understand Norse culture. Whereas the United States was being peopled by 'beaten men from beaten races', the descendants of the Norsemen had implanted the values of freedom and democracy in the British Isles. The spirit of independence, another writer asserted, was even visible in the Anglo-Saxon house, which 'always, if possible, stands detached'. The idea that these characteristics were some kind of racial legacy was soon being conveyed to schoolchildren via history books about their Viking ancestors. John

Ruskin was inclined to accept the idea that they had invented 'Gothic' architecture; William Morris, R. M. Ballantyne and Charlotte Yonge were all Nordophiles; while for people like Percy Grainger, the Teutonic myth was still alive in the 1930s, by which time it had also become part of Nazism.

The first stirrings of nationalism came from middle class intellectuals like Arthur Laurenson, Lawrence Williamson, J. J. Haldane Burgess and Jessie Saxby, the latter a Shetland expatriate living in Scotland. Inspired by the success of Sir Walter Scott's novel of 1821, *The Pirate*, in which the hero was a Scottish earl of ancient Norwegian descent, their ideas were rapidly disseminated by teachers in the new schools. Scholars from other northern lands also began to visit the Shetlands, notably the Faroese linguist Jakob Jakobsen. By 1862, the Viking Club had been founded; its meetings were known as 'Things', the honorary president as the 'Viking-Jarl' and the club's poet as the 'Viking-Skald'.

Vikings were free spirits, men of the sea, unlike the Scots, who lived in a 'rugged and sterile' land. In one of Jessie Saxby's Shetland stories, they had even peopled the American West – a hero of hers discovers Mexico. Inspired by the success of the movement for Irish Home Rule in 1886, liberals and, later, socialists began to dream of an 'Allthing' council for Orkney and the Shetlands, each of which would also each have its own 'Lawthing', with a prince of the royal blood as governor. Resentment of a taxation system under which islanders paid not only Scottish land tax but also taxes to Lord Zetland or to the bishop drove some to canvass the idea of reviving the ancient system of land tenure.

The steam was eventually taken out of the economic grievances by the reform of crofter land-holding in 1886, while the introduction of local government a few years later deflated any idea of Home Rule. Though nationalism persisted, by now it was primarily a largely symbolic movement of cultural self-expression – what has been called 'submerged' or *sub*nationalism. Thereafter Laurenson's energies went into ensuring that the windows of the new town hall (financed by the city of Bergen) showed the arms of the old Norselands and commemorated Norse ancestors: Harald Fairhair, Olaf Tryggvason, Earl Rognvald, St Olaf and others, with the Stewarts represented on one window alone. The pictures inside were copies of portraits of the Danish nobility.

All this appealed to intellectuals. But it was the new ritual of 'Up-Helly-Aa' which was to prove the most popular innovation. It had grown out of the custom in which fantastically dressed 'guizers', on a date prescribed by the old calendar, the twenty-fourth day after Christmas, which ended the Yule holidays, had dragged burning tar-sledges through the streets of the capital Lerwick in an often riotous festival which included throwing fireworks against the premises of some of the 'hard-fisted gentry'.

In 1874, it had been banned by the city fathers on the grounds of the violence and drunkenness which occurred, plus the danger to property from the blazing sledges in the narrow streets. But because of its enduring popularity, a more 'orderly and controlled celebration' had to be devised to replace the old riotous happenings; torches were substituted for the sledges and the ceremony shifted to Christmas Day. By 1882, the editor of the *Shetland Times* had become the 'Worthy Chief Guizer', a title soon changed to 'Guizer Jarl'. Five years later, a Norse galley was ceremonially burned at the market cross – a tradition probably invented by Burgess. A special song, 'The Hardy Norseman', written by C. E. Mitchell, ended:

The Norseman's power is past and gone,
their courage, strength and pride
For now Britannia's sons alone,
In triumph stem the tide;
Then may Victoria rule the land,
our laws and rights defend.
One cheer then give with heart and hand –
the Queen – the people's friend.[78]

This was too much for Burgess, who immediately wrote a more pro-Norse song, 'Up-Helly-Aa', which replaced 'Auld Lang Syne' during the burning of the galley. It ended:

Our galley is the People's Right,
    the dragon of the free;
The Right that, rising in its might,
    brings tyrants to their knees;
The flag that flies above us is the Love of Liberty ...

Although there was a small Shetlands movement in the 1970s – influenced by the Scottish campaign for devolution and Faroese dreams of developing a limited autonomy within the British Isles (but outside the EEC) – it never made any serious impact on political life.

In Scotland, in a referendum in 1979, a bare majority opted for home rule, but not enough to pass the threshold of 40 per cent set by the London government. Wales rejected devolution much more decisively. In the 1992 British general election, despite the growth of feeling that the oil coming from the North Sea was '*our* oil', the Scottish National Party still got less than a quarter of the Scottish vote and won only three seats. The

Welsh Nationalists, Plaid Cymru, won four. 'The proclivities of Scottish voters,' the most authoritative study concluded, in 1992, 'differed little from those of party supporters south of the border.'[79] Yet only a few years later, devolution was to come, not directly, through support for the Scottish National Party, but via the Labour Party, which controlled most of the parliamentary seats in Scotland.

Forging a Republic

I now turn to two major foci of national identity in a country which has been described as the 'First New Nation', the United States of America. One, Thanksgiving, is a ritual, an event; the other, the Statue of Liberty, is an iconic symbol.

When the state sets about creating a myth of national identity, it builds it around people and events who were important in the development of the polity: in the United States, for instance, the Lincoln and Jefferson Memorials and the Washington Monument in the nation's capital, Washington, DC. But the majority of a country's citizens do not usually live in the capital. The major political symbols of the nation-state in Britain, for instance, the war memorials in every town and village, link ordinary individual citizens who gave their lives, by recording the names of the dead from two world wars. Historic disasters, equally, can bind a nation together as effectively as victories. For Serbian extremist nationalists, even though the nation had lost its independence centuries ago, Serbia was 'where Serbian graves were'. For them, the defeat at the hands of the Ottomans at Kosovo in 1389 was a unifying myth. For a much newer country like Australia, their identity as a nation began not with the First Fleet, which brought the convicts to Botany Bay, but with the bloody ANZAC campaign of 1915.[80] The dead were not just corpses; they were *martyrs*, the basis of the myth of the new nation.

It is often uncritically assumed that national rituals express a greater degree of social solidarity than actually exists, even in a country like Israel, where the experience of centuries of being stigmatized and persecuted as Jews, reinforced by the trauma of the Holocaust, provided a powerful ideological basis for a new Israeli national identity. Members of a culture which has produced more than its fair share of intellectuals and has contributed to two other world religions apart from Judaism, Israeli intellectuals set about creating symbols and rituals for Remembrance Day and Independence Day ceremonies,[81] under the direction of the Defence Ministry, with the purpose of uniting state and citizenry. Yet, as Anthony Cohen observes, Israeli national solidarity is in fact still extremely problematic in a society constructed out of culturally highly heterogeneous elements. Modern Zionism, a product of nineteenth-century Europe – 'of the Enlightenment, of emancipation from the ghetto, and of the rise of nationalism' – had bypassed the ultra-Orthodox Jews, for whom truth and history were to be found only in the sacred texts. Since Israel was founded as a secular state, it was not acceptable to them. Nor, therefore, were the symbols of Israeli nationhood. Bitter and complex battles were fought out in the Flag and Symbol Committee of the new state over the choice of national symbols – the menorah, the proposed motif of seven stars, and so on – ending with the elimination from the final design of 'any of the innovative aspirations of modern Zionism for the future'.[82]

A further major social division was the distinction between Ashkenazi Jews of Eastern European origin and Sephardi Jews of Mediterranean origin, divisions which

have become more complex with the huge increase in immigration from the former Soviet Union, with unemployment and underemployment, with the tensions over settlement policy in the occupied territories, with confrontation between secularism and religiosity, with the huge expansion of Hasidic communities and the growth in numbers and political influence of the right-wing, religious settlers.[83]

Then there are the tensions resulting from Israeli occupation of Arab territories which has left large Arab populations within the borders of Israel and has divided Israeli public opinion.

Symbols like these, emanating from the state and focusing on national rituals performed at sacred places, are in any case only one kind of symbol of social solidarity. Other symbols express many kinds of solidarities within civil society, from the older community solidarities of church congregations to urban civic pride expressed in grandiose railway stations and department stores. Here, though, I am concerned with the nation at the societal level, so I will focus on symbols of national identity other than official ones located in the capital, and I will now look at two which have had particular purchase upon the popular imagination.

Attempts to generate national pride do not always come off. Didactic messages such as the display round the viewing floor of the World Trade Center in Manhattan, for instance, tell us that economic growth has been a consequence of trade from time immemorial. It is an interesting display, taking us from the ancient Phoenicians the silk trade to Henry Ford and the space age, and it ends with a celebration of the extraordinary diversity of modern consumer culture, which includes yaks and the zither as well as bread and cheese, candy, toys and wines. But only a few people look at it.

Indeed, most of them have their backs to it, for they are riveted not by words but by the spectacle of capitalism in action, as they look down from the 110th storey of a building where over 50,000 people work and which consumes more electricity than the state capital of Albany, into the canyons of the Financial District and of the rest of Manhattan beyond it. Such 'sermons in stones' can be far more powerful than even the best public-relations presentations.

Major political figures and battles can, of course, become popular symbols, for political change affects everybody and brings social transformation in its wake. The crucial event in America's post-revolution history, the Civil War, which ended slavery and preserved the Union, thus made Lincoln the perfect symbol for modern America, combining the classic American success story – log cabin to White House – with the Christian theme of sacrifice on behalf of one's fellow men. A classic pioneer study of symbolism in American public life between the two world wars, in 'Middletown', found that Lincoln still 'loomed over the memorial rites like some great demigod over the rites of classical antiquity'.[84]

Yet today, as the Civil War itself has become an ever more remote event, Lincoln has diminished in significance. Even 4 July, though still an important public holiday and, as Janet Siskind has written, an important 'occasion for politicians, backyard barbecues and marching bands', is no longer, as it once was, 'a serious ritual event'. Other less overtly political rituals, notably Thanksgiving, on the other hand, have not only persisted but also become an integral part of popular culture.

Thanksgiving

'It is impossible to be American,' Janet Siskind remarks, 'and not be aware of Thanksgiving.' Since it celebrates family, home and nation, it thereby 'expresses and reaffirms values and assumptions about cultural and social unity, about identity and history, about inclusion and exclusion' to the extent that, for most people, it still retains some religious connotations.[85]

Yet the majority of Americans are descendants of people who arrived in the country only in the second half of the nineteenth century. Unlike WASP Daughters of the American Revolution, they cannot trace their families back to the Pilgrim Fathers. Yet the myth of origin appeals even to these descendants of late-comers, for it celebrates not the historical arrival of their own ancestors but the foundation myth of their country: the beginnings of the United States as a nation in the Dreamtime.

At Thanksgiving, the communion is a feast of indigenous American foods. 'Everyone knows that across the nation members of every other household are simultaneously feasting on stuffed turkey, sweet potatoes, pumpkin pie and cranberry sauce.'

The Pilgrims celebrated divine favour with feasts and the displeasure of the deity by fasting. Following English traditions, feasting took place at harvest festivals and other occasions for giving thanks. Such rituals obviously occurred at different times of the year – when, for example, there was a particularly good harvest or a timely rainfall; there was no special single point in the year for feasting. Nor was there any special connection between Thanksgiving and the Plymouth Plantation. Jamestown, for instance, is 'as early and as valid an ancestor' as Plymouth (which lasted only two generations as an autonomous colony), while the three days of feasting in Plymouth in 1621 are purely mythological; thanksgiving, furthermore, occurred in other early Puritan settlements at other dates.

Over time, giving thanks for divine favour became more political, particularly to celebrate success in wars against the Indians: the defeat of the Pequots in 1637 was the first day to be celebrated by the entire New England Church throughout the New England colonies. As New England society gradually ceased to be based on religious fundamentalism, the authority to proclaim days of feasting or fasting became an area of conflict between religious and secular authorities. A year before the Revolution, the issue was finally decided in favour of the secular authorities. After the Revolution, new political struggles between federalists and anti-federalists inhibited the proclamation of further thanksgiving days. Only with the Civil War did Lincoln proclaim several days of thanks to the deity. By the 1860s, the last Thursday in November had been settled upon. Since then, only at times when the Union is troubled or questioned – during the Great Depression under President Hoover, later under President Reagan – have political events markedly influenced Thanksgiving Day.

By the 1860s, people were moving increasingly to the cities and towns. Thanksgiving now became a time for family reunions on the farms, when everyone sat down to a feast of turkey, and particularly stuffed turkey. The turkey, some commentators have argued, 'powerfully symbolizes the Indians', who by the mid-nineteenth century could be viewed sentimentally as 'noble savages' who had lived in a lost Eden, rather than as heathens. By now, the robbing of food from Indian graves in the first traumatic winter was forgotten and a myth of racial harmony between friendly Indians and trusting settlers obscured the long history of genocidal wars. Once they had been exterminated or confined to reservations, though, it was hard to incorporate the Indians into a myth of national solidarity. It was, however, easier than incorporating blacks into Thanksgiving. When they appeared in the illustrated magazines of the nineteenth century, they were serving the white folk their Thanksgiving dinners. And a later generation of Hispanic immigrants celebrated national rituals such as Christmas in their own way, linking it with events in Mexican, not American history: with the Noche Buena, the victory of Cortés after his reverse during the Noche Triste. For Indians, the link was with the Black Virgin of Guadalupe.

In the South, during Reconstruction, Thanksgiving Day was regarded as a cultural expression of Northern domination. In Alabama, in 1875, Governor Houston proclaimed 23 December as a day to celebrate a new policy of keeping blacks out of state government; Georgia and Louisiana announced thanksgivings when all-white government was restored.

It was the beginning of mass immigration which saw the modification of Thanksgiving into a festival in which immigrants had a place. The Pilgrim Fathers were now transformed from 'austere, distant figures' to the very 'model of the good immigrant, imbued with religious conviction, a member of the Chosen People, striving to make a life in the new world'. It is this imagery that was to inform what has now become the classic ritual of the American year.

The Statue of Liberty

'The Statue of Liberty,' writes Marvin Trachtenberg, 'is the symbolic image of America, more than Washington's profile, the eagle, or even the flag.'[86] Yet if things had gone as its sculptor, Frédéric Auguste Bartholdi, had intended, she would have been an Egyptian peasant standing at the entrance to the Suez Canal, symbolizing both the triumph of French technology and the modernization of Egypt along European lines (albeit with the use of slave labour).

Bartholdi possessed a 'swooning passion for the colossal'. His first success, a statue of General Rapp, was so large that it could not be fitted into the exhibition hall of the Salon of 1885. His special interest in patriotic statuary intensified after the Franco-Prussian War of 1871, because he had taken part in the defence of Colmar and had also been aide-de-camp to Garibaldi (who, ever eager to be involved in national struggles, had tried to raise a new French army to fight the Prussians). Bartholdi now experienced defeat and exile from Alsace. After the war, both sides continued to fight symbolically. Bismarck's victorious Germany threw up a 'mass of statuary and masonry' celebrating the new empire's might.[87] The long-mooted monument to Arminius (Hermann), the barbarian hero who had resisted the Romans, was now completed, and the Francophobes who paid for it were well satisfied with the provocative anti-French inscription round its base: 'French arrogance,' it declared, had been chastised by 'all the German races who rallied round the sword raised by the Prussians'.[88] A year later, another massive statue, *Germania*, was erected, gazing westwards into France across the Rhine. France responded with her own monuments of defiance, especially in the border zones where she had been defeated. It was in this climate that Bartholdi made his reputation with statues of Vercingetorix, leader of the Gauls, and to the French Navy and the Artillery. His best-known work, *The Lion of Belfort*, was built into the cliffs below the fortress as a tribute to its heroic defenders, and won him the Legion of Honour.

After his success with the statue of General Rapp, Bartholdi visited Egypt in the company of the Orientalist painters Léon Gérome, Bally and Berchère. There he saw the massive architecture and statuary of Pharaonic Egypt, particularly the Colossi of Memnon. He was receptive, therefore, to later suggestions, possibly on the part of the Empress Eugénie, that Egypt might be a suitable market for his talents. When Ismail Pasha, the modernizing Khedive of Egypt, visited the Universal Exposition in Paris in 1867, Bartholdi put forward the idea of a colossal statue, in the tradition of one of the Seven Wonders of the ancient world, the lighthouse at Alexandria, of an Egyptian woman (a peasant, he later claimed), symbolizing 'Egypt carrying the Light to Asia'. Another proposal was for a colossal statue of Ismail himself, seated on a lion, for a mausoleum at the new city of Ismailia. But just as Verdi's *Aida* was written too late for the festivities at the opening of the (French-designed) Suez Canal (which Bartholdi attended), the statue of the woman never got built.

Bartholdi was not just a fierce patriot; he was also a radical and a Freemason. His patriotism, moreover, included a view of France's civilizing mission which transcended any narrow European focus. After the crushing of the Paris Commune in 1871, radicalism of the kind he espoused was highly politically incorrect. The liberal political circles he moved in brought him to the attention of Edouard-René Lefebvre Laboulaye, the chairman of the French Anti-Slavery Society and Professor of Comparative Jurisprudence at the Collège de France, who, after the death of De Tocqueville, was also the leading French specialist on the constitutional history of the USA. His *History of the United States* depicted Washington, not Napoleon, as the great revolutionary who 'reconciled the world with Liberty'. Despite recent French intervention in Mexico and growing French imperialism in subsequent decades, Laboulaye was concerned to defend republicanism against a possible restoration of the monarchy. He organized the striking of a medal in honour of Lincoln, after his assassination, which would commemorate the historic links between the French and the American revolutions. Twenty-six eminent republicans, including Michelet, Louis Blanc and Victor Hugo, signed the covering letter. But such was the repressive climate of the time that the medal had to be struck in Switzerland and smuggled into France. The project failed, and Louis Napoleon's agents confiscated the funds that had been raised.

The further idea of putting up a radical statue in France was now out of the question. Yet despite these political setbacks, Bartholdi was still determined to win a symbolic victory by erecting 'a colossus', as Trachtenberg remarks, 'in *some* form'. In 1870, Bartholdi had been sent to Bordeaux in order to get arms from America, whose large pro-German population had demonstrated in favour of Germany during the Franco-Prussian War. The very ship's officers, he found, were pro-German. He now conceived of the idea of recycling his Egyptian project by relocating his statue in Manhattan and changing its symbolism to one of Franco-American brotherhood. Progress was made in this direction when the French president, Thiers, gave support to commissioning a statue of Lafayette, to express thanks for American aid to Paris during the siege of 1870–71. Ordinary French citizens in their hundreds of thousands contributed 600,000 francs towards this statue, which was duly erected during the centennial in 1876 and is still there in Union Square, Manhattan. With this stimulus, the much bigger Laboulaye–Bartholdi project was now revived.

While blood was still flowing in the streets of Paris, Bartholdi, backed by a French committee, set off for the United States to explore a new project: the possibility of erecting a monument, to be donated by the citizens of France to the United States, to commemorate the approaching centennial. Matching American funds would be needed; Bartholdi spent five months there and made three more fund-raising visits.

The Statue of Liberty project, then, was very much a French initiative and grew out of French internal politics. Laboulaye, Bartholdi's main patron, 'a retiring man of non-violent principles', was most anxious to reassure potential backers that Liberty would not be as revolutionary as she was in Delacroix's painting of *Liberty Leading the People to the Barricades*, which the public had only recently been permitted to see. She would not be wearing a red bonnet; she would not walk on corpses; she would carry not a rifle but merely a tablet engraved uncontroversially 'July IV MDC-CLXXVII'; the aggressively waved tricolour would be replaced by a 'beacon which enlightens, not an incendiary torch'; and, as Laboulaye was a bachelor and a pious man, Liberty would not be bare-breasted, like Delacroix's figure, but decently clad from neck to toe.

Delacroix's painting is a great work of art; the statue, in Trachtenberg's words, combines 'extravagant ambition' with 'mediocre talent'. Its stern features are those of Bartholdi's mother, a Protestant bigot living in a Catholic community whose prejudice prevented his brother from marrying a Jewess and led to his own mental breakdown, for she kept him from marrying until he was forty-two. When the statue finally arrived in the United States, it was not greeted with enthusiasm. Support for it in France had been considerable – Gounod even composed a 'Liberty Cantata' to help raise funds. But it proved difficult to persuade Congress to accept the statue officially and to provide a site for it. Funds were grudgingly made available for the unveiling ceremony, but in 1883, when the base was half completed, a bill to provide $100,000 failed to pass the session. Finally, when the New York State legislature provided a miserable $50,000, Governor Cleveland vetoed the proposal. San Francisco, Boston and Chicago offered money for the footstool, but for the most part people outside New York thought that the New Yorkers should pay for their lighthouse.[89]

Some objections were cultural rather than financial. The Catholic press objected to the 'pagan goddess' of libertarian values. Rich and cultured New Yorkers thought the whole thing a joke: let it go to Painted Post, NY, or Glover, Vermont, the New York Times suggested, since they were willing to have it. Others suggested parking it on top of the uncompleted Washington Monument, and when the first visible part of the statue – her arm – was exhibited in Philadelphia, the sanity of its creator was questioned; one humorist suggested immersing the statue upside-down in the Central Park Reservoir, 'as if drowned'. When looked at from the Battery, another critic said, the finished statue resembled 'a bag of potatoes with a stick projecting from it'. History repeated itself in the 1990s when a gigantic statue of Columbus was hawked around the United States. Now an archetypal symbol of colonialism and of the extinction of Indian cultures, nobody wanted it.

Though the statue's arrival was imminent, and the tower on which it was to stand was being designed by Eiffel, work on the pedestal actually stopped for lack of funds. But two years later, Grover Cleveland, now President, suddenly became proud to take part in the unveiling ceremony. His volte-face was due to the power of the new popular press. Joseph Pulitzer, an immigrant had served in the Civil War and had acquired the St Louis Post-Dispatch and the New York World, decided that the statue was 'the ideal cause for working-class readers'. And so it proved. His crusade to emulate the French people, by raising the money to pay for the pedestal in a 'people to people' campaign, had the additional merit of increasing his readership from 15,000 to over 100,000. He could now show his detractors, who labelled his papers 'the yellow press', that he had a social conscience. In classic populist style, the rich, notably Jay Gould and William Vanderbilt, were denounced for their miserly lack of interest, together with the 'crooks and the laggards'. Day after day, editorials urged readers to give – and they did. Their names were printed in Pulitzer's papers, together with thousands of letters. The campaign accomplished what 'years of haggling' had failed to bring about. Only five months later, in banner headlines, Pulitzer was able to announce that $100,000 had been collected from over 120,000 contributors and countless fund-raising events.[90]

The statue continued to court disaster. After nearly capsizing en route, it arrived ten years late for the Centennial, while at the unveiling Bartholdi jumped the gun by pulling the cord too soon. But a million excited people displayed the same enthusiasm that the statue has evoked ever since.

It was not, though, a symbol of immigration or of the Americanization of immigrants. When it was proposed to move the Ellis Island immigration station to Bedloe's Island, where the statue stands, Bartholdi declared that it would be 'monstrous' to associate his beloved statue with immigrants whom Emma Lazarus, in her famous poem, had described as 'wretched refuse'. In the 1880s, American Jewry had been rocked by the news of brutal programs in Tsarist Russia. Lazarus, an established poet who had hitherto led a sheltered life, became deeply involved in helping fugitives and wrote her feelings down in verse to assist the Pedestal Fund. Her poem 'The New Colossus' – written before she had seen the statue (it was still in a shed in Paris), which, when erected, was to gaze out towards France – was to become a symbol of American, not French liberty, and was social in its significance rather than political:

'Keep, ancient lands, your storied pomp', cries she
with silent lips. 'Give me your tired, your poor,
your huddled masses yearning to breathe free,
the wretched refuse of your teeming shore.
Send them, the homeless, tempest-tost, to me,
I lift my lamp above the golden door.'

The impact of her poem at the time, however, was minimal; Lazarus was not even invited to the opening ceremonies, at which neither she nor her poem was mentioned, and Whittier's verses, not hers, were recited. A plaque with her poem on was fixed to a wall inside the pedestal only much later, in 1903, by a private philanthropist.

By the turn of the century, though, millions of poor immigrants had passed the statue as they entered the United States. The historian Oscar Handlin records that he once 'thought to write a history of the immigrants in America. Then I discovered that the immigrants *were* American history.'[91] Those who had come earlier and had been successful were often ready to assist their newer fellow ethnics. But they also wished to keep a certain social distance between themselves and these poverty-stricken newcomers, so they paid for them to move on into the new cities and to farms in the newly opening West. But so great was the flood that many stayed in the cities of the eastern seaboard where they had landed, a process which still continues on a small scale. Jewish refugees from the USSR, for example, have been helped by American Jewish organizations which find them jobs and try to win over these largely areligious people for Judaism. Today, they form a large community at 'Little Odessa', in Brighton Beach, adjoining Coney Island.

In South America, rigid Spanish rule had prevented trade between the separate Audiencias. After independence, despite Bolívar's dream of uniting the subcontinent, South America had fallen apart into separate republics. In North America, on the other hand, immigrants were to be the force whose new-found Americanism would weld the area together.

By the turn of the century, Emma Lazarus' verses had become *the* definitive meaning of the statue: Americanization. Like all great symbols, its meaning was infinitely malleable: her crown could be divine or regal, her torch could symbolize any kind of enlightenment. Once mass immigration was closed down in the 1920s, the significance changed once more: now the statue signified not Americanization, which was a *fait accompli*, but *America*. By the time of the Bicentennial, President Reagan, never noted for verbal precision but with the unerring sense of theatre of one trained in Hollywood, made a triumphal spectacle out of the popularity of Liberty against a background of hundreds of small boats, fire hoses and firework displays.

There was only one note of dissent. James Baldwin declared that his ancestors had come to America under conditions which made the sufferings of even the poorest immigrants from Europe look like relative privilege. To blacks, the Statue of Liberty was a 'bitter joke'; it 'meant nothing'.

Unwrapping Christmas

So far we have concentrated on symbols of national identity and on rituals attached to the state. But social and cultural identities have always extended beyond the confines of any state. The great world religions – Buddhism, Islam, Christianity and Hinduism, in particular – have spread across large stretches of the globe. National boundaries have been no impediment either to the worldwide spread of secular ideologies, from liberalism to Marxism.

Though Christianity began in the eastern Mediterranean from the Middle Ages onwards Christendom became coterminous with Europe (Ethiopia, Egypt and Kerala apart). In the modern colonial epoch, Europeans then implanted Christianity outside Europe – notably in the Americas and in Africa – particularly where there were white settlers and state patronage for Christian missions. In the last two centuries, though, a very different value system has come first to conquer the Western world and then to spread to the rest of the globe: materialism.

That change is visible in the transformation of Christmas from what was once a European religious occasion into a de-Christianized secular ritual.

The Romans had celebrated the death and rebirth of the sun, the pre-Christian festival of Dies Natalis Invicti, on 25 December, though only as one of a series of rituals marking the transition from one year to another, the others, especially the rituals at the New Year itself, being equally important. Early Christians who expected the Second Coming of Christ officially disapproved of these popular festivities with their feasting, revels, games, parades and gift-giving, as survivals of the pagan Saturnalia. But the festival celebrated today as Christmas had no biblical authority either, so scholastic debate as to whether Christ had been born not in December but in springtime, in March, April or May, went on for centuries. In England, the matter was finally settled in King Alfred's reign: there would be nine days of Christmas, beginning on 16 December. Though there was biblical authority for the stories about the actual birth and particularly the legend of the Magi, of the four Gospels, Mark and John contain no nativity story at all; in a couple of brief sentences in the other two Gospels Matthew alone refers to a visit from 'wise men from the east' who came to the 'house' where He was born (not a stable), bearing presents of gold, frankincense and myrrh; Luke refers to a visit by shepherds to the manger, but not to any animals or presents.[92]

As Christmas gradually gained acceptance as a Christian festival, other pre-Christian symbols were incorporated from different cultures: for instance, the green, living tree, light and birth, and the celebration of these elements in the setting of the family home. These are primordial symbols which Victor Turner calls 'polysemic' because they have many meanings and can always be invested with new ones.

New elements were now incorporated from many different European cultures, particularly from Scandinavia and Central Europe – reindeer and Yule logs from Scandinavia, Dutch Christmas stockings and German Catholic nativity cribs – while Prince Albert popularized the Christmas tree in England. Other equally ancient elements, though, have been forgotten: while mistletoe is still with us, ivy is not; the horse Santa Claus rode has been replaced by a sledge drawn by reindeer and his 'often sinister' assistant has disappeared altogether. Belsnickel and Christkindel, 'Old World relatives of Santa Claus', as Restad calls them,[93] have virtually dropped out, while the various names by which Santa had been known in Britain, France, Holland, Denmark and Romania – St Aclaus, St Iclaus, Sancte Klaas, St Claas, Santeclaw, St a claus – have become standardized as 'Santa Claus'. One of these versions of Santa, Kris (or Kriss) Kringle, survives only in the Hollywood movie *Miracle on 34th Street*, in which, significantly, he lands in a Bellevue mental ward for claiming to *be* Santa Claus.

Other elements have been given a new content. St Nicholas, whose identity has become fused with that of Santa, was once a miracle-working bishop in what is now Turkey who tossed bags of gold through the windows of poor girls to serve as their dowries, but is now identified with pillows and stockings full of good things.[94] As befitted a saint, he began life as a bachelor and married only late in the nineteenth century. His dress varied from Flemish trunk-hose to fawn-coloured trousers with a blue stripe; sometimes he appeared in high boots, with a short coat and stocking cap; on other ocasions he wore fur, and even lederhosen. It was not until 1862, when Thomas Nast began producing his famous drawings in *Harper's Weekly*, that Santa Claus ceased to be an elf and become the 'traditional' Santa.

Christmas had not always even been the major Christian ritual. It had faced competition from other Christian rituals, above all Easter, a rite of renewal which – as Sir James Frazer reminded the Victorians – predates Christianity. In the Middle Ages, it also faced competition from survivals of the Saturnalia, notably in the form of the medieval Feast of Fools, in which a Lord of Misrule, immortalized in the person of Victor Hugo's (and now Disney's) Quasimodo, was elected, and from festivals such as Bartholomew Fair and Twelfth Night, as well as a variety of riotous festivities in which the everyday order of society was not just suspended but inverted in orgies, cross-dressing, drinking and eating to excess, the mocking of the high and mighty, a good deal of violence and black imagery (Saturn actually *ate* children). Sometimes even open revolt against oppression could be tolerated – though 'for the duration' only. More normally, rituals of inversion went no further than the custom in the British Army by which officers brought the other ranks tea in bed on Christmas Day. On the plantations, even slaves and masters might fraternize at Christmastime. At the festival which opens the Christmas season, Mexicans and their families feast with the dead; American children are allowed to harass their elders by demanding 'trick or treat'. And at office parties the world over, sexual constraints and other things are loosened.

Today, the Saturnalia survives, most famously in the Brazilian and Trinidadian carnivals. So Trinidadians, Miller remarks, have the good fortune to celebrate both Christmas *and* Carnival, with the result that 'the rest of the year could almost be viewed as the necessary rest ... before the country gears itself up for the next festive season'.[95]

Elsewhere, only a few of these subversive elements survive, in very attenuated form, such as the pantomime in England, for they have always been disapproved of by the pious – in the past, as pagan survivals; today, because they represent materialism. In England under Cromwell's Commonwealth, the Puritans 'strongly prohibited' Christmas (and, indeed, *all* saints' days) and declared Christmas Day a day of penance, not feasting. From 1644 to 1652, Parliament deliberately met on Christmas Day.[96] As late as 1951, Lévi-Strauss records, Father Christmas was hanged from the railings of Dijon Cathedral, then burned, in protest against the 'paganization' of Christmas,[97] while a recent US Supreme Court ruling banned nativity scenes in public because they violated the constitutional separation of church and state.

In recent times, the greatest inputs into the mythology of Christmas have come from the two countries whose cultures spread successively along with their political and economic global imperialism: Great Britain in the nineteenth and the United States in the twentieth centuries. From the former came Charles Dickens' enormously popular sentimentalization of Christmas; from the latter, its commercialization.

Though Christmas had been designated a public holiday in Britain a decade before Dickens wrote *A Christmas Carol*, in 1843, the lion's share of the credit (or blame) must go to him. It is still running in London's West End as I write.

When Christmas was exported to the British colonies, it took on very different forms in accordance with the local culture. In New York, where eighteen different languages were spoken at the beginning of the nineteenth century and where there was 'a crazy quilt of timing',[98] there was no single calendar, let alone a shared calendar of festivals. Though a time of respite for some, it was by no means a major festivity for all ethnic communities and religious sects. As in England, Dissenters ignored it.

After the Restoration in England, Charles II had restored Christmas and demanded that Massachusetts repeal its ban on Christmas. Because of Puritan resistance, they took sixteen years to do it. But in the South, as Restad remarks, 'a world of its own', stamped by English culture, 'frolicking', even what she calls 'free-form mayhem', once more prevailed. 'The festive saturnalia stood at the heart of many southern Christmases', with balls, fox-hunting, organized shooting and invasions of the mansions by 'mummers' who were given food and drink (North Carolina's black mummers, called 'John Kooners', disguised themselves as animals, and 'danced, paraded, and begged for money and food'). Though some hard-hearted planters refused it, slaves were usually given 'free time' – sometimes as much as a week. In New Orleans, in addition to the common gentlemen's amusements of billiards and gambling, 'pitching dollars in the streets, and getting drunk' were popular activities at this season.[99]

After the Revolution, when all official British holidays had been revoked, America was left without a festive calendar. There were no national holidays, and the holidays people did have were occasions for letting off firecrackers and drinking alcohol. Christmas Day was the same as any other day and not even Independence Day filled the gap. Different immigrant communities now began to celebrate 'Saints' societies' – those from Britain opting for St George; those of Dutch background choosing 'St Nick' – but these were not celebrated outside those particular communities. Patriots in Philadelphia even chose 'St Tammany', named after a seventeenth-century Delaware chief. What Restad calls 'cities of strangers' yearned for a wider common identity. By now, even Puritans in Boston were no longer opposed to Christmas; what they objected to was the way in which it was celebrated – with 'excess and profane jollity'. What they wanted was a non-denominational Protestant way of celebrating the birth of Christ, focused in the home.

Writers now responded to the new mood. As early as 1809, Washington Irving, in his History of New York, had depicted St Nicholas as the patron saint of the city – a theme taken up and elaborated by his Salmagundi circle of friends. In 1822, one of his acquaintances, Clement Clarke Moore, wrote the verses generally known by the first line, ''Twas the Night Before Christmas' (which is hardly known in England), in which he gave St Nick – 'a right jolly old elf' – his octet of reindeer. In the mid-1850s, Louisa May Alcott equipped him with an entourage of elves.

But the Civil War set back all such thoughts of a season of jollity. Thomas Nast enlisted Santa Claus (as well as Christ) on the Union side in the pages of Harper's. Wearing striped pants and a starred jacket, he visited Union camps and distributed toys and boxes to the soldiers. In December 1864, he accompanied a soldier home on furlough.

But it was not until after the War, when there was a special need for symbols of national unity, that Christmas really took off. Thanksgiving was too closely associated with New England. So new, more national rituals were needed. In Nast's drawings of Santa Claus, he was no longer an elf, but what was to become, from then on, the 'traditional' Santa – a jolly, fat man dressed in a furry red and white coat.

Women played a major part in creating new rituals, bringing religion into family life and rewarding children for good behaviour by giving them presents. Later, even this moral element was removed, as children got more and more gifts, whatever their behaviour had been like during the year. As Christmas flourished, Thanksgiving faded.

One woman in particular dedicated herself to a crusade to turn Christmas into this kind of occasion – Sarah Josepha Hall, who, as editor of *Godey's*, campaigned to have Christmas designated an official holiday, Lousiana being the first state to do so in 1837. *Harper's* joined the new crusade for Christmas.

The nationwide celebration of Christmas now took off. But it was no longer only Old Americans who celebrated it, for by the 1880s the ancestors of most of today's existing population were arriving in what was, for them, a quite New World. Celebrating Christmas became 'a mark of acculturation for nineteenth century and twentieth century European immigrants'.[100]

All kinds of new accretions, such as carols now widely believed to be 'traditional', therefore date only from the mid-nineteenth century: for example, 'We Three Kings of Orient Are' (1857); 'Jingle Bells' (1863); 'O Little Town of Bethlehem' (1868); and 'Away in a Manger' (1885). By 1882, New York's Washington Square bristled with trees; 200,000 were supplied to the city's markets. By 1900, one American in five was estimated to have a Christmas tree.[101] Trees were now elaborately decorated, at first with candles and then – the danger of fire was overcome in a typically American way – by the new technology of electric lights.

Preparations became ever more elaborate – and costly: Christmas stockings for the children, baubles on the tree, presents at its foot. In orgies of conspicuous consumption, front rooms were transformed into 'bowers', with the 'window blinds raised and brightly lighted', thus allowing 'passers-by a full view; friends visited to see them, and people even knocked at the door asking to be admitted to have a closer look'.[102] In the 1960s, this kind of ostentatious display extended to the front lawn – in Saskatoon, Saskatchewan, I saw elaborately decorated and lighted Christmas trees and sleighs drawn by reindeer in front of the larger houses.

Business quickly responded to the market potential of the new vogue of Christmas. The 1,500 gross of tree ornaments which F. W. Woolworth ordered from Germany in 1890 sold out in no time. In 1874, the Boston firm of Louis Prang (of German origin) added Christmas cards to their already large card business, and in the following year introduced them in the United States. Toy stores started special Christmas seasons and the large department stores joined in. In the early 1880s, the large New York department stores had started to dress their windows magnificently. By 1874, Macy's had launched Christmas sales and by 1889 was delivering 162,624 gifts to people's homes. Though a Detroit store got there first,

Macy's efforts to depict itself as the 'store with a heart' and attempts to link Thanksgiving with Christmas reached their peak in 1924 with the launching of the Thanksgiving Day Parade on the third Thursday in November, which still opens the Christmas season. This is a quintessentially American festival, since Thanksgiving Day, of course, is not part of Christmas anywhere else. As Christmas spread, elements from even more cultures became attached. Denmark, for instance, has to maintain a special postal service to handle the flood of letters from all over the world addressed to Santa Claus in Greenland.

However, the materialism of modern Christmas brought some adverse reactions, proponents of the 'Social Gospel' reminding Americans that Christmas was a time for Christian generosity towards worthy 'paupers'.

But Christmas, above all, is an occasion on which people come together in a communion of a shared meal and interpersonal gift exchange. Before the modern commercialization of Christmas, handmade gifts had been especially valued, as evidence of thrift and painstaking work, and simple pleasures like the bran tub predominated. 'The ideal gift,' Restad observes, 'combined an appreciation for the material, objective worth of an object with an appreciation of values loftier than the money which purchased it.'[103]

Today, the ideal gift has to be both expensive and non-utilitarian – not an everyday item. It also involves a sophisticated calculus which calls for the selection of a present which will both be appropriate to the recipient and also reflect something about the character of the donor and the relationship between them.[104] Christmas has therefore become an occasion for much hard work: shopping – 'no laughing matter', as Löffgren remarks, since it involves a tremendous amount of expense and the staging of what he calls the 'cultural organization of anticipation'.[105] The big stores, Daniel Boorstin wryly observed as long ago as 1962, were sending out their Christmas picture-book gift items as early as 4 July. Advent calendars for children have little windows that they open every day, sometimes with a sweet behind them, and long before Christmas Eve cards must be sent to relatives (even those one may not have seen for twenty years), to neighbours and to colleagues at work. Reciprocal visiting is also usually part of Christmastime.

Summer holidays, Searle-Chatterjee observes, may involve 'equally extravagant and commercialized expenditure', but they do not constitute a '*sacred*' period.[106] Though Christmas cards and presents are purchased in shops, they are not just commodities since they are charged with emotions, so before being distributed they have to be ritually displayed at the foot of the tree for all to see (and make judgements upon), elaborately wrapped in paper and ribbons, with special cards, and, when opened, they are expected to be greeted with expressions of surprise and delight. The room in which the exchanges take place is magically transformed by elaborate decorations, especially the tree itself, which has its own special kind of decorations and lights. In Trinidad, for example, the house is made 'immaculate' and ideally should have new furniture, with the hanging of new curtains as the final act.[107] Hard labour on the part of the womenfolk – the 'magic-wand effect' – ensures that by Christmas Eve everything is ready for the elaborate Christmas dinner; as Kuper remarks, 'probably the only annual occasion when virtually everyone in England is doing the same thing at the same time'.[108]

The social framework within which all this takes place is the family – which means the coming together of a conjugal pair with grandparents and other members of the extended family. But Christmas is not really Christmas without children: the essence of Christmas is the *child-centred* family. The tradition that children 'come home' for Christmas, though, becomes problematic with the passage of time, for sons and daughters produce their own families, and their parents become grandparents and are now expected to spend Christmas at the home of the new children, so decisions now have to be made about which of several sons' or daughters' houses will host Christmas.[109]

The commercialization of Christmas has involved standardization of the symbols used. But once Christmas spread to countries outside Europe where holly and plum pudding were difficult to come by, other elements replaced them. The Iñupiaq Eskimo Christmas dinner includes whale and caribou meat and frozen fish; in Trinidad, the season opens at the time of the Hindu festival of Divali. This combination of old and new elements can be seen in Sweden, where girls wear 'Lucia' headdresses with candles in them, and, since the 1960s, the hour of Walt Disney cartoons shown on TV has become *the* most popular show of the entire year.

In the nineteenth century, the dominant ideology of capitalism was the 'Protestant ethic' of work and production. Today, it is an ethic of consumption, nowhere more highly developed than in the richest country on earth, Japan. Traditionally there too the end of the year had been the Taoist season for giving gifts, and was equally significant in Buddhist and Shinto ritual. But the modern Japanese Christmas takes its cue from Macy's. Early in the season, department stores tell their customers to get their orders in early as 'Santa Claus is very busy'.[110] Commercialism also runs riot on Mother's Day, Father's Day, Boy's Day, Girl's Day, Old Peoples' Day, Valentine's Day (reinterpreted as a day women give presents to men), followed, a month later, by White Day (missing in the West), when men give presents to women.

Christmas in Japan has been transformed not so much because it has absorbed older Japanese elements but because it lacks any connection with the birth of Christ and takes place outside the family. It has become part, instead, of Japanese youth culture, with a strong emphasis on young women. As part of the Japanese dating complex, young men woo their girlfriends by booking hotels well ahead – in the summer – to which they hope to take them for Christmas (even, in some cases, before they even *have* girlfriends). Christmas, the big stores have decided, comes from Austria, so that is where you should take your girlfriend for a romantic holiday, complete with 'Mozart balls'. For the rich in a society in which intellectuals listen to Western classical music, the more materialistic take their lead from Fifth Avenue: the ideal gift is Tiffany jewellery, or Lancôme, Givenchy or Elizabeth Arden perfumes. Department stores therefore ransack the globe in their search for new elements for the Christmas meal: the 'delicat[essen] tree, macaroni dishes, an Indian dish "with an ecological touch", French bread with Brie, margaritas, and "Mediterranean fritters"'.[111]

This is, of course, upper-class consumption. Poor people everywhere have to scale down expectations of lavish expenditure, and often denigrate Christmas as a commercial racket. Even in Sweden, a country where the 'discourse of class is rather muted', there is nevertheless dissonance over whether the occasion should be modelled on the kind of Christmas peasants once enjoyed or on Christmas in the manor house.[112]

The World According to Disney

Images of the world outside the society people live in are a crucial part of their system of ideas. Increasingly, because of successive revolutions in modern communications systems, people are likely to draw them from mass media rather than older institutions such as schools and churches.

Images about society are not conveyed solely via print or via visual media such as TV, film and video. For instance, people who go to Las Vegas in their millions every year, go there in part because they have experienced a vast increase in disposable income over the last two decades and in part because they have been persuaded that they might win even more, and that if they don't they can at least live like millionaires for two weeks a year. They are mainly very ordinary folk indeed: from the Midwest, Silicon Valley or the Boeing plants of Washington State. They get a cheap holiday, in first-class accommodation, subsidized breakfast, with floor shows thrown in. Most people gamble with quarters on the 'slots', not with folding money at blackjack. But you still have to go there, and not everyone can. The world which Walt Disney created, on the other hand, was available anywhere where there was a cinema, and the ideas which it communicates about the world have been infinitely more influential than those of intellectuals who win Nobel Prizes. Yet remarkably little attention is given to examining the content of an empire which began with animated cartoons, expanded into films, then into other multi-media enterprise and finally into theme parks, now on three continents.

Though Disney came from small-town Middle America— Marceline, Missouri— the values he was exposed to were ambiguous, for he was the 'son of a disappointed utopian' who drifted between factory jobs and small business ventures that always failed'.[113] Originally a carpenter, his father also had a burning passion for socialism and read a radical weekly called *The Appeal to Reason*, from which young Walt took his models for drawing a fat capitalist and an honest working man.[114] Later, Disney senior tried his hand at farming (which introduced the young Walt to animals), and ended up buying a small local newspaper. His failures, frustrations and ambivalences were taken out on Walt, whom he beat savagely. It was an upbringing that inculcated in the young Walt a Midwestern ethic of hard work, of contempt for high falutin' intellectuals and Easterners, and a yearning for independence from banks unwilling to risk money financing small enterprises like his father's newspaper.

The classic American folk hero, Walt did poorly at school, picking up a little pin-money as a newspaper delivery boy. Later, he served for a year in the Red Cross Ambulance Corps, and was sent to France in 1919.

He then decided to move into another kind of medium from that of his father – animated films. His brother Roy shared his interests, including keeping a file on gags used in burlesque shows. Though his father thought that this new-found interest in drawing was frivolous (and Walt had to survive by working in a jelly factory), his father did eventually pay for him to do a correspondence course in art. When he arrived in Hollywood in 1923 with, legend has it, only $40.15 in his pocket, he survived by making a film on dental hygiene for $500, which enabled him to pay the $1.50 his cobbler was demanding for repairing his shoes.

He then teamed up with Ubbie Iwerks, another pioneer of filmed cartoons. Iwerks' contribution, and that of other animators before him, has been much underestimated – in part because of sustained myth-building by the Disney Corporation, which attributed everything to the genius of Walt. In fact, Walt made very shrewd use of techniques developed by other pioneers of 'continuity cartoons', notably cel animation. Looking at Iwerks' cartoons today, one sees many features – the animals' movements, the jazzy music, the storylines – that we now think of as 'typically Disney'. Both

Disney and Iwerks had successes and failures, including the early 'Laugh-o-Grams' and an *Alice in Wonderland* which initially failed. The relationship between them was off and on for many years, and only became finalized as late as 1940, by which time Iwerks, no great businessman, had given up the attempt to run his own companies and rejoined Disney once more.

Disney had both artistic talent – as a creator of clear narrative stories – and acting ability – he did Mickey's voice until 1946. Although it was Iwerks who drew Mickey, for which he was credited on the early films, it was Disney who received a special Oscar nomination in 1932 for creating him. Bryman's carefully documented and theoretically sophisticated study also highlights his organizational talents and his ability to 'get the best out of people'.[115]

Initially, however, he had little more success than Iwerks in finding backers, for one simple reason – animated cartoons were very expensive to make. And once he did achieve success – with 'Oswald the Lucky Rabbit' – takeover sharks began circling. He lost not only Oswald but very nearly his company too. So he made sure that the next successful animal, Mickey (originally 'Mortimer') Mouse remained in his hands. The breakthrough came with the sensational success of his third Mickey film, *Steamboat Willie* (with sound), in 1928. But Disney then had to fight off a takeover bid by Cinephone, while his subsequent realization that Columbia were making large amounts of money distributing his films and merchandising the cartoon characters made him, ever afterwards, determined to keep all aspects of the business, not just production, under his control as far as possible. To keep control of distribution, he eventually formed a new company Buena Vista.

Disney saw Mickey as a classic American 'little guy', who was also a 'clean' mouse – sentiments which he also projected on to the other cartoon animals, which he drew in bold colours. Sex, Disney declared, 'is of no great interest to Mickey. He is youth, the great unlicked and uncontaminated'. Disney strove to distance himself, he said, from 'ugliness and cynicism' and never paid money for studies in 'abnormality' – he didn't like 'dirty' pictures and didn't have 'depressed moods'. His 'nightmare' was that 'one of his pictures might end up in an art theater'.

His animals have universal appeal. Even cultures which know nothing of pigs or cows know about animals in general. In any case, they came to know *his* animals; they had human characteristics. Mickey was everything by turns, Mr. Everyman:

gaucho, teamster, explorer, swimmer, cowboy, fireman, convict, pioneer, tax driver, castaway, fisherman, cyclist, Arab, football player, inventor, jockey, storekeeper, camper, sailor, Gulliver, boxer, exterminator, skater, polo player, circus performer, plumber, chemist, magician, hunter, detective, clock cleaner, Hawaiian, carpenter, driver, trapper, whaler, tailor, and Sorcerer's Apprentice.[116]

The personality attributes of his friends were also recognizable in any culture: Donald Duck was irascible and combative; Goofy, intellectually challenged; Pluto, friendly and loyal; Clara Cluck, vain and culturally pretentious; two of the three little pigs naughty young things who preferred playing to working. This is what attracted me and my schoolmates as we crowded into my front room to see the black-and-white 8.5mm Disney cartoons I projected on my handcranked machine in north-west England in the 1930s. (My childhood dreams were finally realized when I had my photo taken with my arms round Goofy fifty years later.)

The early Mickey cartoon did not begin to pay off until the arrival of sound, which also led to the first non-Mickey cartoons, notably the *Silly Symphonies*. Ironically, though, the cartoon which won him the first award ever given by the Academy of Motion Pictures and Sciences, in 1932, was not one of these entertaining cartoons, but one about flowers and trees.

When he started on his first full-length cartoon, *SnowWhite*, released in 1937, costs escalated so much that the project, though backed by the Bank of America, became known as 'Disney's Folly'. Yet in 1938–40 he took a further bold step by building new studios in Burbank. Though the Disney Corporation has subsequently taken great pains to present the Disney story as a quintessentially American story of uninterrupted success, and to highlight the role of the Founding Father and his cartoons as the base for the take-off, not only *SnowWhite* but also the next full-length cartoons, including *Pinocchio* and *Fantasia*, though attracting large audiences, still left the Corporation with sizeable losses. *Bambi* too was disappointing from an economic point of view.

During these financially difficult years, many of his employees, including the animators, worked for 'little or nothing'; industrial relations were obviously positive enough to enable Disney to carry on. But in 1940–41, low wages and a concomitant struggle for union recognition transformed Disney's hitherto diffuse social conservatism into a more directly political form, culminating in a showdown with the unions in which employees were threatened with an ultimatum – they would have to sign what the Screen Cartoonists' Guild described as a 'document of surrender'.[117] Though half the employees remained loyal and the settlement favoured the union, one leading animator was denounced to the House Un-America Activities Committee, only getting his job back after war service.

The universal appeal of Disney's characters produced one additional source of badly needed capital, including earnings from abroad – the marketing of goods with Mickey, Goofy, Donald and Pluto on them. In countries like Mexico, where people are still often illiterate and can't always easily get to or afford the cinema, they still 'read' Disney cartoons via a visual medium different from and older than the cinema, *historietas* – cartoon-strip books with no words. By the 1970s, Disney comics were being distributed in twenty languages in sixty-seven countries, with a monthly circulation of nearly 19 million. Sales figures were higher in Brazil and West Germany than in the United States, despite their smaller populations. There were eighteen times as many Disney comics circulating in Chile, per capita, as in the United States.[118]

By now, the Disney Corporation was being criticized not just for its industrial relations policies but for the content of the cartoons. Significantly, it was from a Third World country, Chile, that the most devasting critique came, when Dorfman and Mattelart, two sophisticated left-wing analysts of the mass media, pointed out that a lot that was not so admirable was hidden beneath the surface of these stories about lovable animals. They subjected 103 issues of Disney comics to analysis and discerned hidden capitalist 'subtexts'.[119] In three-quarters of the stories, Donald Duck and his friends are engaged in searching for *treasure*. People in remote countries are savages, living in countries called Inca-Blinca, Sphinxland and Unstableland. In this world, pirates in the Caribbean are engaged in a 'competitive individualistic scramble for wealth and power through the use of ingenuity and force'. But there is no exploitation and no class conflict. There are rich people, like Uncle Scrooge, obsessed with accumulating wealth, and those who sit on their money or steal other people's are shown as villains. But they do not exploit other people's labour. In fact, nobody *produces* anything; they only consume. Money, therefore, is not the expression of a relationship between haves and have-nots; it is a 'fetish' object with powers of its own. That some people are mean and others virtuous, some rich and others poor is completely random, a purely individual matter. Politically, revolutionaries, Latin Americans and South-East Asians, for the most part, are lazy and tyrannical villains; businessmen and the 'good old Navy', as Dorfman and Mattelart put it, are the heroes. On the domestic front, characters represented as manual labourers are also often portrayed as criminals; protest is shown as dangerous or absurd.

Disney himself brushed aside this kind of analysis: 'We make the pictures,' he remarked, 'and then let the professors tell us what they mean.' By now, he was widely accused of a range of sins, from having 'persecuted' Iwerks to being anti-Semitic and an FBI 'spy' – an experience which made the Disney Corporation extremely sensitive to criticism.

One manifestation of this was the attempt to prevent the distribution of an English-language translation of the Dorfman and Mattelart book in the United States.[120] There is some irony that this critique should have emanated from South America, for during the Second World War Disney had turned to making films for the government, such as *Victory Through Air Power* and, addressed to South America, *Saludos Amigos*.

After the war came a radical reorientation – two bold steps which fundamentally changed the nature of a corporation hitherto based upon animated cartoons. The first was the shift to making films with live actors, some (like *Make Mine Music*) still combined with animation and others (like *Treasure Island*, *Davy Crockett*, and *20,000 Leagues Under the Sea*) conventional live-actor full-length films, though still with an 'adventure' content and oriented to child audiences. So whereas *Sleeping Beauty* made only a small loss in 1960, *Mary Poppins* (1964) proved the most successful Disney film to date. Cartoon films now were only part of a more diversified movie business.

The second, more daring, innovation was the opening in 1955 of the first theme park, Disneyland, at Anaheim, California, outside Los Angeles, despite opposition from Roy. The relationship between the Disney brothers has often been seen as a division of labour in which Walt was the creative artist and Roy the businessman. This was not so. Roy was opposed not only to a theme park but even to using the Disney name to promote it.

Walt was proved right and Anaheim was a tremendous financial success. Profits had doubled to over $10 million by 1965. But before he could see the realization of his next, even more ambitious dream – a new kind of park, the Experimental Prototype Community of the Future (EPCOT), in California, he died.

There then followed several indecisive 'years of languish' and descent into 'limbo'. EPCOT was also haemorrhaging money. Yet the troika who took over (which included Roy) were paralysed, constantly asking themselves, 'What would Walt have done?' By the time Roy died, in 1971, and was replaced by *his* son, Roy E. Disney, the Corporation was riven by internal quarrels and had become embroiled in fighting off takeover raiders who used 'Greenmail' methods. Roy E. himself, despite some success with the (animated) *Beauty and the Beast*, in turn resigned in 1977.

The low point came in the early 1980s. By 1984, losses of $64 million led to the announcement of pay cuts and cutbacks in health benefits which ended in a strike – which Disney won. Animators and younger staff members now began to leave what people were beginning to call 'Mouschwitz', which many found 'more like West Point than a creative community'.[121]

On the marketing front, from 1929 onwards, there had been active promotion of Disney toys, toothbrushes, pyjamas, etc., etc., with special sections in major department stores devoted to Mickey Mouse merchandise, plus 150 Mickey Mouse clubs with 150,000–200,000 members across the United States.[122] By the end of 1932, the income from Mickey merchandise was bringing in a third of the studio's net profits; 3 million Mickey Mouse wristwatches had been sold in two years; and there were a million members of the Mickey Mouse clubs, which

rivalled the Freemasons with their arcane hierarchy of Chief Mickey, Chief Minnie, Master of Ceremonies, Cheerleader, Sergeant-at-Arms, et al., all united under the Mickey creed: 'I will be a squareshooter in my home, in school, in the playgrounds, wherever I may be … In short, I will be a good American.'[123]

In the 1950s, Mickey contributed more than a quarter of a billion dollars to the gross national product. But by the 1980s the Disney Corporation was not even bothering to advertise its theme parks.

Disney was also losing ground on the creative front, because children brought up on television were growing too sophisticated for Disney cartoons. 'The real heirs to Walt Disney were creating *Star Wars* and *Raiders of the Lost Ark*. To teenagers who had paid to see *Star Wars* a dozen times, "Disney was for babies".'[124]

The crisis was finally resolved in 1984 with the arrival of Michael D. Eisner from Paramount where his movies had been 'glossy urban fairy tales', his slogan 'No snow, no rural'. He was dismayed to find, at an 'employee recognition' dinner, that employees were singing twenty-year-old Disney songs.

Eisner immediately began to turn the company around, launching a vigorous policy of 'expanding in all directions at once'. Those who had been dragging their feet were fired. Where Roy had been reluctant to make more than five or six films a year (because he feared 'loss of quality'), not only were new films made, including *Pretty Woman*, but a whole production corporation, Miramar (responsible for such successes as *Sex, Lies and Videotape* and *The Crying Game*), was acquired.

On the merchandising front, the stockpile of fifty years of movies and TV shorts were also converted into a goldmine by recycling them in new ways: video-cassettes; developing a Disney TV channel, as well as cutting the rates charged for Disney films on cable TV; syndication rights; the phased reintroduction of old films; the modernization of the marketing of established Disney characters and the launch of new ones. This new income enabled the Corporation to fight off corporate raiders, then to combine with them in new ventures.

The Corporation had never been backward in protecting its assets (even the Academy of Motion Pictures and Sciences had been sued for daring to dress up a young woman as Snow White). But there was now a new aggression on the part of the teams of Disney lawyers and 'paralegals' who hounded down those they suspected of illegal infringement of copyright and were found to be 'ferocious', 'brutal' and 'relentless adversaries' in negotiations. Editors and publishers ran scared, describing the Corporation as 'ravenous and highly combative', 'notoriously litigious' and even 'paranoid'. One writer was reduced to printing a photo of the sky above one of the theme parks, because he was not allowed to use photos of actual *buildings*.[125] Whereas in the 1930s Disney had been concerned about promoting respectable social values, and in the 1940s had directed his fire against the unions on political grounds, now hard-nosed business interest was dominant.

In the theme parks, though, the Founding Father's puritan Midwestern values still had sway for a long time – visitors as well as employees were scrutinized for deviations from the code. A dozen security officers scanned the 2,000 visitors who entered Disneyland every hour, 'looking for glass-eyed evidence of drugs, liquor smells, or large bags or backpacks', which were prohibited. Hot pants and micro-minis were allowed in 'only if not too much of the buttocks was hanging out'. Brassières were preferred and the obviously braless rejected, as were those bearing any controversial or political messages on patches, buttons or T-shirts, such as references to cannabis or slogans like 'Make Love, Not War'.[126]

The Disney parks have been accused of having a virtual obsession about 'control', not only over employees but over visitors too. Bryman, for instance, lists no fewer than six 'levels' of control. The most elemental is the need to ensure the safety of crowds numbered in tens of thousands, which is achieved partly because they mainly move on foot and partly because they are expertly transported in the 'people-moving' vehicles for which the parks are famous. Timing the visitors' progression through the huge series of 'attractions' calls for a 'script' which is far more complex than that of any feature movie. So when the Jungle Cruise was found to be 'too fast', it was retimed from 4½ to 7½ minutes.

The accusation of control over the visitors' imagination, though, is a more serious one. Any attempt at presenting the variety of the world involves a cognitive framework, and a framework of values too. To say this is not to justify the particular frameworks selected – and imposed. Deviations from the scripts are kept under tight control. Though 'guests' are sometimes encouraged to collude in the play-acting – for example, by responding to the guides' patter – the basic purpose of the scripts is to exclude spontaneity. The preservation of fantasy is ensured by strict policing. As one Disney spokesman reminded an employee: 'You are employed to work in one [theme park] land. When you are a cowboy working in Frontierland, you cannot walk through Fantasyland on your way to lunch.'[127]

What critics object to is the fact that just as waste is disposed of underground in the theme parks,[128] all social unpleasantness is also eliminated. Those who play Davy Crockett or Goofy emerge from under the ground too, to put on a new persona as Pluto or Mickey, and to utter scripted banalities: 'Have a nice day', 'Have a nice evening.' Only rarely does the mask slip. 'Please, please, one at a time,' one Snow White pleaded with the kids who were besieging her; 'Oh dear, oh dear, oh shi – ' 'Assholes,' she mouthed, but, well trained, her smile never slipped.[129]

As society changed, much of the old Midwestern puritanism had to go. As one Disney pamphlet put it, 'We couldn't ignore certain major issues that questioned our nation's stand on human liberty and justice.' One sponsor, Coca-Cola, went further: 'The warts-and-all perspective is appreciated by most visitors because our country is not perfect and they know it.'[130] By the 1980s, security guards 'looked the other way' in parks where the banning of single-sex dancing had once ended in a court suit. An Australian who is every bit as hostile to acquisitive values as Dorfman and Mattelart, John Pilger acknowledges that a 'Disney Person' today, is 'relatively well paid and with privileges otherwise regarded as the thin edge of socialism in America: medical care for you and your family'.[131]

Today, then radicals are more likely to object to the manipulation of Disney employees – because they are called 'host(esse)s', in the Disneyspeak language drawn from the cinema, and are said to wear 'costumes', not uniforms, rather than to their working conditions or wage levels – and to the parallel manipulation of customers, who are relabelled 'guests'.

By the 1990s, the Corporation's controls over the behaviour of their employees, like the 'Factor Ten Problem' – undesirable facial hair or hair over the collar – or, more seriously, the unctuous patriotism surrounding the audio-animatronic figures in the Hall of the Presidents, still irked radicals like Pilger. Pilger's overall assessment, though in an article entitled 'The Magic of Disney', is that the end product is 'brilliant child's play': 'America's two enduring gifts to modern civilized life are its music, based on black culture, and Walt Disney'. The cartoons he remembered from his childhood, 'both funny and wry to the point of irony', had been successful not because they subliminally glorified capitalism but because they didn't patronize kids. Where Dorfman and Mattelart had found repugnant values lurking in 'subtexts', Pilger responded to what was on the surface – the charm and amusement of Disney's animal characters.

Anaheim was naturally built, at first, around the cartoon animals. Yet Disney also had the idea of a 'small playground' across the road from the studios. What shape it would take was not clear. All that he did know was what he did *not* want: a jumble of attractions like the usual funfair – Ferris wheel, roller-coaster, hot-dog stands, etc. He wanted a *park*, with unifying *themes*.

The major emphasis which eventually emerged was upon America. But he was also interested in presenting 'attractions' from other countries. In the end, the 'small playground' was eventually to become a microcosm of the *world* in all its cultural variety.

You still enter, though, by walking into Main Street, USA, or at least, a prettified version of a Midwestern small town at the turn of the century (scaled down to seven-eighths scale at ground level and five-eighths at the first floor), with its railroad station, its bank, City Hall, fire station (Walt Disney's favourite spot, they say, was a small apartment above it, from which he could observe people in the square and in Main Street) and the 'emporium' – the world I learned about as a child from Andy Hardy movies. It is irrelevant, though, for intellectuals to remind us that real small towns at the turn of the century were neither very pretty nor, usually, very prosperous, and that a real-life Main Street at that time was likely to have been an unpaved 'equine latrine' flanked by buildings festooned in telephone and telegraph wires,[132] for visitors to Disneyland do not go there to experience the authenticity of horse-dung and piss. They come to relive, with their children, childhood dreams of adventure and to have *fun*.

The dominant theme, in four of the seven major Anaheim 'attractions', is America past. Bear Country celebrates the frontier pioneers of the Davy Crockett era; New Orleans Square celebrates the Old South; Frontierland, with its amalgam of keel boats, Mark Twain steamboats, Big Thunder Mountain Railroad and the girls of the Golden Horsehoe Revue, celebrates the opening of the West. The other attractions cover the rest of the world. Adventureland takes us to the Enchanted Tiki Room (the South Seas); to the Swiss Family Robinson's Family Treehouse; and on a Jungle Cruise up-river, in a boat steered by white guides dressed like Kenyan settlers, past plastic hippos and crocodiles, and the remains of a wrecked safari, with white men and porters alike taking refuge in trees. The cause soon becomes apparent when the boat itself is attacked by painted blacks armed with spears and shields, who are driven off by our protective white hunters.

Though surveys have shown that the typical visitor is white, middle class and affluent enough to afford a car to get there and the cost of a 'total

holiday', according to one cynic, is '$261 per fun-hour', Chicano and
Mexican visitors to Anaheim, and Cubans and Latin Americans at Orlando, nevertheless seem equally amused by a view of Africa they share
with the white American middle class. If Africa is savagery, Europe is history – a Ludwig II Bavarian fantasy: Sleeping Beauty Castle, cobwebs,
witches and all.

What to say about the cultures of other parts of the world had been a
problem for the organizers of the nineteenth-century Great Exhibition at
Crystal Palace in London in 1851, or of the Paris Exposition of 1889, for
England and France were imperialist powers, whose relationship to many
of the countries represented one of political domination. Many, indeed,
were colonies.

One solution, in tune with the celebration of the Victorians' own new
technology, was to concentrate on *products*. Another was to leave the presentation of the cultures of foreign countries to them. So artists like De-
bussy and Ravel were exposed not just to colonial products such as coffee
and rubber but also to Javanese gamelan music.

Disney imagineers had to solve the similar problem of presenting im-
ages of the cultures of the world, past and present. Many of the classic
Anaheim themes were repeated in Orlando – Main Street, for instance.
But Main Street in Florida is bigger, brighter and more ornate than at Anaheim. By the 1980s though, technology and the future were to be the new
dominant themes, rather than nostalgia for the Frontier or for an Old
World Europe or colonial Africa. With the development of EPCOT, the
Disney imagineers had to boldly go into space and into the future. They re-
sponded by writing a new kind of cosmic script.

The site gave them ample latitude for such grandiose ventures. Built on
27,258 acres of Florida swampland, a hundred times the size of Anaheim,
as large as metropolitan San Francisco and twice the size of Manhattan,[133]
it became the world's biggest construction site. In hard economic terms,
to use Roy Disney's words, it was a 'real estate venture for us' from the beginning. Through bond issues, its financing was also largely debt-free,
while a 'no-strike, no-lockout' clause won it the co-operation of the
labour unions.

The new park was also largely independent of local government and
state controls. Disney had experienced a bitter fight to prevent a Sheraton
hotel being built on the edge of the Anaheim site. He was determined,
therefore, to prevent other unsightly developments on the perimeter,
from wiring to motels and car-parks, via 'periphery control'. The solution
was the establishment of the 'Reedy Creek Improvement District', which
the Corporation controlled (on the grounds that people would be *living* at

EPCOT – which they never did). An integrated single district with its own governing body, it was free from interference from county authorities and was therefore able to establish its own building, water and zoning codes. 'Kingdom', then, was no mere metaphor.

Local radio stations were persuaded that the building of the new park was 'news'; the massive publicity they gave Orlando did not, therefore, have to be paid for as 'advertising'. Passengers on Eastern Airlines, by this time an ally of Disney, were targeted as likely visitors to the new park, while potential winners of American beauty contests were contacted in advance so that they could give the correct answer to the question, 'Now that you've been crowned Miss America, what are you going to do next?' The correct answer was, 'I want to visit the Magic Kingdom.'

Disney had intended EPCOT to be home to about 20,000 people:

a ... controlled community, [with] no landowners and therefore no voting control. No slum areas because we will not let them develop. People will rent houses instead of buying them, and at modest rentals. There will be no retirees. Everyone must be employed.[134]

It was a very different vision of a planned Utopia from that which inspired wealthy nineteenth-century owners of giant companies in England, from Lord Leverhulm in Port Sunlight to the Quaker company towns built for the workers at the factories of the Cadbury family at Bournville and the Rowntrees at New Earswick. These looked back to an idealized Middle Ages. Anaheim, again, had been predominantly nostalgic. But EPCOT was to be more *American*, more akin to Edward Bellamy's *Looking Backward* which, despite its title, was forwards-looking – than to English nostalgia for the Middle Ages or Disney's own nostalgia for the Frontier and for small-town America.

The original Disneyland, though, had also taken account of not only the twentieth century but also the future – in Fantasy Land, the Seven Dwarves, Dumbo, King Arthur and the Mad Hatter's Tea Party are to be found side by side with Autopia and Skyway to Tomorrow, while the ten attractions of Tomorrow Land take us from the primeval world of dinosaurs beloved of children into the inner world of the atom, through 'liquid space', via a submarine under the North Pole, and into outer space, on a mission to Mars.

The new park was a success from the start. In its first year, 1971, nearly 11 million guests poured in; four years later, 40 million had passed through the gates. By 1981, over 126 million had visited Orlando, including 10 per cent of foreign visitors to the United States, at a time when

Gettysburg was attracting only 5.2 million people and Yellowstone 2.4 million. So although Disney films still topped the box office in 1988, by that time the Disney Corporation was no longer mainly a film business and nearly 90 per cent of their earnings came from the theme parks.

Many of the themes in the new park – Adventure Land, the celebration of the Frontier, the Magic Castle and the Jungle Ride – were familiar to those who had visited Disneyland in California. But the major authority on Orlando, the anthropologist Stephen Fjellman, calls the notion that Orlando is simply Anaheim writ large 'benighted'.[135] In detail which even he describes as sometimes 'numbing', he takes us through the entirety of the Florida parks, down to the 800,000 vinyl leaves sewn on the Swiss Family Robinson's Treehouse.

Where cultures like that of the Ndembu express the complexity of human relationships, including social conflict, by reducing it to a few powerful symbols, Disney tackles the problem of coping with the enormous cultural variety in the world with the opposite strategy, using a wide range of symbols which can be added to or replaced as the need arises. They are necessarily selective, and what is left out – what Bryman calls the 'many silences' – are as important as what is included. So, in a world in which wars, famines and revolutions are part of ordinary, every day experience for tens of millions of people, these things are dealt with by a social device much beloved of anthropologists: avoidance.

Disney's approach involves using images familiar in popular culture and long exploited in, for instance, travel ads, which use national stereotypes. So Scotch tape, for example – represented by a plaid iconic symbol – is 'Scotch' because it recalls the 'fact' that Scots are mean – that is, *grasping* (things stick to their hands).

'Cultural' symbols of this kind are used for each country. Japan, for instance, is represented by a tea-house, a castle, a summer palace and a five-storey pagoda. Canada is 'the great outdoors'. Norway is a land of stave churches, Viking longboats, trolls, fjords and explorers – 'timeless versions', in Fjellman's words, 'of culture and place through which we learn to think of other nations as theme parks'. He calls this imagery 'Distory'; others have called it 'Mickey Mouse history', even 'historicide'.

The use of such popular stereotypes, presented in stunning high-tech visual forms, makes it possible to go 'round the world in five minutes ... From an Aztec pyramid one can see the Eiffel Tower'. Countries which are relatively unknown, though, present a problem. In a Circle Vision film made jointly with the People's Republic of China, for instance, there is not mention of communism or of Tienanmen Square. Instead, China is the Great Wall, the Temple of Heaven, the Summer palace and so forth.

Only in those rare cases where no such cultural images are available do the Disney imagineers have to fall back on didactic, even political explanations. Hired 'shills', for instance, tell the passer-by that Morocco is significant to Americans because it is a long-standing ally.

Disney had never trusted anyone else to translate his vision of EPCOT into reality, not even Roy. The story that his body was cryogenically frozen after his death may be as much a myth as the motivation attributed to him – that, by being reincarnated, he might be able to reassume control over his project in person. Not only was he not reborn, but his planned community never got off the ground (though at the time of writing, there are plans to revive it).

Once Disney had passed from the scene, however, the Corporation proved very flexible in removing old elements and introducing new ones. The overall ideological framework, plus the capital and hardware invested, was impossible to alter. But new attractions and themes could be added and older ones discarded. By the 1980s, it was acknowledged to a generation which had concluded during the Vietnam War that, in Fjellman's words, 'its elders had lied to it' – the social order was not perfect, or at least had not been in the past. So Susan B. Anthony, Chief Joseph and Frederick Douglass are recognized. Chief Joseph, indeed, is given lines he never spoke: 'I pray that all of us may be brothers, with one country about us, and one government for all.' By the mid 1990s pressures were being put on the Corporation to give more prominence to blacks and gays, while even fundamentalist Christian groups were criticizing Disney attitudes to sex.

It was easier to make room for other cultural legacies in the Disney movies, from Aladdin to Swahili-speaking animals in The Lion King. If it was inevitable that their voices should be American, it was less so that they should be 'wisecracking buddies and streetwise animal sidekicks, folksy figures out of the American tall tale of Huck Finn'.[136]

The historic exhibitions of the past from Crystal Palace to the New York World Fair of 1939, had not just celebrated the past and present, or the exotic; they had also provided visions of the future. And the future they imagined was one governed by technological progress.

Nowhere has this been more evident than at EPCOT, where not only have the boundaries between business, information, advertising, academia and culture become blurred but culture itself has become very big business indeed. Here the attractions were designed and financed by giant corporations. EXXON staff worked for four years with Disney staff to produce the Universe of Energy in Tomorrow Land. 'Energy, you made the world go round' is the theme song of this show, which runs through 275 years of evolution, including such older sources of energy such as coal and oil, in five minutes and ends with a plug for nuclear energy. General Electric's celebration of electricity, on the other hand, is less future-oriented and centres, more traditionally, on 'electrical empowerment' in the home. 'Now,' we are told, 'is the best time of your life', for 'Liberty is spelled e-l-e-c-t-r-i-c-i-t-y'.

The Disney Corporation, though, is not simply in the business of projecting cultural images. It is in the business of business – its own and that of the multinational corporations and their products. But 'products' are no longer what they were in the nineteenth century – 'gears and girders'. 'Product' has now become the standard way of referring to life insurance policies and investment funds.

The transmission of cultural images and the communication of ideas have always required both organization and finance. Thus we have long called one established media of communication, the production and sale of books, the 'publishing *industry*'. Other institutions such as universities, which train young people to think about ideas, have changed from monastic institutions to campuses where business parks and 'think-tanks' house the latest in science and technology. Today much of modern medical research takes place outside the universities in laboratories run by pharmaceutical corporations; Microsoft's innovations in computer software are carried out on a huge site known, significantly, as the 'campus'. In modern times, a gigantic advertising industry has grown up with deals in images about commodities, many of which are services. We are no longer surprised when $500 million is spent on changing the image of Pepsi Cola – a new, blue can – but the same amount can equally be spent on marketing not a material, consumable commodity, such as a drink, but on a new kind of information technology, Microsoft's Windows 95.

The development of the first Disney theme park outside America – in Tokyo – produced a financial slip-up, for the Corporation took only licensing fees and a share of the revenues. The lesson was quickly learned. When Euro Disney opened in France, the Corporation made sure that it owned 49 per cent of the assets.

At home, the Corporation had always had to face the problem of presenting to Americans on holiday images of a world in which, for tens of millions, misery is normal. To counter these bleak thoughts, the accent has always been put upon the positive, upon the non-conflictful and upon non-controversial cultural, technical and scientific achievements. Large areas of the globe too – Eastern Europe and the countries of the former USSR – are under-represented in the cultural geography of Disneyland, and there are very few references to Africa. This is not due to any lack of ingenuity on the part of the Disney imagineers. Rather, it reflects popular ignorance of or lack of interest in those parts of the world.

The development of new theme parks in Asia and Europe was to bring the Corporation up against the problem of accommodating to foreign cultural values more sharply, for the United States, as the only remaining superpower, is looked at with deep suspicion for aiming to impose not only its political and economic interests on the rest of the world but its culture too.

Though half the attractions in the Tokyo theme park are based on those in America, the establishment of new parks abroad inevitably involved modifying the Americanism of the US parks. There are, therefore, both significant concessions to Japanese culture and history and, as usual, new 'silences'. As with the horse-piss on Main Street, one scarcely expects to be reminded of the rape of Nanking, of Pearl Harbor, or of Hiroshima and Nagasaki. But the omission of the submarine *Nautilus* was a more oblique recognition of the association between submarines and nuclear weapons. Nor will most Japanese visitors (75 per cent of whom have visited the Tokyo park more than once) be aware that the animated history of Japan is a replacement for the Hall of the Presidents in the American parks, or that Japanese restaurants (with older people in mind) have been substituted for Main Street shops. More subtly, a Japanese commentator has claimed that the cleanliness and the concern for quality in the Tokyo park are singularly appealing to Japanese. When Euro Disney opened in 1992, on the other hand, there was marked cultural resistance: on the part of the visitors to Disney taboos on alcohol; on the part of employees to being told they could not smoke or chew gum; and on the point of trade unions, objecting to recruitment policies which excluded those with 'unnatural' shades of hair, or who were 'too fat', sweated 'too much' or wore flashy jewellery.

The optimistic notion that the world's problems can be solved via technology, and that technological progress is painless – 'abstracted from industrial production', with conflict 'ironed out'[137] – has been retained even if the technology celebrated is not that of the nineteenth-century iron age, or the steel and automobile technology of the Ford epoch (now denigrated as the 'rustbelt'). Some of the inventions celebrated (voice-operated cookers, for instance) may be trivial, but the stress upon the revolution in mass communications is not. The exponential growth of information technologies, of satellites and computers, is presented as one major ground for hope in the future. For AT&T, the history of the world is therefore the history of communications. So the American Adventure will continue. Engineering the natural environment – the land and the seas – in order to produce more food is now the overall project, both noble and cosmic. (Disney himself had originally planned to cover the entire site with a dome, in order to control the weather.)

In all of this, America has a special global mission – 'the liberation of humanity, the freedom of man and mind … the American Dream'. The statues which symbolize the 'Spirits of America' are the Spirit of Adventure (a sea captain), of Self-Reliance (a farmer), of Knowledge (a female teacher), of Pioneering (an aviator), of Heritage (an (Indian maiden), of Freedom (a Pilgrim), of Discovery (a mountain man). of Compassion (a woman nurse), of Independence (a Minuteman), of Tomorrow (a mother), of Innovation (George Washington Carver, scientist, botanist and agricultural innovator) and of Individualism (a cowboy). 'If we dream it,' we are told, 'we can do it.'

According to General Motors' attraction, American Journeys, in the World of Motion, from the days of the wagon train and of nineteenth-century immigration, America has always been a society on the move, a society based on progress and therefore confident about the future As a land of change, its social institutions too are perennially reborn. 'It's fun to be free', the theme song tells us.

The use of space *outside* the earth constitutes a second new, hopeful frontier. But to achieve this, we – scientists, corporations and people – need to co-operate. Conflict (class struggle, racial and national animosities) simply gets in the way.

So even though it is admitted that resources are finite (solar energy will run out) and even if space on earth is being filled up, there is still hope – in outer space.

Disney, then, still lives – not cryogenically but in this continuing celebration of 'technologism' which is perfectly consistent with his own ideas. For he was 'a tinkerer', the 'first imagineer', who thought of making a movie or building a ride for the most part as 'engineering problems', and, as Fjellman remarks, his ideas about 'life in the future' were also of 'a life amenable to such tinkering'.

But the theme parks do not exist simply to convey an ideology about production. What they actually make money out of is the practice of *consumption*. Even if the ratio of adults to children is four to one, the family is catered for, with different kinds of attractions for those (like me) seeking to recapture their Mickey Mouse youth, or for children who want souvenirs and presents. They also have to be fed, and eating does not come cheap, since food and drink cannot be brought in from outside. Some of the smaller pavilions, indeed, have been described as 'little more than souvenir stands with restaurants'.[138]

The spread of the Disney culture across the modern world has been phenomenal – seen, by some critics, as not just irresistible, but also pernicious, inducing in some of them a virtual 'moral panic'. Winning at the tables in Vegas may be akin to gambling on futures on Wall Street or the Chicago commodity exchanges, but Las Vegas and Disney theme parks are still fantasy worlds, and seen to be so, while in terms of direct messages entertainment is more salient than any direct messages about capitalism. Much of the influence of the theme parks as modes of organizing mass culture has been restricted to consumption styles. In Edmonton West, in Alberta, for instance, the distinction between shopping mall and theme park is hard to discern for the 878 stores and 110 restaurants, with a five-acre water park and a nineteen-storey glass dome, are all parts of *themed* areas spread over 110 acres. In Britain, Gateshead Metro already has a 'Mediterranean Village', and similar developments are planned for London's Gatwick Airport.[139]

But the most spectacular parallel to the Disney parks is Las Vegas, where, as in Disney's worlds, guests are kept happy, comfortable and entertained from dawn to dusk (and all night long) – and are thereby encouraged to spend their money in the hotel's restaurants, bars and, above all, gambling saloons, which are built to resemble swans, dolphins, riverboats, Egyptian pyramids ... or Disney characters.[140]

Those who participate in these fantasies are certainly required to 'willingly suspend' disbelief. But they know what they are in for – and what they have come for. They are not there to look at museums. If they were, the only one worth visiting in Las Vegas is devoted to Liberace. But they are also perfectly aware that Caesar's Palace or the Egyptian Pyramids they are looking at are 'film-sets' façades, built of plastic as often as of stone.

Places like Las Vegas, then, fall into neither of the categories which Bryman examines: 'tourism' and 'post-tourism'.[141] The 'tourist' is a person for whom 'tribal dances' (sometimes modernized as the National Ballet) are staged all over the Third World. He is engaged in

a quest for authenticity ... seek[ing] meaning in far places in their natural, unadulterated state. However, they are invariably thwarted in their quest, since they are unable to penetrate the back regions to which they travel. Instead, they are nudged into the 'front region' where they encounter 'staged authenticity' –

resulting in a condition known as 'touristic shame'.

The 'post-tourist', on the other hand, is a very different kind of animal, a *hip* person who

knows that he is a tourist, not a time-traveller when he goes to stay somewhere historic; not an instant noble savage when he stays on a tropical beach; not an invisible observer when he visits a native compound. Resolutely 'realistic', he cannot evade his condition of outsider. But having embraced that condition, he can stop struggling against it.

It seems élitist, though, to deny a similar criticality to tourists who visit Orlando or Las Vegas, and equally élitist for postmodernist intellectuals to credit those who control the media with the capacity to impose ideas through the images (which they call 'texts') purveyed by the Disney imagineers on uncritical audiences. More Gramscian theorists, such as Stuart Hall, have argued that the 'preferred' texts which the imagineers want to get across may be 'subverted' – 'decoded' – by creating 'opposition' or 'negotiated' readings.[142]

Since the production and consumption of mass culture have themselves become big business, 'show business itself', including the movie industry, has become a further 'attraction', and the Corporation has learned to sell its own history. Disney's beginnings, indeed, have been incorporated into the global marketing spectacle. It would seem that Marshall McLuhan's prophecy, 'The Medium is the Message', has finally come true, for at the Disney-MGM Studios, visitors can see how movies are made, even – since they are allowed to see how the illusion of 'animation' is accomplished – participating in the *destruction* of illusion and fantasy.

5

An Absence of Culture

From Ghetto to Subculture

Before Zionism had become a major force and before the Holocaust, Jews living in countries where they were *not* persecuted identified strongly with the countries they lived in. In the United States, for example, they responded to Emma Lazarus' glorification of their home as a land where oppressed minorities could find freedom, an idea which even Zionists could accept. In Milwaukee in 1919, one of them, Goldie Mabovitz Meyerson (later Golda Meir), dressed herself as the Statue of Liberty at a function held by the Poale Zion Chasidim organization, flanked by a man dressed as Abraham Lincoln, with a tablet inscribed 'The Wanderer Finds Liberty in America' at their feet. It was an ironic anticipation of the future dependence of Israel upon the USA.

It was another Jewish immigrant, this time from Britain, Israel Zangwill, who provided the next major celebration of American democracy in his play of 1925, *The Melting Pot*, a phrase which has passed into everyday currency. In America, he rhapsodized, the 'Great Alchemist' would 'melt and fuse' with his 'purging flame' older nationalities and ethnicities with their ancient, atavistic prejudices:

Jew and Gentile ... East and West, the palm tree and the pine, the pole and the equator, the crescent and the cross ... Here they shall all unite to build the republic of man and the Kingdom of God. Ah ... what is the glory of Rome and Jerusalem where all the nations come to worship and look back, compared with the glory of America, where all races and nations come to look forward.[1]

While Zangwill was hymning the melting pot, the sociologists who founded what became known as the Chicago School were beginning to produce a brilliant series of studies of the life of ethnic minorities in that city, which also generated successive theoretical schools of sociology, over half a century, from the urban sociology of the Chicago School in the 1930s, through interactionist theory, deviance theory and labelling theory, to the work of Erving Goffman.

For the Chicago School, the horizontal antagonisms of class were not, as they would have been for Gramsci (whose ideas were unavailable to them, anyhow), their theoretical starting point. They found that though immigrants identified with America, they did not 'melt' (assimilate), but retained their languages and cultures. But they did not develop counter-cultures, nor did any ethnic group set out to acquire its own territorial state. There was, then, a flourishing, highly localized ethnicity, but no nationalism. The Chicago School therefore began with a spatial mapping of the innumerable districts of the city, each inhabited by a distinctive ethnic group. When plotted systematically on the pull-out map at the front of Frederick Thrasher's classic study, *The Gang*, and taken together, they formed an ethnic mosaic called Chicago.[2]

Chicago sociologists thus emphasized ethnic differences, not counter-cultural oppositions. Their key social concept was that of a *sub*culture inhabiting a limited social *space* – the '*ghetto*'.

Vivid as these thoroughly anthropological studies of how real people lived, face to face, were, they lacked any image of society as a whole. The only great case study which did connect the life of a street gang with national and even international developments came from a Harvard-trained sociologist, William Foote Whyte, who, in his *Street Corner Society* began with one (Italian) gang on a street corner in a Boston slum – and ended with Mussolini.[3]

Some members of these ethnic groups, like Golda Meir, might involve themselves with political movements in their countries of origin, but the second generation were not interested in a Sicily or an Ireland they had never seen. Others, like the Irish in New York, built ethnic political machines, but used them to deliver votes from their community to the two main parties, or, as with the Italians, used wealth generated illegitimately to buy influence in state and national politics. Only the third generation, now thoroughly Americanized, felt secure enough to explore their roots back in Europe.

It is instructive for a European to be taken on a walk round an American city. Where, in England or Italy, they would be told in all but a handful of cities with large, new concentrations of immigrants, 'This is a middle-class area' or 'This is a slum district' – the language of class – in America they are more likely to be told 'This is a Puerto Rican neighbourhood' or 'This is an Irish section.' Over half a century after the Chicago School started their work, in an issue on 'The World of New York', the *New York Times Magazine* asked the question, 'Who lives where?' and answered it in authentically American terms with a map of New York's ethnic groups, resembling, in an ominous simile, a 'map of the tangled Balkans', beginning with 'Asian' and 'Black', going through eight other ethnicities, and ending with 'European-descended Jews' and 'Other Europeans'.[4]

Over time, however, the concept which began life as the 'subculture' of the ghetto became transmuted as Chicago sociologists turned from studying ethnic communities to studying other kinds of deviant and stigmatized groups. They began in the 1930s with gangs and with taxi-dancers; by the 1950s, 'deviance theorists' were studying marijuana smokers and jazz musicians. They also tended to identify with the groups they were studying. All these groups, they found, had their own cultures, with a logic and ethos of their own – not Culture with a capital C, but subcultures, plural, which the bearers of hegemonic WASP subculture would have refused to accord the dignity of the term 'culture'. Since the vast majority of the world's sociologists have always been American, it is this concept, not Gramsci's, which has come to predominate.

For Gramsci, 'counterculture' was part of his revolutionary philosophy. It is significant that the only time it surfaced in American sociology was during the anti-Vietnam youth revolt of 1968, which Theodore Roszak described as 'counterculture'.[5] Otherwise, explorations of expressions of oppositional culture, such as W. F. Wertheim's analysis of what he called 'counterpoint', were rare ventures by maverick, non-American, left-wing sociologists.[6]

Though 'subculture' was not a revolutionary concept, it did have radical implications. In particular, it undermined the élitist conception developed largely by literary critics from Matthew Arnold to T. S. Eliot and F. R. Leavis, of culture as 'high' culture, in the form of 'the arts' – certain kinds (only) of music, painting, sculpture and writing, created and consumed by members of the educated upper and middle classes. What the rest of the population produced and consumed was vulgar, 'low' culture at best – if it deserved that title at all.

Anthropologists, on the other hand, had long argued that even the most material things, from machines, tools and buildings, say, to lavatories even, were products of the human intellect and imagination, and therefore labelled them 'material culture'. Now, interactionist and deviance theorists saw culture as a social, not just an aesthetic/intellectual phenomenon, by no means restricted to one class only. Though popular culture was still distinguished from élite culture, this view was both populist and pluralist. Popular culture was now accepted as culture, its art forms – pop music, football and fashion – every bit as much 'culture' as Bartók quartets.

Not much of this fed through into mainstream sociology, where the culture has been the most underdeveloped theoretical concept of all. Most major sociological theorists have had something to say about it, but few ever bothered to define it very rigorously, and when they did, there was often little agreement between them.[7]

There was, though, one major exception; functionalism, the theoretical school which dominated modern sociology from the 1930s to the 1950s, and especially the work of Talcott Parsons.[8] Social action – a term he preferred to 'behaviour', since that word had been used by a school of psychologists who saw human actions as the result of conditioning – involved three systems: the social system; the personality system of the individual actor; and the cultural system which guided the way they behaved. He defined culture as a *shared* set of symbolic values, which he illustrated mainly by referring to the great world religions. But social structure received far more attention and in the subsequent reaction against functionalism, the baby culture was thrown out with the bathwater.

Thereafter, little attention was paid to the concept of culture. Two decades passed before Zygmunt Bauman's *Culture as Praxis,*[9] in which he identified three uses of the term: the 'universalistic' conception of Culture with a capital C, marking the boundaries between human society and the rest; the 'normative/aesthetic' distinction between 'high' and 'low' cultures (élitism, racism); and the conception of culture as the source of differences between societies or communities within the same society.

Another decade of resounding silence then ensued, finally broken by Margaret Archer's *Culture and Agency.*[10] The concept of culture, she wrote, was more weakly developed than any key concept in sociology, a 'poor relation' of 'structure'. (At a rare conference on the subject, one scholar even asserted: 'we can use the word "culture" as an alternate for "society".'[11])

When they did use the concept, some treated culture as if it was all-powerful – a supremely independent 'prime mover', as Archer put it. Others saw it as a mere epiphenomenon, the outcome of other kinds of social relations. For some, the coherence of any ideology derived ('upwards', as she put it) from the coherence of the social order; for others, ideology worked 'downwards' as an integrating force.

Archer insisted – against both of these positions – that human agency was central in social life and therefore had to be central in sociological analysis too. She therefore denounced all schools of thought which treated culture as something determined by other social forces, from nineteenth-century positivism, which saw social progress as the outcome of technical advance, to the very influential theory put forward in the 1960s by Clark Kerr and his colleagues, who argued that as societies become industrialized they necessarily also 'converged' in terms of both their social structure and their cultural values. Soviet communism would therefore be more liberal – with more freedom for both the market and the expression of opinion, while capitalism would develop mechanisms for distributing wealth more equitably.[12] Before long, it was being asserted that 'the fundamental problems of the industrial revolution had been solved';[13] that we had entered an epoch in which ideologies were redundant – the 'end of ideology'.[14] By the 1980s, Alvin Toffler had updated the theory,[15] hailing the new technological advances in computers and telecommunications as marking the beginning of a new kind of 'information society' (which Archer sarcastically describes as 'positivism with peripherals'). Following the collapse of Soviet communism, Fukuyama told people that we had reached not just the end of ideology but the 'end of history'.[16]

All these theories devalue both culture and human agency: ideas either become redundant or are merely a by-product of technological change. They have no autonomous life of their own: culture merely reflects structure; technical advance determines social progress; and morality is determined by rational thought.[17]

The commonest conception of culture reduces it simply to the cognitive – to a system of ideas – so that people usually use the term 'ideology' instead. But culture also involves, over and above ideas, *values* and forms of *behaviour*. In his philosophy, Kant labelled these three dimensions of culture as the 'cognitive', the 'normative' and the 'conative'; or, to put it in the simpler language of Hannah Arendt, thinking, judging and acting.[18] Culture, that is, does more than simply provide you with an intellectual map of the world and the things (including people) in it; it tells you who your enemies are and who are your friends, and which of the many ways in which people conduct their lives are models you should emulate and which you should shun.

Neither Bauman nor Archer paid much attention to spelling out just what culture *was*; Archer, for instance, dismisses anthropological debate on the matter as mere 'definitional wrangling'.[19] Yet it is anthropology, the study of 'other cultures', which provides us with the clearest conception of culture. More specifically, it is American anthropology, where German immigrant intellectuals had brought with them philosophical idealism. Thus the major intellectual influence on Carl Sauer, the founder of the Berkeley School of geography, was Goethe,[20] though he was further influenced by another immigrant German intellectual, Franz Boas, the founder of modern American 'cultural' anthropology.[21] British anthropology, however, was 'social' anthropology, and concentrated on 'structure', not culture.[22]

Boas had been trained as a natural scientist; he wrote his Ph.D. thesis on the colour of sea-water. According to philosophers like Kant, the natural sciences (*Naturwissenschaften*) were different in kind from the arts because they dealt with human consciousness (*Geist*). The study of human beings cut across this dichotomy. In anthropology, as physical organisms, they were the subject matter of physical anthropology. But as members of cultural communities, which cumulatively develop and elaborate ideas and values and hand them on from generation to generation, humans differ from most other animals.

American anthropologists nevertheless still teach their students that there are four 'tracks' in anthropology: physical anthropology, linguistics, archaeology and cultural anthropology. Yet the last three, being concerned with culture, necessarily entail using different methods of study from those used by physical anthropologists, while archaeologists can't usually find out much that is reliable about the ideas and values of people long dead merely from excavating material objects.

Though Boas did research into physical anthropology, his major contribution was his recognition of the centrality of culture, and he succeeded in persuading other anthropologists of this. Two eminent successors, Kroeber and Kluckhohn, set a young colleague (and later distinguished theorist) to work compiling no less than 164 definitions of cultures which American anthropologists had used. Out of these they distilled a common core of ideas. Culture consisted of 'patterns of and for behavior ... acquired and transmitted by symbols ... the essential core being ideas and especially their attached values'.[23]

It was a definition which reflected the ideas of the 1930s and 1940s, for while it rightly put ideas and values at the centre, it also included what are usually called 'customs' – approved forms of behaviour. But too often the communication of culture was seen simply as the passing-on of *tradition*. Culture was *heritage* – what is acquired, learned and transmitted – an ideology familiar enough today, for instance, in the notion of 'English Heritage', in which castles and stately homes are marketed to tourists by projecting an image of a common past which we all share, whatever the social position of our ancestors might have been. It is an image of continuity and community, not of change and social divisions.

It therefore was an image of culture which tended to underplay innovation and, more widely, to abstract ideas and values from any context of use, treating them as if they were all-powerful determinants of behaviour, rather than as resources *used* by people who commanded power to control behaviour and to validate institutions. In reality, the extent to which this actually happens varies – at times, people do internalize hegemonic ideas; at others, they ignore or reject them.

In previous centuries, images of human society had been much more developmental. The Enlightenment had seen the history of humankind as the story of progress and the gradual extension of human reason; the nineteenth century in terms of the all-conquering theory of evolution. In these philosophies, the emphasis had not been on culture as binding legacy and tradition, but on human innovation, creativity, critical scientific thought and cumulative collective achievement.

Such optimism evaporated after the blood bath of the First World War, long before such modern developments as concentration camps, brainwashing, Hiroshima and Nagasaki and the prospect of global nuclear annihilation or total ecocide. But social evolutionalism also died because nineteenth-century models of the 'stages' of social evolution did not stand up to scrutiny, and because people began looking at society in a quite different way. They now asked not about the *origins* of customs, but about how they worked in everyday life, a mode of inquiry which provided a much more dynamic picture of everyday life, though at the price of losing any sense of historical development.

The view of culture as tradition is also a conservative view of human life. It lacks any place for countercultures or subcultures: a culture is said to possess a single 'ethos of the total culture' (Kroeber); cultures are 'coherent wholes' (Malinowski); or form 'patterns' (Benedict). Later, even more idealist writers went further: values were 'over-arching' or 'deep', but either way 'ineffable', so 'sacred' that they were unchallengeable and unproblematically efficacious.

Yet Parsons himself, usually accused of having too 'integrated' a model of society, in fact paid a lot of attention to contradictions. For various reasons, people *failed* to internalize the values of their culture adequately. He also noted that though cultural values did shape behaviour, they also emerged out of people's social relations.[24] So culture could no more be seen simply as a system of values projected on to society than the other way round. Culture was *not* simply 'ineffable' and all-determining. Even where what he called 'pattern-consistency' existed – for example, logical coherence within a philosophy, or a dominant art style – these might not fit well with other elements of culture or society.

The view of culture as tradition did not pass unchallenged even within the American anthropology of the time. Some pointed to the coexistence of different sets of values within the same society; others emphasized human creativity, innovation and imagination. Though functionalist anthropologists taught their students to look at the societies they were studying as if they were taking snapshots at a single point in time, archaeologists, who necessarily had to deal with change, often over long periods, were constantly confronted with evidence that some forms of culture get lost while new ones emerge, whether they were studying great empires like Mohenjo Daro or Angkor Wat, which have disappeared, or technologically simpler cultures like that of the Anasazi of the Rocky Mountains, who lived for many centuries at Mesa Verde, then disappeared (probably owing to climatic changes) within a couple of generations. Such changes sometimes occurred gradually and at others suddenly.

In concentrating on culture in this book, though, I am not preaching 'culturalism', underestimating the importance of the other two dimensions of social action: the political (the exercise of power) and the economic (the production and distribution of goods and services). I emphasize culture only because it is usually simply ignored by those who give us political economy but call it 'sociology'. The study of religion – a singularly 'cultural' field – particularly of Asian religions commonly thought of as singularly mystical, 'otherworldly' kinds of religion, tempted some people to concentrate exclusively on beliefs rather than behaviour. But historians have shown that Asian kings struggled to bring temples under their control, because of their wealth and because those who dominated these institutions thereby gained power over the faithful.[25] So though anthropologists like Fuller, in his study of the great temple of Minakshi at Madurai, in southern India,[26] and Seneviratne, in his study of the Temple of the Tooth at Kandy, in Sri Lanka,[27] both carefully examine the beliefs on which religious worship is based, they also show that because these are major centres of pilgrimage, they are also complex economic organizations which have to handle large flows of wealth, over which struggles take place within the temple, while outside the temple, by patronizing religious rites, politicians use the appeal of religion to build up support.

In his classic study of the genesis of modern capitalism, Max Weber emphasized the importance of a set of cultural values, the Protestant ethic, which were favourable to capitalism because they motivated people to work hard and to accumulate. His emphasis was upon motivation. Capitalism, which many have described purely in terms of a 'material base', for him also further depended upon crucial ideal elements (in the sense in which Godelier uses the term *idéel* – that is, things of the mind). Capitalism, indeed, is based upon two central *non-economic* ideas which are not just normative – *rights* – but are enshrined in law: the sanctity of private property and the right to transmit accumulated wealth to one's kin or any other legatee one designates. Though capitalism could not flourish without these principles, they are usually ignored by economists and left for lawyers and social scientists to worry about. By contrast, in Australian Aboriginal culture, as we saw, such ideas would be as unthinkable as the right to own air.

Thus, though the BBC is a cultural institution, governments seek to influence or totally control the media (not just the news) because they recognize that the media influence people's behaviour, not just their ideas.

Parliament, likewise, is a political institution, but its decisions – on all policies, not about taxes alone – have consequences for the distribution of wealth and the uses to which wealth is put. Banks, again, though primarily financial institutions, take decisions which are quite as fateful for ordinary people as those taken by their governments.

One major non-anthropologist theorist of culture, Raymond Williams, has paid particular attention to the relationship between ideas and values and the 'apparatuses' through which they are disseminated and reinforced. Unfortunately he described his approach as 'cultural materialism' (a term also used by Marvin Harris for his very different kind of theory which reduces ideas to responses to stimuli). What Williams should have called it was *dialectical* sociology, for it involves a relationship between ideas and social structures. Thus he looks at the ownership and control of the means of cultural production – in the modern world, the ownership of newspapers, TV and other media of mass communication. There is no simple formula, though: some private owners use their newspapers simply as a 'licence to print money'; others as a means for the ideological control of the masses; while some aim at both. Collective, 'public' forms of ownership vary from liberal newspaper 'trusts', which open their columns to debate, to (more commonly) state or party ownership, where the purpose is ideological control pure and simple. Williams also uses the term 'cultural materialism' to describe not so much the ownership of the means of cultural production as the ways in which the producers of culture – writers, editors, movie-makers – produce it, and their relationship to those who employ them (which may include a certain degree of 'relative autonomy'). Finally, he uses the term to describe the study of the *ideas* conveyed through cultural products about *everything* in social life from sex roles to dress styles, not just national politics.[28]

At the end of the day, one has to say that culture, since it deals in ideas and values, is *not* material; it is, to use Godelier's term again, *idéel*. While material objects certainly exist, even the most material of them, from stone axes to CD-ROMs, could not have been brought into being without the use of the human intellect: Mr Crapper could not have succeeded in inventing the lavatory had he not thought long and hard about it and even the most routinized kinds of manufacture depend upon human skills and judgement. We cannot, indeed, understand what an object from another culture *is* unless we understand what it means to those who produce and use it, and it may mean something quite different to us – or nothing. A mask which one culture symbolizes a god is, to us, a work of 'art', to exhibit in a museum. Even less can behaviour be labelled 'purely material'.

The opposite, idealist assertion is equally mystifying: ideas and values do not float about in the air, nor do all of them have the same significance for social behaviour. Their importance depends upon the ways in which they are *used*, put into action, by groups and individuals. To understand when, why and how culture may be sometimes successfully communicated, imposed or internalized, or, at other times, ignored or resisted, we have to set these questions within contexts of power. Social relations, then, have to be looked at in dialectical terms, as an interplay *between* ideas and other kinds of constraints on behaviour, from hunger to social pressures.

Global Village, Global Culture?

We said earlier that social identity and membership exist at levels which are both narrower than the polity and wider than it. Even tiny island societies have had to reckon with neighbours who were likely to threaten their security from time to time. But where, a generation ago, they would have fought each other with spears, today they would be more likely to use Kalashnikovs. For the last two millennia, most people on earth have been part of large empires too, or have belonged to religious communities which transcend any particular society. But the wars which have ravaged the Third World since 1945 – more than 120 of them, causing 22 million deaths – have not been small-scale wars against traditional ethnic enemies but consequences of the Cold (actually very hot) War, when even the most remote peoples were sucked into new global conflicts by élites who took power in new states and allied their countries with one camp or the other, importing vast quantities of high-tech weaponry in the process, and often – as in Korea and Somalia – doing the fighting as surrogates for the super-powers.

In the economic sphere as well, workers in factories in Britain have long been sensitive to foreign competition. Today, they are even more aware that the plant they work in can be shut down or transferred overnight, by the transnational corporation which owns it, to other countries, not just in Europe but even in the South, where labour costs are lower.

At first the colonies were cheap-labour, raw-materials-producing zones, where a predominantly male labour force was employed in mines and on plantations. Later, increasing numbers of both men and women became workers in low-tech urban factories or in domestic 'putting-out' production in the home. But growing numbers of women also began to work outside the home, at first in industries like textiles, today as part of a large unskilled and non-union labour force, employed in niches within a global division of labour determined by transnational corporations, often in quite high-tech industries, such as the routine assembly of electronic goods or, as in the 'Special Economic Zones' of China, the production of a large proportion of the toys sold in Western markets.

A new term, 'newly industrializing', soon had to be invented for countries where this process had begun earliest, notably the four 'Little Dragons' of East Asia (Hong Kong, Taiwan, South Korea and Singapore), plus Brazil and Mexico, which have since become major industrial economies or financial centres.

It should not be assumed, though, that all countries will inevitably follow the same path; that it is evidence of the 'end of the Third World' as a whole.[29]

American and Japanese corporations with branch-plants in East Asia, for instance, still locate their innovatory research and development and high-tech manufacturing back home. They have, though, selected a few formerly 'Third World' countries as 'cores' of whole regions, where intermediate levels of R & D now take place.[30]

These global economic processes had already begun to affect colonies from New Guinea to West Africa long before the twentieth century. Peasants cultivating cash crops experienced wild and, to them, mysterious swings in the prices they received; workers in plantations and mines found themselves driven to class struggle over wages and working conditions.[31]

These remote areas had also been radically transformed by global cultural forces, for they were now introduced to new ideas, mainly a diet of biblical lore, in mission and other colonial schools. But few got into these schools. For the most part, therefore, in their efforts to make sense of all this, people still drew upon traditional knowledge. Increasing numbers, though, did learn to read and write – which made it possible for them to enter a new world.

Thirty years ago, Marshall McLuhan created a sensation when he showed that the invention of movable type had sparked off cultural revolution not just in Europe, where it began, but across the entire planet. In the 1930s, a West African prince recorded the intellectual shock he experienced when he first realized what *print* was. The only crowded space in the local missionary's house, he wrote, was his bookshelves:

I gradually came to understand that the marks on the pages were *trapped words*. Anyone could learn to decipher the symbols and turn the trapped words into speech ... I shivered with the intensity of my desire to do this wondrous thing myself.[32]

Several centuries had to elapse before the Gutenberg revolution reached the corners of the earth. Since then, that revolution has been overtaken by a whole set of linked exponential revolutions in communications technology within a very few decades – transistor radios, TV, audio and then video cassettes, CDs, PCs and word processors, satellite dishes, fax machines and mobile phones, CD-ROMs, e-mail, the Internet – which have grown out of the development of microchips during the exploration of space and have made electronic communications a larger and more profitable industry than the automobile industry.

Making sense of all this is not easy. So another industry, the education industry, has grown up to provide just such interpretations. In the developed world, an increasing proportion of all children now go on to higher education. Their homes too are jam-packed with electronic gadgetry. My grandchildren, who cannot speak or read yet, know a lot about pressing buttons. Soon, they will have video games. Yet even in the developed world many people still do not get beyond secondary education, while in the 'South' they generally get only a rudimentary schooling which stops long before their teens.

All of them, though, are exposed to the electronic media. Even in the Amazon, men own transistors as well as bows and arrows, and I have seen very poor agricultural labourers in villages in Brazil for whom renting a TV is among their highest domestic priorities – and it is switched on all day long. The programmes, like the radio programmes the Amazonian Indians listen to, are often the same as those being listened to and watched by people in Los Angeles.

Yet it was not until 1991 that Leslie Sklair produced the first study which devotes as much space to cultural (he calls it 'culture-ideology') as to economic and political globalism.[33] Even so, he still treats culture in the 'arts' sense and looks at it in largely economic terms as a consumer *industry* in which First World tastes and wants are exported to the Third World. The Third World merely *receives* these things.

The *content* of culture – what it is that is being communicated – receives little attention. Media institutions themselves simply log figures of programmes sold and transmitted and viewing audiences. A more dialectical, and qualitative, approach would show that although ownership is decisively concentrated in the hands of a few Western transnationals, so that the profits flow back to the 'North' (which includes Australia and Japan!), the cultural traffic is *not* all one-way. The great forms of popular music in the twentieth century, indeed, have been *black*, from jazz and calypso to reggae, rock and beyond. The cultural source of the world's modern popular music, then, has been the South. But its main market is the North, where it is consumed by mass audiences. Jazz itself incorporated white influences, such as Sankey and Moody harmonies. Today, there has been so much more crossover of styles, including new syntheses of music from very diverse cultures of both the North and the South (Mali, Zaïre, Bangladesh), that a special name has had to be coined to describe them: 'world music'.

Likewise, even habits of eating – which one might think were much less volatile, more 'material', more 'primordial' forms of culture, less prone to change – are being rapidly transformed with the global spread of Western fast foods, which, as a recent study of McDonald's shows, involves not just the consumption and marketing of hamburgers but their production too, in accordance with methods laid down in Hamburger University, Oak Park, Illinois. Some writers see this as merely an extension, in the sphere of food consumption, of 'post-Fordism', in which Henry Ford's classic methods of rationalizing production, based on the principles of 'scientific management' – efficiency, calculability and predictability – and operationalized via the assembly line and bureaucratic supervision of the work process – time-and-motion studies – have now been carried much further by using *non*-human technology in place of unreliable human labour.[34]

McDonald's has, indeed, expanded in spectacular fashion across the globe. Franchising began in the United States in 1955 and in 1967 was extended abroad, though no further than to Canada. In 1974, McDonald's opened up in London; by 1984, it became the first foreign food firm permitted to operate in Taiwan after the ending of martial law. Outlets in Korea, Greece, India and even Mecca, and, of course, in Moscow and Beijing followed. By 1992, 60 per cent of profits were coming from abroad.

Most writers discuss the emergence of fast-foodism solely in economic terms. Where they do touch upon its cultural significance, as with music, they usually treat it merely as one-way traffic. However, Watson and his colleagues, researching McDonald's in East Asia,[35] have shown that the attempt to impose standardized Western-based cultural norms ran into unexpected problems. In India, a beef-less burger and a 'veggieburger' had to be invented; for Japan, riceburgers.

Back in the USA, pyschologists had selected the bright orangy-red colour as being optimally attractive for luring customers in, but so bright that people would want to move on after about forty minutes. It seemed to be the ideal, culture-free way of ensuring a continuous throughput of customers.

But some of the problems McDonald's came up against abroad were indeed cultural factors, some traditional, some novel. We saw earlier how one Western cultural form, Christmas, has been transformed among the Japanese upper classes. Outside America, McDonald's has long been an archetypal symbol of US culture, and, in the 1970s, commonly a negative one: branches of McDonald's from Mexico to Paris were singled out as eminently appropriate targets for protests against US cultural imperialism. But in Hong Kong, in a culture in which the consumption of food has always been a central value, and where the consumption of fast food on the street has long been a feature of public life, eating at McDonald's fitted in easily. Unlike street-market food, though, McDonald's now became a by-word for scrupulous cleanliness, and therefore modern living standards and styles. In Japan too, eating at McDonald's became a symbol of American modernity for children who dropped in on the way home from school (many of them didn't actually like the food, at first at least). It was also prestigious, whereas in the homeland of McDonald's, the middle classes had come to look down on hamburger culture, and the educated were often proud to announce that they had never been into a McDonald's. Japanese children, on the other hand, with money to spend and with a new consumer-consciousness, transformed their local McDonald's into centres of fun, familiarity and friendship. McDonald's branches became virtual high-school clubhouses where schoolchildren hung out for hours, even doing their homework there. The children also developed a whole new culture of birthday parties, held at McDonald's, in which parents participated and to which McDonald's responded by providing party hostesses and a new clown/host, Ronald McDonald.

The cultural traffic, then, has not been entirely one-way. In the post-1945 era, Western cultural influence over Japan was, of course, great, from political institutions to golf and baseball. In a study of Disneyland Tokyo, one Japanese writer shows that it was only a latter-day instance of a much wider and earlier importation of Western culture in which whole life-sized 'foreign villages' (*ikoku-mura*) were specially constructed, all over Japan, as showcases to inform the Japanese what life in the West was like, with special emphasis on advanced technology and consumerism. By the 1960s, consumerism had become possible for the Japanese too. Yet, as after the Meiji Restoration a century earlier, Yashimoto sees all this as a singularly powerful extension of *Japanese* nationalism.[36]

Much more than music, food and consumer goods has been diffused from the West, though. In the nineteenth century, Western political ideas – liberalism, nationalism, Darwinism and, later, socialism and Marxism – were freely borrowed, and were very prestigious. But they always had to be adapted to indigenous ways of thought and to indigenous political cultures. Though Marx had thought the state would wither away under communism, for example, the state became all-powerful in a Russia inured over centuries to autocracy, to centralized rule, the millennial rule of the landlord and a religious orthodoxy tied to state and Tsar. China borrowed institutions like the single party and state planning from the USSR. But her far longer history had also included long periods in which the central state had disintegrated, so although the religion most closely linked to the state, Confucianism, had died as a *religious* cult before the end of the nineteenth century, the millennial tradition of the mandarinate as a meritocratic administrative élite still survives today in the form of the party. In Russia, the party is dead; in China, it is still in control.

The internationalist ideals of nineteenth-century communism too have been replaced by national communisms. China and Vietnam eventually even went to war, not jointly against world capitalism but against each other. Similarly, Islam, a religion which lays claims to universal validity and to being a religion of peace based on the community of the faithful, has generated virulent modern nationalisms, deriving from older cultural differences, resulting in conflicts between Muslim states, notably the war between Sunni Iran and majority-Shia Iraq which left over a million dead.

But though the past shapes the present, modernizers are obviously not simply conservatives. What is described as 'fundamentalism' does include traditional elements, but also highly innovative, even radical ones, while even traditional ideas are reinterpreted and harnessed to modern ends. In the colonial epoch, they were used to mobilize people against foreign colonialism. Thus what have been called the 'Little Traditions', from Melanesia to southern Africa, used ancient beliefs to interpret a world turned upside down by the arrival of the whites. For the Xhosa in the 1850s, the loss of most of their cattle from a new disease and their final military defeat at the hands of the British sparked off a movement inspired by a fifteen-year old prophetess who proclaimed the imminent return of the dead – after which there would be such abundance they should kill off all their cattle and cease cultivating the land.[37] (As a result, 100,000 people starved to death.) In New Guinea, similar 'cargo' movements were only the first in a long series of reactions to colonial rule, and then to independence, in which phases of total non-co-operation with the state were followed by periods of participation in the parliamentary system.[38]

Little Traditions had always had to come to terms with expanding world religions such as Christianity and Islam. At first, local religions – notably cults of the earth and of the ancestors – which had existed long before the arrival of Islam, coexisted with Islam, but they were too parochial in the end to maintain their cultural autonomy and were replaced by Islamic beliefs and practices, though distinct traces can still be discerned.[39]

Even the Great Traditions, though, had to come to terms with the domination of the new global system by modern Western European colonialism, whose power was not just military, political and economic but also claimed cultural superiority.

In the Islamic world, for instance, there had been profound debates for centuries about what the ideal relationship between the state and the religious *ulema* should be. At first, modernizers – in Egypt, Turkey and Iran – had often been deeply influenced by the new secular Western philosophies. Even what people today call fundamentalism – which they think of as some kind of unproblematic return to unambiguous and rigid tradition, enshrined in the Koran and the *hadith* – involves new 'readings' of Islamic ideas. Ayatollah Khomeini's conception of the *nation*, for instance, and of the right of the mullahs to rule and legislate, or Ali Shari'ati's more radical-populist conception of the people as *masses* and as victims of oppression – and therefore the main agent for bringing about social transformation – are *new* ideas, as novel as Khomeini's technological innovation of using audio tapes to spread them.[40]

Today, such is the power of modern communications that art forms, economies, religions and entire ways of life are vulnerable to fundamentalist Christianity, as US-sponsored evangelistic sects, equipped with their own planes, satellite dishes and schools, move into tribal areas, into Central American peasant villages which hardly see a Catholic priest from one end of the year to the other and into the city shanty towns where the dispossessed live.

Major cultural traditions such as these do not disappear easily. Rather, they undergo revival, transformation and synthesis. In Bali, in colonial times, reformers fought indigenous aristocrats and religious leaders, backed by the Dutch, who all worked together to preserve both the traditional privileges of the high castes as well as many newly invented ones, in struggles which reflected both old and new kinds of social divisions. During the Second World War, some nationalists used traditional culture as a source of solidarity in the struggle against Japan; others saw the entire social order as archaic, compromised and therefore needing to be made over. After independence, some modernizers attacked both the caste system and Hinduism; others tried to use religion as a unifying mechanism, converting Hinduism from a religion with a whole pantheon of gods (10,000 it has been said) into a monotheistic world religion fit to stand alongside Islam and Christianity.[41]

So colonialists were not the only agents of oppression, nor was class the only basis for oppression. In all cultures, people have been exploited, throughout history, because of their ethnicity, their nationality or their religion. Older inequalities, based not on class but on caste, existed in India, for example, long before British rule and still persist. From the beginning, therefore, the British inevitably found themselves embroiled, like the kings they displaced and the Congress Party later, in social struggles, such as rights of access to the great temple of Minaksi, in southern India, visited by over 15,000 people a day, where priests and temple servants profited from economic privileges – from fees and the control of temple lands – but, before 1939, denied access to Harijans (Untouchables) and the similarly polluting Nadar caste.[42] Similar social struggles took place in Sri Lanka at the Temple of the Tooth.[43]

Marx was right to emphasize that class struggle grew out of a differential relationship to the means of production – those who owned capital and those who provided the labour. This particular kind of inequality is, indeed, one historic, major source of continuous struggle. But people do not lead economic lives. They live in civil society and may be victims of a variety of forms of what has been called 'structured social inequality' other than economic inequalities. Rather, as Weber pointed out long ago,[44] economic exploitation and social stratification are only particular *forms* of inequality. In South Africa, inferiority in the economic sphere has been a *consequence* of the political and cultural ideology of apartheid, since skilled jobs were reserved for whites and blacks were denied any access to superior positions, not just in the economy but in public life generally on the basis of their *colour*.

Any explanation of social and political change in Europe needs an equally strong infusion of both historical and cultural explanation: to look at social and not only political and economic institutions, and at the values and ideas people use to make sense of what is happening to their world, together with the 'cultural apparatuses' through which explanations about the meaning of it all are supplied to them or forced on them.

Most explanations of the chaotic state of Russia following the collapse of communism, for instance, emphasize the absence of political and economic institutions adequate to cope with the gigantic task of replacing a command economy and an authoritarian, centralized party-state with one based on the market and on a participatory democracy. The reorganization of the economy does indeed require institutions appropriate to a market economy – a stock exchange, a merchant-banking system, an insurance industry, a modern and equitable system of taxation, and so on – none of which existed under Soviet communism.

But no economy exists 'in itself'. Wealth is socially produced and socially distributed. The socialist dream that democracy applied to the economy would mean new kinds of rights in ownership, in administration and in the labour process has been massively damaged by the experience of the USSR and by its successor economy, in which property is in the hands of a new political class. If this is capitalism, it is 'booty capitalism', made possible by control over the state, often by corrupt and criminal means, and very different from developed capitalist economies, which recognize that democracy has an economic as well as a political dimension, and that people are optimally motivated to work by systems of reward and recognition which they accept as reasonable returns for their labour. The problem for the countries of the ex-USSR, then, is not just one of developing economic institutions. It also derives, as one Western journalist with lengthy experience of Russia has pointed out, from underdevelopment not of the economy but of *civil society*,[45] for a democratic civil society never developed in either Tsarist Russia or in the USSR, and, in Jonathan Steele's words, is still a 'mirage'. The separation of powers, and the notion that government, central and local, should be accountable to the governed, never took root. There was no tradition that ordinary citizens, not just élites and especially political élites, have rights and also a duty to concern themselves with public policy; no legacy of non-state institutions, from a free press to independent trade unions; no contending political parties reflecting sectional interests; no praxis of participation in national political life – in short, no democratic political *culture*.

Social change initiated by the state has massive consequences for civil society. But the opposite is also true: changes in civil society, notably the major social movements of our time, have brought about great changes in the economy and in government policies. The emergence of the women's movement in the West in the 1960s, for instance, was the outcome of profound social and cultural changes. In the First World War, women had volunteered for or been conscripted into the Armed Forces and the munitions factories in their millions. Within a decade, they were voting in national elections. They were equally involved in the Second World War, after which, for the first time in human history, they entered higher education in large numbers. Within a few years, a new phase of the feminist movement took off. Young men too, in their hundreds of thousands, got into universities and colleges which had been unavailable to their parents. By the late 1960s, campuses across the world were racked by student protest which, though largely a protest against the Vietnam War, widened to include a criticism of Western materialist values (though it never threatened the positions of either the older classes and élites which have historically dominated capitalist society – the 'establishment' – or the newer political classes and dynasties from the Kennedys to the Nehrus). The very considerable amount of social mobility in developed capitalist society – in which American students were privileged participants – ensured that most of them, in the end, were absorbed into a new kind of 'postmodern' society; and many, too, into new kinds of conservatism.

In the underdeveloped world, culture has never been to the forefront, for these are states are controlled by local political élites and by domestic and foreign corporations and global economic institutions, notably the IMF and the World Bank. Development policy has been couched in terms of political economy – the maximization of GNP or the strengthening of the power of the state and the ruling party. Large wealthy classes have indeed emerged as a result – new 'political classes' whose wealth derives not from the private ownership of the means of production but from control over the state. The obverse of this is that poverty remains endemic, both in the shanty towns and in the still vast rural backlands, while at the macro level, countries like Mexico and Brazil – which are not 'newly industrializing' but already *industrialized* – cannot pay the gigantic debts they have accumulated in the process, and so are mired in desperate financial crisis.

This kind of development has failed because it rewards only the successful and the privileged. The theories on which it is based treat economic growth as an end in itself, as a problem of how to maximize production not of how the product is distributed, resulting in political cultures which put the interests of the state before the needs of ordinary people. It is political economy devoid of any democratic conception of civil society.

I hope that I have made some contribution towards destroying that kind of thinking. But I do not wish to drive a stake through the heart of political economy altogether. Politics do matter, and decisions certainly have to be taken and are taken about how wealth is to be produced and distributed. Rather, I hope that, by adding the dimension of culture, including counterculture and subculture, to black-and-white, two-dimensional political economy, and to the kind of sociology (most of it) that has a place for civil society but not for culture, we might begin to develop a three-dimensional social science, in colour, not in black-and-white, and thereby be better able to think about how to create a more humane world.

Notes

Introduction

1 Mills, 1961, p. 2.
2 Durkheim, 1954.
3 Radcliffe-Brown, 1930.
4 Worsley, 1956.
5 Worsley, 1961.
6 Lévi-Strauss, 1966.
7 Lévi-Strauss, 1969.
8 Worsley, 1967.
9 Waddy, 1988.
10 Levitt, Dulcie, 1981.
11 Vygotsky, 1962.
12 Needham, 1954–96.
13 Blainey, 1976.
14 Berger and Luckmann, 1967, p. 57.
15 Koestler, 1968.
16 Beattie, 1964.

Chapter 1

1 Turner, David, 1974, Fig. 1, pp. 4, 5.
2 Warner, W. L., 1937, p. 140.
3 Worsley (unpublished).
4 Porteus, 1931, p. 401.
5 Ibid., pp. 119–21.
6 Baker, 1989, p. 184.
7 McKnight (in press), Chap. 6.
8 Roughsey, 1984.
9 Herbert, 1938, pp. 68–9, 22.
10 Rose, 1947.
11 Baker, 1989, p. 117.
12 Levitt, Dulcie, 1981, Chap. 4.
13 Ibid., p. 23.
14 Ibid., pp. 12–13.
15 Ibid., Chap. 8.
16 McArthur, 1960, pp. 190–91.
17 Tindale, 1925, p. 82.
18 Baker, 1989, pp. 162, 166.
19 Ibid., p.166.
20 Harney, n.d., p. 176.
22 Cited in Baker, 1989, p. 189.
22 Levitt, Dulcie, 1981, p. 43.
23 Sahlins, 1972.
24 Ibid., p. 15.
25 Ibid., pp. 15–21, Figs. 1.1, 1.23 and Tables 1.1, 2.1, 3.1, based on data in McArthur, 1960, and McCarthy and McArthur, 1960.
26 Reynolds, 1981, p. 61.
27 Friedl, 1975, pp. 18–19.
28 Engels, 1948.
29 Radcliffe-Brown, 1952.
30 McKnight (in press), Chap. 7.
31 Turner, David, 1974, p.18.
32 Radcliffe-Brown, 1930.
33 Rose, 1960.
34 Worsley, 1992.
35 Tindale, 1925, pp. 70–72.
36 Levitt, Dulcie, 1981, p. 19.
37 Wilkins, 1928, pp. 244–5.
38 Tindale, 1925, p. 68.
39 McKnight (in press), Chap. 4, my italics.
40 Elkin, 1945.
41 Hart and Pilling, 1960, p. 94.

42 Ibid., pp. 79–80.

43 Ibid., p. 67.

44 Wolf, 1982.

45 Blainey, 1976, p. v.

46 Worsley, 1994.

47 Blainey, 1976, p. 237.

48 Worsley, 1955.

49 Reynolds, 1981, pp. 11–12.

50 Durack, 1967.

51 Searcy, 1909, 1912.

52 Tindale, 1925, p. 131.

53 Long, 1992, pp. 1–8.

54 Turner, David, 1974, pp. 13–14.

55 Ibid.

56 Hart and Pilling, 1960, pp. 102, 107–9.

57 Kaberry, 1939, pp. 115–130.

58 Worsley, 1954a.

59 Turner, David, 1974, p. 94.

60 Waddy, 1988, Vol. 1, pp. 50–51.

61 Turner, David, 1988.

62 Waddy, 1988, Vol. 1, p. 102.

63 Ibid., pp. 101–2.

64 Levitt, Dulcie, 1981, Chap. 9.

65 Ibid.

66 Hazan, 1986.

67 Beeton, 1898.

68 Smith, Delia, 1978, 1979, 1985.

69 Lévi-Strauss, 1970.

70 Worsley, 1967.

71 Mintz, 1986.

72 Goody, 1982, p. 105.

73 Ibid., 216–220.

74 Cunningham, 1980.

75 Martin, 1983.

76 Zukin, 1991, pp. 206–214.

77 Waddy, 1988, Vol. 1, p. 106.

78 Ibid.

79 Ibid., pp. 99–100.

80 Ibid.

81 Sahlins, 1976.

82 Thomson, 1946, p. 167.

83 Waddy, 1988, Vol. 1, p. 71.

84 Ibid., pp. 73, 83.

85 Atran, 1990, p. 5.

86 Waddy, 1988, Vol. 1, p. 89.

87 Ibid.

88 Thomas, Keith, 1983.

89 Dobbs, 1975, p. 196.

90 Ibid., p. xi.

91 Ibid., p. 6.

92 Ibid., p. 197.

93 Ibid., p. 61.

94 Hill, 1964.

95 Hoyles, 1991, p. 236.

96 Mayr, 1969, p. 55.

97 Ibid., pp. 54–8.

98 Ibid., p. 58.

99 Waddy, 1988, Vol. 1, p. 173.

100 Walter, 1984, p. 311.

101 Ibid., pp. 312–14.

102 Ibid., pp. 316–17.

103 Thomas, Keith, 1983, p. 19.

104 Ibid., p. 147.

105 Ibid., p. 109.

106 Douglas, 1966.

107 Thomas, Keith, 1983, p. 191.

108 Ibid., pp. 67, 69.

109 Ibid., p. 17.

110 Ibid., Chap. IV.

111 Ibid., p. 292.

112 Rackham, 1986, p. 147.

113 Thompson, 1975.

114 Hoyles, 1991, pp. 34–42.

115 Ibid., p. 38.

116 Thomas, Keith, 1983, p. 218.

117 Hoyles, 1991, p. 47.

118 Blythe, 1969, pp. 103–5.

119 Thomas, Keith, 1983, Chap. V.

120 Hoyles, 1991, Chap. 4.

121 Brockway, 1979.

122 Thomas, Keith, 1983, p. 66.

123 Hoyles, 1991, pp. 269–71.

124 Ibid., p. 271.

125 Ibid., p. 171

126 Hoskins, 1955, pp. 231–2.

127 Reader's Digest, 1972.

128 Heinzel, Fitter and Parslow, 1972.

129 Ibid., pp. 10–11.

130 Hay and Synge, 1969.

131 Reader's Digest Association, 1978.

132 *Dictionary of American Biography*, 1928, pp. 423–7.

133 Peterson and Peterson, 1981.

134 Saunders, 1975.

135 More and Fitter, 1980.

136 Stokoe, n.d.

137 Capell, 1942, p. 376.

138 Worsley, 1954b.

139 Waddy, 1988, Vol. 1, p. 169.

140 Stokes, 1982.

141 Harris, John, 1982, p. 174.

142 Stokes, 1982, p. 59.

143 Ibid., p. 83.

144 Ibid., p. 103, my italics.

145 Ibid., pp. 120–21.

146 Harris, John, 1982.

147 Sayers, 1982, my exclamation mark.

148 Harris, John, 1982, pp. 169–73.

149 Murphy, 1985, p. 216.

150 Quirk and Greenbaum, 1973.

151 Waddy, 1988, Vol. 1, Table 17.

152 Chatwin, 1989, p. 271.

153 Magnusson, 1960, p. 17.

154 Bosley, 1990.

155 MacKnolty and Wamburranga, 1988, p. 128.

156 Waddy, 1988, Vol. 1, p. 128.

157 Durkheim and Mauss, 1963, p. 82.

158 Turner, David, 1988, p. 470.

159 Anderson, Perry, 1983, p. 43.

160 Lévi-Strauss, 1966, pp. 13–15.

161 Nadel, 1957, Chap. 4.

Chapter 2

1 Howard and Borofsky, 1989, p. 241.

2 Worsley, 1984, Chap. 1.

3 Smith, Bernard, 1960.

4 Worsley, 1964, p. 13.

5 Sahlins, 1985, pp. 10, 12–13, 26.

6 Ibid., p. 51.

7 Lewis, David, 1972, p. 15.

8 Ibid., p. vii.

9 Ibid., map on p. 295.

10 Ibid., pp. 17–18, 20–21.

11 Irwin, 1992, pp. 21–3.

12 Lewis, David, 1972, p. 275.

13 Irwin, 1992, p. 1.

14 Thomas, Stephen, 1987, p. 4.

15 Lewis, David, 1972, p. 253.

16 Ibid., p. 274.

17 Feinberg, 1988, p. 82.

18 Gladwin, 1970.

19 Feinberg, 1988, p. 273.

20 Ibid., p. 89.

21 Gladwin, 1970, p. 113.

22 Firth, 1954, p. 91.

23 Thomas, Stephen, 1987, Appendix 2.

24 Gladwin, 1970, p. 157.
25 Feinberg, 1988, pp. 110–11.
26 Thomas, Stephen, 1987, Appendices 3, 4.
27 Feinberg, 1988, p. 92.
28 Gladwin, 1970, p. 64.
29 Ibid., p. 153.
30 Ibid., p. 144.
31 Ibid., pp. 182–3.
32 Lewis, David, 1972, pp. 84ff.
33 Gladwin, 1970, p. 161.
34 Lewis, David, 1972, p. 87.
35 Ibid., p. 248.
36 Gladwin, 1970, p. 164.
37 Lewis, David, 1972, p. 208.
38 Spate, 1979, p. 115.
39 Stavrianos, 1981, p. 145.
40 Spate, 1983, p. 298, note 1, and Chap. 9.
41 Lewis, David, 1972, p. 93.
42 Gladwin, 1970, p. 131.
43 Lewis, David, 1972, Plate viii and Fig. 31a, pp. 184, 185.
44 Thomas, Stephen, 1987, between pp. 148 and 149.
45 Lewis, David, 1972, pp. 193–205.
46 Ibid., p. 213.
47 Thomas, Stephen, 1987, p. 119.
48 Ibid., Appendix 6.
49 Ibid., p. 88.
50 Gladwin, 1970, p. 202.
51 Nadel, 1957, p. 93.
52 Thomas, Stephen, 1987, pp. 83, 162.
53 Ibid., p. 202.
54 Ibid., p. 132.
55 Ibid., Appendix 9.
56 Ibid., p. 105.
57 Riesenberg and Elbert, 1971, p. 219.
58 Peter Ochs, 'Learning Sea Lore on Puluwat Atoll', cited in Thomas, Stephen, 1987, p. 97.
59 Lewis, David, 1972, pp. 235–6.
60 Alcalay, 1987.
61 Gladwin, 1970, p. 124.
62 Ibid., p. 155.
63 Irwin, 1992, p. 212.
64 Thomas, Stephen, 1987, p. 127.
65 Feinberg, 1988, Chap. 7.
66 Lewis, David, 1972, p. 279.
67 Malinowski, 1915, 1922.
68 Sahlins, 1972, pp. 143–4.
69 Sharp, 1957, pp. 146–7.
70 Updike, 1987, pp. 107–8.
71 Lewis, David, 1972, p. 275.
72 Golson, 1963.
73 Levinson, Ward and Webb, 1973.
74 Lewis, David, 1972, p. 153.
75 Spate, 1979, p. 24.
76 Williamson, 1933.
77 Sahlins, 1985, p. 60.
78 Ibid.
79 Best, 1922, p. 8.
80 Ibid., p. 28.
81 Thomas, Stephen, 1987, p. 168.
82 Shore, 1989.
83 Thomas, Stephen, 1987, p. 162.
84 Ibid., p. 90.
85 Hallpike, 1979.
86 Piaget, 1932.
87 Vygotsky, 1962.
88 Ibid., p. 59.
89 Ibid., p. 76, my italics.

90 Ibid.
91 Gell, 1992, p. 104.
92 Yearley, 1988, p. 43.
93 Kuhn, 1962.
93 Atran, 1990, pp. 265–8.
95 Garfinkel, 1967.
96 Ibid., p. 24.
97 Ibid.
98 Thompson, 1967.
99 Spencer, 1897, p. 180.

100 Gell, 1992, p. 107.
101 Ibid., pp. 108–9.
102 Hallpike, 1979, p. 33.
103 Vygotsky, 1962, p. 75.
104 Hallpike, 1979, p. 59, my italics.
105 Ibid., p. 24.
106 Ibid., p. 35, my italics.
107 Ibid., p. 206.
108 Ibid., p. 279.

Chapter 3

1 Helman, 1990, p. 65.
2 Lomnitz, 1981, p. 49.
3 Ibañez-Novión, et al., 1978.
4 Pelling, 1978a.
5 Janzen, 1978.
6 Ibid., p. 52.
7 Ibid., p. 28.
8 Ibid., p. 44.
9 Lewis, Gilbert, 1979, p. 132.
10 Evans-Pritchard, 1937.
11 Ibid., p. 367.
12 Festinger, Riecken and Schachter, 1956.
13 Janzen, 1978, p. 136.
14 Ibid., pp. 206–7.
15 Freidson, 1970, pp. 293–4.
16 Janzen, 1978, p. 115.
17 Desmond and Moore, 1991, p. 324.
18 Porter, 1989, p. 24.
19 Pelling, 1978b, pp. 30–32.
20 Loudon, 1987, p. 109, Table 6.1.
21 Stacey, 1988, pp. 43–8.
22 Griggs, 1981, p. 89.
23 Holloway, 1987, p. 155.
24 Foster, 1978.
25 López Austín, 1967.
26 Arber, 1986, p. 52.

27 Webster, 1982, pp. 47–50.
28 Arber, 1986, p. 250.
29 Griggs, 1981, p. 160.
30 Ibid., p. 160.
31 Porter, 1989, pp. 1, 11.
32 Ibid., p. 46.
33 Ibid., pp. 66ff.
34 Griggs, 1981, pp. 127–31.
35 Holloway, 1987, pp. 142–7.
36 Shryock, 1936, p. 76.
37 Porter, 1989, pp. 27, 31.
38 Parry and Parry, 1976, p. 139.
39 Ibid.
40 Ibid., pp. 140ff.
41 Pelling, 1978a.
42 Loudon, 1987, p. 122.
43 Parry and Parry, 1976, p. 104.
44 Helman, 1990, p. 61.
45 Parssinen, 1979, p. 112.
46 Saks, 1992, p. 5.
47 Stacey, 1988, p. 102.
48 Parry and Parry, 1976, p. 130.
49 Larkin, 1983, p. 192.
50 Stacey, 1988, p. 131.
51 Larkin, 1983, p. 19.
52 Stacey, 1988, p. 237.

53 Ibid.
54 Larkin, 1980, pp. 225–7.
55 Larkin, 1983, p. 21.
56 Ibid., Chap. 5.
57 Ibid., p. 188.
58 Larkin, 1992.
59 Larkin, 1983, p. 184, my italics.
60 Parry and Parry, 1976, pp. 197–9.
61 Ibid., p. 208.
62 Desmond and Moore, 1991, Chap. 44.
63 Parssinen, 1979, p. 68.
64 Inglis, 1992, p. 124.
65 McKeown, 1971.
66 Wadsworth et al., 1971; Levitt, Ruth, 1976, p. 95.
67 Helman, 1990, pp. 45, 63.
68 Ibid., p. 91.
69 Dunnell and Cartwright, 1972; Jefferys et al., 1960; Stacey, 1988, pp. 142, 177–9.
70 Helman, 1990, p. 55.
71 Zborowski, 1982.
72 Zola, 1966.
73 Helman, 1978, pp. 103–4.
74 Ibid., pp. 107–8, my italics.
75 Ibid., pp. 130–31.
76 Payer, 1988.
77 Ibid., pp. 86–7.
78 Ibid., p. 37.
79 Ramsey, 1987, pp. 80–81.
80 Payer, 1988, p. 61.
81 Ibid., pp. 66, 118.
82 Lipset, 1960.
83 Griggs, 1981, Chap. 12.
84 Payer, 1988, p. 128.
85 Ibid., p. 139.
86 Lasch, 1980.
87 Payer, 1988, p. 122.
88 Griggs, 1981, Chap. 16.
89 Vogel, 1970.
90 Weatherford, 1988, p. 192.
91 Griggs, 1981, p. 164.
92 Ibid., p. 175.
93 Warner, John, 1987, p. 253.
94 Griggs, 1981, p. 175.
95 Janzen, 1978, p. 192.
96 Illich, 1977.
97 Leslie, 1976, p. 370.
98 Wallis and Morley, 1976, p. 10.
99 Press, 1971, p. 161.
100 Taussig, 1980.
101 Werbner, 1977; Romano, 1965.
102 López Austín, 1967.
103 Holland, 1963, p. 202.
104 Igun, 1977.
105 Taylor, 1976, p. 290.
106 Jaspan, 1976.
107 Prins, 1979.
108 Lewis, Gilbert, 1979.
109 Obeyesekere, 1976.
110 Beals, 1976, p. 188.
111 McKnight, 1981.
112 Friedrich, 1971.
113 Horton, 1967.
114 Foster and Anderson, 1978, pp. 775–6.
115 Holland, 1963.
116 Taylor, 1976, p. 5.
117 Jaspan, 1969, pp. 29–30.
118 Janzen, 1978, p. 161, Plates 24, 25.
119 Press, 1971.
120 Holland, 1963, p. 217.
121 Taylor, 1967, p. 287.
122 Beals, 1976, p. 197.
123 Otsuka, 1976, p. 335.

124 Unschuld, 1976, pp. 300–321.
125 Ibid., pp. 304, 314.
126 Basham, 1976, p. 27.
127 Beals, 1976, p. 191.
128 Freidson, 1970, p. 7.
129 Prins, 1979, p. 287.
130 Holland, 1963.
131 Lambo, 1962.
132 Feierman, 1979, p. 277.
133 *Development Dialogue*, 1995.
134 Chapin and Wasserman, 1981.
135 Cajka, 1978.
136 Lewis, Gilbert, 1979, pp. 118, 115.
137 Beals, 1976, p. 192.
138 Mackie, 1994, p. 10.
139 Allen, Tim, 1992.
140 Helman, 1990, pp. 39–40.
141 Haslemere Group, 1976, p. 6; for a study of one country, Mexico, see de María y Campos, 1977.
142 Brass, 1972.
143 Revolutionary Health Committee of Hunan Province, 1978.

144 Haslemere Group, 1976.
145 Taylor, 1967, p. 289.
146 Foster and Anderson, 1978, p. 262.
147 Goffman, 1961.
148 Roth, 1963.
149 Stacey, 1988, p. 158.
150 West, 1995, p. 206.
151 Fulder, 1992, p. 168, Table 13.1.
152 *Independent*, London, 2 June 1993.
153 *Times*, London, 29 November 1994.
154 West, 1992, p. 202.
155 Fulder 1992, p. 170.
156 Foucault, 1977.
157 Goffman, 1961.
158 Rollin, 1990, p. 109.
159 Ibid., pp. 109–10.
160 Ibid., p. 111.
161 Helman, 1990, p. 167.
162 Foster and Anderson, 1978, p. 93.
163 Sen, 1994.
164 Wartovsky, 1976, 1978.
165 Kramer, 1993.

Chapter 4

1 Griaule and Dieterlen, 1954, 1965.
2 Griaule, 1965, p. xvi.
3 Ibid., p. 52.
4 Griaule and Dieterlen, 1965, p. 230.
5 Griaule and Dieterlen, 1954, pp. 94–5.
6 Dieterlen, 1952.
7 Ibid.; Griaule, 1952.
8 Bosley, 1990, p. xxv.

9 Berndt, 1952, p. xxi.
10 Berndt, 1951.
11 Lawson and McCauley, 1990, p. 155.
12 Mimica, 1988.
13 Srinivas, 1952.
14 Wolf, 1982, pp. 46–7.
15 Brown, in Rigaldi, 1964, p. xxii.
16 Le Roy Ladurie, 1980.
17 Hussey, 1967, p. 136.

18 Gorer, 1955, pp. 252–3.

19 Berger, 1961.

20 Hays, quoted in Waddy, 1988, Vol. 1, p. 224.

21 Gramsci, 1957, p. 121.

22 Wagner, 1940, p. 204.

23 Griaule, 1965, pp. 14–15, 63–4.

24 Ibid., p. 217.

25 Thomas, Stephen, 1987, p. 126.

26 Ibid., p. 163.

27 Ibid., p. 190.

28 Ibid., p. 92.

29 Ibid., pp. 172, 177.

30 Turner, V. W., 1967, p. 187.

31 Turner, V. W., 1957.

32 Mouffe, 1979, p. 187.

33 Atran, 1990, p. 269.

34 Urry, 1991.

35 Cirese, 1982, p. 243.

36 Mouffe, 1979, pp. 194, 197.

37 Sassoon, 1980.

38 Worsley, 1984, pp. 244ff.

39 Horne, 1984, p. 181.

40 Moloney, 1978.

41 Stolcke, 1995.

42 Smith, Anthony, 1994, p. 707.

43 Kohn, 1944.

44 Gellner, 1983.

45 Nairn, 1977.

46 Anderson, Benedict, 1983.

47 Worsley, 1984, p. 258.

48 McLuhan, 1965.

49 Anderson, Benedict, 1983, p. 39.

50 Horne, 1984, p. 181.

51 Anderson, Benedict, 1983, p. 26.

52 Ibid., p. 27.

53 Worsley, 1984, pp. 256–8.

54 Gilbert, 1994, p. 4.

55 Ibid., p. 277, fn. 1.

56 Oberg, 1940; Maquet, 1961.

57 Anderson, Benedict, 1983, p. 80.

58 Cannadine, 1983, p. 103.

59 Ibid., p. 102.

60 Ibid., p. 109.

61 Ibid., p. 116.

62 Cohn, 1983, p. 166.

63 Ibid., p. 184.

64 Ibid., p. 200.

65 Morgan, 1983, p. 100.

66 Horne, 1984, p. 30.

67 Ibid., p. 203.

68 Gellner, 1983, p. 59.

69 Horne, 1984, p. 136.

70 Ibid., p. 111.

71 Trevor-Roper, 1983, p. 15.

72 Ibid., p. 19.

73 Ibid., p. 24.

74 Ibid., p. 41.

75 Morgan, 1983.

76 Ibid., p. 66.

77 Cohen, Bronwen, 1983.

78 Ibid., Appendix.

79 Butler and Kavanagh, 1992, pp. 131, 280.

80 Kapferer, 1988, Chap. 5.

81 Handelman, 1990.

82 Handelman and Shamgar-Handelman, 1990.

83 Cohen, Anthony, 1994, pp. 164–5.

84 Warner, W. L., 1959, p. 273.

85 Siskind, 1992, pp. 167–8.

86 Trachtenberg, 1986, p. 8.

87 Hobsbawm, 1983, pp. 174–5.

88 Trachtenberg, 1986, p. 98.

89 Allen, Leslie, 1985, p. 33.

90 Ibid., pp. 35–6.

91 Juliani, 1974, p. 1.

92 Searle-Chatterjee, 1993, p. 187.

93 Restad, 1995, p. 65.

94 Belk, 1993, p. 77.

95 Miller, 1993, p. 137.

96 Restad, 1995, p. 7.

97 Lévi-Strauss, 1993.

98 Restad, 1995, p. 20.

99 Ibid., p. 26.

100 Belk, 1993, p. 81.

101 Restad, 1995, p. 111.

102 Ibid., p. 115.

103 Ibid., p. 72.

104 Carrier, 1993, p. 63.

105 Löffgren, 1993, p. 219.

106 Searle-Chatterjee, 1993, p. 183.

107 Miller, 1993.

108 Kuper, 1993, p. 157.

109 Searle-Chatterjee, 1993, pp. 183–4.

110 Moeran and Skov, 1993, p. 105.

111 Ibid., p. 112.

112 Löffgren, 1993, p. 223.

113 Zukin, 1991, p. 222.

114 Cooke, 1993.

115 Bryman, 1995.

116 Schickel, 1968, pp. 115–17.

117 Wallace, 1985, p. 51.

118 Real, 1977.

119 Dorfman and Mattelart, 1972.

120 Schmucler, ibid.

121 Bryman, 1995, p. 51.

122 de Cordova, 1994.

123 Romney, 1996, p. 6.

124 Harmetz, 1985.

125 Bryman, 1995, p. 64.

126 Real, 1977, p. 52.

127 Bryman, 1995, p. 85.

128 Johnson, 1981, p. 161.

129 Pilger, 1992, p. 300.

130 Wallace, 1985, pp. 56–7.

131 Pilger, 1992, p. 300.

132 Francaviglia, 1981, p. 144.

133 King, 1981.

134 Quoted in Zukin, 1991, p. 224.

135 Fjellman, 1992.

136 Showalter, 1996.

137 Zukin, 1991, p. 231.

138 Bryman, 1995, p. 64.

139 Ibid., p. 155.

140 Venturi et al., 1977.

141 Bryman, 1995, pp. 175ff.

142 Hall, 1980; Bryman, 1995, pp. 185–6.

Chapter 5

1 Zangwill, 1925.

2 Thrasher, 1927.

3 Whyte, 1943.

4 New York Times Magazine, 1985.

5 Roszak, 1970.

6 Wertheim, 1974.

7 Alexander and Seidman, 1990.

8 Parsons, 1951.

9 Bauman, 1973.

10 Archer, 1988.

11 Tenbruck, 1989, p. 21.

12 Kerr et al., 1962.

13 Lipset, 1969, p. 406.

14 Bell, 1962.

15 Toffler, 1981.

16 Fukuyama, 1992.

17 Archer, 1990, p. 117.

18 Worsley, 1984, pp. 42–43.

19 Archer, 1988, p. 2.

20 Jackson, 1989, Chap. 1.

21 Lowie, 1937; Trindell, 1969.

22 Radcliffe-Brown, 1956.

23 Kroeber and Kluckhohn, 1952, p. 357.

24 Parsons, 1951, p. 357.

25 Gunawardana, 1979.

26 Fuller, 1984.

27 Seneviratne, 1978.

28 Williams, 1962, 1982.

29 Harris, Nigel, 1986.

30 Henderson, 1989.

31 Worsley, 1968, Chap. 1.

32 McLuhan, 1965, p. 81.

33 Sklair, 1991.

34 Ritzer, 1993.

35 Watson, forthcoming.

36 Yashimoto, 1994.

37 Peires, 1989.

38 Wanek, 1993.

39 Osman, 1989.

40 Zubaida, 1989, Chap. 1.

41 Vickers, 1989, pp. 150–55, 164–7.

42 Fuller, 1984.

43 Seneviratne, 1978.

44 Weber, 1947, pp. 25off.

45 Steele, 1994.

References

Alcalay, Glenn. 'Pax atomica: US nuclear imperialism in Micronesia', in Peter Worsley and Kofi Buenor Hadjor (eds.), *On The Brink: Nuclear Proliferation and the Third World*, Third World Communications, London, 1987, pp. 107–21.

Alexander, Jeffrey C., and Steven Seidman (eds.). *Culture and Society: Contemporary Debates*, Cambridge University Press, Cambridge, 1990.

Allen, Leslie. *Liberty: The Statue of the American Dream*, The Statue of Liberty-Ellis Island Foundation, New York, 1985.

Allen, Tim. 'Upheaval, affliction, and health: a Ugandan case study', in Henry Bernstein, Ben Crow and Hazel Johnson (eds.), *Rural Livelihoods: Crises and Responses*, Open University/Oxford University Press, Oxford, 1992, pp. 217–48.

Anderson, Benedict. *Imagined Communities: Reflections on the Origin and Spread of Nationalism*, Verso, London, 1983.

Anderson, Perry. *In the Tracks of Historical Materialism*, Verso, London, 1983.

Arber, Agnes. *Herbals: Their Origin and Evolution – A Chapter in the History of Botany, 1470–1670*, Cambridge University Press, Cambridge, 1986.

Archer, Margaret. *Culture and Agency: The Place of Culture in Social Theory*, Cambridge University Press, Cambridge, 1988.
— 'Theory, culture and post-industrial society', in *Global Culture*, special issue of *Theory, Culture and Society*, Vol. 7, Nos. 2–3, June 1990, pp. 97–119.

Atran, Scott, *Cognitive Foundations of Natural History*, Cambridge University Press, Cambridge, 1990.

Baker, Richard Munro. 'Land is life: continuity through change for the Yanyuwa of the Northern Territory of Australia', Ph.D. thesis, University of Adelaide, 1989.

Basham, A. L. 'The practice of medicine in ancient and medieval India', in Charles M. Leslie (ed.), *Asian Medical Systems: A Comparative Study*, University of California Press, Berkeley, 1976, pp. 18–43.

Bauman, Zygmunt. *Cultare as Praxis*, Routledge and Kegan Paul, London, 1973.

Beals, A. R. 'Strategies of resort to curers', in Charles M. Leslie (ed.), *Asian Medical Systems: A Comparative Study*, University of California Press, Berkeley, 1976, pp. 184–200.

Beattie, John. *Other Cultures*, Cohen and West, London 1964.

Beeton, Isabella. *The Book of Household Management*, Ward, Lock, London 1898.

Belk, Russell W. 'Materialism and the making of the modern American Christmas', in Daniel Miller (ed.), *Unwrapping Christmas*, Clarendon Press, Oxford, 1993, pp. 75–104.

Bell, Daniel. *The End of Ideology*, Collier, New York, 1962.

Berger, Peter. *The Sacred Canopy*, Doubleday, New York, 1961.

Berger, Peter, and Thomas Luckmann, *The Social Construction of Reality: Everything That Passes for Knowledge in Society*, Doubleday, New York, 1967.

Berndt, Ronald M. *Kunapipi*, Cheshire, Melbourne, 1951.
— *Djanggawul: An Aboriginal Cult of North-east Arnhem Land*, Routledge and Kegan Paul, London 1952.

Best, Elsdon. *The Astronomical Knowledge of the Maori: Genuine and Empirical*, Dominion Museum Monograph N. 3, Government Printer, Wellington, New Zealand, 1922 (new edition 1986).

Blainey, Geoffrey. *The Triumph of the Nomads*, Macmillan, London, 1976.

Blythe, Ronald. *Akenfield: Portrait of an English Village*, Allen Lane/Penguin Books, Harmondsworth, 1969.

Bosley, Keith (trans. and ed.). *The Kalevala*, Oxford University Press, Oxford, 1990.

Brass, P. R. 'The politics of Ayurvedic education in a case study of revivalism and modernization in India', in S. H. and I. L. Rudolph (eds.), *Education and Politics in India*, Harvard University Press, Cambridge, Mass., 1972, pp. 342–459.

Brockway, Lucile H. *Science and Colonial Expansion: The Role of the British Royal Botanic Gardens*, Academic Press, New York, 1979.

Bryman, Alan. *Disney and His Worlds*, Routledge, London, 1995.

Butler, David, and Dennis Kavanagh. *The British General Election of 1992*, Macmillan, London 1992.

Cajka, Frank. 'Peasant Commercialization in the Serranos of Cochabamba, Bolivia', Ph.D. thesis, University of Michigan, 1978.

Cannadine, David. 'The context, performance and meaning of ritual: the British Monarchy and the "invention of tradition"', in Eric Hobsbawm and Terence Ranger (eds.), *The Invention of Tradition*, Cambridge University Press, Cambridge, 1983, pp. 101–64.

Capell, A. 'Languages of Arnhem Land, North Australia', *Oceania*, Vol. XII, No. 4, 1942, pp. 364–92.

Carrier, James. 'The rituals of Christmas giving', in Daniel Miller (ed.), *Unwrapping Christmas*, Clarendon Press, Oxford, 1993, pp. 55–74.

Chapin, G., and R. Wasserman. 'Agricultural production and malaria resurgence in Central America and India', *Nature*, Vol. 293, 17 September 1981, pp. 181–5.

Chatwin, Bruce. *What Am I doing Here?*, Jonathan Cape, London, 1989.

Cirese, Alberto Maria. 'Gramsci's observations on folklore', in Anne Showstack Sassoon (ed.), *Approaches to Gramsci*, Writers and Readers, London, 1982, pp. 212–47.

Cohen, Anthony P. *Self Consciousness: An Alternative Anthropology of Identity*,

Routledge, London, 1994.

Cohen, Bronwen. 'Norse Imagery in Shetland: an historical study of intellectuals and their use of the past in the construction of Shetland's identity, with particular reference to the period 1800–1914', Ph.D. thesis, University of Manchester, 1983.

Cohn, Bernard S. 'Representing authority in Victorian India', in Eric Hobsbawm and Terence Ranger (eds.), *The Invention of Tradition*, Cambridge University Press, Cambridge, 1983, pp. 165–209.

Cooke, Alistair. 'Disney: a folk hero's farewell', *Guardian*, 16 December 1993.

Cunningham, Marion, with Jeri Larber (eds.), *The Fannie Farmer Cookbook*, Knopf, New York, 1980 (originally published 1896).

de Cordova, Richard. 'The Mickey in Macy's windows', in Eric Smoodin (ed.), *Disney Discourses: Producing the Magic Kingdom*, Routledge, London, 1994, pp. 203–14.

de María y Campos, M. 'La industria farmaceutica en México', *Comercio Externo*, 27, 1977, pp. 288–912.

Desmond, Adrian, and James Moore. *Darwin*, Michael Joseph, London 1991.

Development Dialogue: A Strategy Paper and Six Country Stories, Dag Hammerskjold Foundation, Uppsala, 1995, No. 1.

Dictionary of American Biography, Vol. I, American Council of Learned Societies, Scribner, New York, 1928.

Dieterlen, Germaine. 'Classification des végétaux chez les Dogon', *Journal de la Société des Africanistes*, Vol. XXII, 1952, pp. 115–58.

Dobbs, Betty Jo Teeter. *The Foundations of Newton's Alchemy, or 'The Hunting of the Greene Lyon'*, Cambridge University Press, Cambridge, 1975.

Dorfman, Ariel, and Armand Mattelart. *How to Read Donald Duck: Imperialist Ideology in the Disney Comic*, International General, New

York, 1975. The Spanish-language original, *Para Leer al Pato Donald* (Siglo XXI, Mexico City, 1972), contains Hector Schmucler's account ('*Donald y la política*') of the attempt by the Disney Corporation to prevent circulation of the Dorfman-Mattelart book in the USA).

Douglas, Mary. *Purity and Danger: An Analysis of the Concepts of Pollution and Taboo*, Routledge, London, 1966.

Dunnell, K., and A. Cartwright. *Medicine Takers, Prescribers and Hoarders*, Routledge and Kegan Paul, London, 1972.

Durack, Mary. *Kings in Grass Castles*, Corgi Books, London, 1967.

Durkheim, Emile. *The Elementary Forms of the Religious Life*, Allen and Unwin, London, 1954 (originally published 1912).

Durkheim, Emile, and Marcel Mauss. *Primitive Classification*, Cohen and West, London, 1963 (originally published 1903).

Elkin, A. P. *Aboriginal Men of High Degree*, Australasian Publishing Company, Sydney, 1945.

Engels, Friedrich. *The Origin of the Family, Private Property and the State*, Foreign Languages Publishing House, Moscow, 1948 (originally published 1884).

Evans-Pritchard, E. E. *Witchcraft, Oracles and Magic among the Azande of the Anglo-Egyptian Sudan*, Clarendon Press, Oxford, 1937.

Feinberg, Richard. *Polynesian Seafaring and Navigation: Ocean Travel and Navigation in Anutan Culture and Society*, Kent State University Press, Kent, Ohio, 1988.

Feierman, S. 'Change in African therapeutic systems', *Social Science and Medicine*, B, 13, 1979, pp. 277–84.

Festinger, Leon, Henry W. Riecken and Stanley Schachter. *When Prophecy Fails: A Social and Psychological Study of a Modern Group That Predicted the Destruction of the World*, Harper, New York, 1956.

Firth, R. 'Anuta and Tikopia: symbiotic elements in social organization',

Journal of the Polynesian Society, Vol. 63, No. 2, 1954, pp. 87–131.

Fitter, Richard, Alastair Fitter and Marjorie Blamey. *The Wild Flowers of Britain and Northern Europe,* Collins, London 1974.

Fjellman, Stephen M. *Vinyl Leaves: Walt Disney World and America*, Westview Press, Boulder, Colorado, 1992.

Foster, G. M. 'Humoral pathology in Spain and Spanish America', in *Homenaje a Julio Baroja,* Centro de Investigaciones Sociológicos, Madrid, 1978, pp. 357–70.

Foster, G. M., and B. G. Anderson. *Medical Anthropology*, Wiley, New York, 1978.

Foucault, Michel. *Discipline and Punish: the Birth of the Prison*, Allen Lane/Penguin Books, Harmondsworth, 1977.

Francaviglia, Rchard V. 'Main Street U.S.A.: a comparison/contrast of streetscapes in Disneyland and Walt Disney World', *Journal of Popular Culture*, Vol. 15, No. 1, 1981, pp. 141–56.

Freidson, Eliot. *The Profession of Medicine: A Study of the Sociology of Applied Knowlege,* Harper and Row, New York, 1970.

Friedl, Ernestine. *Women and Man: An Anthropologist's View*, Holt, Rinehart and Winston, New York, 1975.

Friedrich, Paul. *La Calavera*, Biblioteca Era, Mexico City, 1971.

Fukuyama, Francis F. *The End of History and the Last Man*, Hamish Hamilton, London, 1992.

Fulder, Stephen. 'Alternative therapists in Britain', in Mike Saks (ed.), *Alternative Medicine in Britain*, Clarendon Press, Oxford, 1992, pp. 166–82.

Fuller, C. J. *Servants of the Goddess: The Priests of a South Indian Temple*, Cambridge University Press, Cambridge, 1984.

Garfinkel, Harold. 'The rational properties of science and commonsense activities', in *Studies in Ethnomethodology*, Prentice-Hall, Englewood Cliffs, New Jersey, 1967, pp. 262–83.

Gell, Alfred. *The Anthropology of Time: Cultural Constructions of Temporal Maps and Images*, Berg, Oxford, 1992.

Gellner, Ernest. *Nationals and Nationalism*, Blackwell, Oxford, 1983.

Gilbert, Martin. *First World War*, Weidenfeld, London, 1994.

Gladwin, Thomas. *East is a Big Bird: Navigation and Logic on Puluwat Atoll*, Harvard University Press, Cambridge, Mass., 1970.

Goffman, Erving. *Asylums: Essays on the Social Situation of Mental Patients and Other Inmates*, Anchor, Garden City, New York, 1961.

Golson, Jack (ed.). *Polynesian Navigation*, Polynesian Society, Wellington, Memoir 34, 1963.

Goody, Jack. *Cooking, Cuisine and Class: A Study in Comparative Sociology*, Cambridge University Press, Cambridge, 1982.

Gorer, Geoffrey. *Exploring English Character*, Cresset Press, London 1955.

Gramsci, Antonio. *The Modern Prince and Other Writings*, Lawrence and Wishart, London, 1957.

Griaule, Marcel. 'Classification des insectes chez les Dogon', *Journal de la Société des Africanistes*, Vol. XXII, 1952, pp 7–71.
— *Conversations with Ogotemmêli: An Introduction to Dogon Religious Ideas*, Oxford University Press, Oxford, 1965.

Griaule, Marcel, and Germaine Dieterlen. 'The Dogon of the French Sudan', in Daryll Forde (ed.), *African Worlds: Studies in the Cosmological Ideas and Social Values of African Peoples*, Oxford University Press, Oxford, 1954, pp. 83–110.
— *Le Renard Pâle*, Vol. 1, *Le Mythe Cosmogonique*, Fascicule 1: *La Création du Monde*, Institut d'Ethnologie, Paris, 1965.

Griggs, Barbara, *Green Pharmacy: A History of Herbal Medicine*, Jill Norman and Hobhouse, London 1981.

Gunawardana, R. A. L. H. *Robe and Pough: Monasticism and Economic Interest in Early Medieval Sri Lanka*, Monograph No. XXXV, Association for Asian Studies, University of Arizona Press, Tucson, 1979.

Hall, Stuart. '"Encoding"/"Decoding"', in S. Hall, D. Hobson, A. Lowe and P. Willis (eds.), *Culture, Media, Language*, Hutchinson, London 1980.

Hallpike, C. R. *The Foundations of Primitive Thought*, Clarendon Press, Oxford, 1979.

Handelman, Don. 'State ceremonies of Israel – Remembrance Day and Independence Day', in Don Handelman, *Models and Mirrors: Towards an Anthropology of Public Events*, Cambridge University Press, Cambridge, 1990, pp. 190–233.

Handelman, Don and Lea Shamgar-Handelman, 'Shaping time – the choice of the national emblem of Israel', in Emiko Ohnuki-Tierney (ed.), *Culture Through Time: Anthropological approaches*, Stanford University Press, Stanford, California, 1990, pp. 193–226.

Hargrave, S. (ed.). *Language and Culture: Work Papers of the SIL-AAB*, Series B, Vol. 8, Summer Institute of Linguistics, Australian Aboriginal Branch, Darwin, 1982.

Harmetz, Aljean. 'The man re-animating Disney', *New York Times Magazine*, 29 December 1985.

Harney, W. E. *North of 23°: Ramblings in North Australia*, Sydney, n.d.

Harris, John. 'Facts and fallacies of Aboriginal number systems', in S. Hargrave (ed.), *Language and Culture: Work papers in the SIL-AAB*, Series B, Vol. 8, Summer Institute of Linguistics, Australian Aboriginal Branch, Darwin, 1982, pp. 153–81.

Harris, Nigel. *The End of the Third World: Newly Industrializing Countries and the Decline of an Ideology*, Penguin Books, Harmondsworth, 1986.

Hart, C. W. M., and Arnold Pilling, *The Tiwi of Northern Australia*, Holt, Rinehart and Wilson, New York, 1960.

Haslemere Group. *Who Needs the Drug Companies?*, War on Want and Third World First, London 1976.

Hay, Roy, and Patrick M. Synge. *The Dictionary of Garden Plants*, Ebury Press/Michael Joseph, London 1969.

Hazan, Marcella. *Marcella's Kitchen*, Macmillan, London 1986.

Heinzel, Herman, Richard Fitter and John Parslow. *The Birds of Britain and Europe*, Collins, London 1972.

Helman, Cecil G. 'Feed a cold, starve a fever: folk models of infection in an English suburban community, and their relation to medical treatment', *Culture, Medicine and Psychiatry*, 2, 1978, pp. 107–37.
— *Culture, Health and Illness: An Introduction for Health Professionals*, John Wright, London, 1990.

Henderson, Jeffrey. *The Globalization of High Technology: Society, Space, and Semiconductors in the Restructuring of the Modern World*, Routledge, London, 1989.

Herbert, Xavier. *Capricornia*, Angus and Robertson, North Ryde, New South Wales, 1938.

Heyerdahl, Thor. *American Indians in the Pacific*, Rand McNally, Chicago, 1952.

Hill, Christopher. 'William Harvey and the Idea of the Monarchy', *Past and Present*, No. 27, April 1964, pp. 54–72.

Hobsbawm, Eric. 'Mass-producing traditions: Europe 1870–1914', in Eric Hobsbawm and Terence Ranger (eds.), *The Invention of Tradition*, Cambridge University Press, Cambridge, 1983, pp. 263–307.

Hobsbawm, Eric, and Terence Ranger (eds.). *The Invention of Tradition*, Cambridge University Press, Cambridge, 1983.

Holland, W. R. *Medicina Maya en los Altos de Chiapas*, Instituto Nacional Indigenista, Mexico City, 1963.

Holloway, S. W. F. 'The orthodox fringe: the origins of the

Pharmaceutical Society of Great Britain', in W. F. Bynum and Roy Porter (eds.), *Medical Fringe and Medical Orthodoxy, 1750–1850*, Croom Helm, London, 1987, pp. 129–57.

Horne, Donald. *The Great Museum:The Re-presentation of History*, Pluto Press, London, 1984.

Horton, Robin. 'African traditional thought and Western science', *Africa*, 37, 1967, pp. 50–71, 155–87.

Hoskins, W. G. *The Making of the English Landscape*, Hodder and Stoughton, London, 1955.

Howard, Alan, and Robert Borofsky (eds.). *Developments in Polynesian Ethnology*, University of Hawaii Press, Honolulu, 1989.

Hoyles, Martin. *The Story of Gardening*, Journeyman Press, London, 1991.

Hussey, Maurice. *Chaucer's World:A Pictorial Companion*, Cambridge University Press, Cambridge, 1967.

Ibañez-Novión, Martin Alberto, Olga C. Lopez de Ibañez-Novión and Ordep José Trinidade Serra, *O Anatomista Popular: Um Estudo de Caso*, Faculty of Social Sciences, Universty of Brasilia, 1978.

Igun, U. A. 'Health-seeking behaviour: a case-study among the Urhobo of Bendel State, Nigeria', Ph.D. thesis, University of Manchester, 1977.

Inglis, Brian. 'Unorthodox medicine after the establishment of the National Health Service', in Mike Saks (ed.), *Alternative Medicine in Britian*, Clarendon Press, Oxford, 1992, pp. 124–34.

Irwin, Geoffrey. 'Against, across, and down the wind: a case for the systematic exploration of the remote Pacific islands', *Journal of the Polynesian Society*, Vol. 98, 1989, pp. 167–206.
—— *The Prehistoric Exploration and Colonisation of the Pacific*, Cambridge University Press, Cambridge, 1992.

Jackson, Peter. *Maps of Meaning*, Unwin Hyman, London, 1989.

Janzen, John M. *The Quest for Therapy: Medical Pluralism in Lower Zaïre*, University of California Press, Berkeley, 1978.

Jaspan, M. A. 'Traditional medical Theory in South-East Asia', inaugural lecture, University of Hull, 1969.
— 'The social organization of indigenous and modern medical practices in southwest Sumatra', in Charles M. Leslie (ed.), *Asian Medical Systems: A Comparative Study*, University of California Press, Berkeley, 1976, pp. 227–42.

Jefferys, M., J. H. F. Brotherston and A. Cartwright. 'Consumption of medicine on a working-class housing estate', *British Journal of Preventive and Social Medicine*, 14, 1960, pp. 64–76.

Johnson, David M. 'Disney World as structure and symbol: re-creation of the American experience', *Journal of Popular Culture*, Vol. 15, No. 1, 1981, pp. 157–65.

Juliani, Richard N. *Immigration and Ethnicity in North America*, Balch Institute Historical Reading List, No. 1, Philadelphia, 1974.

Kaberry, P. M. *Aboriginal Woman: Sacred and Profane*, Routledge, Sydney, 1939.

Kapferer, Bruce. *Legends of People, Myths of the State: Violence, Intolerance, and Political Culture in Sri Lanka and Australia*, Smithsonian Institution Press, Washington, 1988.

Kerr, Clark, et al. *Industrialism and Industrial Man*, Heinemann, London, 1962.

King, Margaret. 'Disneyland and Walt Disney world: traditional values in futuristic form', *Journal of Popular Culture*, Vol. 15, No. 1, 1981, pp. 157–65.

Koestler, Arthur. *The Sleepwalkers: A History of Man's Changing View of the Universe*, Hutchinson, London, 1968.

Kohn, Hans. 'Nationalism', in D. L. Sills (ed.), *International Encyclopaedia of the Social Sciences*, Vol. 11, Macmillan, New York, p. 63.

Kramer, Peter D. *Listening to Prozac*, Fourth Estate, London 1993.

Kroeber, A. L. and C. Kluckhohn. 'Culture: a critical review of concepts and definitions', Papers of the Peabody Museum of American Archaeology and Ethnology, No. 47, Harvard University, Cambridge, Mass., 1952.

Kuhn, Thomas S. *The Structure of Scientific Revolutions*, University of Chicago Press, Chicago, 1962.

Kuper, Adam. 'The English Christmas and the family: time out and alternative realities', in Daniel Miller (ed.), *Unwrapping Christmas*, Clarendon Press, Oxford, 1993, pp. 157–75.

Lambo, T. A. 'Patterns of psychiatric care in developing countries', in A. Kiev (ed.), *Magic, Faith and Healing: Studies in Primitive Psychiatry Today*, Free Press, New York, 1962, pp. 443–53.

Larkin, Gerald. 'Professionalism, dentistry and public health', *Social Science and Medicine*, 14A, 1980, pp. 223–9.
— *Occupational Monopoly and Modern Medicine*, Tavistock, London 1983.
— 'Orthodox and osteopathic medicine in the inter-War years', in Mike Saks (ed.), *Alternative Medicine in Britain*, Clarendon Press, Oxford, 1992, pp. 112–23.

Lasch, Christopher. *The Culture of Narcissism: American Life in an Age of Diminishing Expectations*, Abacus, Sphere Books, London, 1980.

Lawson, Thomas and Robert N. McCauley. *Rethinking Religion: Connecting Cognition and Culture*, Cambridge University Press, Cambridge, 1990.

Le Roy Ladurie, Emmanuel. *Montaillou: Cathars and Catholics in a French village, 1294–1324*, Penguin Books, Harmondsworth, 1980.

Leslie, Charles M. (ed.). *Asian Medical Systems: A Comparative Study*, University of California Press, Berkeley, 1976.

Lévi-Strauss, Claude. *The Savage Mind*, Weidenfeld and Nicolson, London, 1966.
— *Totemism*, Pelican Books, Harmondsworth, 1969.
— *The Raw and the Cooked*, Jonathan Cape, London 1970.

— 'Father Christmas Executed', in Daniel Miller (ed.), *Unwrapping Christmas*, Clarendon Press, Oxford, 1993, pp. 38–51.

Levinson, Michael, R. G. Ward and J. W. Webb. *The Settlement of Polynesia: A Computer Simulation*, University of Minnesota Press, Minneapolis, 1973.

Levitt, Dulcie. *Plants and People: Aboriginal Uses of Plants on Groote Eylandt*, Australian Institute of Aboriginal Studies, Canberra, 1981.

Levitt, Ruth. *The Reorganized National Health Service*, Croom Helm, London, 1976.

Lewis, David. *We the Navigators: The Ancient Art of Landfinding in the Pacific*, Australian National University Press, Canberra, 1972.

Lewis, Gilbert. *Knowledge of Illness in a Sepik Society: A Study of the Gnau, New Guinea*, Athlone Press, London, 1979.

Lipset, S. M. *The First New Nation: The United States in Comparative and Historical Perspective*, Heinemann, London, 1960.
— *Political Man*, Heinemann, London, 1969.

Löffgren, Orvar. 'The great Christmas quarrel and other Swedish Traditions', in Daniel Miller (ed.), *Unwrapping Christmas*, Clarendon Press, Oxford, 1993, pp. 217–34.

Lomnitz, Larissa. 'El congreso científico: una perspectiva antropológica', *Vuelta*, 56, Mexico City, 1981.

Long, Jeremy. *The Go-Betweens: Patrol Officers in Aboriginal Affairs Administration in the Northern Territory 1936–1974*, North Australia Research Unit, Australian National University, Darwin, 1992.

López Austin, Alfredo. *Textos de Medicina Náhuatl*, UNAM, Mexico City, 1967.

Loudon, Irvine. 'The vile race of quacks with which this country is infected', in W. F. Bynum and Roy Porter (eds.), *Medical Fringe and Medical Orthodoxy, 1750–1850*, Croom Helm, London, 1987, pp. 106–28.

Lowie, R. H. *The History of Ethnological Theory*, Harrap, London, 1937.

McArthur, Margaret. 'Food consumption and dietary levels of groups of Aborigines living on naturally occurring foods', in C. P. Mountford (ed.), *Records of the American-Australian Scientific Expedition to Arnhem Land*, Vol. 2, Melbourne University Press, Melbourne, 1960, pp. 90–135.

McCarthy, Frederic M., and Margaret McArthur, 'The food quest and the time factor in Aboriginal economic life', in C. P. Mountford (ed.), *Records of the American Australian Scientific Expedition to Arnhem Land*, Vol. 2, Melbourne University Press, Melbourne, 1960, pp. 145–94.

McKeown, T. 'A social approach to the history of medicine', in G. MacLachlan and T. McKeown (eds.), *Medical History and Medical Care*, Nuffield Provincial Hospitals Trust and the Joseph Macy Foundation, 1971, pp. 1–16.

Mackie, Robert. 'The British Disease', *Observer*, London, 16 October 1994, p. 10.

McKnight, David. 'Sorcery in an Australian tribe', *Ethnology*, 20, 1981, pp. 31–44.
— *People, Countries and the Rainbow Serpent: Systems of Classification among the Lardil of Mornington Island*, Oxford University Press, New York (in press).

MacKnolty, Chips, and Paddy Wamburranga, 'Too many Captain Cooks', in Deborah Bird Rose and Tony Swan (eds.), *Aboriginal Australians and Christian Missions*, Australian Association for the Study of Religions, Adelaide, 1988, pp. 355–60.

McLuhan, Marshall. *Understanding Media: The Extensions of Man*, McGraw-Hill, New York, 1965.

Magnusson, Magnus (trans. and ed.), *Njal's Saga*, Penguin Books, Harmondsworth, 1960.

Malinowski, Bronislaw. 'The Natives of Mailu', *Transactions and Proceedings of the Royal Society of South Australia*, Vol. 39, 1915, pp. 494–706.
— *Argonauts of the Western Pacific*, Routledge, London, 1922.

Maquet, J. J. P. *The Premise of Inequality in Rwanda: A Study of Political Relationships in a Central African Kingdom*, Oxford University Press, Oxford, 1961.

Martin, Judith. *Miss Manners' Guide to Excruciatingly Correct Behavior*, Hamish Hamilton, London, 1983.

Mayr, Ernst. *Principles of Systematic Zoology*, McGraw-Hill, New York, 1969.

Miller, Daniel. 'Christmas in Trinidad', in Daniel Miller (ed.), *Unwrapping Christmas*, Clarendon Press, Oxford, 1993, pp. 134–53.

Miller, Daniel (ed.). *Unwrapping Christmas*, Clarendon Press, Oxford, 1993.

Mills, C. Wright. *The Sociological Imagination*, Grove Press, New York, 1961.

Mimica, Jadran. *Intimations of Mortality: The Mythopoeia of the Iqwaye Counting System and Number*, Berg, Oxford, 1988.

Mintz, Sidney W. *Sweetness and Power: The Place of Sugar in Modern History*, Penguin Books, Harmondsworth, 1986.

Moeran, Brian, and Lise Skov. 'Cinderella Christmas: kitsch, consumerism, and youth in Japan', in Daniel Miller (ed.), *Unwrapping Christmas*, Clarendon Press, Oxford, 1993, pp. 105–33.

Moloney, Mick. 'Stereotypes in the media: the Irish-American case', in Randall M. Miller (ed.), *Ethnic Images in American Film and Television*, Balch Institute, Philadelphia, 1978, pp. 83–5.

More, David, and Alastair Fitter. *Collins Gem Guide: Trees*, Collins, London, 1980.

Morgan, Prys. 'From a death to a view: the hunt for the Welsh past in the Romantic period', in Eric Hobsbawm and Terence Ranger (eds.), *The Invention of Tradition*, Cambridge University Press, Cambridge, 1983, pp. 43–100.

Mouffe, Chantal (ed.), *Gramsci and Marxist Theory*, Routledge and Kegan Paul, London, 1979.

Mountford, C. P. *Records of the Australian-American Expedition to Arnhem Land, Vol. 2: Anthropology and Nutrition*, Melbourne University Press, Melbourne, 1960.

Murphy, Raymond. *English Grammar in Use*, Cambridge University Press, Cambridge, 1985.

Nadel, S. F. *The Theory of Social Structure*, Cohen and West, London, 1957.

Nairn, Tom. *The Break-up of Britain: Crisis and Neo-colonialism*, New Left Books, London, 1977.

Needham, Joseph. *Science and Civilization in China* (6 vols.), Cambridge University Press, Cambridge, 1954–96.

New York Times Magazine, 'One City, Many Nations', 3 November 1985.

Oberg, Kalervo. 'The Kingdom of Ankole in Uganda', in M. Fortes and E. E. Evans-Pritchard (eds.), *African Political Systems*, Oxford University Press, Oxford, 1940, pp. 121–62.

Obeyesekere, Gananath. 'The impact of Ayurvedic ideas on the culture and the individual in Sri Lanka', in Charles M. Leslie (ed.), *Asian Medical Systems: A Comparative Study*, University of California Press, Berkeley, 1976, pp. 201–26.

Osman, Mohd. Taib. *Malay Folk Beliefs: An Integration of Disparate Elements*, Dewan Bahasa dan Pustaka, Kuala Lumpur, 1989.

Otsuka, Y. 'Chinese traditional medicine in Japan', in Charles M. Leslie (ed.), *Asian Medical Systems: A Comparative Study*, University of California Press, Berkeley, 1976, pp. 322–40.

Parry, Noel, and José Parry. *The Rise of the Medical Profession: A Study of Collective Mobility*, Croom Helm, London, 1976.

Parsons, Talcott. *The Social System*, Routledge and Kegan Paul, London 1951.

Parssinen, T. M. 'Professional deviants and the history of medicine: medical Mesmerists in Victorian Britain', in Roy Wallis (ed.), *On the Margins of Science: The Social Construction of Rejected Knowledge*, *Sociological Review*, Monograph No. 27, University of Keele, 1979, pp. 103–20.

Payer, Lynn. *Medicine and Culture: Varieties of Treatment in the United States, England, West Germany and France*, Henry Holt, New York, 1988.

Peires, J. B. *The Dead Will Arise: Nongqawuse and the Great Xhosa Cattle Killing Movement of 1856–7*, Ravan Press, Johannesburg, 1989.

Pelling, Margaret. *Cholera, Fever, and English Medicine 1825–1865*, Oxford University Press, Oxford, 1978a.
— 'Medical Practice in Norwich, 1550–1640', *Bulletin of the Society for Social Research in Medicine*, 1978b, pp. 30–32.

Peterson, Roger Tory, and Maria Peterson. *Audubon's Birds of America*, Audubon Society Baby Elephant Folio, Heinemann, London, 1981.

Piaget, Jean. *The Moral Judgment of the Child*, Routledge and Kegan Paul, London 1932.

Pilger, John. *Distant Voices*, Vintage, London, 1992.

Porter, Roy. *Health for Sale: Quackery in England, 1660–1850*, Manchester University Press, Manchester, 1989.

Porteus, Stanley D. *The Psychology of a Primitive People: A Study of the Australian Aborgine*, Arnold, London, 1931.

Press, Irwin. 'The urban curandero', *American Anthropologist*, 73, 1971, pp. 741–56.

Prins, Gwyn. 'Disease at the cross-roads: towards a history of therapeutics in Bulozi since 1876', *Social Science and Medicine*, B, Vol. 13, 1979, pp. 285–316.

Quirk, Randolph, and Sidney Greenbaum, *A University Grammar of English*, Longman, London, 1973.

Rackham, Oliver. *The History of the Countryside*, Dent, London, 1986.

Radcliffe-Brown, A. R. 'The social organization of Australian tribes', *Oceania Monographs*, No. 1, Nos. 1–4, Sydney, 1930.
— 'The mother's brother in South Africa', in *Structure and Function in Primitive Society*, Cohen and West, London, 1952, pp. 15–31.

Ramsey, Matthew. 'Property rights and the right to health: the regulation of secret remedies in France, 1789–1815', in W. F. Bynum and Roy Porter (eds.), *Medical Fringe and Medical Orthodoxy*, 1750–1850, Croom Helm, London, 1987, pp. 79–105.

Reader's Digest. *Classification of the Animal Kingdom: An Illustrated Guide*, English Universities Press/Reader's Digest Association, London, 1972.

Reader's Digest Association. *Reader's Digest Encyclopaedia of Garden Plants and Flowers*, Reader's Digest Association, London, 1978.

Real, Michael R. 'The Disney universe: morality play', in Michael R. Read (ed.), *Mass-mediated Culture*, Prentice-Hall, Englewood Cliffs, New Jersey, 1977, pp. 45–89.

Restad, Penne L. *Christmas in America: A History*, Oxford University Press, New York, 1995.

Revolutionary Health Committee of Hunan Province, *A Barefoot Doctor's Manual*, Routledge, London, 1978.

Reynolds, Henry. *The Other Side of the Frontier: Aboriginal Resistance to the European Invasion of Australia*, Penguin Books, Victoria, Australia, 1981.

Riesenberg, Saul and Samuel Elbert. 'The *Poi* of the Meeting', *Journal of the Polynesian Society*, 80 (2), 1971, pp. 217–27.

Rigaldi, Eudes (Odo Rigaldus or Rigaud). *The Register of Eudes of Rouen*, Sidney M. Brown (trans.) and Jeremiah F. O'Sullivan (ed.), Records of Civilization Sources and Studies No. LXXVII, Columbia University Press, New York, 1964.

Ritzer, George. *The McDonaldization of Society: The Changing Character of*

Contemporary Social Life, Pine Forge Press, Newbury Park, California, 1993.

Rollin, Henry R. 'The dark before the dawn', *Journal of Psychopharmacology*, 4(3), 1990, pp. 109–14.

Romano, O. I. 'Charismatic medicine, folk-healing, and folk-sainthood', *American Anthropologist*, 67, 1965, pp. 1,151–73.

Romney, Jonathan. 'The Mouse That Soared', *Guardian*, London, 14 October 1996, pp. 6–7.

Rose, F. G. G. 'Malay influence on Aboriginal totemism in northern Australia', *Man*, Vol. XLVII, 142, 1947, p. 129.
— *Classification of Kin, Age Structure and Marriage among the Groote Eylandt Aborigines: A Study in Method and a Theory of Australian Kinship*, Akademie-Verlag, Berlin, 1960.

Roszak, Theodore. *The Making of a Counter-culture: Reflections on the Technocratic Society and its Youthful Opposition*, Faber and Faber, London, 1970.

Roth, Julius. *Timetables: Structuring the Passage of Time in Hospitals and Other Careers*, Bobbs-Merrill, Indianapolis, 1963.

Roughsey, Elsie (Labumore). *An Aboriginal Mother Tells of the Old and the New*, Paul Memmot and Robyn Horsman (eds.), McPhee Gribble/ Penguin, Victoria, Australia, 1984.

Sahlins, Marshall. 'The original affluent society', in *Stone Age Economics*, Aldine-Atherton, Chicago, 1972, pp. 1–39.
— *Culture and Practical Reason*, Aldine, Chicago, 1976.
— *Islands of History*, University of Chicago Press, Chicago, 1985.

Saks, Mike (ed.). *Alternative Medicine in Britain*, Clarendon Press, Oxford, 1992.

Sassoon, Anne Showstack. *Gramsci's Politics*, Croom Helm, London, 1980.

Saunders, David. *RSPB Guide to British Birds*. Hamlyn, London, 1975.

Sayers, Barbara J. 'Aboriginal mathematical concepts: a cultural and linguistic explanation for some of the problems', in S. Hargrave (ed.), *Language and Culture: Work Papers of the SIL-AAB*, Series B, Vol. 8, Summer Institute of Linguistics, Australian Aboriginal Branch, Darwin, 1982, pp. 183–200.

Schickel, Richard. *The Disney Version: The Life, Times, Art and Commerce of Walt Disney*, Simon and Schuster, New York, 1968.

Searcy, A. *In Australian Tropics*, Robertson, London 1909.
— *By Flood and Field*, Bell, London, 1912.

Searle-Chatterjee, Mary. 'Christmas cards and the construction of social relations in Britain today', in Daniel Miller (ed.), '*Unwrapping Christmas*', Clarendon Press, Oxford, 1993, pp. 176–92.

Sen, Kasturi. *Ageing: Debates on Demographic Transition and Social Policy*, Zed Press, London, 1994.

Seneviratne, H. L. *Rituals of the Kandyan State*, Cambridge University Press, Cambridge, 1978.

Sharp, Andrew. *Ancient Voyagers in the Pacific*, Penguin Books, Harmondsworth, 1957.

Shore, Bradd. '*Mana* and *tapu*', in Alan Howard and Robert Borofsky (eds.), *Developments in Polynesian Ethnology*, University of Hawaii Press, Honolulu, 1989, pp. 137–73.

Showalter, Elaine. 'Fallen icon', *Guardian* Review, London, 21 June 1996, pp. 2–3.

Shryock, Richard Harrison. *The Development of Modern Medicine: An Interpretation of the Social and Scientific Factors Involved*, Knopf, New York, 1936.

Siskind, Janet. 'The invention of Thanksgiving: a ritual of American nationality', *Critique of Anthropology*, Vol. 12 (2), June 1992, pp. 167–91.

Sklair, Leslie. *The Sociology of the Global System: Social Change in Global*

Perspective, Harvester/Wheatsheaf, New York, 1991.

Smith, Anthony D. 'The politics of culture: ethnicity and nationalism', in T. Ingold (ed.), *Companion Encyclopaedia of Anthropology: Humanity, Culture, and Social Life*, Routledge, London, 1994, pp. 706–33.

Smith, Bernard. *European Vision and the South Pacific*, 1768–1850, Clarendon Press, Oxford, 1960.

Smith, Delia. *Delia Smith's Cookery Course* (3 parts), Hodder and Stoughton, London, 1978, 1979, 1985.

Smoodin, Eric (ed.), *Disney Discourses: Producing the Magic Kingdom*, Routledge, London, 1994.

Spate, O. H. K. *The Spanish Lake*, Croom Helm, London, 1979.
— *Monopolists and Freebooters*, Croom Helm, London 1983.

Spencer, Herbert. *The Study of Sociology*, Kegan Paul, Trench, Trubner, London, 1897.

Srinivas, M. N. *Religion and Society among the Coorgs of South India*, Clarendon Press, Oxford, 1952.

Stacey, Margaret. *The Sociology of Health and Healing: A Textbook*, Unwin Hyman, London, 1988.

Stavrianos, L. S. *Global Rift: The Third World Comes of Age*, Morrow, New York, 1981.

Steele, Jonathan. *Eternal Russia: Yeltsin, Gorbachev and the Mirage of Democracy*, Faber and Faber, London, 1994.

Stokes, Judith. 'A Description of the mathematical concepts of Groote Eylandt Aborigines', in S. Hargrave (ed.), *Language and Culture: Work papers of the SIL-AAB*, Series B, Vol. 8, Summer Institute of Linguistics, Australian Aboriginal Branch, Darwin, 1982, pp. 33–152.

Stokoe, W. J. *The Observer's Book of British Wild Flowers*, Warne, n.d.

Stolcke, Verena. 'New boundaries, new rhetorics of exclusion in

Europe', *Current Anthropology*, Vol. 36, No. 1, 1995, pp. 1–24.

Taussig, Michael. *The Devil and Commodity Fetishism in South America*, University of North Carolina Press, Chapel Hill, 1980.

Taylor, C. E. 'The place of indigenous medical practitioners in the modernization of health services', in Charles M. Leslie (ed.), *Asian Medical Systems: A Comparative Study*, University of California Press, Berkeley, 1976, pp. 285–99.

Tenbruck, Friedrich H. 'The cultural foundations of society', in Hans Haferkamp (ed.), *Social Structure and Culture*, Walther de Gruyter, Berlin, 1989, pp. 15–35.

Thomas, Keith. *Man and the Natural World: Changing Attitudes in England 1500–1800*, Allen Lane, Harmondsworth, 1983.

Thomas, Stephen D. *The Last Navigator*, Holt, New York, 1987.

Thompson, E. P. 'Time, work-discipline and industrial capitalism', *Past and Present*, Vol. 38, 1967, pp. 56–97.
— *Whigs and Hunters: The Origin of the Black Act*, Penguin Books, Harmondsworth, 1975.

Thomson, Donald F. 'Names and naming among the Wik Monkan tribe', *Journal of the Royal Anthropological Insitute*, Vol. LXXVI, 1946, pp. 157–68.

Thrasher, Frederick M. *The Gang: A Study of 1,313 Gangs in Chicago*, University of Chicago Press, Chicago, 1927.

Tindale, N. B. 'Natives of Groote Eylandt and of the west coast of the Gulf of Carpentaria', *Records of the South Australia Museum*, Vol. III, Nos. 1 and 2, Adelaide, 1925, pp. 61–134.

Toffler, Alvin. *The Third Wave*, Pan, London 1981.

Trachtenberg, Marvin. *The Statue of Liberty*, Penguin Books, Harmondsworth, 1986.

Trevor-Roper, Hugh. 'The invention of tradition: the Highland tradition of Scotland', in Eric Hobsbawm and Terence Ranger (eds.), *The Invention of Tradition*, Cambridge University Press, Cambridge, 1983, pp. 15–41.

Trindell, R. T. 'Franz Boas and American geography', *Professional Geographer*, Vol. 21, No. 5, 1969, pp. 328–32.

Turner, David H. *Tradition and Transformation: A Study of Aborigines in the Groote Eylandt Area, Northern Australia*, Australian Aboriginal Studies No. 53, Australian Institute of Aboriginal Studies, Canberra, 1974.
— 'The Incarnation of Nambirrirrma', in D. Rose and T. Swain (eds.), *Aboriginal Culture and Christian Missions*, Australian Association for the Study of Religions, Sydney, 1988, pp. 468–83.

Turner, V. W. *Schism and Continuity in an African Society: A Study of Ndembu Village Life*, Manchester University Press, Manchester, 1957.
— 'Muchona the Hornet, interpreter of religion', in *The Forest of Symbols: Aspects of Ndembu Ritual*, Cornell University Press, New York, 1967, pp. 131–50.

Unschuld, P. U. 'The social organization and ecology of medical practice in Taiwan', in Charles M. Leslie (ed.), *Asian Medical Systems: A Comparative Study*, University of California Press, Berkeley, 1976, pp. 300–321.

Updike, John. 'The blessed men of Boston', *Forty Stories*, Penguin Books, Harmondsworth, 1987, pp. 98–109.

Urry, John. *The Anatomy of Capitalist Societies*, Macmillan, London, 1991.

Venturi, Richard, et al., *Learning from Las Vegas*, MIT Press, Cambridge, Mass., 1977.

Vickers, Adrian. *Bali: A Paradise Created*, Penguin Books, Victoria, Australia, 1989.

Vogel, Virgil J. *American Indian Medicine*, University of Oklahoma Press, Norman, Oklahoma, 1970.

Vygotsky, Lev Semenovich. *Thought and Language*, MIT Press, Cambridge, Mass., 1962.

Waddy, J. A. *Classification of Plants and Animals from a Groote Eylandt Point of View* (2 vols.), North Australia Research Unit Monograph, Australian National University, Darwin, 1988.

Wadsworth, M. E. J., W. J. H. Butterfield and R. Blaney. *Health and Sickness: The Choice of Treatment*, Tavistock, London, 1971.

Wagner, Gunter. 'The political organization of the Bantu of Kavirondo', in M. Fortes and E. E. Evans-Pritchard (eds.), *African Political Systems*, Oxford University Press, Oxford, 1940, pp. 196–236.

Wallace, Mike. 'Mickey Mouse history: portraying the past at Disney World', *Radical History Review*, 32, 1985, pp. 33–57.

Wallis, Roy and Peter Morley (eds.). *Marginal Medicine*, Peter Owen, London, 1976.

Walter, E. V. 'Nature on trial: the case of the rooster that laid an egg', in R. Cohen and M. Wartovsky (eds.), *Methodology, Metaphysics and the History of Science*, Reidel, Dordrecht, 1984.

Wanek, Alexander. *Fighting Lucifer: The State and Its Enemies in Papua New Guinea*, Department of Social Anthropology, Stockholm University, 1993.

Warner, John Harley. 'Medical sectarianism, therapeutic conflict, and the shaping of orthodox professional identity in antebellum American medicine', in W. F. Bynum and Roy Porter (eds.), *Medical Fringe and Medical Orthodoxy, 1750–1850*, Croom Helm, London, 1987, pp. 234–60.

Warner, W. L. *A Black Civilization*, Harper and Row, New York, 1937.
—— *The Living and the Dead: A Study of the Symbolic Life of Americans*, Yale University Press, New Haven, Connecticut, 1959.

Wartovsky, M. W. Editorial, *Journal of Medical Philosophy*, Vol. 1, 1976, pp. 289–300, continued in Vol. 3, 1978, pp. 265–72.

Watson, James L. (ed.). *Golden Arches: McDonald's in East Asia*, forthcoming.

Weatherford, Jack. *Indian Givers: How the Indians of the Americas Transformed the World*, Fawcett Columbia, New York, 1988.

Weber, Max. *The Theory of Social and Economic Organization*, Free Press, Glencoe, Illinois, 1947.

Webster, Charles. 'Paracelsus and Paracelsianism: basic data', *Bulletin of the Society for Social Research in Medicine*, Nos. 30–31, June–December 1982, pp. 47–50.

Werbner, R. P. (ed.). *Regional Cults*, Academic Press, New York, 1977.

Wertheim, W. F. *Evolution or Revolution: The Rising Waves of Emancipation*, Penguin Books, Harmondsworth, 1974.

West, Ruth. 'Alternative medicine: prospects and speculation', in Mike Saks (ed.), *Alternative Medicine in Britain*, Clarendon Press, Oxford, 1992, pp. 201–10.

Whyte, William Foote. *Street Corner Society: The Social Structure of an Italian Slum*, University of Chicago Press, Chicago, 1943.

Wilkins, G. H. *Undiscovered Australia*, Benn, London, 1928.

Williams, Raymond. *Communications*, Penguin Books, Harmondsworth, 1962.
— *Culture*, Fontana, London 1982.

Williamson, R. W. *Cosmic and Religious Beliefs of the Central Polynesians*, Cambridge University Press, Cambridge, 1933.

Wolf, Eric R. *Europe and the People without History*, University of California Press, Berkeley, 1982.

Worsley, Peter. 'Emile Durkeim's theory of knowledge', *Sociological Review* (Keele), vol. 4, No. 1, new series, 1956, pp. 47–62.
— *The Third World: A Vital New Force in International Affairs*, Weidenfeld and Nicolson, London, 1964.
— 'Groote Eylandt totemism and *Le totémisme aujourd'hui*', in Edmund Leach (ed.), *The Structural Study of Myth and Totemism*, ASA Monograph No. 5, 1967, pp. 141–159.

—— *The Trumpet Shall Sound: A Study of 'Cargo' Cults in Melanesia*, second edition, Schocken Books, New York, 1968.

—— *The Three Worlds: Culture and World Development*, University of Chicago Press, Chicago, 1984.

—— 'The practice of politics and the study of Australian kinship', in Christine Ward Gailey (ed.), *Dialectical Anthropology: Essays in Honor of Stanley Diamond, Vol. 2: The Politics of Culture and Creativity*, University Press of Florida, 1992, pp. 252–62.

—— 'The nation-state, colonial expansion and the contemporary world-order', in T. Ingold (ed.), *Companion Encyclopaedia of Anthropology: Humanity, Culture, and Social Life*, Routledge, London, 1994, pp. 1,040–66.

—— 'The measurement of cross-cultural group-differences in intelligence: an experiment in the construction of 'culture-bound' tests' (unpublished).

Worsley, P. M. 'The Changing Social Structure of the Wanindiljaugwa', Ph.D. thesis, Australian National University, 1954a.

—— 'Noun-classification in Australian and Bantu: formal or semantic?', *Oceania*, Vol. 24, No. 4, 1954b, pp. 275–88.

—— 'Early Asian contacts with Australia', *Past and Present*, No. 7, April 1955, pp. 1–11.

—— 'The utilization of food resources by an Australian Aboriginal tribe', *Acta Ethnographica*, Hungarian Academy of Sciences, Vol. X, Nos. 1–2, Budapest, 1961, pp. 153–90.

Yashimoto, Mitsuhiro. 'Images of empire: Tokyo Disneyland and Japanese cultural imperialism', in Eric Smoodin (ed.), *Disney Discourses: Producing the Magic Kingdom*, Routledge, London, 1994, pp. 181–99.

Yearley, Steven. *Science, Technology and Social Change*, Unwin Hyman, London, 1988.

Zangwill, Israel. *The Melting Pot: A Drama in Four Acts*, AMS Press, New York, 1925.

Zborowski, M. 'Cultural components in responses to pain', *Journal of Social Issues*, 8, 1982, pp. 16–30.

Zola, I. K. 'Culture and symptoms: an analysis of patients' presenting complaints', *American Sociological Review*, 31, 1966, pp. 615–30.

Zubaida, Sami. *Islam, the People and the State: Essays on Political Ideas and Movements in the Middle East*, Routledge, London, 1989.

Zukin, Sharon. *Landscapes of Power*, University of California Press, Berkeley, 1991.

Spirit of Micronesia, a sound-recording by David Fanshawe, includes star-path chants by master navigators Piailug and Hipour and others, as well as material about life on the islands in general, from pre-colonial women's dances, toddy-cutting songs and Yap stone money songs to Spanish-influenced stick dances, mission and independent church choirs, nineteenth-century hornpipes, a song recording the arrival of the first aeroplane; a Gilbertese version of 'It's a Long Way to Tipperary' from the Second World War Battle of Tarawa; songs of people deported during the Second World War by the Japanese, and by the Americans from Eniwetok atoll, used for nuclear-bomb testing; songs sung to welcome a visiting Chinese delegation; and the sounds of canoes being launched, of canoes and copra boats at sea, and the sounds of birds in a very remote reef. Stereo-cassette CSDL414; compact disc CD SDL414, Saydisc Records, Chipping Manor, The Chipping, Wotton-under-Edge, Gloucester, GL12 7AD, UK.

Index